The Essential Guide to Internet Business Technology

D1368713

ISBN 0-13-042820-5

90000

9 780130 428202

Prentice Hall PTR
Essential Guide Series

**THE ESSENTIAL GUIDE TO KNOWLEDGE MANAGEMENT:
E-BUSINESS AND CRM APPLICATIONS**

Tiwana

**THE ESSENTIAL GUIDE TO APPLICATION SERVICE
PROVIDERS**

Toigo

THE ESSENTIAL GUIDE TO STORAGE AREA NETWORKS

Vacca

THE ESSENTIAL GUIDE TO MOBILE BUSINESS

Vos & deKlein

**THE ESSENTIAL GUIDE TO COMPUTING:
THE STORY OF INFORMATION TECHNOLOGY**

Walters

**THE ESSENTIAL GUIDE TO RF AND WIRELESS,
SECOND EDITION**

Weisman

The Essential Guide to Internet Business Technology

GAIL HONDA
KIPP MARTIN

Prentice Hall PTR, Upper Saddle River, NJ 07458
www.phptr.com

Library of Congress Cataloging-in-Publication Date

Honda, Gail
    The essential guide to internet business technology / Gail Honda, Kipp Martin.
        p. cm. – (The essential guide series)
    Includes bibliographical references and index.
    ISBN 0-13-042820-5
        1. Information technology–Management. 2. Management information systems. 3. Business networks.
    4. Electronic commerce. 5. Internet. I. Martin, Kipp II. Title. III. Essential guide series (Prentice-Hall, inc.)

    HD30.2 .H659 2002
    658'.054678–dc21

                                                                                          2001058073

Editorial/Production Supervision: *Jan H. Schwartz*
VP, Executive Editor: *Tim Moore*
Marketing Manager: *Debby vanDijk*
Manufacturing Manager: *Alexis R. Heydt-Long*
Buyer: *Maura Zaldivar*
Art Director: *Gail Cocker-Bogusz*
Interior Series Design: *Meg VanArsdale*
Cover Design Direction: *Jerry Votta*
Cover Design: *Kiwi Design*
Editorial Assistant: *Allyson Kloss*

© 2002 Prentice Hall PTR
A Division of Pearson Education, Inc.
Upper Saddle River, NJ 07458

Prentice hall books are widely used by corporations and government agencies for training, marketing, and resale.

The publisher offers discounts on this book when ordered in bulk quantities.
For more information, contact

    Corporate Sales Department
    Prentice Hall PTR, A Division of Pearson Education, Inc.
    One Lake Street
    Upper Saddle River, NJ 07458
    Phone: 800-382-3419; FAX: 201-236-7141
    Email (Internet): corpsales@prenhall.com

Printed in the United States of America

10 9 8 7 6 5 4 3 2 1

ISBN 0-13-042820-5

Pearson Education LTD.
Pearson Education Australia PTY, Limited
Pearson Education Singapore, Pte. Ltd.
Pearson Education North Asia Ltd.
Pearson Education Canada, Ltd.
Pearson Educación de Mexico, S.A. de C.V.
Pearson Education—Japan
Pearson Education Malaysia, Pte. Ltd.

Dedication

To our parents

Sadao and Jean Honda

Bruce and Phyllis Martin

Contents

Part 3

Nuts and Bolts
of Internet Business   161

Part 4
Back End: Support   263

Preface

This book originated as a set of notes for an MBA course entitled "Computing Technology for the General Manager," first taught at the University of Chicago Graduate School of Business (GSB) in January 1994. The course was one of the first in the country to cover the Internet. Back then, the technologies introduced in the course included Gopher, a predecessor to the Mosaic browser, which was the earliest widely used browser.

Kipp Martin, developer of the course and a co-author of this book, saw that computers and the Internet were becoming increasingly important for all business professionals, not just for the "techies," or IT (information technology) experts. He created this course as a way to teach MBA students all they would need to know about using the computer in business. In the beginning, there were no appropriate textbooks for the course, so he pieced together a reading list that comprised books on MIS (management information systems) and a user's guide to the Internet, as well as a packet of articles from the popular press.

Even as the Internet grew in importance in the late 1990s and books on the Internet proliferated, he still needed to rely on parts of a number of books for his syllabus, for there was no book that satisfactorily covered all the relevant topics. Finally, he realized he needed to write his own book. He teamed up with Gail Honda, whom he had known since 1984 when she was an MBA student at the GSB. With his technical knowledge, and her business and writing credentials and experience, they decided to write a book that would clearly explain, in nontechnical language, the technology behind the Internet and how to use it in business. This book is the result of that decision.

The material in this book has been expanded and enhanced since 1994, thanks to the feedback of hundreds of Kipp's students. Kipp's MBA course, now called "e-Business Technology," has been constantly updated to take into account changing technology in the Internet business world. Kipp's Executive Education seminar, "Information Technology for Non-IT Managers: Foundations of e-Business," taught at the GSB and abroad, has been well received and has provided an additional source of information on what's really important to real-life executives who need to know more about technology in their everyday work lives.

This book was written as a trade business book intended for a general audience, rather than as a textbook intended for students, though it certainly can be used as a textbook. Business professionals who find that computers and the Internet are becoming increasingly important to their jobs and who need to expand their knowledge of the same will benefit from reading this book. They include those who make technology-based decisions; talk frequently with CIOs (chief information officers) , CTOs (chief technical officers), and IT (information technology) personnel; have been promoted to CIO or CTO from a functional area such as finance or marketing; want to go into Internet business consulting; need to evaluate Internet business companies; or are starting an Internet business.

As a textbook, the book is appropriate for an MBA or advanced undergraduate course on Internet business or Internet commerce. It could also be used for more general courses on business technology or IS (information systems). If you would like to find out more about Kipp's MBA course, log on to `http://gsbkip.uchicago.edu/ htmls/coursework/b372/b372.html`. For more information and readings by the authors related to this book, go to `www.globaloptima.com`. If you have comments you would like to share with the authors or questions regarding this book, please write to the authors at the email address, `InternetBusiness@globaloptima.com`.

Please note that throughout the book, numbers in hard brackets, [ ], refer to a citation from an entry in the bibliography toward the end of the book.

In sum, if you are looking for a book that explains a lot of important business technology in plain, precise, and (we think) interesting language, this book is for you.

Acknowledgments

Many of our colleagues, students, friends, and family contributed generously of their time and knowledge to help make this book the clearest and most thorough we could write. John Borse and Syam Menon read parts of the manuscript and sharpened a number of chapters. Computing Services at the University of Chicago Graduate School of Business (GSB) helped Kipp over the years deepen his understanding of computers. Former and current students in Kipp's MBA course, "Computing Technology for the General Manager," now called "e-Business Technology," on which this book is based, contributed to the development of the course and the clarity of the manuscript. Material for this book also comes from students in his Executive Education seminar, "Information Technology for Non-IT Managers: Foundations of e-Business," taught at the GSB.

Kipp would like to thank his seminar colleagues Mark Jeffery and Mohan Sodhi. He has learned much from them. He would also like to thank Ed Mondek of Microsoft for his time helping Kipp with SQL Server and BizTalk Server. Linus Schrage, Kipp's longtime colleague in the GSB, applied his formidable knowledge of computers and operations management to reading the entire manuscript and made numerous cogent suggestions. Kipp would also like to thank Linus for the many years that Kipp was able to ask him for advice and the answer to a computing question, to which Linus would invariably know the answer.

This book has become a reality thanks to our publisher, Prentice Hall. We would like to thank our anonymous business reviewer, our technical reviewer, Corinne Gregory, and our main reviewer, Russ Hall, for their many helpful comments, and especially Russ for smoothly managing the review process. Our editor, Tim Moore, has been a constant source of encouragement, insight, wit, and market knowledge throughout the entire journey, from idea to final product. We have enjoyed our professional affiliation with him, the reviewers, the field representatives, and the production managers with whom we have worked.

Finally, we would like to thank our parents, Sadao and Jean Honda, and Bruce and Phyllis Martin, to whom this book is dedicated. Sadao and Jean contributed their ever-fresh enthusiasm and constant anticipation of seeing the finished product to increase the enjoyment of writing the book. Bruce and Phyllis applied their considerable writing expertise to reading the entire manuscript and helped to strengthen the syntax and style. We are grateful to both sets of parents for being such wonderful people and supporters.

Part 1

Technology Basics

In order to make informed decisions about technology, it is necessary to understand the basic elements of any system: hardware, software, and the Internet. In Chapter 1, "Say 'Yes' to Internet Business," we discuss why understanding Internet business is important if you are to remain competitive in today's technology-driven business environment. We show why Internet business is critical even in the post dot-com crash era. In Chapter 2, "What Do I Need to Know About Hardware," we provide you with the fundamental concepts of computer hardware, such as the different types of computers, the essentials of how a computer works, and how information is stored and accessed. We discuss the managerial implications of purchasing hardware and integrating it into an Internet business system. In Chapter 3, "Software Is Everywhere," we present the major operating systems and the different kinds of application software and programming languages. Current topics such as object-oriented programming, Java, and the open source movement are covered. In Chapter 4, "Internet and Web Technology," we explain how the Internet works with its protocols, packet switching, and domain name system. You will also learn about different Internet tools, such as FTP and Telnet.

1 Say "Yes" to Internet Business

In this chapter ...

INTERNET BUSINESS IS MORE THAN E-COMMERCE

· ·

WHY YOU NEED TO KNOW ABOUT INTERNET BUSINESS

Internet business, or business conducted over the Internet, encompasses much more than buying and selling goods online (Internet commerce or e-commerce). **Internet business is about the efficient exchange of information.** Almost any type of information exchange can be conducted more efficiently using the Internet. This efficiency results in tremendous cost savings as well as new channels for generating revenues. A company that does not understand how to create these efficiencies will be at a severe disadvantage vis-a-vis its competition. Those who do not understand the true power of Internet business will find their potential for career advancement diminished.

Internet commerce has taken a beating since the peak of the dot-com revolution in the last quarter of 1999 and the first quarter of 2000. Online retailers have folded, and many business-to-business (B2B) marketplaces have closed. Internet stocks are at a fraction of their peak values and are in danger of being delisted. But there are lessons to be learned from these failures, which we cover in this book. More importantly, Internet commerce, while the best known and most hyped aspect of Internet business, accounts for only a piece of the whole.

Some of the most revolutionary changes due to the Internet are occurring within companies rather than between. Dubbed the "Dell Computer Inc. of the fashion industry," Spanish clothing designer and retailer Zara turns orders for clothing around in a matter of days. It restocks its 924 stores in 31 countries twice a week and churns out 12,000 different designs annually. How does it do this? By equipping its store managers with handheld computers to place orders, computerizing its design and production processes, and manufacturing most of its clothing in Spain, which cuts assembly and shipment time to two weeks [43].

Companies everywhere are adopting "back end" technology to streamline their in-house operations. What is back end? It is the computer hardware and software that most managers never see but are critical to a business, like servers and databases. There are companies that provide back end hardware services for those who choose not to do it them-selves. They are called "managed service providers" or MSPs. Their services range from "colocation services"—hosting your company-owned hardware in their data center—to pro-viding all the hardware for you. On the software end, "application service providers" or ASPs will provide all of your software needs remotely over the Internet so you need never worry about upgrades and maintenance on individual PCs.

Internet business also includes software that can enhance your customer service, sales force, supplier relationships, and supply chain. One example of savvy Internet business is Carrier Corporation, the world's largest manufacturer of air conditioners, with close to $10 billion in annual revenue. Carrier's president since December 1999, Jonathan Ayers, has saved the company $100 million by moving a good part of Carrier's operations to the Internet. In Brazil, Carrier's dealers, retailers, and installers now transact over 80 percent of their business, about $280 million in 2000, over the World Wide Web (Web). This resulted in greater customer satisfaction and higher inventory turnover. In Korea, Carrier transacts 50 percent of sales over the Web, which reduced the cycle time for an order from 33 to 18 days. Carrier has also implemented online bidding auctions for suppliers, which has reduced the cost of components by about 15 percent. More transparency over the Web has enabled Carrier to become much more efficient and to build air conditioners on demand, instead of on forecasts. And because the company has moved so quickly, suppliers are committed to working with Carrier's Web-based purchasing system instead of its competitors'. Internet business is totally transforming the way companies are doing business, and this book will show how you can contribute to your company's efficiency and profitability [86].

These exciting ways that Internet business is being used to help companies stay at the top of their game demonstrate that Internet commerce is only a small part of Internet business. Thus, even though the dot-com shakeout has caused many dot-coms to go belly-up, this by no means signals the end of Internet business. Quite the contrary. We are just beginning to see how companies are realizing the potential of the Internet to outpace their competitors. The ingenuity behind Internet business technology has spurred the creation of brand new forms of traditional business tools like viral marketing and electronic cash, both of which are discussed in this book. This is a fascinating time to be in business if you take advantage of the evolving Internet world around you. The future belongs to those who understand Internet business and leave their competitors in the dust.

INTERNET BUSINESS IS BIG........................

The number of occupations in computer-related fields is growing quickly due to the explosive growth of the Internet, according to Mike Pilot, an economist in the Office of Employment Projections of the U. S. Bureau of Labor Statistics [110]. This means that those who understand Internet business will be in greatest demand among all workers in the United States. The median cash compensation for someone working in Internet business is $83,000, including salary, bonus, and commission [25]. If you would like to learn what you need to know for an Internet business job, this book is for you.

Other studies have shown that the volume of Internet business is predicted to rise from $400 billion in 2000 to $7 trillion in 2005 in the United States alone [25]. Seven trillion dollars is an astonishing volume, nearly a quarter of the entire world economy as measured in 2000 [179]. If you're interested in compensation, there were 5.3 million information technology (IT) workers in 1998, and they were earning almost double that of non-IT workers [25]. If you haven't yet engaged in Internet business, you most certainly will in the coming years. The Internet has revolutionized the way we do business, from

Amazon's trail-blazing retailing model to eBay's wildly successful auction site. Still, we have experienced only the tip of the iceberg when it comes to exploiting the Internet's potential to conduct business that's more efficient, fun, and profitable. Those who are savviest will no doubt come out on top in the business world. Will this be you?

....

EVEN AFTER THE DOT-COM CRASH INTERNET BUSINESS REMAINS BIG

In 2001, well after the peak of the dot-com revolution and well into its crash, studies show that the future of Internet business remains big. IDC, an Internet business and technology research firm, predicts that worldwide investment in Internet business will remain strong, growing from $700 billion in 2001 to $2.152 trillion in 2004. In addition, according to the U.S. Bureau of Labor Statistics, the top five fastest-growing occupations through 2008 are computer-related, thanks to the growth of the Internet.

This book, *The Essential Guide to Internet Business Technology*, is for anyone who wants to be at the forefront of Internet business. Internet business is driven by technology, and understanding technology is key to understanding Internet business. You may be in a position to make important decisions that depend on your knowledge of technology, or at least the ability to ask the right questions of technology experts. You may find yourself confronted with a whole slew of new Internet business software that you must quickly master. You may be contemplating a career switch to the field of Internet business where demand for workers outstrips supply. If Internet business is, or will soon be, a part of your work day, this book is for you.

Knowledge of technology, which you will gain from reading this book, is a powerful business tool. Until recently, understanding technology in business has been the purview of the information technology, or IT, specialists. They are the ones you call upon to install new software on your PC, reboot your hard drive when it crashes, or network your company's computers. Until recently, there wasn't any compelling reason to know much about technology yourself, except perhaps how to send email and surf the Internet. But as we have seen, companies have been harnessing the power of Internet technology to transform themselves into cost-cutting and revenue-enhancing organizations.

Dollars saved and generated within a single company have reached the billion dollar mark. Oracle claimed to save $1 billion using its own software. General Electric (GE) announced that $1 billion worth of goods was ordered on its Web site [15]. To attain numbers like this, it is certain that knowledge and use of new technologies were virtually company-wide, far beyond the reaches of the IT department. Indeed, at the urging of former GE Chairman and CEO Jack Welch, thousands of top GE executives and Mr. Welch himself each hired a mentor to help them understand the power of the Internet. Furthermore, GE has as its goal to have every single person in its company use the Internet to perform all kinds of management tasks, from team-building to customer service [89]. Thus, it is not just those who work in IT departments or at dot-coms who need to understand Internet business technology, but those in all departments at even the most established companies.

WHY TECHNOLOGY IS KEY ....

According to Haim Mendelson, a professor at the Stanford University Graduate School of Business, "One of the core messages we are trying to convey is that there is no clear-cut distinction between the technologists and the general managers." Demand for knowledge on technology in the Information Age, spurred by growth in Internet business, has never been higher. The *New York Times* sports a Technology/Internet section, *The Wall Street Journal* has added a Technology Journal, and *Business Week* features a section on Technology, in both newsstand and online versions. Type "technology" in an Amazon book search, and the site returns tens of thousands of titles for your perusal. A search on "technology" at Google yields well over 33 million Web pages. People everywhere are clamoring for up-to-the-minute information to increase their technological savvy because their jobs depend on it.

Why technology? Because technology is changing the way we do business. Technology allows information to flow instantaneously, communities to be built in a day, and market research to be conducted from a single computer. Technology is everywhere. PCs on company desks used to be as foreign as typewriters are today. With email, telephone tag is a thing of the past. How many of you still receive timely correspondence via the postal service? What company, start-up or established, doesn't need an informative, interactive Web site? Suddenly, a small-business owner can have a global audience. As we have seen in the examples above, the best companies are continuously searching for ways to exploit technology to become even more efficient. Understanding how technology works is critical. The blurring between technologists and general managers is occurring because smart business practices are becoming increasingly technology-driven. This is not to say that the human element is diminishing in importance. Rather, human initiative, creativity, and interaction will always be the engines for progress in business. It's just that the human element has so many more channels for innovation, if one understands the underlying technology.

The problem with understanding technology for many people is that most books on technology are written for a technical audience. As a result, the average business professional who wants to learn is often turned off by the bewildering acronyms, challenging diagrams, and daunting technospeak. For the uninitiated, reading a technical book is much like trying to read in a foreign language. Moreover, many books on technology are written in a straightforward and somewhat dry manner. Thus, the reader often ends up frustrated and bored and putting the book back on the shelf.

In this book, we make a concerted effort to reach out to the nontechnical business professional. On our writing team, we have both the technologist and the business generalist who collaborate on every sentence to ensure that you are getting the most precise and up-to-date technical information presented in a way that is clear, engaging, and fun. You will learn a lot and enjoy yourself in the process. We feel that this emphasis on explaining technological concepts in a way that is accessible and interesting to the nontechnical person is what sets our book apart from others on Internet business. You will be amazed at how much you learn and you will soon amaze others with your grasp of Internet business technology. You probably never realized that technology could be so fascinating. Then with these concepts under your belt, you, too, can be an agent of Internet business change and ride the crest of progress.

OBJECTIVES OF THE BOOK . . . .

We realize there is a growing number of you who recognize that staying on top of technology is becoming critical to your job. Perhaps you hear acronyms or unfamiliar jargon being tossed around, words like "firewalls," "best of breed," and "server" sliding into the everyday vocabulary. Perhaps you need to learn how to query a database, submit a purchase order online, or manage an automated supply chain. Maybe your boss has asked you to look into the advantages and disadvantages of going with an ASP versus purchasing software in-house. You may even be responsible for combining traditional and online means of selling, or "channel bundling," to increase market share. There are countless examples of how Internet business is becoming a part of our everyday work lives.

This book is designed to give you the tools you need to manage these tasks and more. The following is a list of what you will be able to accomplish once you have read this book. You will be able to:

- Ask informed questions and make sound business decisions on technology investments such as selecting a Web hosting service or adding features to your Web site.

- Comprehend the latest technological achievements in Internet business so you can begin to apply them to your own workplace.

- Understand the different types of Internet business initiatives available.

- Understand the modern Internet business N-tier architecture.

- Communicate effectively with IT specialists and your chief information officer (CIO) to get their support for your projects.

- Determine the technology you need to support your Internet business initiatives.

- Save time and money by streamlining your operations using the Internet.

- Understand the trade-off in time and money between creating a Web site that has a large capacity ("scalability") versus creating one that is up and running quickly ("speed to market").

IS THIS BOOK FOR YOU? . . . .

This book is for you if you would like to understand how Internet business technology can help you and your company save and make money. It is expressly written for you if you have little to no knowledge of technology. However, if you consider yourself a technologist, you might also enjoy this book and share it with the nontechnical people in your life so they, too, can enjoy the wonders of technology. Thank you for selecting this book. We hope it will help you in your future endeavors.

NAVIGATING THE BOOK ....

We have designed this book to progress logically from the most fundamental aspects of Internet business to the most sophisticated. Each chapter builds upon the previous chapters to arrive at new insights and deeper understanding.

The book is divided into five parts. Part I, "Technology Basics," is devoted to providing you with the necessary background for understanding how Internet business works. This part includes this chapter on saying "yes" to Internet business, and Chapters 2 through 4, which are primers on hardware, software, and Internet and Web technology. Part II, "Front End: Presentation," refers to the "front end" of Internet business architecture, the layer through which Internet business presents itself to its customers, business partners, and other constituents. This part comprises Chapters 5 through 7, which cover what you need to know about the best ways to design and establish an Internet presence. Part III, "Nuts and Bolts of Internet Business," focuses on the key strategies of getting an Internet business up and running. In this part we discuss in Chapters 8 through 11 the different Internet business models, security, transactions, and marketing on the Internet. Part IV, "Back End: Support," is a reference to the "back end" of Internet business architecture, which supports the front end. In this part we cover in Chapters 12 through 14 the power of databases, Internet business architecture, and enterprise application software. Note that we cover the back end after Part III on business models, rather than immediately after Part II on the front end. We feel that it is important for you to understand basic models and how Internet business is conducted before you take a behind-the-scenes look at the more sophisticated technological aspects. Finally, Part V, "Additional Help," provides more technical details and references for the adventurous and curious reader. This part includes technical appendices, a suggested reading list, and a glossary. A more detailed part and chapter analysis follows.

Part I − TECHNOLOGY BASICS: In order to make informed decisions about technology, it is necessary to understand the most basic elements of any system: hardware, software, and the Internet.

Chapter 2 − What Do I Need to Know about Hardware?: We live in the Information Age, and understanding how information is stored and retrieved is critical to knowing how to use it to your advantage. In this chapter we provide you with fundamental concepts of computer hardware, like the different types of computers, the essentials of how a computer works, and how information is stored and accessed. After reading this chapter you will know what to consider when purchasing a computer, and will have a better idea of how to integrate hardware into an Internet business system. We also present the managerial implications of this hardware technology.

Chapter 3 – Software Is Everywhere: In this chapter we discuss the crucial role of software in all modern corporations, regardless of size. Software is crucial because every Internet business function depends on software. Making the wrong software decision can wreak havoc on a firm and waste millions of dollars. Software with all the upgrades is expensive, too. We briefly describe the software development process so you can understand what you are paying for when you purchase software. We discuss less expensive alternatives to shrink-wrapped software that are becoming available. The choice of an operating system is a fundamental Internet business decision, and we examine the advantages and disadvantages of different operating systems. We look at the trend toward open source computing and the increasingly important battle between Microsoft and the Java/Unix community, which will affect every firm interested in Internet business.

Chapter 4 – Internet and Web Technology: The essence of the Internet can be summed up in three words: efficient information exchange. Understanding how this information exchange works gives you an advantage when weighing decisions such as whether to host your Internet business in-house or outsource. We begin this chapter with a brief history of the Internet and the fascinating people who made it what it is today. You will learn about packet switching and the TCP/IP protocol, the language of the Internet. We discuss the basic tools for navigating the Internet, as well as for uploading and downloading information. After reading this chapter you will understand the Internet addressing and naming system for computers.

Part II – FRONT END: PRESENTATION: In the second part of the book, we build on concepts and vocabulary introduced in the first part to show you how to integrate hardware, software, and the Internet to build an Internet presence. The chapters in this part of the book are devoted to what is called the presentation layer of Internet business architecture. It is the "interface," or site of interaction, between a firm engaged in Internet business and the world. The fundamental component of the presentation layer is a Web site with which customers or business partners can interact.

Chapter 5 – Languages of the Internet: Information exchange over the Internet requires that different computers be able to "talk" to each other. To do so, a common language that all computers recognize is necessary. In this chapter we introduce the concept of a markup language. A markup language uses a set of commands to control how the recipient sees the information. It's important to distinguish between a markup language and a "what you see is what you get" (WYSIWYG) language like Microsoft Word. We explain all of this in this chapter. We introduce HTML, XML, and XHTML. HTML and XHTML are used for the front end of Internet business architecture and XML is becoming a cornerstone for the back end. We also describe the different options you have for developing a Web page, like using HTML, a converter, or specialized software like Microsoft FrontPage. We also introduce the technologies for making Web pages dynamic.

Chapter 6 – Web Site Design and Content: Just as branding, corporate identity, public relations, signage, and advertising have been the face that companies have traditionally presented to the world, a Web page is the Information Age face to the world that Internet business presents. What works and what doesn't? In this chapter we explore designing

Web pages and discuss how to create a Web site that won't turn customers away (which many do) and will keep them coming back for more. The quality of Web page design and ease of use are very important aspects of building a Web presence. We discuss major considerations when designing a Web page such as target audience, clarity, and the "non-linear" nature of surfing the Web. We discuss how Web search engines work and how to get a search engine to give your page a high ranking.

Chapter 7 – Getting Your Business Online: A major Internet business decision is whether to develop an online presence in-house or outsource. In this chapter, we discuss a spectrum of options in selecting a Web hosting service available to you. We cover everything from the technology necessary for an in-house solution to selecting an MSP and an ASP to manage your Internet business hardware and software. To broaden your understanding of options available to you, we include a discussion of basic networking and telecommunications technologies such as wireless and DSL.

Part III – NUTS AND BOLTS OF INTERNET BUSINESS: Behind a Web presence lie the operations of Internet business. In this part of the book we cover the different Internet business models as well as functions such as financial transactions and marketing. Because the medium of Internet business exists in a world where hackers abound, no company can afford to be without security. Even a pure brick and mortar company – a traditional company not doing business on the Internet – is affected by the Internet because of what its competitors can do with the Internet to take market share away. Thus, every company must engage in Internet business. This part of the book gives you the nuts and bolts.

Chapter 8 – Rethinking Internet Business Models: What are the different ways a firm can use the Internet for business? In this chapter we explore the ingenious models that continue to transform the way people do business. We have already made a distinction between Internet business and Internet commerce. We examine this distinction in greater detail and present a number of Internet business models, including the Internet Retailing Model, Auction Model, Portal Model, Content Model, B2B Exchange Model, and Bricks and Clicks Model.

Chapter 9 – Security and Internet Business: Regardless of whether a firm is using any one of the models featured in Chapter 8 or working with in-house enterprise application software, security is of foremost importance. A firm must guard against theft and destruction of highly sensitive information such as credit card information, customer databases, new product designs, employee records, pricing schemes, and confidential email memos. In this chapter we describe the different means by which you and your firm can protect yourselves. We discuss password safety, encryption, public and private key systems, digital signatures, digital certificates, firewalls, and legal issues.

Chapter 10 – Internet Business Transactions: Once your Web presence is established, your Internet business model up and running, and your firm's infrastructure secure, the next thing to do is to start filling those orders. What's involved with order fulfillment? A lot, it turns out, and may make the difference between a profitable and unprofitable company. In this chapter we discuss how to build a storefront, the different ways you can receive payments online, and how you can most efficiently fulfill orders.

Chapter 11 – Marketing on the Internet: Generating orders for your Internet business is both an art and a science. We discuss both aspects in this chapter. In the first part of the chapter, we discuss Internet marketing strategies like branding, one-to-one marketing, permission marketing, viral marketing, partnering, and doing more with less. We write about what not to do based on the culture of the Internet. Because the nature of the Internet makes it easy to track and measure movements of customers and prospective customers, Internet marketing is approaching more of a science. The second part is devoted to tracking and measuring your customers' movements once they arrive at your site and deciding what to do with the data you collect. In the third part we discuss the different media of Internet marketing like channel bundling, banner ads, and email marketing.

   Part IV – BACK END: SUPPORT: When a customer visits the Amazon Web site he is interacting with the presentation layer of Internet business architecture. That is, a Web page is the "interface" between Amazon and the customer. If the customer is a repeat customer, Amazon will serve up a Web page of suggested customized readings based on what other customers who share similar reading interests with him have bought. For ease of purchasing, the customer may opt to use the Amazon "1-Click" shopping, which saves him from re-entering all of his billing and shipping and credit card information each time he makes a purchase. These kinds of Internet business functions trigger a great deal of activity past the presentation layer and deep into architecture; that is, into the middle tier, or business logic layer, and into the back end, or database tier. In this part of the book, we hope to convey to the reader a basic understanding of how more complex activities such as these are realized.

Chapter 12 – The Power of Databases: A revolution not fully appreciated by many is the ability of modern computers to store, organize, and analyze enormous amounts of data. This may not seem exciting on the surface, yet the ability to store and analyze corporate data is critical if a firm is to gain competitive advantage. One way to do this is to keep data on your customers and their preferences so you can market to them accordingly. Another is to keep track of suppliers, their products, prices, quality, and delivery lead times to make ordering more efficient. Customized correspondence, invoices, and purchase orders can be created in seconds using databases. In this chapter we provide an introduction to databases and their many uses. We describe how to get information you need in and out of a database, how to design databases for optimum efficiency, and how to create and mine data warehouses.

Chapter 13 – Internet Business Architecture: In the early days of computing, every-thing was based around a monolithic mainframe computer, one of those huge gorillas of a computer that sometimes filled an entire room and to which many users were hooked up through terminals. With the advent of the PC in the early 1980s, computing shifted to individual desktops. Then computers were networked and a shift occurred back to the model of a central server (previously the mainframe, now an enterprise server) for multiple clients or users. At first this model was a simple two-tier system represented by a client and a server. As Internet business has grown in size and complexity it has become necessary for client/server systems to "scale," or increase in size to fit the need. This has led to more complicated N-tier architectures. In this chapter we discuss the latest N-tier architectures that provide the backbone for large-scale Internet business applications.

Chapter 14 – Enterprise Application Software: The discussion of Internet business architecture in the previous chapter leads naturally into this chapter on enterprise application software. This software is used for managing customer relationships, sales force, manufacturing, accounting, and a host of other jobs. There is also a growing trend toward integrating different software systems within a firm and between different firms. This hot new area is called B2Bi (business-to-business integration). We address the important problem of integrating different software systems within a firm. We introduce a number of important software technologies for "gluing" together different software applications in a distributed environment.

Part V – APPENDIX: ADDITIONAL HELP: The book concludes with additional material designed to help the reader interested in pursuing Internet business technology in greater depth.

Technical Appendix: For the more technologically curious, we include an appendix containing sections on representing numbers in digital form, IP addressing, object-oriented programming, XML, JavaScript, Active Server Pages, Web services, and middleware technologies. These are designed for the more advanced reader wishing to understand some of the details behind the technologies covered in this book.

Suggested Reading: In this appendix we provide a brief annotated bibliography on a wide variety of Internet business-related books. They run the gamut from strategy and programming to histories of technology.

Glossary: We have provided, for your ease of reading and reference, definitions of key terms used in the book. Use this if you come across a word or acronym you don't recognize. If we don't define a word where you encounter it, it may have been that we defined it earlier in the book. We try our best to define all vocabulary related to Internet business.

2

What Do I Need to Know about Hardware?

In this chapter ...

IS THE PC DEAD? . . . .

Key to making sound decisions about the hardware behind Internet business is understanding where computing power should reside. Should it be diffused on desktop PCs or centralized on an enterprise server? PCs saw their heyday in the 1980s and early 1990s, but with the spread of the Internet, many critics of PCs claimed that it would be replaced by a centralized model in which users would access computing power over the Internet from "dumb" terminals. Critics claimed the PC was dead. This hasn't quite panned out as predicted, but a fierce debate continues to rage. Which side will triumph has important repercussions for hardware decisions being made today. In this section we trace the development of computing power to give you perspective on the debate, which should inform your hardware decisions. Moreover, this understanding provides the foundation for comprehending sophisticated Internet Business Architecture, the subject of Chapter 13.

In the beginning, all computing was done on monolithic mainframes. This phase of computing is depicted by the 12 o'clock position in Figure 2–1. In the late 1940s and into the 1950s a mainframe was a very large machine that filled an entire room and relied on vacuum tubes for computing power. The *user interface*, or the means by which the user interacted with the computer, was through punch cards (actually by hand wiring in the very beginning). The user sat at a large key punch machine and punched holes in a card. A sequence of punched holes corresponded to an instruction to the computer. The cards were then read through a card reader that often had an unfortunate tendency to destroy the cards. Yes, hanging chads were a problem even back then. A hanging chad resulted in an incorrect instruction. These massive vacuum tube computers vanished by mid-century with the invention of the transistor.

The transistor was invented in December 1947 at Bell Labs. William Shockley was the leader of the research group. It is difficult to overestimate the significance of this discovery, for without the transistor there would be no desktop computers and no Internet. By the mid-1950s millions of transistors were being sold in various electronic devices. In 1955 Shockley left Bell Labs and ventured out on his own to stake a fortune in transistors. He created Shockley Semiconductor Laboratory in 1956. Perhaps Shockley's greatest strength as a manager was his ability to hire outstanding people. Two such hires were Gordon Moore and Robert Noyce. He also hired Gene Kleiner, who later went on to help found the famous venture capital firm of Kleiner, Perkins, Caufield, & Byers.

However, Shockley was notoriously paranoid and held many beliefs that would today be considered politically incorrect, to put it mildly. Shockley's management style resulted in an exodus of his top talent. Moore and Noyce left Shockley Semiconductor Laboratory on September 18, 1957, as part of the now infamous "Traitorous Eight." The Traitorous Eight was a core group of engineers who left together to form a new company. At that time, millions of transistors were being produced each year. Moore and Noyce formed Fairchild Semiconductor. At Fairchild, they took computing to the next level by figuring out how to produce the integrated circuit; that is, how to put many transistors on the same wafer of semiconducting material. (Independently, Jack Kilby at Texas Instruments also developed the integrated circuit and was awarded the Nobel Prize in Physics in 2000 for his work.)

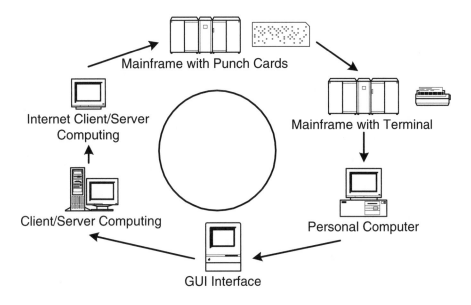

Figure 2–1 The cycle of computing.

The transistor and integrated circuit gave rise to the second and third generations of computers in the 1960s and 1970s. Although these machines were continuously improving in speed, a problem remained: the world was still mainframe-centric and using a mainframe was still too difficult and cumbersome for the average layperson. Nevertheless, with second and third generation computers came a major improvement in the user interface: rather than punching and feeding cards through a machine, the user could submit instructions to the computer remotely through a terminal and keyboard and actually interact with the computer. This was called *time sharing*. No more hanging chads! Moving clockwise in our cycle of computing this development brings us to 2 o'clock in Figure 2–1. Yet it was still difficult to communicate with a computer, and using one required a fair amount of training and skill. For example, a general manager who wanted information from a corporate database stored in a computer had to ask a trained specialist to probe the database and generate a report. There was as yet no hands-on access to data for a general manager. The work of the Traitorous Eight was not yet complete.

Moore and Noyce eventually became dissatisfied with Fairchild Semiconductor and left to found Intel in 1968. A cofounder of Intel, employee number four, was Andy Grove (who just stepped down as CEO in 1998). The founders wanted to do something new and great and not just compete in the integrated circuit market. It turns out they did two great things. The first had to do with memory—where a computer's information is stored. They wanted to make memory smaller and work faster by developing memory chips. Intel became the first company to produce RAM, or random access memory chips. Intel began marketing these memory chips in the spring of 1969.

Then in 1971, thanks to Ted Hoff (employee number 12), Intel did a second great thing by introducing the first microprocessor (the brain of the computer). What the microprocessor did was reduce what used to be contained in a mainframe the size of a room to the size of a single chip, or about the size of a thumbnail. A chip comprises a base, usually made of silicon, and a set of transistors. The first Intel chip was the 4004 and contained 2,300 transistors. While the 4004 was clearly a breakthrough, developments in computing power and speed have since been breathtakingly rapid. Take, for example, the Pentium III chip introduced by Intel in 1999. It has approximately 9.5 million transistors. See Table 2–1 for the increases in microprocessor power with each new chip. The significance of this improvement is stated in Moore's Law, which is still remarkably accurate since Moore declared it in 1965: The number of transistors on a new chip doubles every 18 months.

Table 2–1 Microprocessor Power [81]

	Year	Transistors	Clock Speed	Data Path Width
4004	1971	2,300	108 KHz	4 bits
8080	1974	6,000	2 MHz	8 bits
80286	1982	134,000	6 -12.5 MHz	16 bits
386 DX	1985	275,000	16 - 33 MHz	32 bits
486 DX	1989	1,200,000	25 - 50 MHz	32 bits
Pentium	1993	3,100,000	60 - 66 MHz	64 bits
Pentium Pro	1995	5,500,000	150 - 200 MHz	64 bits
Pentium II	1997	7,500,000	200 - 300 MHz	64 bits
Pentium III	1999	9,500,000	650 MHz-1 GHz	64 bits
Pentium 4	2000	42,000,000	1.3 - 1.5 GHz	64 bits

The microprocessor made the desktop computer possible. This brings us to 4 o'clock in our cycle of computing in Figure 2–1. The first personal computer was the Altair 8800 released in 1975 by the MITS Corporation founded by Ed Roberts. Bill Gates dropped out of Harvard to write software for the Altair. However, the Altair was really just a computer for hobbyists. It had to be assembled from a kit.

The first personal computer to hit it big was the Apple II computer released in 1977. Once IBM realized that desktop computers were not just a toy, but a serious business tool, it entered the business. The first IBM personal computer hit the market in August 1981. Initially, the personal desktop computer was not a serious business tool. The "killer app" (short for "killer application," a term for any hot, revolutionary computer application tool in great demand—you buy the computer so you can use the killer app) for the first generation of personal computers was the spreadsheet. For the Apple II the spreadsheet was VisiCalc and for the IBM PC the spreadsheet was Lotus 123. To some extent, word processing was also a killer app.

One feature of the early personal computer that prevented it from becoming hugely successful in business was the operating system. The operating system is software that controls how the computer works and how the user interacts with the computer. A key aspect of an operating system is the user interface, or how the user issues commands to and retrieves information from the computer. The early personal computers had a "command line interface," which meant the user had to remember and type arcane commands into a somber, all-text screen that was hardly user-friendly.

Then in 1984 another revolution occurred. It was the introduction of the *graphical user interface or GUI*. Instead of facing an unfriendly text screen and typing in commands, the user clicked on friendly pictures and graphical icons with a mouse to get things done. Apple Computer, with its Macintosh, was the first company to introduce an affordable GUI-based computer into the marketplace, although the origins of the GUI trace back to work done earlier at Xerox PARC (Palo Alto Research Center). The GUI-based personal computer brings us to 6 o'clock in the cycle of computing (See Figure 2–1).

Tech Talk

Moore's Law: An empirical observation of Gordon Moore of Intel states that the computing power of a new chip doubles every 18 months.

Even with a GUI, the personal computer was still not a full-blown business tool. This required still another revolution called file sharing—the ability to share data across a computer network. Users at different desktop computers could now exchange information across a network that connected their computers. A leader in this technology was Sun Microsystems. The word Sun came from Stanford University Network. Sun introduced its network file sharing technology, NFS, in 1984. The Apple Macintosh had its own technology called AppleTalk.

Although Sun computers were used mainly in the scientific community, networking technology was quickly adopted in the personal computer marketplace. Networking technology brings us around the cycle of computing to 8 o'clock, where we arrive at "client/server computing." As the name implies, there is a client computer that retrieves something from another computer that acts as a server. The server may simply serve up data files, or it might do more sophisticated things like run tasks requested by the client. For example, the client might be a desktop PC running an application that receives payroll information stored on the server. Typically, many client machines use a single server or cluster of servers. Client/server computing is the main topic of Chapter 13.

Now with the Internet, we are coming full cycle to the 10 o'clock position. The Internet has caused an explosion in client/server computing because it acts as the network through which the client and server communicate. This explosion is also due to the ubiquitous Internet browser, such as Microsoft Internet Explorer or Netscape Communicator, which allows a user to browse Web pages and use other tools of the Internet. A browser is on virtually every user's computer and is rapidly becoming a universal piece of client software. Indeed, in 1995, Larry Ellison declared that the personal desktop computer was a "silly device" and that the network computer (NC), a client computer interacting with a server over the Internet, would replace desktop computing.

Although his prediction has not yet been borne out, we are in the process of a major paradigm shift in hardware. With the power of the network, it is no longer necessary to have a powerful desktop machine, or strong client, as it is called. Rather, it is now possible to use an inexpensive, weak client and depend on the server for data and computing. (Weak and strong clients are also called thin and fat clients, respectively.) In the weak client paradigm the server needs to be powerful. Thus, the server is evolving into a mainframe and we have come full circle back to our mainframe days, at 12 o'clock. Hence, our cycle of computing model.

. . . .

Larry Ellison

> Larry Ellison is the swashbuckling Chairman and Chief Executive Officer of Oracle Corporation. He is one of the best known personalities in the Internet era. He has a love of fast cars, boats, and planes. He is the embodiment of conspicuous consumption. Through his vision, Oracle became the number one database company in the world. He is a leading proponent of network-based computing and is constantly attacking Microsoft for its devotion to the PC. An appropriately titled biography is *The Difference Between God and Larry Ellison: Inside Oracle Corporation* by Mike Wilson [175].

However, the mainframe that once took up an entire large room is now a server often the size of a pizza box. There are also two other key differences from the original mainframe days. First, the browser is a universal GUI that interacts with the server as opposed to punched cards. Second, the Internet is an open, universal network of which any company can take advantage. In the early days of client/server computing there were many networking standards, which made it difficult to communicate across company networks. It was also virtually impossible for customers to access the company network. The new Internet-based paradigm has major implications for Internet business and for many important players like IBM, Microsoft, Sun, and Oracle. We revisit this topic in Chapter 3, "Software Is Everywhere" and Chapter 13, "Internet Business Architecture." The book *The Silicon Boys* by David Kaplan [88], the Intel Web site, and the Sun Web site provided information for this section.

HOW INFORMATION IS STORED . . . .

As we wrote in the first chapter, Internet business is all about making information exchange more efficient. The hardware is simply a tool, albeit a powerful one, to effect this exchange. One of the reasons Internet business is becoming so big is that it results in dramatic cost savings and increases in productivity. An international air mail invoice may take days if not weeks to arrive at its destination and could cost close to a dollar to send. An international invoice sent via email may take a few seconds and is essentially free. Before Internet business, company employees offsite could not access a corporate database for information they might need for a sale. They would have to call the office and ask someone to retrieve the information. With the Internet, they can access the database remotely and instantly, thereby greatly improving their productivity.

So how is information produced and stored with hardware and transmitted over the Internet? If you understand this, you understand one of the fundamental building blocks of Internet business. All information that can be stored on a computer and transmitted over the Internet, whether it be text, numbers, sound, graphics, or video, can be represented as a series of the numbers 0 and 1. This is what computers are all about—transforming human knowledge, thought, and creativity into 0s and 1s. The secret is in the chip. Intel's Pentium III chip contains 9.5 million transistors. What does this mean? Each transistor is used to store a single 0 or 1. The computer registers "0" if an electrical charge is not flowing through a transistor, and "1" if it is. The ability to transform information into 0s and 1s is what makes the computer a digital device. In fact, whenever you see or hear the word "digital" you now know this means that whatever is represented, whether a movie, your favorite song on a compact disc, or a graphic, has been translated into 0s and 1s. How can this be possible? We shall see in the rest of this section.

Storing Text

Text, i.e., letters and words, is easy to store on a computer. In order to store text one simply develops a code consisting of a string of 0s and 1s for each letter of the alphabet and for special characters like the "@" sign and the dollar sign. To illustrate, let's store the sentence: SEE SPOT RUN. Each letter with the corresponding code is given in Table 2–2.

Table 2–2 Example of ASCII Code

S	1010011
E	1000101
E	1000101
S	1010011
P	1010000
O	1001111
T	1010100
R	1010010
U	1010101
N	1001110

In Table 2–2 each letter of the alphabet takes up seven 0s or 1s. Each 0 or 1 represents a *bit*, or the smallest unit of information on a computer; that is, whether or not an electrical charge is flowing through a transistor. The standard code for representing text as 0s and 1s, what you see in Table 2–2, is called the ASCII (American Standard Code for Information Interchange) coding scheme. The ASCII code is universal and virtually any piece of software capable of creating documents can read an ASCII file. Files containing ASCII data are often called *text files*. These files often have a `.txt` extension after the name of the file.

Although bits represent the smallest unit of information in a computer, data are not moved around in a computer one bit at a time. The smallest chunk of data which the computer moves around is called a *byte*, which comprises eight bits. Since ASCII requires only seven bits, the extra bit is set to 0 when storing the standard ASCII characters. Different computer systems may use the leading bit to store other non-ASCII symbols. How many different characters can you represent in ASCII? Unfortunately, only 2^7 characters, or the possibility of either 0 or 1 for each of the 7 bits, which is 128 characters. This is not a problem with the English language since it uses a 26-letter alphabet, but there is a problem with the Chinese language because its characters are based on pictographs and number in the tens of thousands. The answer to the problem of a limited ASCII character set is a new coding scheme. Such a code is called "unicode," which uses 16 bits, rather than 7 bits, to represent a character. This allows for over 65,000 characters. Using unicode we can represent in 0s and 1s every language from Arabic and Chinese to Greek and Russian.

In an ASCII text file, only seven bits are used to encode the 128 ASCII characters. The extra bit is used in what are called *binary files*. Most software applications store their documents as binary files. For example, a Microsoft Word document, a .doc file, or a Microsoft Excel spreadsheet, an .xls file, is a binary file. The entire software applications themselves, Word and Excel, are also binary files. On a Windows machine, software application files end with the suffix .exe. For example, the actual Word program is stored on the computer as WINWORD.EXE. These files are usually stored in a proprietary format. This means that the company that developed the binary (proprietary) encoding scheme may not freely release the coding scheme. This contrasts with the ASCII coding scheme for text files, which is open and can be freely used by anyone.

There are many problems associated with binary files. Binary files cause problems with upgrades. If a company alters its binary file format, someone with an older version of the software may not be able to read a file created with a newer version of the software. It also turns out that computer viruses are often spread through emailing binary files. Viruses cannot be spread using text files. So, if possible, try to exchange text files rather than binary files. Finally, it is a good idea to store, or at least back up, mission-critical data as text files. Virtually any word processing, spreadsheet, or database program can read text files, whereas binary files require special software which may not always be available.

Most units of measurement for the computer are based on a byte. You may have heard these units of measurement bandied about when referring to a computer's memory. A *kilobyte* (KB) is $2^{10} = 1,024$ bytes. The amount of main memory on your computer is usually measured in megabytes where one *megabyte* (MB) is 2^{20} bytes or 1,048,576 bytes. The sentence, SEE SPOT RUN, stored as in the previous example, takes only 12 bytes. Your average novel on the best-seller list would take about one megabyte or "meg" of memory. The amount of main memory in a modern computer is generally 64 to 256 megabytes. This number is increasing rapidly. In the early 1980s, 640 kilobytes of main memory was considered a lot. A *gigabyte* (GB) is 2^{30} bytes or 1,073,741,824 bytes. Most high-end PCs now come with at least 10 gigabytes of memory on the hard drive. All of these units are a power of 2, which reflects the binary nature of the transistor.

Storing Numbers

Developing a code in 0s and 1s to represent letters of the alphabet was relatively easy because every language has a finite number of letters. How can 0s and 1s be used to represent numbers? Let's first consider the easier case of integers, or whole numbers. We could, in theory, store a number like 56 as the "character" 5, a textual representation of "5" with no numerical meaning, followed by the character 6. (Storing the *character* 5 is like typing 5 using word processing software—the 5 cannot be added or subtracted. Storing the *number* 5 is like typing 5 into a spreadsheet model, which can be added or subtracted.) It would be totally impractical to perform mathematical operations on numbers represented as characters. We need to store a number as a number. The logical choice is to store integers using the "base 2" number system. For example, in Table 2–3 we represent the integer 37 using the base 2 number system.

Table 2–3 Base 2 Representation of 37

1×2^0	$=$	1
0×2^1	$=$	0
1×2^2	$=$	4
0×2^3	$=$	0
0×2^4	$=$	0
1×2^5	$=$	32
0×2^6	$=$	0
0×2^7	$=$	0
TOTAL	$=$	37

If we look at the first column of 0s and 1s and line them up from last to first (largest power of 2 to smallest power of 2), we see that 37 is stored in binary as 00100101. Here we are assuming an 8 bit (1 byte) unit. Not counting a bit to store the sign of the number as either positive or negative, the largest integer that a byte can represent is $2^8 - 1$ which is 255. This is rather limited, so most integers are stored in unit sizes of at least 32 bits. What is the largest unsigned integer you can represent in a unit of 32 bits? (Answer: $2^{32} - 1 = 4,294,967,295$, which is large enough to cover most integers used in everyday life.)

In the real world, however, there are numbers like interest rates and stock prices which are not integers. These noninteger numbers are called *floating point* numbers. Simply rounding these numbers to the closest integer in a computer would obviously lead to severe inaccuracies. The problem with storing floating point numbers is that we don't know ahead of time how many decimal places there are in a number so we don't know how many bits to allot to it. The solution to this problem is to use a form of scientific notation based on the base 2 number system and fix the number of nonzero elements allowed after the decimal point. The details of this method appear in the Technical Appendix at the end of the book.

The reader should be aware that there are several problems with working with floating point numbers on a computer. First, even a simple number like 0.1 = 1/10 cannot be stored precisely using 32 bits (or any finite number of bits using a base 2 scheme). There is a loss of accuracy because of the fixed number of bits. Second, operations on floating point numbers cannot be executed as quickly as on integers. Floating point operations are measured in MFLOPS, or 1 million floating point operations per second. There are computers capable of executing over one teraflop per second, or TFLOPS, which is 1 trillion floating point operations per second. It comes as no surprise that some Wall Street firms have purchased supercomputers to perform the number crunching necessary for rocket scientists to build their mathematical models for sophisticated financial instruments.

Storing Sound

You may have gone to the movies and seen on the big screen that the movie has been recorded in "Dolby Digital Surround Sound." You probably never gave much thought to the word "digital" as you sat there munching on popcorn and waiting for the movie to begin. Thanks to reading this book, however, you now know that this means the movie's sound track has been "digitized" or reduced to a series of 0s and 1s. We've seen how complicated digitizing can be for numbers, but how can this be possible for sound? And why do movie producers make a big deal about the sound being digital?

Storing sound on a computer is a problem because sound is naturally captured as an *analog* phenomenon. Sound is a *continuous* waveform passing through the air. You hear because these sound waves hit your eardrum. Sound is captured on a telephone line by electromagnetic waves that vary in amplitude and frequency in proportion to the voice. This electromagnetic wave is continuous. The problem with storing sound in a computer is that 0s and 1s are discrete, or *noncontinuous* units. So how can a continuous sound wave be represented by noncontinuous 0s and 1s?

In order to store sound in a computer, it is "digitized." That is, the sound wave is "interpolated" at a finite number of points. What does this mean? This means that the shape of the waveform of sound, which is actually made up of an infinite (continuous) number of points, is estimated at a finite (noncontinuous) number of points. This process is called *sampling*. In Figure 2–2 we see how the sound wave is "cut up" into a finite number of grid points at which the amplitude (height) of the wave is measured. The number of grid points represented by the vertical lines in the figure is the *sampling rate*. The greater (more accurate) the sampling rate, the greater the number of vertical lines. It is usually measured in KHz (cycles per second is known as Hertz, and KHz is a measure of a thousand cycles per second). For example, a sampling rate of 44.1 KHz is 44,100 cycles per second, or in this case, samples per second. The amplitude or height at each of the points is recorded as a base 2 number. Converting this height to a base 2 number is called *quantization*. Typically the height is stored as either a one or two byte number. CD (compact disk) quality sound uses 44.1 KHz sampling and two byte quantization. The number of bits required to sample one hour of music at CD quality is $44,100 \times 16 \times 3,600 = 2,540,160,000$ where 44,100 is the samples per second, 16 is the number of bits in 2-byte quantization, and 3,600 is the number of seconds in an hour.

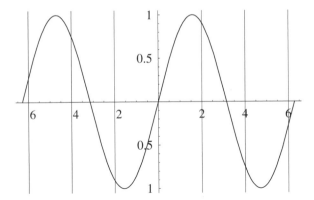

Figure 2–2 Interpolating a wave.

This converts to

$$2,250,160,000/(8 \times 2^{20}) \approx 303$$

or 303 megabytes to store one hour of music since there are (8×2^{20}) bits in a megabyte. Adding a second channel in sound quality for stereo increases the number of megabytes required to about 600. That is why only about one hour of music can be stored on a CD. A newer technology, DVD (digital versatile disk or digital video disk), has even higher exacting standards. It uses a 96 kHz sampling rate and 20–24 bit quantization.

Another way to conceive of how sound is stored in a computer is to think of the difference between a vinyl phonograph record and a CD. A vinyl record uses analog technology to record the sound. Those grooves you see on the record's surface are actually a replica of the sound waves being recorded. When the needle of the turntable passes over the grooves, the sound is reproduced. A CD, on the other hand, uses digital technology to record. A computer is used to transform the sound waves being recorded into 0s and 1s using sampling. The advantage of listening to a CD, in addition to its size and convenience, is that the sound remains crisp even after much use because the 0s and 1s on the CD do not "wear down" after repeated listening. The grooves on a vinyl record will wear down after much use, and can become scratched and distorted, which is why much of the recording industry has switched to digital technology. There are some true audiophile experts, though, who claim that the sound reproduced on a new vinyl record is superior to that on a CD. This is because the sampling process in recording a CD cannot capture the entire continuous sound wave, and the resulting quality, the audiophiles argue, is not as rich as that captured on a record.

Storing Graphics and Video

If storing sound as 0s and 1s seemed counterintuitive, storing graphics, or lines and shapes, may seem slightly more intuitive. This is because we can visualize a flat surface as a grid with an x-axis along the bottom and a y-axis along the side with points on the grid defining the line or shape. (We're going back to geometry in high school math.) The location of the points can be stored as numbers along the x- and y- axes, which are in turn stored as 0s and 1s in the computer. This image of a grid does indeed form the basis for the two general approaches to storing graphics. Graphics are stored as either *bitmap graphics* (also called *raster graphics*), or as *vector graphics*.

With bitmap, or raster graphics, each picture is stored as a set of *pixels*. Think of a picture, as we did above, as a grid with x and y coordinates. Each cell of the grid is a pixel. For example, a pixel might be location x = 20, y = 30. As we saw with the sound waves, the continuous lines and shapes of the graphic are approximated using a finite number of pixel locations. But the pixels are close enough together so that the eye is "tricked" into seeing a continuous line or shape. The amount of memory required to store each pixel depends upon whether the picture is stored in black and white or in color. The amount of memory required for a pixel is called the *bit depth*. Bit depths for different kinds of graphics are given below.

- Black and white - one bit

- Grayscale - one byte (8 bits)

- True color - three bytes

The use of three bytes for true color requires a little explanation. Three bytes are used for each pixel, one for red, one for green, and one for blue. Any color on the spectrum detectable by the human eye can be represented by a mixture of these three colors. Thus, the byte for say, red, represents the amount of red in the mixture. Because each byte consists of 8 bits, there are $2^8 = 256$ shades of red (represented by the numbers from 0 to 255) that can be present in a particular color. Since three bytes are used to represent a color pixel, this means there are $2^{24} = 16,777,216$ possible colors represented in this scheme. The bytes are stored in the order: red, green, and blue. Thus, a true red is represented by 11111111 00000000 00000000 (255, 0, 0), white, or the absence of color, is represented by 00000000 00000000 00000000 (0, 0, 0), and purple, or a mixture of red and blue, is represented by 11111111 00000000 11111111 (255, 0, 255). Of course, each byte could also represent a number between 0 and 255, depending on the shade of the color.

Tech Talk

CMYK : cyan, magenta, yellow, and black. This is a color scheme alternative to RGB (red, green, and blue) and is used for color printers. CMYK is called a subtractive color scheme because when light is reflected from colored pigments each added color absorbs (subtracts) more shades of the spectrum.

The bitmap graphics approach to storing graphics also applies to color monitors. Each grid or pixel on a color monitor contains three subpixels. These subpixels contain phosphors that can glow red, green, or blue when hit by an electron beam. How much red, green, or blue glows depends upon the 0s and 1s stored for each subpixel. The pixels are so close together the eye thinks it is seeing a continuous spectrum of colors. The VGA (video graphics array) standard for a color monitor is 640 times 480 (307,200) pixels on the "grid" of the monitor. A high resolution monitor is 1024 times 768 (786,432) pixels. If each subpixel contains eight bits then we have true color and the monitor can represent over 16 million colors.

On the Internet many of the pictures you see are stored in *GIF* (graphics interchange format). These GIF files are one of the two most common graphics file formats on the Web. The other is called *JPEG* (joint photographic experts group). As you can imagine, bitmap or raster graphics files such as GIF and JPEG can become very large because of the number of pixels and the use of color. In order that files be transmitted more quickly or stored more efficiently, the files are subjected to a compression scheme. Compression is discussed in the next subsection.

Tech Talk

GIF: A compression scheme for storing graphics developed by Compuserve. It can handle only 8 bit color. It is slowly being replaced by the PNG (portable network graphics) format developed by the World Wide Web Consortium.

Tech Talk

JPEG: A compression scheme for photographic images. Unlike the GIF compression scheme, with JPEG some information is lost.

Vector graphics are descriptions of objects represented by circles, rectangles, lines, and other geometric shapes. A horizontal blue line 30 pixels long could be described as:

1. Start point x = 5, y = 30

2. End point x = 34, y = 30

3. RGB (red, green, blue): 0, 0, 255

Two advantages of the vector scheme over the bitmap scheme is that it is easy to scale and size shapes, and graphics stored as vectors require much less memory than bitmapped graphics. The disadvantage is that it cannot store photographic images easily. The various fonts printed or shown on your computer screen can be stored either way, that is, as bitmap fonts or outline (vector graphic) fonts. TrueType fonts, used by both the Windows and Macintosh operating systems, are stored in vector format.

Postscript is a vector graphics file format and much more. It is actually a page description programming language. Postscript can store bitmap graphics with vector objects. It describes the text and graphics layout to a printer, and Postscript files can be transformed into *PDF* (portable document format) for easy downloading. *PICT* is another vector graphics file format. It was developed by Apple Computer in 1984 and can hold both vector graphics and bitmap graphics. PICT is supported by all graphics programs that run on Macintosh computers. For more information on how computer data storage works we highly recommend the book by Fortner [51].

Compression

Earlier we saw that a single channel of an hour of CD quality music required approximately 300 megabytes of storage. When you consider that stereo sound requires multiple channels, in addition to error checking bits, etc., CD quality sound requires about 1.5 megabits to store one second of music. Video is much more information-intensive, requiring up to 10 megabits per second. The problem with video is that in order for the picture not to look jerky it must store 30 frames or pictures per second.

The massive amount of memory required by sound and video necessitates that the data be compressed. Perhaps the best known video and audio compression scheme is *MPEG*, which stands for Motion Picture Experts Group. There are MPEG standards 1 through 4 at the present time. MPEG is an example of *lossy* compression, so named because there is a loss of data in the compression. The MPEG standard of lossy compression uses *perceptual coding* to eliminate or reduce data that cannot be perceived by the human eye or ear. It also uses *temporal compression*. The basic idea of temporal compression begins with examining consecutive frames in a movie for parts in a scene that may not change much from frame to frame. For example, in a John Wayne western shot in Monument Valley, the background mountains may not change very much from scene to scene. There is no need to keep storing the same data in every scene, so repetitive data appearing in many frames is encoded only once. Again, actual data are lost when using the MPEG compression scheme.

The MPEG standard is used for both sound and video. For example, the *MP3* (MPEG-1 Audio Layer-3) is one of the best known compression schemes for reducing sound files to a fraction of their original size. You may have heard of MP3 in news about the battle between Napster, a Web site where music can be downloaded free as MP3 files and shared among users, and the music industry, which claims Napster is violating copyright laws by allowing music to be freely downloaded and shared (called *P2P*, or peer-to-peer, computing). The MP3 compression algorithm works by reducing some of the data generated in digitizing CD quality sound. The data reduced are those that cannot be perceived by listeners, so the sound quality remains high.

Not all compression methods are lossy. For example, the GIF compression scheme for graphics uses the LZW algorithm, which is named after its inventors Abraham Lempel, Jacob Ziv, and Terry Welch. The idea behind LZW is to look for patterns in the file. For example, the pattern,

xyzwxyzwxyzwxyzw

could be coded as xyzw[4]. The LZW compression algorithm is an example of *lossless* compression; that is, no information is lost by compressing it.

HOW A COMPUTER WORKS ....

If you've ever had to wait for a computer to perform a task, you know how important it is to have a powerful and fast computer. The more powerful and faster a computer, the more valuable and expensive. In this section, we show how most of the major developments in computers made them operate more quickly. Internet business is growing because it allows for rapid and efficient information exchange. In this section we learn how computers achieve this great speed.

Regardless of whether a computer is a mainframe, desktop, or handheld device, the basic logic of how a computer works is the same. In fact, the way virtually all computers work is based on a model described in a paper by Arthur Burks, Herman Goldstine, and John von Neumann in 1946. A computer has the following key components:

- A central processing unit or CPU

- Cache

- Main memory

- Secondary storage

- Input and output units

- System or memory bus

- Chipset

Tech Talk

Chipset: This is the glue of the computer. A set of chips that coordinate communication among the various subsystems of the PC. The chipset provides the necessary buses for the CPU, main memory, secondary storage, and input/output devices to communicate.

In Figure 2–3 we show how these components relate to one another. Often the term CPU is used synonymously with the word microprocessor. The microprocessor, such as an Intel Pentium III or Sun UltraSparc III, is the brain of the computer. It controls how the computer works. It comprises a control unit, a decode unit, an arithmetic logic unit (ALU), a quartz crystal clock, a cache, a bus unit, and a set of registers where data and instructions are temporarily held. All of the components of a microprocessor are located on a single integrated circuit or chip, which is why the terms microprocessor and chip are also used interchangeably. Sometimes the control unit, decode unit, and ALU are called the CPU. John von Neumann, considered a mathematical genius, was the first to write about the concept of a *stored program*. (Although J. Presper Eckert, Jr. and John W. Mauchly of the ENIAC (Electronic Numerical Integrator and Computor) project at the University of Pennsylvania also wrote about the concept of a stored program.) This is the idea that the computer works by executing a set of instructions on data, and that both the instructions and the data are stored in main memory. Any microprocessor executes the following four steps:

- Fetches instructions and data from the main memory

- Decodes the instructions

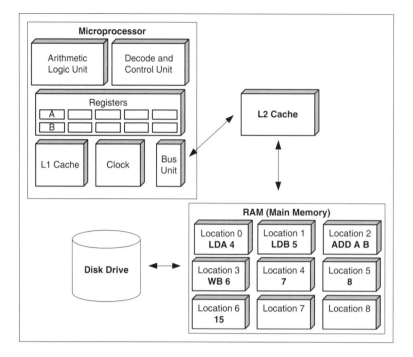

Figure 2–3 Executing an instruction from RAM.

- Executes the instructions
- Stores the results of the execution

The decode unit and control unit are in charge of interpreting and executing the instructions. Mathematical operations are controlled by the arithmetic logic unit (ALU). Instructions, data, and the results of executing instructions are stored in the microprocessor in both registers and an L1 cache. The instructions and data come in and out of the microprocessor via the system or memory bus. Think of a bus as a pathway that carries information from one part of the computer to another. Registers are storage locations on the chip that can be accessed very quickly. Most microprocessors will have different types of registers. There might be registers for integer numbers, floating point numbers, referencing memory addresses, etc.

It is very important to understand that different microprocessors have different sets of instructions. This is why an application written for an Apple Macintosh will not run on an IBM machine or why a Macintosh PowerPC chip does not understand instructions written for an Intel chip. This is a critical issue for software developers. Also, as the architecture of a chip family changes over time it causes a problem for software developers. When Intel increased the number of registers on its chip it had to include a mechanism for translating old register instructions to new ones.

The primary or main memory on a modern computer is also called random access memory or RAM. Think of RAM as a set of locations with specific addresses, as shown in Figure 2–3. Each location may contain data or may contain instructions. The number of bits in a location is called the *word length*. This is the amount of information a computer can process at one time. The word length affects the speed of a computer. The first Intel chip, the 4004, used a word length of 4 bits. The Pentium III uses 4-byte or 32-bit words. The Sun UltraSparc III uses an 8-byte (or 64-bit) word. On modern personal computers, RAM is volatile memory and its contents are lost when you turn the computer off.

To deepen your understanding of how a computer works, think of a very simple task such as adding 7 + 8 to get 15. A computer can execute this task incredibly quickly, but must follow an excruciatingly precise set of instructions to do so. For example, the location numbered 0 in Figure 2–3 might contain an instruction such as LDA 4. In this instruction the LDA is called the *op code* (operation code) and the number 4 is called the *operand*, or the data the opcode works on. This instruction says to load the contents of location 4 (the number 7) into register A, located in the microprocessor. The instruction in location 1 is LDB 5, which is to load the contents of location 5 (the number 8) into register B. Location 2 contains instruction ADD A B which is to add the contents of register A and B (resulting in the number 15) and store the result in register B. Finally, in location 3 we have the instruction WB 6, which is to write the contents of register B (the number 15) to location 6. These memory locations are illustrated in Figure 2–3. Table 2–4 below shows how much cheaper RAM has become over the last 30 years.

Table 2–4 Cost of 1 Meg of RAM

Year	Cost
1994	$45.00
1996	$35.00
1997	$12.50
1998	$6.25
1999	$2.80

Data can be retrieved very quickly from the registers that are located in the microprocessor. Retrieving data from main memory, or RAM, is relatively much more time-consuming. In order to speed up the process most CPUs have a *cache* that acts as a temporary staging area where data and instructions are held before being used by the control unit and the ALU in the CPU. Although faster than RAM, cache memory is more expensive. There are two types of cache memory, *L1* and *L2*. The L1 cache is physically on the microprocessor, whereas the L2 cache sits between the microprocessor and RAM. The Pentium III, for example, has a 32K (32 kilobyte) L1 cache and 512K L2 cache. From an efficiency standpoint, it is important to have the instructions and data that the CPU needs next in cache rather than in RAM. When an instruction or data must be fetched from RAM this is referred to as a "cache miss." A good programmer writes code to minimize cache misses.

The cache memory is sometimes also called SRAM for static RAM. What is in static memory remains there as long as there is power being fed to the computer. It is more expensive and faster than DRAM (dynamic random access memory). Dynamic memory needs a fresh electronic charge every few milliseconds. When people say RAM, they usually mean DRAM. Although SRAM is faster than DRAM it has several disadvantages, such as, for a given capacity it requires more transistors than DRAM and is more expensive. You may also hear about SDRAM which is synchronized DRAM. SDRAM is very fast DRAM synchronized with the clock of the CPU. Intel is also developing *Rambus* or RDRAM for the Pentium 4, which Intel claims has greater performance than SDRAM.

What is clock speed? Each microprocessor has an internal clock that determines the speed of operations. The clock in a CPU is a quartz crystal that is used to synchronize operations on the computer. The amount of elapsed time necessary to execute an instruction is controlled by the clock speed and the complexity of the instruction. The clock speed is measured in cycles per second. It may take several clock cycles to execute a single instruction. Recall from the discussion on storing sound that cycles per second is known as Hertz. A 500 megahertz machine, i.e., 500 MHz, would execute 500 million cycles per second. When it comes to clock speed, many people are misled by looking only at the megahertz figure for a personal computer. It is not necessarily true that the higher the megahertz, the faster the computer. Other factors such as word length, size of the system bus (which connects the CPU and main memory), speed of memory access, and chip architecture greatly affect performance. For example, some chips are designed to be very fast at doing floating point calculations. The amount of RAM a computer has also affects performance. More is better!

Secondary storage refers to hard drives, CD-ROM (compact disk, read only memory), Zip drives, Jaz drives (a Jaz drive is similar to the more common Zip drives, but has a greater memory capacity), tape drives, floppy drives, etc. The applications and operating system are stored on the hard drive. Zip and Jaz drives are very popular for backing up important files. Unlike RAM, secondary storage is not volatile and does not lose information when the computer is turned off (you hope). Secondary storage is much slower than RAM and its size is usually measured in megabytes or gigabytes. Most personal computers produced in 2001 will have at least a 10 gigabyte or "gig" hard drive. The latest and greatest storage technology is the DVD mentioned earlier. A DVD can store about 4.7 gig per side. Some DVDs have two layers on each side for about 17 gig. Accessing secondary storage is not nearly as fast as accessing primary storage. As you move from the chip registers to secondary storage (the disk drive) access times increase dramatically. Another type of memory, flash, is growing in popularity. Flash memory is nonvolatile but it has speed similar to DRAM. However, it is more expensive than DRAM for similar capacity. Flash memory is popular in handheld devices. It is also used to store information which is used when the computer boots up (is turned on).

Modern microprocessors use a number of sophisticated techniques to make them faster. One such technique is called *pipelining*. The idea behind pipelining is to have one part of the chip fetching instructions, another part decoding instructions, and another part executing instructions, all at the same time, or "in parallel." To illustrate the concept of pipelining, assume you have two loads of laundry to do. Further assume the wash cycle takes one-half hour and the dry cycle takes one-half hour. If you do not pipeline it takes two hours to do the two loads because you wait for the first load to complete the dry cycle before starting the second load. With pipelining it takes 1.5 hours since you start the wash cycle for the second load when you start the dry cycle for the first load. Microprocessors with multiple pipelines are called *superscalar*.

Another important technique for making microprocessors faster is called *single-instruction, multiple-data technology* (SIMD). The idea behind SIMD is to execute the same arithmetic operation (for example add or multiply) on multiple data streams simultaneously. The Intel MMX used this operation on a pipeline that could manipulate 64-bit wide data. The Pentium III extended this idea to work on two 64-bit wide data pipelines simultaneously.

An extension of the idea of SIMD is *very long instruction word (VLIW)* microprocessors. The essential idea of a VLIW microprocessor is to improve speed by fetching and decoding long words—for example, a 64-bit word that is composed of two 32-bit instructions—and process these instructions in parallel. The Intel Itanium uses the "Intel Architecture-64," a chip configuration that will process two 32-bit word instructions in a clock cycle simultaneously. The new Pentium 4 makes extensive use of pipelining and is superscalar.

In order to improve efficiency and speed, there have been two distinct chip design trends for personal or desktop computers. One is CISC (complex instruction set computer) and the other is RISC (reduced instruction set computer). The philosophy behind the CISC chip was to reduce the number of times an instruction must be fetched from RAM, or the number of "cache misses," which took time and were inefficient. In order to do this, the instructions for each fetch became more complicated, but the number of times the RAM had to be accessed was reduced. Hence, the term "complex instruction set computer" or CISC, arose. However, with further development, access times decreased and it became more efficient to simplify instructions while making more frequent fetches into main memory. This is the philosophy behind RISC chips. Properties of RISC chips include:

1. A small instruction set
2. Simple addressing modes
3. Many registers
4. Heavy use of pipelining
5. A common instruction word length

Historically, the Intel chips have been of the CISC variety while Sun Microsystems has been a leader in the RISC technology. The Apple Power Macintosh also uses a RISC-based chip made by Motorola. The Intel Pentium now has many RISC-based features.

Before closing the discussion of microprocessors, we want to mention the Crusoe chip from Transmeta. This chip has received a lot of play in the press. One of the major investors in Transmeta is Paul Allen, cofounder of Microsoft with Bill Gates. The Crusoe chip takes instructions compatible with the Pentium family and, through software stored on Flash memory, converts them into VLIW instructions. By doing this the chip requires fewer transistors and can run all day by battery. It is designed for mobile computing.

TYPES OF COMPUTERS AND HARDWARE SELECTION . . . .

Locking into the wrong hardware structure can be very expensive. If you are going to make any kind of Internet business hardware purchasing decision, it is important that you understand the options available to your company. Before the microprocessor, there was only one kind of computer—the mainframe. Back in the early days of computing there wasn't much choice. If you wanted a computer you bought a mainframe from IBM, or perhaps Amdahl. If you wanted a smaller computer called a *minicomputer* you might go to DEC or Honeywell. Things are different today. If you are making a computer purchase for your company, you are faced with a confusing array of possibilities. In this section we categorize the different kinds of computers and their capabilities.

Mainframe: The term mainframe has always been used for a large powerful computer. However, the term mainframe is on the wane. Companies such as Sun and Fujitsu do not refer to their high-end machines as mainframes. Indeed, even IBM, the former king of the mainframe, has rebranded its entire line of corporate computers as eServers. What used to be a mainframe is often now called a *server,* an *eServer,* an *enterprise server,* or a *supercomputer.*

Supercomputer: A supercomputer refers to the fastest computer money can buy, often well over a million dollars. Seymour Cray was a pioneer in the field of supercomputing; hence, a supercomputer once referred primarily to computers manufactured by the Cray Computer Corporation. In the world of supercomputing, fast usually refers to the ability to perform numerical calculations. Supercomputers are designed to perform floating point operations quickly. Recall that floating point operations are arithmetic operations such as multiplying and dividing real numbers (not necessarily integer). These operations can be time consuming and result in loss of accuracy. If the ability to perform an extremely large number of rapid complex calculations on floating point numbers is critical to your company, the purchase of a supercomputer might be justified. Merrill Lynch was the first Wall Street investment firm to install a Cray supercomputer. It was used to price and hedge complex financial instruments. IBM recently produced a $110 million supercomputer commissioned by the Department of Energy to simulate nuclear weapon explosions [146]. This machine, called ASCI White, weighs 106 tons, has 8,192 CPUs, takes up the space equivalent to two basketball courts, and can perform at the rate of 12.3 TFLOPS (trillion floating point operations per second). Supercomputers are also used for complex weather simulation models, atomic research, gene research, and the solution of very complex systems of equations in business and science applications. Other companies producing supercomputers include Fujitsu, Hitachi, NEC, and Sun.

More detailed information about the global supercomputer market was provided in an interview with Mr. Hideo Mita, General Manager of the Fujitsu Hawaii Office. Since 1977 Fujitsu (www.fujitsu.com) has installed over 400 supercomputer systems worldwide for a total of over 10 TFLOPS of computing power. According to Mita, most of Fujitsu's supercomputers, called the VP and VPP systems, are used for scientific applications, such as weather and climate prediction, computational fluid dynamics for airplane and automobile, seismic simulation for oil field exploring, crash simulation for automobiles, structural analysis for the manufacturing industry, computational chemistry, and gene research. Universities and national institutes of research are Fujitsu's primary market for supercomputers, followed by weather centers. Mita, who held previous posts as General Manager of Fujitsu's International Computer Business Group and President of Fujitsu Spain and Fujitsu Italy, said that about a quarter of Fujitsu's supercomputer sales are in Europe, primarily Germany, France, and the UK. Fujitsu is also involved in Internet business and has installed large Web hosting systems with its Windows NT servers and Unix servers.

Server: This is a computer dedicated to serving clients in the client/server model of computing. These servers might be presentation servers that serve up Web pages for a company, or they might be application servers that perform back end calculations related to an Internet business, or they might be database servers. They might be servers hosting software applications for weak clients. The demand for such machines has exploded with the growth of the Internet. Companies like IBM, Sun, and Dell all sell computers designed to act as servers. These machines vary tremendously in power and price. The lower-end machines (say under $10,000) that serve the needs of small groups or departments are referred to as servers. Servers priced in the $10,000 to $100,000 range are what used to be called minicomputers. High-end servers, or enterprise servers, are often sold in *clusters*. A cluster is a group of CPUs linked together in a high-speed network acting as one computer. The cluster of servers might be mounted together on a rack. The term "mainframe" is being replaced by "server," usually a high-end machine. Fujitsu has replaced its mainframe line with its "Global Server" line of products. IBM and Sun use the term "Enterprise Server."

Workstations: It used to be easy to define a workstation. It was a desktop machine with a RISC (reduced instruction set computer) chip running the Unix operating system on its own hard drive. It was much more powerful than a Windows or Macintosh desktop computer. Now, with the Power Macintosh machines using RISC chips and powerful Intel processors running on Windows NT or 2000, the distinction between a workstation and desktop machine is becoming blurred. Currently, most people would define a workstation as a high-end desktop computer. By high-end we mean a machine with one of the faster chips available and a sophisticated operating system such as Unix, Linux, or Windows 2000. At one time workstations were used primarily by engineers and scientists. Today, a workstation is a desktop machine for the user who needs more power than a standard PC can provide, but whose needs do not require a top-of-the-line numbers-crunching supercomputer (sometimes called a *power user*). Software developers often do their work on workstations.

Desktop Machines: As the name implies, this is a computer that can, loosely speaking, fit on a desktop. A desktop computer was made possible by the invention of the transistor. In our cycle of computing, think of a desktop machine as a strong client, a self-contained machine with a hard drive for storing data, an operating system, and software applications. As of this writing a low- to medium-end desktop machine is priced under $1,000. As we mentioned, Larry Ellison, CEO of Oracle, declared in 1995 that the PC was "dead" and would be replaced by the network computer, a weak client operating over the Internet with a server. However, one reason that the network computer did not succeed as Ellison predicted was that it was less powerful than a desktop computer but not priced substantially below a desktop computer. Users asked: why buy a network computer when you can purchase a more powerful desktop computer for approximately the same price? The difference between a desktop computer and a workstation, some would say, is that the desktop uses a lower-end chip such as the Intel Celeron while a workstation uses the more powerful Pentium III or 4.

Laptop: This is a generic term used for personal computers that are portable. It is a self-contained device with a keyboard and monitor that usually weighs eight pounds or less. Some individuals refer to the heavier end of the spectrum as laptops and the lighter end of the spectrum as notebooks or even subnotebooks. The subnotebooks do not have internal CD-ROM drives or floppy drives. They have smaller keyboards and typically weigh four pounds or less. As employees of companies become more mobile, a recent trend is to purchase notebooks rather than desktop computers for them. With the advent of wireless Internet connections, employees can now take their notebooks with them wherever they want to work (outside of their cubicles and onto the stairways or to a nearby cappuccino stand) and can still be connected to their company's intranet and databases.

Thin (Weak) Clients: With a thin client, everything from data to the operating system and the software is on the server, a computer separate from the thin client and accessible through a network like the Internet. In fact, a true thin client is nothing more than a monitor or terminal that gives the user access to a server. The thin client typically has no hard drive on which to store data. The monitor is usually attached to a small box that manages the screen and network connection. Everything is preloaded on the box and does not need to be managed. Examples include the NetVista from IBM, the Sun Ray from Sun Microsystems, and the Citrix Terminal.

Internet Devices: An Internet device is similar to a thin client and is designed for home use. It is not directly connected to a server as it might be in a business. Rather, when turned on, it connects directly to the user's Internet Service Provider and allows for easy access to email and browsing the Web. It is a consumer product designed for easy access to the Internet, whereas the weak client as described above is a business tool. We include in this category *set-top boxes*, which are cable television devices that sit on top of a television and give the user access to the Internet. Another example of an Internet device is Web TV. As the market for desktop computers declines, PC computer manufacturers hope to make money selling Internet devices for music, video, email, etc.

Handheld Devices: These devices are the ultimate in mobile computing: a computer you can hold in the palm of your hand. One of the first entries into this market was the Apple Newton, which was the brainchild of then CEO John Sculley. This so-called PDA, or personal digital assistant, turned out to be a dismal failure, partly due to its inability to read handwriting. The big breakthrough in handheld devices was the 3Com PalmPilot. The PalmPilot is still the leader in the handheld computing market, although others that use the Microsoft Pocket PC operating system are gaining ground. These handheld devices are turning cellular phones into devices that can function as cell phones, check email, and surf the Web. These devices are crucial to *m-commerce*, or mobile commerce.

One of the problems preventing wireless computing from becoming more dominant is the lack of wireless standards, which makes it difficult for the same wireless telephone to be used in different part of the United States, let alone in different parts of the world. Other important hindrances are the size of the screen on a handheld device and the difficulty of inputting text on the miniature keyboard of a PDA or on the keypad of a cellular phone. In Japan, NTT DoCoMo's "i-mode" standard of wireless computing has garnered close to 20 million users, many of whom send email and surf the Web for stock quotes, astrological predictions, and weather forecasts on their cellular phones. The reason it has caught on in Japan and not in the United States is that most Japanese do not have PCs in the home and are not spoiled by surfing the Web on a comfortably visual 17-inch screen. Japanese users are happy with the limited use provided by screens on cellular phones. Many pundits, in the United States and elsewhere, see handheld devices as the future of computing. If implemented correctly, handheld devices could be the next big thing, though there are still many hurdles to overcome.

FUTURE TRENDS AND IMPLICATIONS. . . . .

We began this chapter by introducing the cycle of computing and the revolution brought about by the transistor. We looked at Moore's Law, which states that computing power on a chip doubles every 18 months, and examined the incredible resulting changes in computing technology. We wrote about the digitizing of information and how computers are designed to process information. This material, while interesting in its own right, leads to important implications for managing Internet business. How can you use this information to help you and your company in your day-to-day activities? What can you extrapolate about computing trends that will help you in future decisions?

1. Be aware that although the unit cost of a computer continues to decrease while its power continues to increase, overall costs to a firm for information technology will increase. Consider Table 2–5. These data are taken from advertisements in various PC magazines. Look at the dramatic decrease in cost as processor speed increases. We discussed earlier in the chapter that MHz measures clock speed. The amount of time necessary to execute an instruction is determined by the clock speed and the complexity of the instruction. Note the change in clock speed even within a year. Between 1997 and 1998, for example, the clock speed stayed the same while the cost was cut by more than half. What this table does not reveal is that in addition to increasing clock speed, there have been great strides in adding and improving peripheral devices which come attached to the computers, even as costs were decreasing. Many of the prices in Table 2–5 include speakers, subwoofers, printers, and CD-ROM drives (with access speeds also increasing dramatically).

Looking at Table 2–5 you might be tempted to conclude that your firm's total cost of computing will decline. Unfortunately, the exact opposite is likely to be true. The reason is an arcane law in economics called *Say's Law* which states that supply creates its own demand. As a case in point, while computers have become more powerful and available they have also created tremendous demand for their use. Twenty years ago computer use in business was limited to basic data processing, and budgets for information technology were relatively small. Today, few in business can function without a computer, which drives up the overall cost of information technology to a firm. Information technology is the brain of a corporation. Information technology to support a burgeoning Internet business industry will become even bigger and more important to a firm. Thus, while the unit cost of the hardware will continue to decline, the increase in demand for computing power will more than keep pace, thereby raising the total cost of hardware to a firm. You should expect to see a similar trend in wireless or mobile computing. As the supply of low cost wireless mobile computing devices increases, new applications and demand for these devices will arise.

Table 2–5 Cost of Desktop Computers

Computer	Cost	Speed
1981 IBM PC	$3000	4.77 MHz
1994 Gateway P5-90XL	$3999	90 MHz
1996 Gateway P5-133	$2799	133 MHz
1997 Gateway P5-166	$2999	166 MHz
1998 Gateway GP5-166	$1299	166 MHz
1999 Gateway GP6-400	$1749	400 MHz
2000 Gateway GP-650	$1599	650 MHz
2001 Gateway V733Cse	$699	733 MHz

2. Do not underestimate computing power when planning new business ventures and applications. Some estimate that Moore's Law will be valid at least until 2005–2008 [102]. Other more optimistic predictions based on current semiconductor research at places like IBM estimate that Moore's Law will hold for another 15–20 years [151]. There is even research being done on methods of computing that will not rely on the transistor. Two such esoteric lines of research are DNA and quantum computing. It is important for management to be aware that as good as things have been in terms of computing power, they will only get better. Do not kill a project just because it requires more computing power than you currently have. Computing power is plentiful and readily available at reasonable cost.

3. Keep in mind, when making any kind of managerial decision regarding computing, the *total cost of ownership* (TCO). From Table 2–5 we see the dramatic decrease in hardware cost. However, the actual cost of the hardware may be small relative to TCO. The cost of updating and maintaining software, establishing help desks, and training users for new upgrades may dwarf the actual cost of hardware. The TCO is a critical issue for management when selecting the type of desktop computing environment for employees. For example, a firm may be deciding whether to go with a thin client or fat client model of computing. In the thin client model, employees use cheap and weak terminals to access a powerful server that houses the software and where the bulk of the actual work of computing is executed. In the fat client model, employees use powerful PCs at their desks, each of which requires its own software. Because of the ease of managing all of the software and data centrally, and reduced support staff requirements, the thin client model is often

cheaper than the fat client model. It is interesting to note that Microsoft has marketed Windows 2000 as a means of reducing TCO. One study [139] claimed a substantial drop in PC-related help desk calls after Windows 2000 was installed.

4. Although there is a mind-boggling array of computers to choose from, including the latest and greatest sleek and powerful models, select the computer that best suits your environment and meets your needs. If your main computing task is word processing, you need not be overly concerned with clock speed. An 800 MHz machine is not necessary for word processing. On the other hand, if you will be doing some serious number crunching and speed is of the essence, you may wish to invest in extra clock speed. If the computers you are considering will not be used for sophisticated purposes, consider a thin client model with a lower overall TCO. Do not be afraid to mix and match thin and fat clients, depending on the different needs of users. This is easy to do with networking.

Tech Talk

XML (extensible markup language): A new language for exchanging documents and information over the Internet. Later, in Chapter 5, "Languages of the Internet," we introduce XML and all of its wonderful features. In the future it will be easy to store files in XML format because all of the major database vendors are adding XML features to their products.

5. Always save and back up mission-critical data as a text file. We have discussed the difference between a text file and a binary file. Files stored as text are open, which means the coding scheme is freely available, whereas binary files are often proprietary. Files saved as text files will always be available and never go out of date. However, new versions of applications often do not support binary file formats that are several generations old. Also, saving important data in an application-specific binary format is a problem when the application is no longer supported. Fortunately, saving data as text files is becoming easier with the growing popularity of XML which is a text-based format. Make sure your company has plans to get mission-critical data into XML format. Also, store your mission-critical files on several different media, for example, on tape and DVD. As one medium becomes outdated (e.g., punch cards) copy your data to a modern medium.

6. Harness the power of the computer to revise your business plans continuously and to find optimal solutions, not just good solutions. As Hammer and Champy point out in their book, *Reengineering the Corporation: A Manifesto for Business Revolution* [69], before modern computing, business plans would get revised only periodically and infrequently. Business moved glacially and having a 5-year or 10-year plan was considered normal. With the introduction of high-performance computing, a so-called "disruptive technology," constant and continuous revision of plans has become the norm. Especially in the rapidly evolving world of Internet business, what holds today may not hold tomorrow, so it is all the more vital to keep revising plans.

Yet another virtue of high-performance computing is that it gives management the ability to search for an optimal, or best solution, not just a satisfactory solution. For example, a very successful mathematical modeling effort (often called optimization) in supply chain management led to pretax annual savings of over $200 million for the Procter &

Gamble Co. and motivated the company to establish its Analytics Center of Expertise (ACOE) [24]. Solving a mathematical optimization model such as this requires a tremendous amount of computing power, so the savings Procter & Gamble realized would not have been possible without high-performance computing at a reasonable cost. The complex scheduling models used by airlines to generate minimum cost routes also require phenomenal amounts of computing power. Looking for optimal solutions and revising plans continuously are good examples of Say's law in action: the supply of powerful computing creating its own demand.

3 Software Is Everywhere

In this chapter ...

SOFTWARE: SOLUTION OR PROBLEM? . . . .

From the time you drive to work in your car with its in-dash Global Positioning System, throughout the day as you access data on your desktop PC, notebook, or handheld device, until the time you watch the late night news on your television with digital set-top box, software is everywhere. The era of *pervasive computing* is upon us. Pervasive computing allows us to download or upload information of every kind in our everyday lives using "smart" devices networked to provide a single continual seamless computing experience.

A large part of pervasive computing is, of course, Internet business. Increasingly, firms are relying on the Internet for all aspects of doing business. By virtue of its definition, every Internet business transaction requires some piece of software in order to access the Internet. Thus, it is difficult to fully grasp the importance of Internet business and how it can work for you without some understanding of how software works. Moreover, software is an industry with market value in the hundreds of billions of dollars, and this is a particularly fertile time in software development. Understanding who the key players are in the software industry and why they are at war with one another will afford you much greater depth in your grasp of technology as you peruse articles and features appearing every day in all major media.

In terms of power, software has kept pace with hardware. With each "doubling" of computing power as predicted in Moore's Law, software has been developed to exploit the increasing power. Software is the critical link between the user and the computer, which has allowed the user to manipulate data and perform calculations as quickly as the hardware can process them. It terms of reliability, however, software has not kept up with hardware. Competitive pressure, increasing complexity of software design, working on "Internet time," quarterly earnings reports, and stock prices have forced many software companies to roll out their software products before they should be released, meaning they can be loaded with bugs (errors in the code) and glitches. This has wreaked havoc with some companies who purchased software, and has even forced the shutting down of some previously prosperous firms. Some examples follow.

- FoxMeyer was once a $5 billion drug distributor. According to Bart Brown, the bankruptcy trustee for FoxMeyer, bad inventory-control software played a big role in its downfall. The company is suing both SAP, the software manufacturer, and Andersen Consulting (now Accenture), the firm that installed the software, for $500 million dollars each. Allegedly, the new R/3 software from SAP could handle only 10,000 orders per day, down from the 420,000 of FoxMeyer's previous system [176]. SAP produces enterprise resource planning (ERP) software, which is discussed in Chapter 14, "Enterprise Application Software."

- Hershey Foods estimates that its rollout of SAP software caused the company to report a loss of $60.4 million for the third quarter of 1999 [31].

- A flaw in a type of software called a "driver" (drivers link the operating system with peripheral devices such as modems and printers) prevented modems of certain Gateway and HP (Hewlett-Packard) laptops from placing outgoing calls beginning at the stroke of midnight on February 21, 2001. For some reason, the computer's internal date change triggered the lockup. Although fixing the problem won't financially affect the company that made the drivers, ESS Technology CEO Robert Blair found the problem humbling. He admitted that the software had been "bitten by a Feb. 21 bug," rather than the expected Y2K bug [68].

- On May 5, 1999, a software glitch at Chicago's O'Hare International and Midway airports' main air traffic control center caused numerous flight delays and cancelations. The center was trying out new software that would display a plane's size on radar screens, but resulted in United Airlines cancelling 164 flights and American Airlines cancelling 42 of its flights [3].

- On June 10, 1999, eBay suffered a 22-hour outage due to a software glitch.

- Computer viruses, such as Melissa in 1999 and the Love Bug in 2000, shut down numerous corporate mail servers.

Application software bugs cost companies $85 billion per year in lost revenue and extra expenses [65]. As we have seen, even some of the largest and best-known companies are not immune to software bugs and viruses that plague all of us at some point. What does this mean for Internet business if all of it depends on software in order to function? It means that the open source movement, whereby the code for a product is open via the Internet for all programmers to see and improve, and the movement toward establishing software standards and bug-free modules by the likes of the National Science Foundation and the Pentagon become all the more critical. It means that programming languages that allow the programmer to easily incorporate previously tested "objects" into new code will be necessary for large software development projects. It also means that if you are responsible for software purchases for your company, the more you know about these issues, the better. Of course, software has become an integral part of our lives and the information economy as we know it would not exist without it. However, we do want to increase awareness of the problems with Internet business software because billions of dollars and you and your company's success depend on it. Consider the following information on software development:

- 30 percent of all applications launched on high-end Web sites will fail because these types of sites are not able to successfully integrate legacy (older) applications with applications built specifically for the Web site [173].

- Industry and government spent about $100 billion to fix the Y2K problem [85].

- In 1998, 46 percent of big corporate software development projects were either late or over budget, and 28 percent failed completely [136].

- 42 percent of software projects are abandoned before being completed [1].

Clearly, software bugs, late delivery times, missed budgets, and security problems are enormous problems for business. These problems will only continue, if not mushroom, in the future. There are several reasons for this:

- Companies developing software used for Internet-related business are competing on Internet time. There is incredible pressure for companies to establish an early beachhead in their market. This results in a decrease in software development time.

- The increased power of the computer has led to a demand to solve more difficult problems, which in turn has led to an increase in the demand for more powerful software. The Windows 2000 operating system has over 30 million lines of code.

- The increased demand for integrated software applications has caused problems. In Chapter 14 we talk about B2Bi and the growing trend of integrating back end software products with front end presentation software. The trend for integration is not just intrafirm, but also interfirm. A bug in just one part of the system affects the entire interfirm system. This high level of integration also introduces security problems. For example, the tight integration of the Microsoft Office suite with its VBA (Visual Basic for Applications) is both powerful and dangerous. The Melissa virus, which infected Word documents, spread rapidly because of the integration of Word with the Outlook email address book in the Office suite of products.

- Due to the incredible proliferation of software, it is unlikely that any two individuals have exactly the same combination of software and software settings. Because all these software applications may interact with each other as well as with the operating system, it is challenging for a software company to find in advance every bug that might arise from the interaction of any of an impossibly large combination of software products on a computer or network of computers. This is why many companies are turning to the weak client-strong server model rather than the individual desktop PCs model for their employees. With the weak client-strong server model, all of the software applications reside on the server and the employees access the applications via their weak clients, so everyone shares the same software and software settings.

People often use the terms program, software, and software program interchangeably. We use the term software. In this chapter we break software down into two basic types: operating systems and application software/programming languages. In the next section we talk about operating systems. An operating system determines how your computer works and how you interact with it. Then in the section "Programming Languages" we discuss software applications (software or specific programs designed for certain functions such as word processing or spreadsheets) and programming languages. Most people do not really understand or appreciate how applications are created. In this section we also introduce the concept of a programming language and provide detail on how an application is created. We feel that it is important for a manager to have some feeling for how this process works. This is an incredibly dynamic time in software development, and in the section "Modern Software Development" we discuss object-oriented programming, visual programming environments, and the use of Java. The chapter concludes with a discussion of future trends and implications. These trends include the open source movement, the emergence of Web services, the increasing use of the Java programming language, and the growing intensity of the Microsoft versus Java/Unix war.

OPERATING SYSTEMS ....

Have you ever wondered what the true difference is between a Macintosh and a "Wintel" machine (a PC like that of Compaq, Dell, Gateway, IBM with a Windows operating system and an Intel chip), beneath the marketing and the hype? And why all the fuss about something called Linux? The true difference among the three is a kind of software called the *operating system*. A computer cannot run without an operating system. The operating system gives instructions to the computer. It interacts with the CPU and controls how the computer operates. It also provides the *user interface* or *shell*. The user interface or shell is the user's window to the operating system.

When you sit down at the computer and work, you are interacting with the operating system. In some sense, you are engaging in an interactive dialog with the computer through the operating system. For example, when you double-click on the icon for an application like Word or Quicken you are telling the operating system to load the application into main memory and run it. It did not always work this way. In the earlier days of the mainframe—refer back to the 12 o'clock and 2 o'clock positions in Figure 2–1 in Chapter 2, "What Do I Need to Know about Hardware,"—applications were called *jobs* and they were submitted in *batch mode*. The operating system then put the jobs into a queue and executed them based on a priority system such as first in first out. Each job had a set of instructions with it called JCL (job control language). The user could not interact with the job once it started to execute. This is fine if the job consists of running the monthly payroll calculation, but is totally impractical if the user's input is required, say, for constructing a spreadsheet application or creating a document with a word processor. Modern operating systems allow for interactive processing.

The operating system is stored on the hard drive. To run the computer it is loaded into main memory when the computer is turned on. We say the computer *boots* or *boots up* as the operating system is being loaded into main memory. This is what is happening from the time you turn the computer on until the time you can actually execute an application, which may take a minute or two. On most computers main memory is composed of *RAM* or random access memory, which is volatile (its contents are lost when the computer is turned off), and another kind of memory called *ROM* or read only memory (or *flash memory* on newer computers) which is nonvolatile. A small piece of the operating system sits in ROM or flash and is first executed as the computer boots up. When the computer is turned on, the CPU knows the exact location of the first instruction in ROM or flash, and so it knows how to begin. The small piece of the operating system in ROM or flash then instructs the CPU to load the rest of the operating system.

The Shell

An operating system consists of two main parts, the shell and the kernel. The shell is what the user sees, while the kernel controls how the computer works. There are basically two types of shells or ways a user can interface with the computer. There is the command line interface and the GUI (graphical user interface). Both have their advantages as well as their disadvantages.

Command Line: In the old days (before 1984) all operating systems were command line-based. You typed in what you wanted the computer to do. MS-DOS and Unix are two well-known examples of command line-based operating systems. In Table 3–1 are some simple commands and what they do in MS-DOS and Unix.

Table 3–1 *Unix and MS-DOS Commands and What They Do*

Unix Command	MS-DOS Command	What Command Does
ls	dir	lists files in a directory
lpr	print	prints a file
cp	copy	copies a file
kill	Control C	terminates a running application
mkdir	mkdir or md	makes a directory for files
diff	compare	compares two files

The big advantage of a command line user interface is that a simple command can accomplish a complicated task. Let's say you wanted to compare the contents of two files to see if they were identical. To do this in Unix you would simply type in the command:

```
diff file1 file2
```

This is done in MS-DOS with the *compare* command. Let's see you do that in Windows or on the Mac in one step. Now say you wanted to concatenate the contents of two files into a third file. In Unix, just type in:

```
cat file1 file2 > file3
```

In MS-DOS this is done with the *copy* command and a + sign. You don't need to go into a word processor, copy, and paste: just type four words and one symbol. Another advantage of the command line interface is that it is relatively easy to collect a sequence of frequently used commands into a single command file. This way, whenever you need to execute this sequence, you issue just one command to execute the entire command file.

However, there is a disadvantage of a command line interface. You have to remember the commands. This is not an inconvenience if you work frequently with the command line-based operating system. It is a problem for the new or infrequent user. Also, to do a simple thing like copying a file from one directory to another requires a lot of typing because specifying a particular file requires typing in the file path to that file.

GUI (Graphical User Interface): The Macintosh computer, introduced in 1984, (positioned at 6 o'clock in Figure 2–1 in Chapter 2) is responsible for the wide popularity of a GUI. The Macintosh allowed a user to interface with the operating system using a mouse. (Note: Not all GUIs are mouse-based. For example, some GUIs work by having the user select commands by touching a screen.) The Macintosh's GUI (which originated at Xerox PARC) idea was copied by Microsoft with its Windows operating system. The big advantage of a GUI is that it is easy to learn and to use. The big disadvantage is that some tasks, like those mentioned above, require more steps than a command line interface. Given the proliferation of GUI based operating systems, it is clear that its advantages outweigh its disadvantages.

The Kernel

The kernel is the nucleus of the operating system and serves all other parts of the operating system. The following are important functions of the kernel:

- File management – keeps track of all the files in the systems and their location in memory
- Memory management – controls the loading and location of applications into main memory
- Peripheral control – controls the system's interaction with peripheral devices such as monitors, CD-ROM drives, printers, etc., through device drivers
- Process management and scheduling
- Network communication control

The Multis

The kernel also controls what we call the "multis." A bewildering family of terms beginning with the prefix "multi" is used to describe modern operating systems: multitasking, multithreading, multiprocessing, and multiuser. They all sound similar but mean very different things. When your vendors start throwing these terms around, will you know what they're talking about? Understanding these terms can make the difference between a smart purchase and a clueless one. Know what you are paying for.

First, we need to define some concepts. A software program is a set of static instructions written in code that is stored on the hard drive until executed. When executed, it is loaded into main memory. The software program, such as Word, is executed when you double-click on the program icon and the program window opens up. When you execute the program, the operating system creates a *process*, which is a set of resources used to manage the program. The resources include a private address space in memory allocated to hold the program instructions and data on which the instructions operate, as well as operating system resources such as files and windows. Each process requires its own space in memory.

Also created upon execution of a program is at least one *thread* associated with the process. A thread, also called a *subprocess*, is a sequence of instructions to execute within the process. For example, if you are editing a file in Word while Word is printing a document, the operating system will create two threads within the same process for these two activities. Multiple threads for the same process share memory space and system resources. The fact that multiple threads share memory is significant.

To illustrate this significance for Internet business and the usefulness of threads, consider the case of a popular Web-based retailer selling thousands of products online. Information on all of its products is entered into a database that users can access from the retailer's site in order to find out more about a product before purchasing it. Now consider the number of users who visit the retailer's Web site at any given point in time, which could be in the thousands. If a new *process* was required every time a new user wanted to access the database at the same time thousands of other users were accessing its database, the memory needed in the retailer's servers would figuratively blow up, because every process requires its own memory space. However, this is not the case. The only way the retailer's database model could work is for a new *thread* to be created each time a new user wants to access the database. Because threads share memory, considerable memory is saved. Impress your CIO and ask if your Web database server supports multiple threads.

Just as it is possible to have different threads for a single process, it is possible to have different processes for a single program. Look at Figure 3–1. Note that there are two processes, both called IEXPLORE.EXE, which were created by executing the same program, Internet Explorer, twice. This can happen in the following way. Say, for example, you are very impatient and cannot wait for Web sites to download. You click on Internet Explorer, type in a Web site address, and while it is downloading, click on Internet Explorer again to download yet another site. Then you can switch back to the first, which has probably downloaded by now, read what you wanted in the initial site, then switch back to the second. Thus, you can have two browser windows open simultaneously and switch back and forth between them, and can, for example, read two online newspapers at the same time. This is an illustration of two processes occurring for a single program.

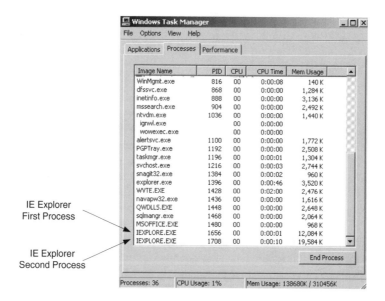

Figure 3–1 Multiple processes in Windows 2000 Server.

Figure 3–1 is perhaps a bit misleading. Look at all of the processes running. There are 36 (not all are shown in the screen capture). There are also over 300 threads associated with these 36 processes. Are they all running simultaneously? Not exactly. There are 36 processes running seemingly simultaneously but the operating system kernel is actually allocating time slices of the CPU to each process. A process runs in its time slice and then hands over another time slice to another process. This all happens so quickly that it *appears* to the user that the processes are executing simultaneously, but in fact they are all sharing the same CPU, which is dividing its time in very thin slices to each of them in rapid succession. We are now ready to define the "multis":

- **Multitasking** is the ability of an operating system to appear as though it were performing multiple processes at the same time. In reality, it is dividing the time of the CPU into thin slices, each devoted to a different process and occurring in rapid succession so as to give the appearance of multiple processes occurring simultaneously. With multitasking you could, for example, be printing a document in Word, calculating a function in Excel, and browsing the Web all "at the same time."

  There are actually two kinds of multitasking: *preemptive multitasking* and *cooperative multitasking*. In preemptive multitasking the *operating system* controls when a process can be interrupted in order to run another process. In cooperative multitasking the *process* controls when it can be interrupted, e.g., only at preprogrammed times such as when it requests data input. This means that in cooperative multitasking a process can run a long time without giving up control.

- **Multithreading** takes the concept of multitasking and applies it to a single process. An operating system that supports multithreading can perform multiple threads within a single process seemingly simultaneously. For example, in Excel you could print a spreadsheet in the background while performing calculations on another spreadsheet in the foreground. You do not have to wait for the print job to finish before working on a second spreadsheet.

- **Multiprocessing** is the ability of a single operating system to *truly* manage multiple processes simultaneously without sharing time slices from a single CPU. Multiprocessing requires two or more CPUs so that each CPU can be completely devoted to performing a single process. Many high-end enterprise servers have two or more CPUs that can perform multiprocessing. Web sites that have to manage millions of hits a day use clusters of enterprise servers to handle numerous concurrent requests and to balance the load of requests equally among all the CPUs. There are various kinds of multiprocessing. A common form is symmetric multiprocessing (SMP) where all of the microprocessors are equal and all have access to the same memory. A detailed discussion of multiprocessing is beyond the scope of the book.

- **Multiuser** refers to the ability of an operating system to support multiple users concurrently. Concurrently does not mean two or more people are using the same CPU simultaneously, rather it means that each user is allocated very small time slices alternately by the CPU so that from the users' standpoints they appear to be accessing the operating system simultaneously. Multiuser operating systems have been around for a while (for example, the Unix operating system). Typically, in this paradigm users connect via a terminal or weak client to a server running a multiuser operating system. Each user has his or her own account and work area. To see if you understood this section, consider the following statement: a multiuser operating system must be multitasking in order to accommodate the different users' requests, but a multitasking operating system need not necessarily be multiuser.

Important Operating Systems

In this section we discuss some of the most popular operating systems for servers, desktop computers, workstations, notebooks, and handheld devices.

Server Operating Systems

The most popular operating system for servers is Unix. Unix was originally written at Bell Labs in 1969 by Dennis Ritchie and Ken Thompson. It is a very powerful and robust operating system that supports all of the multis. It was an operating system originally given away free, which contributed greatly to its success. Because Unix was developed as a nonproprietary system and freely given away, there are many variants of Unix. Some popular variants include HP-UX from Hewlett-Packard, Solaris from Sun Microsystems, and FreeBSD, an open descendant of code developed at UC Berkeley which is currently managed by the "Core." An increasingly popular variation is Linux. IBM offers a Unix-based server operating system called AIX as well as other non-Unix based server systems such as OS/390, OS/2 Warp, and OS/Z. If Unix and Linux server sales are combined, in 1999 they led the worldwide server market with a 39 percent share (24 percent Linux, 15 percent Unix), followed by 32-bit Windows with 36 percent, and Novell Netware with 19 percent [80].

An important feature of Unix is that there are variations that run on both Intel-based chips and RISC-based chips. Unix was written by "techies" for techies and was not designed for the masses. It is command line-based and the typical user would probably consider it unfriendly. There are GUIs for Unix, such as KDE and GNOME, that provide a user-friendly interface. The biggest advantage of Unix and its variants is reliability. It is considered to be the most reliable operating system. This no doubt explains why the majority of Web servers run the Unix operating system.

Microsoft is attempting to parlay its dominance in the desktop market to the server market. Its current server software family line is Windows 2000 Server, Windows 2000 Advanced Server, and Windows 2000 Datacenter. These operating systems support all of the multis and differ in the level of symmetric multiprocessing and scalability (ability to expand capacity in order to handle increased traffic) that they support. These are all built on the older NT operating system which was Microsoft's first attempt to break into the server software market. The NT system did not have a good reputation in terms of reliability and scalability. Microsoft is very sensitive to this. Witness their numerous ads for 99.999 percent uptime. The initial reviews on the reliability of Windows 2000 are very favorable. The user interface for the Windows 2000 server family is the same as for its desktop operating systems. The Windows 2000 server family is designed for the Intel Pentium family of chips (hence, the "Wintel" moniker we discussed earlier).

Desktop, Workstation, and Notebook Operating Systems

According to legend, Gary Kildall went flying and lost out on the opportunity to make a fortune. Bill Gates did not, and we all know what he did. In Chapter 2 we talked about the first microprocessor, the Intel 4004, introduced in 1971. Gary Kildall, while a professor at the Naval Post-Graduate School in Monterey, California, purchased an Intel 4004 so he and his students could tinker with it. He developed an operating system, PL/M (programming language/microprocessor) for this chip and extended it to the Intel 8080. Later on in the 1970s, Gary developed CP/M (control program/microcomputer) for the Intel 8080. It could read files to and from a disk and many of its commands were based on the Digital Equipment Corporation (DEC) VMS operating system. CP/M was the first DOS, disk operating system, for personal computers. At the same time, Bill Gates and Paul Allen were developing BASIC (an early programming language) interpreters in Seattle for Microsoft.

Gary and his wife formed a company, Intergalactic Digital Research Inc. IBM, searching for an operating system to put into the line of personal computers it was developing, flew executives to Seattle to see if they could purchase one from Bill Gates, whom they had heard about. Gates told them they had the wrong person and directed them to Kildall. The executives flew to California and went a-courting to Intergalactic. Evidently, Kildall did not think a meeting with IBM was very important and chose to go flying in his airplane when the executives showed up. Kildall's wife met with them and was less than enthusiastic about the hard-line terms of the contract the IBM executives were proposing. It is not clear whether or not Gary missed the entire meeting because he was flying (there are different variations of the legend). However, it is clear that he could not reach an initial agreement over the terms of the contract.

The IBM executives tried to get Gates to intervene for them with Kildall. Presented with a golden opportunity twice, Gates realized the importance of the operating system and immediately purchased the rights to QDOS, quick and dirty operating system, from Tim Patterson. Microsoft modified it and sold it to IBM as MS-DOS (Microsoft disk operating system). MS-DOS had a command line operating system, worked with 16-bit words, and had no multis available. Eventually, Kildall came to an agreement with IBM. However, when IBM rolled out its PCs with MS-DOS and CP/M on different models, the PC loaded with MS-DOS was considerably cheaper than that with CP/M. The reason for the price discrepancy is not clear, but the rest is history, as companies chose the cheaper computer, and MS-DOS, followed by Windows, came to dominate in business.

The Macintosh operating system released in 1984 was the first successful desktop operating system with a GUI. Although very popular in the educational market, the Macintosh operating system was never as popular in business. One of the reasons was that Microsoft was able to establish a positive feedback loop for its MS-DOS operating system. MS-DOS had the bigger market share, hence more software applications were written for MS-DOS. Because there were more applications written for MS-DOS, people were more likely to buy an MS-DOS machine. It was also much easier to write business applications for the simpler MS-DOS, and hard drives were available earlier for the more open IBM PC. In another strategic coup, Microsoft did not give an exclusive license for MS-DOS to IBM and sold its operating system to IBM clone manufacturers. Microsoft understood early on how important it was to capture market share.

Later in 1991, Microsoft released Windows 3.1, which was its first successful GUI-based operating system. It allowed for cooperative multitasking. Following Windows 3.1 was the Windows 95/98/ME family. The Windows 95/98/ME family uses a 32-bit word length and supports multitasking and multithreading. It does not support multiprocessing, and the different versions are not multiuser systems. The newest Windows for the desktop is Windows XP. XP incorporates a very new look and feel to the user interface and is built upon the NT/2000 kernel. It has many consumer-oriented multimedia features.

The new Macintosh operating system OS X is an exciting development for Macintosh fans. It has the Apple user interface but a Unix kernel based on the technology developed by NeXT, the company Apple purchased when Steve Jobs returned to Apple after founding NeXT. It remains to be seen what impact OS X will have in business or in the arena of server operating systems.

Until the late 1990s the Windows and Macintosh operating systems were the only significant players in the desktop computing market. This has changed with Linux. The Linux operating system, a variant of Unix that runs on Intel chips, is becoming an increasingly popular operating system. People are even using Linux on their notebook computers. Others are buying systems that allow for a dual boot of either Linux or one of the Windows operating systems. Just as Linux is gaining a foothold in the desktop market, an interesting trend is developing in the workstation market. At one time the workstation market was, for the most part, the sole domain of Unix. Microsoft is now making headway in that market with NT and the new, more robust Windows 2000 Professional.

Handheld Operating Systems

In the area of handheld computers, there are three main operating systems: the Palm OS for the PalmPilot, Epoc, and Windows CE. The Epoc operating system is from Symbian, a consortium of telecommunications heavyweights including Motorola, Nokia, and Ericsson. It is interesting to note that in the handheld market, Microsoft has not been able to successfully use its muscle to dominate. Windows CE has not been very successful.

A growing trend in this market is the convergence of handheld devices and mobile phones. People want to access the Internet and check email from their mobile phones, and they want to make phone calls from their handheld computers. This has led to devices that do all of these things. These devices require a small operating system. Again, Palm, Symbian, and Windows CE are the competing operating systems.

PROGRAMMING LANGUAGES . . . .

Software applications are used at both the enterprise level and the desktop level. An example of enterprise application software is the Oracle9i database management system for storing and retrieving information in large corporate databases. Examples of desktop application software are Macromedia's Dreamweaver for designing Web sites, as well as commonly used word processing and spreadsheet programs. Software applications are created using another type of application software called a *programming language*. In this section we focus on programming languages.

Recall we defined a program as a set of instructions to the computer. These instructions, also called *code* or *source code*, are written in a programming language. Just as you need to understand the syntax and semantics of a particular language in order to communicate with another person in that language, so the programmer must understand the syntax and semantics of a particular programming language in order for the program to communicate with the computer.

Writing good, robust code for complicated programs with many features requires great skill. The best programmers take pride in writing elegant code: logical, sparse, and powerful. In the introduction to this chapter we mentioned the high percentage of programming projects that were late, exceeded budgets, or were outright failures. It is often the case that this is not the fault of the programmer but of those managing the software development process. In this section we provide some insight into the software development process so you know what you are paying for when you purchase software. Once the software is developed (the code is written), the per-unit cost of replicating it for sale, whether it be copied onto a CD-ROM or downloaded off the Web, is virtually zero. Therefore, what you are paying for primarily is the intellectual capital of writing the code and managing such a highly complex and multifaceted process.

Early Programming Languages

The only way to program the first computers was by hand wiring or flipping switches. Once magnetic storage became available a program could be stored in the computer. However, because the computer's brain is composed of transistors, it only understands 0s and 1s. Hence, the first generation of programming languages for computers was called *machine language* and the syntax of machine language consisted of strings of 0s and 1s conforming to the circuitry of the computer. Trying to program instructions as sets of 0s and 1s, as you can imagine, is very cumbersome. The programmer had to remember the code of 0s and 1s for each instruction as well as for all kinds of data.

This led to the development of the second generation of languages, called *assembly languages*. Assembly languages improved upon machine languages by using code (called op code or operation code), albeit very rudimentary code, instead of 0s and 1s. Recall Figure 2–3 from Chapter 2, a schematic of how a computer works. In the main memory of the figure are instructions in assembly language. For example, the instruction LDA 4 says to load what is in memory location 4 into register A. Although op codes were a vast improvement over a string of 0s and 1s, imagine trying to write a sophisticated application like a Web site design program or a database by giving assembly language instructions to the CPU. It was still very cumbersome to keep all of the registers straight and keep track of where numbers were kept in main memory. The next development in programming languages allowed programmers to focus on writing simpler and more human-comprehensible instructions.

High-Level Languages

The third generation of languages, or "high-level" languages, allowed a programmer to write "English-like" commands. The set of commands or instructions written by the programmer, as we mentioned above, are called source code, or code. For example, a high-level set of instructions to add two integers and print the result might look like this:

```
int x, y, z;
x = 7;
y = 8;
z = x + y;
System.out.println( z );
```

The above code first declares x, y, and z to be integers, then assigns values to them. The final instruction tells the computer to print the result z. The commands are pretty straightforward and leave all of the details about registers and memory to the CPU. The following are some popular high-level languages that have been used to create applications.

COBOL (common business-oriented language): This is an old language from the 1950s which was designed for accounting and transaction processing. When people talk about legacy applications, they are often talking about COBOL applications running on older mainframe computers. A lot of time and money was spent trying to remove Y2K bugs from COBOL applications. Although few people are learning COBOL these days, there is still considerable support for it because there is so much legacy code. Fujitsu, IBM, Unisys, and Hitachi all have modern development environments for COBOL.

FORTRAN (formula translation): This is an excellent language for numerically intensive work. Although an old language, it is still quite popular in the scientific community, e.g., in physics. If programmers know FORTRAN they are probably over 40. This is not a Gen X programming language!

C, C++: The C language was developed by Dennis Ritchie (and popularized in the book *The C Programming Language* with coauthor Brian Kernighan) in the early 1970s in conjunction with the Unix operating system. In fact, Unix is written in C. However, C is not tied to the Unix operating system and is used to write applications for other operating systems such as Windows and Macintosh. C is good for numerical applications and scientific computing. It is also used for writing many desktop applications. C has been "extended" to be object-oriented, which we discuss later in this chapter. The extended version of C with object-oriented features is C++. Often, the "guts" of an application might be written in C and the GUI or user interface written in C++.

BASIC: (beginners all-purpose symbolic instruction code): BASIC was initially developed at Dartmouth College back in the mid 1960s. It was designed as a language for teaching students about programming. It is easy to learn, but has never been considered a good language for large, numerically intensive data processing applications. Paul Allen and Bill Gates got their start writing BASIC interpreters. An interpreter is an application that executes source code line by line. In fact, as we learned earlier in the chapter, Microsoft was initially selling BASIC interpreters and not operating systems. This product has evolved into Visual Basic, which is a popular product for building applications, often of the client/server variety. Each version of this language has been more and more object-oriented. Microsoft Visual Basic is very different from the original Dartmouth BASIC.

Java: This is a language developed by Sun Microsystems. It is an extremely popular language for developing Internet business applications. Java is an object-oriented language.

C#: This is a new language from Microsoft designed to facilitate the development of Internet business applications. It is part of the company's Microsoft .NET initiative.

How a High-Level Language Communicates with the Computer

A programmer uses a programming language to write a set of instructions that constitute a program. However, there is still the fundamental problem that the CPU can only understand 0s and 1s. Therefore, it is necessary to translate the "English-like" instructions of the source code into machine language. There are two ways this can be done: through a *compiler* or an *interpreter*. There are advantages and disadvantages to each, as we shall see.

The compiler is an application program that runs on the programmer's computer and takes the instructions in the source code written by a programmer and converts them into a set of machine language instructions that the computer can understand. The set of machine language instructions constitutes the application that users would buy and run on their own machines. In a Windows environment these applications have an .exe extension. This process is illustrated in Figure 3–2.

It is important to understand that the application created by the compiler is operating system dependent. This means that a program compiled to run on one operating system would not run on a different operating system. If a particular application like TurboTax by Intuit is to run on different operating systems, say, Macintosh and Windows, the source code must be written and compiled for each operating system. This is a nontrivial process and has tremendous implications for software development. We alluded earlier to Microsoft creating a positive feedback loop for MS-DOS and applications written for it. Indeed, most desktop applications are first developed for the Windows operating system because that is where the biggest market is. In turn, because the Windows operating system has the greatest number of applications written for it, people are inclined to choose Windows over other operating systems.

The second way a high-level language can communicate with a computer is through an interpreter. Like a compiler, an interpreter is also an application. However, rather than compiling the entire set of instructions into a stand-alone application, an interpreter executes the source code directly, line by line. The application cannot run without the interpreter. From a programmer's point of view this is a form of instant gratification and executing the code line by line in an interpreter makes it easy to debug the program. Languages written for interpreters are called *scripting languages*. They are usually less complicated than a full blown programming language designed for generating compiled applications.

Scripting languages such as Visual Basic Script (VBScript) and JavaScript are often used to add functionality to a Web page. Both VBScript and JavaScript are simpler languages than Visual Basic and Java, respectively. They do not require a compiler and are very easy to use and test. Also, Internet Explorer and Netscape Communicator contain

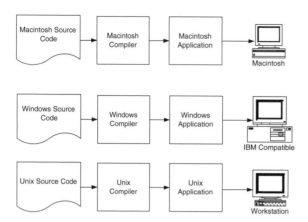

Figure 3–2 The compilation process for different operating systems.

JavaScript interpreters so that anyone viewing a Web page with one of these browsers can interpret the script that the page uses. Internet Explorer contains a VBScript Interpreter. The downside of using an application based on a scripting language is that it runs more slowly than an application that has been compiled into executable code. If you are writing a big, complex program for a Web site and are concerned about the user getting a quick response you would probably choose a compiled program.

Fourth-Generation Languages

High-level third-generation languages such as BASIC, COBOL, C, C++, FORTRAN, and Java are called *procedural languages* because the instructions spell out step by step what is to be accomplished and how to accomplish it. Fourth-generation languages (4GL) are called *nonprocedural* because their instructions simply state the form of the desired results, not the procedure for doing it. A good example is structured query language (SQL) which is used to extract information from databases. For example, say you wanted to know the email addresses of sales representatives supplying a part with SKU number 577 in the database called Retailer. The SQL statement for this query is:

```
SELECT DISTINCT Retailer.rep_e_mail, Retailer.sku_num;
FROM Retailer;
WHERE Retailer.sku_num = 577
```

Notice that in this SQL statement the query to the database is merely telling the computer what result is desired, not how to do it. The visual programming tools we discuss later for creating desktop applications and the desktop applications themselves are also considered fourth-generation languages. There is no precise definition of a fourth-generation language.

MODERN SOFTWARE DEVELOPMENT ....

While the subsequent generations of programming languages certainly eased the difficulty of writing code, the software development process itself became more complicated as operating systems and applications grew more complex. It became increasingly difficult to debug large programs. Moreover, with a multitude of operating systems, applications written for one operating system (e.g., Windows) had to be partially rewritten to work on other operating systems (e.g., Macintosh and Unix). Development times for a single application became very long and costly! Software developers, desperate to improve the development process, have made headway in aiding this process. Indeed, much has been written about managing the software development process. Version management and the daily build are now commonplace. In the appendix at the end of the text, we provide the reader with a number of books about scientific software management. We concentrate here on three important technologies that cut development time and expense: 1) object-oriented programming, 2) visual programming, and 3) the Java programming language.

....

VERSION MANAGEMENT

Regardless of the programming language selected for a software development project, coding a sophisticated application is very difficult. For example, Windows 2000 is over 30 million lines of code. Management of a large software project requires configuration management/version control tools. In a large software project there are numerous programmers working on a large collection of files and documents. Version management tools are designed to manage this process so that all of the programmers can work simultaneously on the project without using the wrong version of a file or overwriting what another programmer has done. Tracking product enhancements and bugs is also important. Good examples of this software are ClearCase and ClearQuest by Rational Software.

Tech Talk

Daily Build: This is the process of having programmers check their code in by a certain time each day and then compiling all of the source into an executable program. The purpose of this is to give rapid feedback to the project team. This concept was popularized by Microsoft in developing its operating systems and Office products. Prior to the daily build, software project milestones were often measured in months.

The basic idea of object-oriented programming is to develop reusable software modules called *objects* and make it easy to modify or extend the objects for use in different applications. Visual programming follows in a similar vein. The programmer can click and drag visual objects such as text boxes and radio buttons and use these in an application without writing the code to do so. The idea behind Java is, as Sun Microsystems says, to "write once, run anywhere" in order to eliminate the time and expense of rewriting applications to run on different operating systems. We now elaborate on these topics in the following three subsections.

Object-Oriented Programming

Object-oriented programming is built around the concepts of a *class* and an *object*. A class is an abstraction of a real-world object and describes the essence of the object. For example, think of a pattern for a suit cut for a particular individual as a class. It describes the specs of the suit: the shape of shoulder, the length of the arms, the taper of the waist, etc., but it is not a suit. The actual suit the tailor cuts from the pattern is an *instance* of the class and is called an object. There can be many instances of a class, i.e., objects, just as many suits can be cut from the same pattern. For example, a navy herringbone is one object, a gray flannel is a second object.

In the world of programming a class is composed of 1) data (often called primitives or data members) and 2) methods (often called functions) that operate on the data. In object speak we say the data and methods are encapsulated into objects. For example, consider software written for supply chain management. An example of a class is a generic product that moves through the supply chain. This class might consist of data members such as an SKU, price, color, etc. It might also have methods or functions that estimate demand, calculate levels of inventory, etc. In this example a specific product is an instance of the generic product class.

To illustrate concretely how a business might use object-oriented programming to write code more quickly for its services, consider the example of a bank offering different kinds of accounts. One example of a class is a savings account. Consider Figure 3–3. In this class, `new_balance`, `old_balance`, `int_rate`, `tax`, and `tax_rate` are data members. There are two methods in the class: `calcbal()` and `calctax()`. `Calcbal()` calculates the interest on a savings account for tax purposes based on the continuous compounding formula and `calctax()` calculates the tax owed on the interest. The method `calcbal()` calculates the new balance using the formula

```
new_balance = old_balance*exp(int_rate)
```

and the method `calctax()` calculates the taxes owed using the formula

```
tax = tax_rate*(new_balance - old_balance)
```

Using the class `account` as a model, the bank would create an instance of the class (an object) for each of its customers opening a savings account. Suppose Mr. David Crockett would like to open a savings account at the bank. In Figure 3–4, the bank would create the object `dcrockett` as an instance of the class `account` for Mr. Crockett. Note how the "." is used. For example, `dcrockett.int_rate` refers to the interest rate used for the object `dcrockett` in the class `Account` and `dcrockett.calcbal()` calls the method `calcbal()` using the data values for the object `dcrockett`.

Class Account	
Data	new_balance old_balance int_rate tax tax_rate
Methods	calcbal() calctax()

Figure 3–3 The class account.

Object dcrockett	
Data	dcrockett.old_balance = 1000 dcrockett.int_rate = 0.09 dcrockett.tax_rate = 0.31
Methods	dcrockett.calcbal() dcrockett.calctax()

Figure 3–4 The object dcrockett.

Other examples of classes are:

- An employee
- A loan account
- A stock keeping unit
- A window (as in a GUI)
- An option (as in finance)

Examples of instances or objects of these classes are:

- Mary Washington is an instance of the class employee
- John Fernandez's loan is an instance of the loan account class,

- A red widget is an instance of the stock keeping unit class

- A text box in PowerPoint is an instance of a window

- A Procter & Gamble call option expiring December 31, 2002, is an instance of an option class

So how does object-oriented programming help the bank become more efficient and write better code? When writing very complicated code, for example, building a GUI, the main idea is to avoid introducing new errors. Ideally, we would like to use building blocks of code (e.g., classes) that have already been debugged and can be reused. This saves large amounts of time and money. Let's go back to our example with the bank account. We can use the class account for any kind of savings or checking account that requires calculating interest. Even more fundamental, and what really makes a programming language object-oriented, is *inheritance*.

To understand the idea of inheritance, consider the the class account that has the method calcbal() that calculates interest based on the continuous compounding formula. Assume that there is a second kind of savings account that operates just like the first kind of account, except the interest is compounded for a finite number of time periods, perhaps monthly, rather than continuously. Instead of having to write a lot of code from scratch for this new kind of savings account, a new class can *inherit* all the data members and methods from the class Account that are appropriate for the new class and override the ones that are not. Consider Figure 3–5.

Class AccountPeriodic Extends Account	
New Data in addition to Data from Class Account	num_periods
New Method that overrides calcbal() from Class Account	calcbal() that is calculated by new_balance = old_balance*(1.0 + int_rate/num_periods) $^{num\_periods}$

Figure 3–5 The Class AccountPeriodic extends the class Account

The class AccountPeriodic is very similar to the class Account, but extends it. It inherits all the data members of the class Account and adds the new data member num_periods. It also inherits the method calctax(). However, note from Figure 3–5 that interest is now compounded periodically rather than continuously. Thus the method calcbal() in the class AccountPeriodic now overrides the method calcbal() in the class Account.

Suppose bank customer Mr. William Travis would like to open a savings account of the second type. Consider Figure 3–6. The object wtravis created by the bank for Mr.

Object wtravis	
Data	wtravis.old_balance = 1500 wtravis.int_rate = 0.08 wtravis.tax_rate = 0.39 wtravis.num_periods = 12
Methods	wtravis.calcbal() wtravis.calctax()

Figure 3–6 The object `wtravis`.

Travis also has a method `calcbal()`. When it's time for the bank software to calculate the interest, the version of `calcbal()` called depends upon which class the object belongs to. Object `dcrockett` of class `Account` will call the continuously compounded version of `calcbal()` and object `wtravis` of class `AccountPeriodic` will call the periodically compounded version. A feature of object-oriented programming called *polymorphism* ensures that the correct method is called. Polymorphism and inheritance save the bank from having to write new code for each class and result in seamless extension of one class to another. It is the characteristics of polymorphism and inheritance that make a language truly object-oriented. These features allow developers to write code quickly and efficiently for the burgeoning software market. The actual Java code for this example appears in the Technical Appendix.

Visual Programming

Visual programming is related to object-oriented programming. As in object-oriented programming, the idea is to spare the programmer from writing new code if possible. In a visual programming development environment, programmers can click or drag on an icon (hence, the term visual) and the visual software will automatically generate the underlying code. This is particularly helpful to programmers when building a GUI for the application they are writing. The process is greatly enhanced by being able to click on icons such as radio buttons and text boxes and have the code automatically generated. These icons can be thought of as classes that get "instantiated" into objects when the programmers select them and make decisions about their data members such as background color, size of the window, etc.

Microsoft led the way with visual programming with its Visual Basic. The company now has a programming environment called Visual Studio. Visual Studio provides a programmer with Microsoft Foundation Classes (MFC), or reusable classes. These classes allow the programmer to develop applications without going through the laborious process of writing code from scratch for the GUI. There are a number of competitors in this market. JBuilder from Borland is one such competitor. JBuilder is a visual environment for developing Java applications. Visual Cafe from WebGain is also a highly regarded development environment.

Java

Java is a high-level object-oriented procedural language as are C++ and Visual Basic. However, Java is getting much more publicity in the popular press than the other languages. Why all the fuss? It turns out that the compilation process for Java is a bit different than for other programming languages. This has huge ramifications for Internet business, client/server computing, and the shrink-wrap software industry. By shrink-wrap we mean the prepackaged software on a CD-ROM with a manual included that you might purchase from a retail outlet or order from a computer catalog warehouse.

Suppose you wish to write and distribute an application that will run on the Macintosh, Windows, and Unix operating systems. Then, as illustrated in Figure 3–2, three separate versions of the same application must be coded, debugged, and compiled. Although the underlying logic of the application may not depend on the operating system, the code that is written for the GUI may differ considerably. This development problem is well documented by Michael Cusumano and D.B. Yoffie in their book, *Competing on Internet Time* [35]. They describe the battle for the browser between Netscape Communicator and Internet Explorer. Netscape wanted to develop a browser for the Macintosh, Windows, and Unix operating systems. However, the Internet Explorer browser from Microsoft was fine tuned and very efficient for the Windows operating system. Thus, Netscape was faced with the dilemma of trying to allocate programming resources across all platforms or going head-to-head with Microsoft on the Windows operating system.

Enter Java, the brainchild of James Gosling at Sun Microsystems. Gosling went to Scott McNealy, the CEO at Sun, and told him he wanted to do something great. McNealy had the foresight to let him try. Gosling delivered *big time* when he developed Java. The key to Java is that the compilation process is operating system independent! This means that a programmer needs to write only one Java program, regardless of the operating system. Hence the expression "write once, run anywhere." The developer writing code in Java does not need to know what operating system the client software uses! The operating system used to create the application is also irrelevant.

Rather than create an executable program that depends on the operating system, the Java compiler compiles the program into something called *bytecode*, which is operating system independent. The application in the form of bytecode is then distributed (possibly over the Internet) to users with different operating systems. In order to run on a given operating system, the bytecode requires a *virtual machine* that interprets and runs the bytecode on the user's operating system. Thus, it is the virtual machine that is operating system dependent. Any user with a browser has the virtual machine appropriate for her computer. Browsers like Netscape Communicator and Internet Explorer have virtual machines built into them. (In a very controversial move, Microsoft has deleted the Java virtual machine in the Windows XP operating system and Internet Explorer. However, users may download a virtual machine from Sun Microsystems.) Virtual machines for all the major operating systems are also distributed freely by Sun Microsystems. Numerous other companies also distribute Java virtual machines free of charge. This process is illustrated in Figure 3–7.

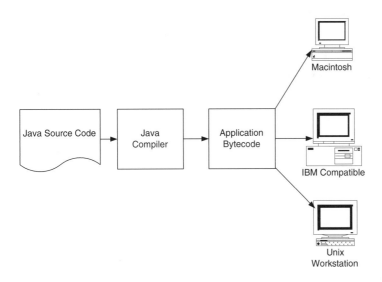

Figure 3–7 Developing an application for multiple operating systems using Java.

The Java virtual machine is operating system dependent, but once a user has a Java virtual machine she can run any Java application regardless of the platform the Java application was created on. Thus, the thousands of software developers can write applications in Java and assume that the users of their software will have a virtual machine for their computers. Note however that the software developer must have a Java compiler that is written for the operating system they are using. Currently, there are numerous free and commercial Java compilers for every operating system.

Tech Talk

JRE (Java Runtime Environment): The JRE consists of a Java virtual machine and important Java classes and libraries. A JRE for all of the major operating systems is available for free download from java.sun.com. With a JRE installed, a user can run Java applications on his machine.

There is, however, a downside to Java. Because of the Java virtual machine which must translate bytecode into native machine code, Java applications will not run as fast as applications written specifically for a given operating system. For example, all else being equal, a C++ application will run faster than a Java application. However, this speed gap is narrowing as Java virtual machines become faster. Many companies feel that ease and lower cost of developing applications outweigh the loss in speed.

FUTURE TRENDS AND IMPLICATIONS ....

We conclude the chapter with three very important software trends: the open source movement, the growing use of Java, and Web services. We also discuss the important battle between Microsoft and the Java/Unix world. This is an important theme we revisit throughout the book.

The Open Source Movement

There is a very important trend toward open source software (sometimes called free software). As the name implies, with open source software, the source code of an operating system or application is not proprietary but open and generally available for free download over the Internet. A good example of this is Linux, a Unix-based operating system. The Linux operating system is the brainchild of Finnish programmer Linus Torvalds. He developed this software because he wanted to run Unix on Intel-based PCs. The source code for the Linux operating system can be downloaded from the Internet. Anyone can modify it and fix bugs, although Torvalds has the final say on changes. Linux is a command line operating system. One development that has led to an increase in its popularity is the KDE and GNOME GUIs for Linux. Both KDE and GNOME are open source software.

Tech Talk

GNU/Linux: GNU is an acronym for GNU's not Unix. The GNU project was started by Richard Stallman in an effort to write a free, portable, Unix-like operating system. It is actually more accurate to call Linux "GNU/Linux" because Linux is just a kernel. The kernel is only one part of the operating system, and Linux makes heavy use of command processors, compilers, editors, etc., that were developed as part of the GNU project.

Another example of a popular (although it does not get as much press) open source operating system, which is yet another variant of Unix, is FreeBSD. This variation of Unix has its roots in BSD (Berkeley Software Distribution), a version of Unix developed at UC Berkeley in the late 1970s and early 1980s. It is popular for Internet servers. For example, Yahoo! uses FreeBSD. At one point Microsoft used FreeBSD, not Windows NT, on its Hotmail servers. FreeBSD is administered by a group of fifteen individuals called the "Core." Unlike with Linux, software developers can use FreeBSD as a software component in a commercial package and put restrictions on the use of that commercial product. Other examples of open source software are MySQL, a database package, and Apache, a Web server.

Actually, this trend toward open source software is a philosophy coming full cycle. In the early days of software development, developers were more open about sharing code, and many firmly believed that software should be free. It took time before people considered software a commercial product. While software was a big industry in the sixties and seventies, people like Bill Gates and Larry Ellison came along and made fortunes from selling software. Oracle is an interesting example. In Chapter 12, "The Power of Databases," we study relational databases, which are used by all large corporations. The theory behind relational databases originated at IBM, where the developers published their results. Oracle used these ideas and built the first successful commercial relational database package. See Kaplan [88] for more details on the Oracle story.

. . . .

FREE SOFTWARE

The free software concept originates with Richard Stallman who founded the Free Software Movement in 1984. In this context, free does not mean zero price. The term free means that the owner of free software is free to use the software, copy it, modify it, and distribute it. Stallman defines four levels of freedom. Freedom zero allows the owner of the software to run the program for any purpose. Freedom one allows the owner of the software to alter the source code. Freedom two allows the owner to distribute copies of the software. Finally, freedom three allows the owner to modify and distribute the modified source code. Access to source code is a necessary condition for freedoms one and three. Software is still considered free if the owner charges for the modified source code, as long as no restrictions are placed on its use or redistribution.

In order to prevent a distributor from adding restrictions on free software, Stallman introduced the concept of *copylefted* software (as opposed to copyrighted). If party two obtains copylefted free software from party one and distributes (possibly after modification) the software to party three, then party three must be granted the same rights of modification and distribution as party two. The key idea of copylefted software is to preserve freedom of use as software is distributed from party to party.

A good example of a copyleft license is the GNU GPL (general public license). Linux is distributed under the GNU GPL. The key point of the GNU GPL pertains to portions of the original or modified source code in a new software product. A new software product derived from software copylefted under the GNU GPL and distributed to a third party must transfer all the freedoms associated with the original work to the third party. The GNU GPL for Linux does not put any restrictions on software developed to run on the Linux operating system as long as this software does not use Linux source code.

There are other models of open source licenses available at the OSI (open source initiative) Web site. Some licenses such as the BSD Unix license allow for modification of source code and allow adding restrictions on the software when it is redistributed. The OSI organization is adamant about open source being more than just access to source code. In the OSI view, to be truly open source there shouldn't be any restrictions on using the open source code as part of other software systems, nor on the redistribution of the software.

Following are some questions and problems associated with an open source software development program:

1. If the source code for a software application is available for free download off the Internet, how do you make money?

2. Managing a software development project over the Internet, with perhaps thousands of contributors, is difficult.

3. If people don't like decisions regarding changes and additions to code made by the "core" group managing the project, they may try to create their own version of the software, which leads to product cannibalization.

A successful business model that involves open source software is employed by companies selling Linux such as Caldera and Red Hat. Although you can download Linux without charge, installing it without support is difficult for the average user. For a fee, these companies provide the CD with the software, documentation, and support. Many companies are not inclined to use software without support and are willing to pay for it.

Emergence of Web Services

In Chapter 2 we presented the cycle of computing. We showed that as a direct result of the Internet and the ubiquitous nature of the browser as an interface, there is a strong movement toward the weak client-strong server paradigm. This has important ramifications for desktop operating systems and applications. Since the very beginning of the introduction of the PC, the trend has been toward more powerful PCs with more powerful operating systems. With the weak client-strong server paradigm, however, a weak client does not need a powerful operating system since it can use the operating system of the server. This implies that server operating systems are going to become even more important. Clearly, Microsoft has realized this and is increasing emphasis on the Windows 2000 Server family.

The effect of the weak client on desktop applications is just as dramatic. Rather than buy a shrink-wrap tax preparation package to put on your desktop, you can prepare your taxes online. Rather than buy a package to balance your checkbook, you can do this online with your bank. Intuit, the king of shrink-wrap tax preparation and checkbook applications, now offers a database service online. With Sun Microsystems' Sun Ray weak client you can run Sun's StarPortal online suite. The emergence of Web services make the weak-client model of computing even more viable. Very loosely speaking, a Web service is a service such as a software application or storage space available over the Web. A more formal definition and description of Web services is given in Chapter 14, "Enterprise Application Software." These services can be sold on a subscription basis and the consumers can buy only what they need. For example, users may require nothing more than simple word processing and can just "rent" the time they spend using the word processing application online rather than having to purchase the entire shrink-wrap package with all the features they'll never use. Companies are also turning to Web services in the form of application service providers (ASPs) that will provide all the software the company needs remotely over the Web.

Growing Use of Java

Java is becoming a very popular programming language. Because Java is "write once, run anywhere" the user's operating system is not relevant. This is an incredible threat to the Windows hegemony. With Java, software developers do not need to write specifically for the Windows platform. Many Web service applications and Web servers are being written in Java. Witness the emergence and growing power of companies like BEA Systems that produce Java-based application servers. The use of Java makes the operating system irrelevant. Consequently, users can move to a free (or nearly free) operating system such as Linux.

Microsoft Versus Java/Unix

A battle is shaping up that will affect every decision maker at every company engaged in Internet business. Internet business companies are going to have to decide which type of desktop model to choose (weak or strong client), which operating system to use, which servers to use, which operating system to use for the servers, which programming language to use for software development, and whether or not to contract out everything to an application service provider. All of these decisions will be affected by a growing dichotomy—a Microsoft solution or a Java/Unix non-Microsoft solution. This dichotomy is typified by the constant barbs between Microsoft and Sun and as witnessed in the new Sun ONE (open network environment) and Microsoft .NET technologies. Both companies realize the necessity of winning the battle for providing Web services technology.

On the Sun side, CEO Scott McNealy has stated that, "the lessons of the dot-com era are clear: open beats proprietary; platform-independent beats platform-specific; choice beats single-vendor lock in." As stated on one of the pages of its Web site [154], the Sun philosophy is:

- Software should be free. Software you pay for should provide a significant competitive advantage for your company.

- Your software choices should not determine which hardware you need to buy. Application software should be open source, support universal file formats, and be available on multiple platforms.

Microsoft, the king of the proprietary desktop operating system Windows, realizes the importance of the Internet and Web services. Hence, its Microsoft .NET, which is a game plan for developing the software and services for the next generation Internet. However—and this has caused tremendous controversy within Microsoft—it plans to tie .NET services to the Windows operating system. In explaining the decision to link Windows with .NET, Bill Gates says [63]: "There are separate businesses, and there are separate competitive battles. But it's got to be within one jihad. A thousand startups are doing pieces of things. Some of those pieces are good, but if you really want to get people involved in using this stuff, you've got to create solutions—full, integrated, experiences for computer users. We've got all the pieces."

Perhaps the proprietary versus open source battle is best summed up in Table 3–2. Every Internet business is going to have to make the choice of whether or not to go with the integrated Microsoft .NET solution or an open source multivendor solution. This book provides you with the knowledge to make an intelligent choice.

Table 3–2 Microsoft Versus Java/Unix

Java/Unix	Microsoft
Network Power	Desktop Power
Universal Interface	Windows Interface
Open Standards	Proprietary Standards
Choice	Single Vendor
Java	C#, Visual Basic
Linux, Unix	Windows

Implications

1. Be careful in taking advice on operating systems because once someone becomes wedded to an operating system that person will defend continuing its use, even if there is something better. The operating system is a religion for many IT people.

2. Accept market-driven standards.

3. Generate positive feedback loops. The idea here is to get market share, which is a common Internet strategy. Get people to use your standard and create a feedback loop. A perfect example is the acceptance of MS-DOS over CP/M.

4. Realize that the best technology will not always win. Consider the case of Apple. It had an operating system superior to both MS-DOS and Windows 3.1, but it lost the war. Why? Because its market share was insufficiently large and it was too costly for companies using MS-DOS to switch.

5. Create value by bundling. Don't give people reason to look elsewhere. A good example of bundling is Microsoft Office. Microsoft was able to compete very effectively against Lotus and Word Perfect by creating a bundle so a customer did not have to buy two separate applications.

4   Internet and Web Technology

In this chapter ...

FROM SOAP OPERAS TO TIDAL WAVES · · · · · · · · ·

The Internet is the core of Internet business and the Web is the core of the Internet. What exactly is the Internet? What is the Web? How do they differ? First the Internet. The Internet can trace its roots back to the Soviet launch of the *Sputnik* satellite in October, 1957. This Soviet achievement created quite a crisis in the United States. If people were not worried about the Soviets launching missiles from outer space at the United States, they were at least disturbed that the Soviets had leapt ahead in science and technology. At the time, the newly appointed Secretary of Defense was Neil McElroy, the former President and CEO of the Procter & Gamble Company. While he was at the helm of the company, he had a brainchild (in addition to the concept of brand management), which was to sell soap during radio and television dramas; hence, the name "soap opera." It was clear that the United States needed to regain the upper hand in science and technology. As a means to do so, McElroy, a strong believer in research while running Procter & Gamble, proposed creation of the Advanced Research Projects Agency (ARPA). Funding was approved by Congress in 1958 and the agency was established.

Fast forward to 1966. Bob Taylor was the Director of the Information Processing Techniques Office (IPTO) at ARPA. He had three computer terminals in his office (we are at 2 o'clock in Figure 2–1, our cycle of computing). One terminal was connected to a computer in Boston, one to a computer in San Francisco, and one to a computer in Santa Monica. Each computer had its own set of commands and programs and was unable to "talk" to the others. Taylor was frustrated by this, and his frustration led to the creation of what was known as ARPANET.

The ARPA network was based on a technology called packet switching and led to the development of the networking *protocol* called TCP/IP (transmission control protocol/Internet protocol). For most people, the word protocol is usually associated with diplomatic relations. The use of the word protocol in networking is probably due to Tom Marill and a project he did for ARPA in 1966 [66]. In the world of networking, the word protocol refers to a set of rules for exchanging messages over a network. So think of a protocol as a set of rules computers use on a network in order to talk to each other. A network protocol would include rules for acknowledging message receipt, error checking, and data formatting. In the next section, "Computer Network Basics," we provide a very brief introduction to computer network technology. Most computer networks communicate using packet switching, and this is the focus of the section, "Packet Switching and TCP/IP." The ARPANET evolved into the Internet. In fact, the Internet can be defined as a network of computers using TCP/IP.

In 1995, Bill Gates said, "The Internet is the most important single development to come along since the IBM PC was introduced in 1981. It is even more important than the arrival of graphical user interface (GUI) · · · The Internet is a tidal wave. It changes the rules." For a number of years the Internet was used mainly by universities. It was a research tool, not a tool for commerce. Email was the most commonly used Internet tool. This changed when Tim Berners-Lee created the World Wide Web. In the section "The Web" we learn what makes the Web unique and how it uses the Internet, but is not the same thing as the Internet. The Web became popular with the common user when Marc Andreesen, then a student at the University of Illinois at Champaign-Urbana, developed a graphic user interface (GUI) for the Web called Mosaic. Microsoft's realization of the importance of the browser and the Web led to the famous and well-documented "browser war" between Microsoft and Netscape. The competitive (or anticompetitive) strategies used by Microsoft in this war led to its Department of Justice lawsuit. The browser has become a universal interface, and more than any other software tool, led to the Internet business revolution. The browser is most certainly the killer app of the World Wide Web.

In the section "The Web" we introduce the three key components of the Web—the URL, HTML, and HTTP. These three things define the Web. Of course, the Web is just one Internet technology or tool. In the section "Basic Internet Tools" we learn about other tools such as FTP and Telnet that are also important for Internet business. Part of the URL is based on a naming (and underlying numbering) scheme for computers. The naming and numbering scheme has important implications for Internet business. The process of resolving the name of a computer into its address is covered in the section "The Domain Name System." Also important for Internet business is to know where to go to get what you need on the Web, whether you're looking for information, products, or services. How to conduct more directed and time-saving searches is covered in "Advanced Searches on the Web." The chapter concludes with the section, "Future Trends and Implications."

COMPUTER NETWORK BASICS . . . .

Internet business would not exist without a computer network. In fact, it was the ability to network personal computers that made the computer an incredibly powerful tool for business. Imagine having to send someone a floppy disk or Zip disk by mail or courier every time you wanted to send information in digital form. Imagine not being able to submit an order using the Internet. In this section we look at some basic network concepts. A very simple computer network is illustrated in Figure 4–1. For obvious reasons this is called a *star network*. The *hub* at the center of this network is a very simple piece of networking hardware that takes the data from one computer in the network and passes them on to the other computers in the network. The network illustrated in Figure 4–1 is known as a *local area network* or *LAN*. A LAN is a communications network consisting of cables, computers, and network devices confined to a very small geographic region such as a single building, or floor of a building.

Tech Talk

Packet: When sending a message over a network (e.g., an email), the message is usually broken up into a smaller set of messages called packets.

A very important LAN technology is *ethernet*. This technology was developed by Robert Metcalfe and David Boggs at Xerox PARC. With ethernet, any computer on the network can send data packets to any other computer on the network. However, no two computers can "talk on the line" at the same time. If two computers send a packet at the

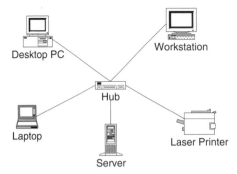

Figure 4–1 A basic Local Area Network (LAN).

same time there is a "collision." Ethernet is a technology for handling these collisions and retransmitting the packets. When a collision occurs the packets are retransmitted after a very small random interval. Ethernet is a very effective protocol and it is easy to connect a computer into the network.

Tech Talk

Bandwidth: When talking about computer networks, bandwidth refers to the capacity of a network. Bandwidth is often measured in kilobits per second (Kbps), megabits per second (Mbps), or gigabits per second (Gbps). The terms broadband, narrowband, and midband are often used to describe the bandwidth. These are not precisely defined, except in an ordinal sense, and the actual bandwidth associated with these terms is changing rapidly over time as network capacity increases. We will define broadband as at least 10 Mbps, midband as 1–10 Mbps, and narrowband as less than 1 Mbps.

....

ALOHAnet

ALOHAnet was a radio network designed to allow computers in the Hawaiian Islands to communicate with each other. It was developed by Norman Abramson, a professor at the University of Hawaii and a surfing (on real waves, not the Internet) enthusiast. ALOHAnet was built on the idea of retransmitting packets after a small random interval if there is a collision on the network. This is the basic idea used in ethernet.

When an organization's local area networks are connected together over a larger geographical region, perhaps the world, they are called a *wide area network* or *WAN*. This is illustrated in Figure 4–2. A *router* is a network device used to send or route packets from one LAN to another LAN. The LANs may be connected by dedicated leased phone lines, fiber optic cable, or through various wireless technologies.

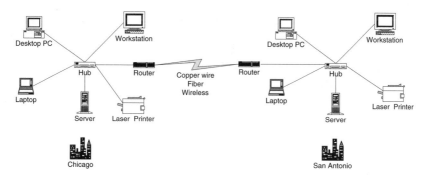

Figure 4–2 A basic Wide Area Network (WAN).

If you are planning to install or upgrade your company's network, you should be concerned about the following:

- Which kind of data are transmitted–voice, text, video?

- What is the network bandwidth? Is it narrowband, midband, or broadband?

- How reliable is the network?

- Will it provide the bandwidth to meet future needs?

- How is speed degraded by traffic load?

- How much does it cost to operate?

- How secure is it?

- What protocols are used? Are they compatible with other networking protocols?

We will touch on a number of these issues throughout the book. The emphasis of this chapter is the Internet and we want to concentrate on TCP/IP, which is the networking protocol used by the Internet.

PACKET SWITCHING AND TCP/IP ....

Consider the computer network illustrated in Figure 4–3. Assume computer A in Chicago wants to communicate with computer B in San Antonio. There are different paths on this network between Chicago and San Antonio. One potential way to communicate is to select one of these paths and then establish a connection between computers A and B on this path. This path would be dedicated to A and B for the duration of their message exchange. Establishing a connection between two points using a specific path on a network for the duration of a message exchange is called *circuit switching*. This is exactly how the public switched telephone network (PSTN) works. It is also referred to as POTS, for plain old telephone service. The public telephone system is also analog, which means that information travels over it in wave form.

The problem with circuit switching is that the line is tied up regardless of how much information is exchanged. To see this, consider circuit switching applied to a highway system. Assume Figure 4–3 now represents a highway system and a person wants to drive from Chicago to San Antonio. With the circuit switching philosophy, you would select a path, say, Chicago to Memphis to San Antonio, on the highway system between these two cities and then reserve all of the highways on this path for the period of time it takes the person to drive from Chicago to San Antonio. This means that if a second person wanted to drive from Chicago to Nashville he would be blocked from using the Chicago to Memphis link until the first person arrived in San Antonio.

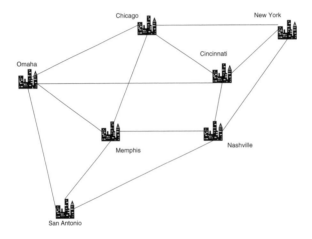

Figure 4–3 Packet switching network.

Circuit switching is a big problem for computers because their information exchange is typically "bursty" rather than even and constant. Two computers might want to exchange a file, but after that file is exchanged the computers may not engage in communication again for quite some time. Thus, we call the need to exchange data between computers "discrete," not continuous. An alternative to circuit switching is *packet switching*. The concept of packet switching was developed independently by Paul Baron and Donald Watts Davies in the 1960s. The interested reader may wish to see one of Paul Baron's original memos [9] at the RAND Corporation describing packet switching. This work was done during the time of the Cold War and part of his motivation for developing packet switching was the design of a network that could withstand a nuclear attack.

To understand packet switching, now consider sending a letter from Chicago to San Antonio. Rather than sending the entire letter over a particular route, we could cut the letter into a set of packets. The packets are cut, addressed, and sent in a particular way, that is:

- The packets are numbered so they can be reassembled in the correct sequence at the destination.

- Each packet contains destination and return addresses.

- The packets are transmitted over the network as capacity becomes available.

- The packets are forwarded across the network separately and do not necessarily follow the same route; if a particular link of a given path is busy, some packets might take an alternate route.

Packet switching was radical thinking at the time. AT&T stated flatly that packet switching would never work. However, the work on packet switching very much influenced Larry Roberts at ARPA, who had been hired by Bob Taylor. He opened bidding to build a packet switched network for ARPA. Two important companies, IBM and AT&T, did not even bid. The contract was awarded to the Boston consulting firm Bolt Beranek and Newman, known as BBN. The project was led by Frank Heart.

Packet switching is a philosophy of network communication, not a specific protocol. The protocol used by the Internet is called TCP/IP. The TCP/IP protocol is due to Robert Kahn and Vint Cerf. The IP in TCP/IP stands for Internet protocol and is the protocol used by computers to communicate with each other on the Internet. Computers using the Internet must have IP software. Packets that follow the IP specification are called IP datagrams. These datagrams have two parts: header information and data. To continue with the letter analogy, think of the header as the information that would go on an envelope and the data as the letter that goes inside the envelope. The header information includes such things as:

- Total length of the packet

- Destination IP address

- Source IP address

- Time to live—the time to live is decremented by routers as the packet passes through them; when it hits zero, the packet is discarded; this prevents packets from getting into an "infinite loop" and tying up the network

- Error checking information

The IP packets are independent of the underlying hardware structure. In order to travel across different types of networks, the packets are encapsulated into frames. The underlying hardware understands the particular frame format and can deliver the encapsulated packet.

The TCP in TCP/IP stands for transmission control protocol. This is software that, as the name implies, is responsible for assembling the packets in the correct order and checking for missing packets. If packets are lost, the TCP software requests new ones. It also checks for duplicate packets. The TCP software is responsible for establishing the session between two computers on a network. The TCP and IP software work together.

An important aspect of packet switching is that the packets, just like a letter, have forwarding and return addresses. What should an address for a computer look like? Since it is a computer, and computers only understand binary (0/1) information, the most sensible addressing scheme is one based on binary numbers. Indeed, this is the case and the addressing system used by IP software is based on a 32-bit *IP address*. An example IP address is:

```
128.135.130.201
```

All IP addresses have this format: four sets of numbers separated by three periods. This is called *dotted-decimal* notation. Each of the four sets of numbers requires one byte (eight bits), for a total of 32 bits. By convention, we are stating the IP address in decimal rather than binary format. For more details on the IP addressing scheme we refer you to the Technical Appendix.

Tech Talk

NAP: These are switching points in large cities where the very high bandwidth network backbones of major telecommunications companies meet.

We have defined the Internet as a network of computers using the TCP/IP. Who built the network and how do you get connected? The Internet backbones, the high bandwidth fiber-optic cable connecting major cities in the United States, are controlled by major telecommunications companies like MCI WorldCom, Sprint, AGIS, PSINet, and BBN. Large Internet service providers are connected directly into the backbone at NAPs like San Francisco, Chicago, New York, and Washington D.C. A person or company connects to the Internet using an Internet service provider. This is discussed in more detail in Chapter 7, "Getting Your Business Online."

You should be aware that there are many networking protocols other than TCP/IP. One of the great innovations of the Macintosh, in addition to the GUI, was easy networking. At one point it was much easier to network Macintosh computers than IBM PCs. The Macintosh networking protocol was called AppleTalk. Other well-known protocols include Token Ring and Novell NetWare.

THE WEB.................................

The Internet is a network of computers using TCP/IP. What is the Web? It is the creation of Tim Berners-Lee and is based on his major insight to combine hypertext with the already existing Internet.

First, the idea of hypertext. This term is due to Ted Nelson. The standard way of reading a book is in a linear fashion, starting with page one. The concept of hypertext is to allow a person to read or explore in a nonlinear fashion. The key concept is that hypertext contains "links" to other text. By following the links the reader is not constrained to follow any particular order. Hypertext may contain links that do not necessarily lead to other text, but to sound or video files. Before the Web came into being there were hypertext products in the marketplace. One such commercial product was Guide, distributed by Owl

Ltd. If you clicked on a link in Guide, a new document would be inserted in place of the link. Also, in keeping with its tradition of being a great innovator, Apple Computer had a product called Hypercard that implemented hypertext. However, these products did not use the Internet.

Tim Berners-Lee was working at CERN (a European particle physics laboratory located near Geneva, Switzerland) in a department charged with processing and recording the results of the scientific experimental work being done there. At CERN there were scientists from many different countries, so there were many different computer operating systems and document formats in use. It was difficult for a scientist working with one computer system to obtain information from a colleague using a different computer system. This is the same problem that faced Bob Taylor at ARPA. Berners-Lee realized that it would not be feasible to force the wide mix of researchers at CERN to reorganize their way of doing things to fit a new system. It was crucial that everyone work with his or her own operating system, but still easily share information. Berners-Lee's solution was to marry hypertext with the Internet. This marriage is the World Wide Web and consists of three key components, HTTP, HTML, and URL, all developed by Berners-Lee.

1. HTTP (hypertext transfer protocol): Recall that a protocol is a set of rules for exchanging information on a network. HTTP is a high-level protocol used to exchange information between a browser and a server. The HTTP protocol uses TCP/IP to locate and make a connection between the browser and the server. The messages sent between the browser and server are either request or response messages. The request message contains 1) a request line containing the name of the requested file and whether the request is a GET or POST (see Tech Talk in this section), 2) a header containing information such as the type of browser and operating system, and 3) a body containing data, for example, data entered into a form. The response from the server will contain 1) a response line with a code indicating that the requested file was found or an error code (almost everyone has had to deal with the dreaded HTTP 404 Error - file not found) if there was a problem, 2) header information such as the type of server software, and 3) a body containing the HTML of the requested file. An HTTP request and response is illustrated in Figure 4–4.

Tech Talk

GET and POST: In the request line sent from the browser to the server is an HTTP command called the method. The method is usually a GET or a POST. The GET method is a request for a specific URL. With a GET request, the body is empty. The POST method tells the server that data will be sent in the body of the request. The POST method is used when you submit forms.

2. HTML (hypertext markup language): This is the language used by the browser to display the text and graphics on a Web page. In the next chapter we describe what a markup language is, and how to create a Web page using HTML.

3. URL (uniform resource locator): This is the "address" of a Web page. When you click on a link in a Web page, you are taken to a new location. The link contains the URL for your destination and the URL must follow a very specific syntax used in naming the destination.

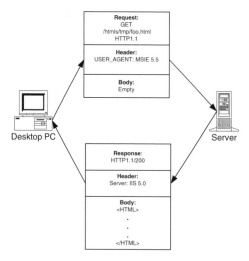

Figure 4–4 An HTTP request.

There are three parts to a URL. They are:

- The Internet protocol used, e.g., HTTP (or FTP or Telnet as discussed later)
- The address or name of the server
- The location and name of the file on the server

Consider the URL in Figure 4–5. In this example, the protocol is HTTP. The name of the server or host machine is gsbkip.uchicago.edu. The target file being requested by the browser is named foo.html. It is located in the directory tmp which is a subdirectory of htmls. Thus, the URL specifies the directory path for the requested file.

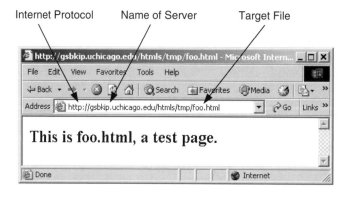

Figure 4–5 The parts of a URL.

Suppose a user with a browser views a Web page that has a link in its hypertext to the file `foo.html` on the machine `gsbkip.uchicago.edu`. The text and graphics of the Web page are displayed according to the underlying HTML. The link contains the URL given above in the example so the packets know what server to go to and what file to retrieve. When the user clicks on that link an HTTP request for the file `foo.html` is sent over the Internet to the server machine, `gsbkip.uchicago.edu`. The server machine then returns the requested file. The beauty of this process is that the operating systems used by the desktop machine and by the server machine are irrelevant. They do not have to be compatible.

There are two pieces of software required for this process to take place. The desktop PC must have a browser such as Netscape Navigator or Internet Explorer. The server machine must have an HTTP server. The HTTP server software is "listening" for packets addressed to it. When we use the term server we are referring to two things. Server refers to both the physical machine as well as the software on the machine that is serving up the files. When the server software receives packets requesting files, it sends the requested file back to the desktop PC.

There are a number of server software packages on the market. The current leader is Apache with almost 60 percent of the market [122]. Apache is open source software. It runs in the Linux, Unix, and Windows environments. The name Apache came about because the software is "a patch" work of code from the numerous independent coders who worked on it. The Windows 2000 operating system comes bundled with Internet Information Server, which is Microsoft's HTTP server. It has about 20 percent of market share. Sun Microsystems' iPlanet is a distant third, with about 6.5 percent of the market.

BASIC INTERNET TOOLS ....

It is important to understand that there are important Internet protocols other than HTTP. The other protocols work in much the same way as HTTP in that there is a piece of client software making requests to a server machine running the appropriate server software. Here are some of the most common and useful protocols.

FTP (File Transfer Protocol): This existed before HTTP and as the name implies is a protocol for exchanging files over the Internet. There are two types of FTP: nonanonymous and anonymous. With nonanonymous FTP, you are required to have an account name and password on the server in order to access files on the server. When using nonanonymous FTP client software you must provide three things: 1) the name of the server, 2) the account name, and 3) your password.

When you use nonanonymous FTP you are connecting to a server and have access to certain files on the server for which your account has permission. Figure 4–6 shows the screen when you FTP to the server `gsbkip.uchicago.edu` using the account `kmartin` (that is, when you enter `ftp://kmartin@gsbkip.uchicago.edu` on your browser). As the figure indicates, you can click on file folder icons and "drill down" through the file structure in a hierarchical fashion just as though the server were your own machine. Note the contrasts between HTTP and FTP. First, when you FTP to a server and click on folder or file icons, you remain connected to that server machine. This is in contrast to HTTP, where a click on a hypertext link may take you to a different server altogether. The second difference between HTTP and FTP is that with HTTP you can see the actual content of the files you request displayed using HTML, whereas with FTP you can see only the folders and directories where your requested file is housed. With FTP you must first download a file from the server onto your computer and then open that file, assuming you have the required software to read it. Note also that when using FTP, the only service we require from the server is to serve up files. We are not using the server CPU for computing.

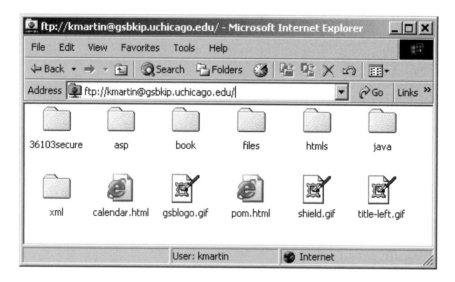

Figure 4–6 Using FTP.

FTP is an important protocol for Internet business. It is an excellent way for a company to exchange files quickly and securely with customers or partner companies. Perhaps the most common example is in distributing software. Many software companies offer their customers the option of using FTP to download software after making a purchase rather than sending a CD-ROM via the postal service. Another typical example is provided by a company like Hewlett Packard. You can go to the HP Web site and download via FTP the most current version of their printer drivers (software used by an application such as a word processor to communicate with a specific type of printer). Netscape has always used FTP as a means to distribute its browser. Of course, FTP use is not restricted to software companies. Companies might also use FTP to exchange purchase orders. It is also quite common in the Web development process to create and design Web pages on a client machine and then FTP the resulting work to the server machine of the Web-hosting company.

If you download software over the Internet using FTP, it is important to understand the following distinctions:

- Public domain software—this is software that is free, carries no copyright, and there are no restrictions on redistribution of the software. In this context, free refers to price, not free in the sense of the GNU GPL as developed by Richard Stallman and described on page 65. Public domain software may well be an executable binary file with no source code provided.

- Freeware—this is software that is free, but is copyrighted. There may be restrictions on the redistribution of freeware. Again, in this context, free refers to price, not free in the sense of the GNU GPL as developed by Richard Stallman and described on page 65. Freeware software may well be an executable binary file with no source code provided. Also, the policy on use and redistribution may be considerably more restrictive than in the GNU GPL.

- Shareware—this is copyrighted software that is distributed on a "try-before-you-buy" basis. You download the software using FTP. The software will often have an expiration date. You use the software until the expiration date. If you like the software, you purchase it after the trial period ends. Often there is no trial period and the users are on their honor to purchase this software if they decide to keep it. This is a surprisingly effective business model. John McAfee used this shareware model to build a very successful software company based upon his anti-virus software. Shareware software often requires a purchase of the software in order to get technical support. The technical support appeals to large corporations, which motivates them to pay for the software.

Shareware and freeware are often distributed using anonymous FTP. With anonymous FTP the user does not need a password. When using FTP client software, the word anonymous is used as the account name and any string of characters can be used for the password. Distributing files with anonymous FTP is a good way to maximize their availability.

Client software is necessary in order to FTP files from a server. There is much dedicated FTP client software available as shareware or freeware. You can also use a browser as an FTP client. When Tim Berners-Lee was developing the Web protocols he made a conscious decision to incorporate the already existing FTP protocol into the Web. This allows users of the Web to easily access the numerous documents available on FTP servers. The URL syntax for using anonymous FTP with a browser is:

```
ftp://name_of_server
```

and for nonanonymous FTP it is

```
ftp://account_name@name_of_server
```

In the latter case you will be prompted for the password associated with `account_name`.

In Chapter 2, "What Do I Need to Know about Hardware?," we discussed file compression algorithms. Many files stored on the Internet for download are compressed. A summary of the most common file extensions and associated compression programs is given in Table 4–1. Shareware or freeware programs are available on the Internet that allow a user to uncompress compressed files. Some programs provide the capability to uncompress without charge, but you are required to pay for a version of the program if you want to compress a file. This is yet another example of the classic Internet business model to give a useful product away free but charge for enhanced versions of the product.

Table 4–1 Compression Programs and Extension

Extension	Compression Program
.Z	Compress (Unix)
.sit	Stuffit Deluxe
.sea	Self-extracting archive (Stuffit Deluxe)
.zip	Pkzip or Winzip - Windows and DOS
.exe	Windows/DOS self-extracting archive

Just as with the HTTP protocol, special FTP server software must be running on the server computer. A server computer may run more than one piece of server software simultaneously. However, for a company serving many users, there may be separate computers that are dedicated FTP servers. The Microsoft Internet Information Server comes bundled with both an HTTP and FTP server.

Telnet: In a sense, Telnet is the converse of FTP. With FTP you are using a dumb server—the server is only providing files and all the computing is done on the client machine. With Telnet, the client machine is nothing more than a dumb terminal. You connect to the server machine running Telnet server software and all the computing is done on the server machine. The Telnet URL has the form

```
telnet://name_of_server
```

In order to use the Telnet protocol you need Telnet client software. You cannot Telnet using a browser without this additional client software. When you Telnet to a server machine, you are given a command line (not GUI) interface to the server machine. This is akin to being at the 2 o'clock position in Figure 2–1, the old time-sharing mode of the late 1960s and early 1970s. Telnet is still widely used, especially in Unix environments. It is a great way to access the CPU of another machine and test software. Telnet is often used by systems administrators to connect remotely to computers they are managing.

News: Internet newsgroups are a very common way of exchanging information. There are newsgroups on everything from archery to zen. An example news URL is

```
news://uchinews.uchicago.edu/rec.backcountry
```

In this URL, news is the service required, uchinews.uchicago.edu is the news server, and rec.backcountry (a newsgroup devoted to backpacking) is the target newsgroup desired. In order to access a newsgroup you need client software, such as Microsoft Outlook, and the server needs to be running the appropriate server software.

Newsgroups are asynchronous. That is, you post a message, someone responds at a later date, and you go back to the newsgroup and read the response to your message. Chat rooms and instant messaging are becoming increasingly popular because they are synchronous.

Mailto: Electronic mail, better known as email, is perhaps the most popular Internet protocol. As with all Internet software tools, you need client software and server software to use email. Indeed, when configuring your client email software to use programs like Eudora or Microsoft Outlook, you have to provide the name of the server where you send and receive mail. You can also send email using your browser and the mailto protocol. There is a mail URL for the browser that has the format

```
mailto:johndoe@company.com
```

where mailto is the service required, `johndoe` is the name of the person (or whatever name the person chooses to go by) to whom you're sending email, and `company.com` is the mail address. The mailto tool is similar to Telnet and news, in that you can execute the URL in a browser, but additional client software is needed in order to actually use the tool.

File or Path: Unlike the other URLs, this URL is used on the client machine only. It has a very useful function, which is to let a developer test a Web page before putting it on a server. Using this URL allows the developer to view a Web page through a browser where both the browser and Web page are on the client machine. For example, assume you have a file `test.html` that you wish to view in a browser. Assume this file is in the directory `temp` on the C drive of a Windows machine. Then the URL

```
C:\temp\test.html
```

will allow the user to view `test.html` in the browser. The client machine does not need to be connected to the Internet in order to use the file URL.

THE DOMAIN NAME SYSTEM · · · · · · · · · · · · · · · · · · ·

The URL naming scheme developed by Tim Berners-Lee is very powerful. Recall that a URL has three parts, one of which is the name of the server. This name is called a *domain name*. An example of a domain name is `gsbkip.uchicago.edu`. The domain name is ordered right to left. The *top level* domain in this name is `.edu`, the domain for educational institutions. The current top level domains are given in Table 4–2. Besides the domains listed in Table 4–2 there are extensions that denote a foreign country. For example, `.jp` is the extension for Japan and `.de` for Germany. Reading right to left, the next part of the domain name in our example is `uchicago` (note that dots separate levels of the domain name). This is a *second level* domain, in this case, the University of Chicago. Finally, `gsbkip` represents a host machine within the University of Chicago.

When you click on a link with an underlying URL, you are taken to the computer named in the URL. Having a name for a server is important for Internet business. For example, if you wanted to go to the IBM Web site, you would naturally guess the name to be `www.ibm.com`. Certainly names like `amazon.com` have become valuable trademarks. Indeed, there have been numerous law suits over domain names. Many businesses invest a

Table 4–2 Top Level Domains

Domain Type	Description
.com	commercial users
.net	network providers
.edu	educational institutions
.org	nonprofit organization
.gov	United States government
.mil	United States military
.aero	(new)
.biz	commercial use (new)
.coop	(new)
.info	all uses (new)
.museum	(new)
.name	for individuals (new)
.pro	(new)

great deal of time and money in selecting an appropriate domain name. It is important to have a name that is easy to remember. A good domain name can also be a marketing tool.

In an earlier section we saw that TCP/IP software uses IP addresses, not names, for addressing packets. This means that somehow the domain names must get converted or *resolved* into IP addresses. This is done through an Internet service called the *domain name system* (DNS). This system makes use of special servers called domain name servers. The process is illustrated in Figure 4–7.

For example, assume an employee sitting at a desktop PC makes a request for a file to the machine with domain name gsbkip.uchicago.edu. The domain name gets resolved from right to left. The first thing that would happen is that the local DNS server would make a request to a *root server* for addresses in the .edu domain. There are multiple copies of root servers throughout the world that do nothing but serve up addresses in top level domains. This root server would then provide the address for a DNS server that had the address for the second level domain uchicago.

In Figure 4–7 this is the server with the address 128.135.4.2. This server knows all of the addresses of host machines for the uchicago domain including the host machine gsbkip. It then responds to the local DNS, sending it the IP number 128.135.130.201, which is the IP address for the domain name gsbkip.uchicago.edu. The local DNS server then passes that IP number to the desktop PC that originally made the request. It now has an IP address associated with the domain name gsbkip.uchicago.edu and can send packets out over the Internet requesting files from the server (labeled enterprise Web server in the figure) with this domain name. All of this happens in a matter of seconds or even less. Simple!

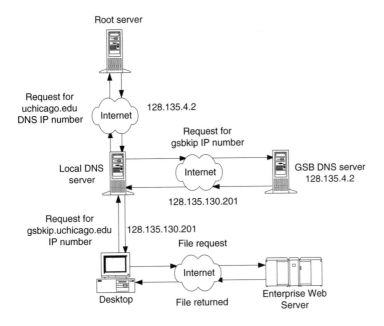

Figure 4–7 Domain name resolution.

Clearly, in order for the process outlined in Figure 4–7 to work properly, the IP addresses and domain names must be globally unique. The organization entrusted with ensuring this is the Internet Corporation for Assigned Names and Numbers (ICANN). This organization was established by the United States Commerce Department for the purpose of making the Internet run smoothly. At one time, Network Solutions Inc., which is now owned by VeriSign, had a monopoly on assigning domain names. They no longer have a monopoly on assigning domain names, but they still have control of the domain name database for `.com` and `.net` and get $6 per year per name for maintaining this database. Now, if a company wants to register a domain name they can contact one of the ICANN Accredited Registrars. Many Internet service providers will, for a fee, take care of the process of getting an IP address and registering a domain name.

Many companies are discovering that if they want to register a domain name, the name is already taken. To help alleviate this problem, ICANN has approved seven new top level domain names. They are `.aero`, `.biz`, `.coop`, `.info`, `.museum`, `.name`, and `.pro`. Not surprisingly, there are companies trying to usurp the power of ICANN. One such company is New.net. They have come up with their own top level domain names like `.family`, `.tech`, and `.xxx`. However, because they are not approved by ICANN, their domain names are not part of the root server system. In order to reach host computers using the New.net domain names, a user, or the user's Internet service provider, must use special software that adds the extension `new.net` onto every address [29].

. . . .

CYBERSQUATTING

Cybersquatting is the practice of registering a domain name for the purpose of reselling it at a later date. Early in the domain name registration process, clever individuals registered domain names related to well-known products or company names, e.g., `Mcdonalds.com`, with the express purpose of charging a large ransom fee on the name when the company finally decided to use it. This is also called domain name hijacking. This is now much more difficult to do. In October of 1999, ICANN approved a set of rules for the Uniform Domain Name Dispute Resolution Policy. This policy is followed by all domain name registrars for the top level domains of `.com`, `.org`, and `.net`. Victims of cybersquatting can make a formal complaint under this policy and be heard by an ICANN-approved dispute-resolution service provider. If someone has registered a domain name in "bad faith," there is high probability he will be forced to give it up. We refer the reader to the ICANN Web site for what constitutes "bad faith."

How can New.net establish new top level domain names without being given the authority to do so? No government or company owns the Internet. Organizations such as the W3C try to provide standards on HTML and HTTP, and ICANN tries to control domain names and numbers, but there is no central worldwide authority. Perhaps that is why the Internet has worked so well to date.

ADVANCED SEARCHES ON THE WEB . . . .

In addition to using Internet tools, you may wish to conduct advanced searches on the Web for your Internet business as another way to take advantage of what the Web has to offer. You may have already conducted basic searches using one of the search engines like Yahoo!, Google, Lycos, or Altavista. Yahoo! offers a "directory" form of search where users "drill down" through increasingly specific topic areas to arrive at the subject they are seeking. The other search engines offer an "index" form of search where users enter a keyword and the search engine returns a list of Web pages in which the keyword is used. See the section, "How to Get a High Ranking for Your Web Site" in Chapter 6, "Web Site Design and Content," for information on how search engines find Web pages and determine their ranking.

Some of the newer search engines even have features like categorizing the entries for you to help narrow your search. Vivisimo, for example, not only returns standard entries when the word "books" is entered, but also categories such as "music," "children," "rare-print," and "art" that can be clicked on for more efficient searches. Wisenut is another categorizable search engine that offers a feature called "Sneak-a-Peek" that allows users to catch glimpses of listed sites without ever leaving the Wisenut site. This allows for faster searching without having to wait for the browser to switch between the listings and the search engine site [172].

For more sophisticated and directed searches that can help save time and money, more than one keyword with advanced search code words and syntax can be entered at a time. Say for example that you are interested in learning about different ways to promote your company's Web site. It is difficult to think of a single keyword that would provide you with the information you need. However, once you have mastered the advanced search techniques listed here, you will find whole new worlds of information opening up for you. Advanced search code words and syntax differ from search engine to search engine, so check with each before using them. For more information on search engines see [13] and [57]. Here are a few of the more commonly used advanced search techniques:

- " " Quotation marks are used around a multiword phrase that you want searched verbatim. Using the example of wanting to learn about different ways to promote your Web site, you might enter "Web site promotion" as is, in quotations. The search engine would return a list of Web pages with the phrase Web site promotion in them. Without quotes around the phrase, each word in the phrase may be searched for separately (depending on the search engine). For example, if you enter the phrase Web site promotion without quotes, your search engine may do a search for pages with the word Web, or the word site, or the word promotion in it.

- **+** Inserting a plus sign before a keyword indicates that the keyword must be on a page returned. Just entering a keyword by itself may not necessarily return a page with that word in it. For example, if you're searching for a consultant who might help you with your Web site promotion, if you enter +"Web site promotion" consultant some search engines will return pages with Web site promotion in it, but not necessarily the word consultant (some search engines rank pages with both phrases Web site promotion and consultant in it higher than pages with Web site promotion alone). In order to have pages returned with both entries in it, you would have to enter both terms with plus signs before each term, i.e., +"Web site promotion" +consultant.

- **AND** The word AND entered between keywords will find pages that have all of those keywords in a page. For example, if you are searching for software that will help you with Web site promotion, a search on "Web site promotion" AND software will find pages with both Web site promotion and software in it. Note that entering "Web site promotion" AND software is equivalent to entering +"Web site promotion" +software.

- **OR** The word OR entered between keywords will find pages that have at least one of the keywords in it, but not necessarily all keywords on a page. For example, a search on "Web site promotion" OR software finds pages with the phrase Web site promotion in it as well as pages with the word software in it, but not necessarily both entries in a single page.

- **NEAR** The word NEAR entered between keywords will find pages with the keywords in close proximity to one another in the page. For example, suppose you wanted to search Web pages that not only have the phrase Web site promotion in it, but also phrases like promotion of Web site. Then you would want the phrase Web site in close proximity to the word promotion in a page, and you would enter "Web site" NEAR promotion.

- **NOT** The word NOT entered before a keyword will find pages that do not contain the keyword. For example, suppose you're interested in Web site promotion, but not in banner ads. Entering "Web site promotion" NOT "banner ads" will return pages with the phrase Web site promotion in it, but not the phrase banner ads. Note that a hyphen works in the same way as NOT; that is, entering "Web site promotion" NOT "banner ads" is equivalent to entering "Web site promotion" - "banner ads".

- **( )** Parentheses used around keywords can create a much more sophisticated search. If you enter "Web site promotion" AND (consultant OR software) the response will have the entries Web site promotion and consultant in it, *or* the entries Web site promotion and software in it.

FUTURE TRENDS AND IMPLICATIONS ....

Understand the power of a network and the effect of connecting people to the network. What makes the telephone network so useful is that virtually everyone is connected to it. It has become a standard by sheer number of the people using it. By Metcalfe's Law (the same Robert Metcalfe who developed ethernet), the power or utility of a network does not grow as a simple linear function of the number of people in the network; rather, it grows as the *square* of the number of people connected. This growth is illustrated by the graph in Figure 4–8. As a consequence of Metcalfe's Law, you want to use open, not proprietary, networking protocols. Make it easy to use your company network.

A critical mistake by management is to underestimate bandwidth availability when planning new business ventures. Do not kill a project just because it will require a great deal more bandwidth than you currently have. There is not a Moore's Law for bandwidth, but there should be. Bandwidth is growing exponentially and becoming cheaper.

The networks discussed in this chapter (for example, the network in Figure 4–1) are client/server networks. There is a central server machine that serves the client machines on the network. When you use a browser on the Internet, you are working in client/server mode. The browser is downloading files from an HTTP server. This is currently the main paradigm in networking. However, peer-to-peer (P2P) networks in which each machine is both client and server are growing in popularity. An example of a P2P network is Gnutella. This is a file-sharing system on the Internet that allows you to directly search other computers for files and software. In order to do this you need special software that allows your machine to be both a client and a server. When using Gnutella you connect directly to other computers using an IP address (not DNS).

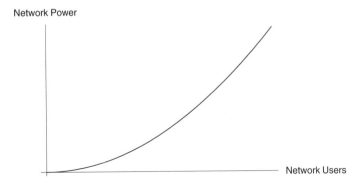

Figure 4–8 *Graphical illustration of Metcalfe's Law.*

The browser has had an amazing effect on computing. By providing the user with a universal interface to the Internet, the browser is replacing the operating system shell as the user's interface to the computer. In addition, the Internet is replacing the computer. The Internet is making Sun Microsystem's saying, "the network is the computer" look more and more prophetic. Plan your business model around your employees' and customers' having low-cost client machines with high bandwidth connections to the Internet.

Tech Talk

GigaPOP: Gigabit Point of Presence. Very high-speed switching points that connect the backbone of the new Internet2.

The government sponsored ARPANET project was initially used for connecting university computers. It eventually morphed into the Internet and is currently overloaded. The *Internet2* is a joint government, university, and industry project to accelerate the creation of tomorrow's Internet. The Internet2 is being administered by UCAID (University Corporation for Advanced Internet Development). Currently, the network is designed to be a leading edge network for the national research community and to foster the development of new Internet technologies. Eventually, these services and technologies will be transferred to the broader community. The original intent of the Internet was to exchange text; the Internet2 is being developed to exchange multimedia data at high-speed. The Internet2 is based upon two very high-speed optical backbones: one is MCI Worldcom's vBNS (very high-speed Bandwidth Network Service), the other is Abilene, also an optical network developed specifically for Internet2 by UCAID. Abilene is initially designed to run at 2.4 Gbps. Connections to the backbone are through GigaPOPs located throughout the country. Internet2 uses the IPv6 addressing scheme (see the Technical Appendix).

Part 2

Front End: Presentation

In the second part of the book, we build on concepts and vocabulary introduced in the first part to show you how to integrate hardware, software, and the Internet to build an Internet presence. The chapters in this part of the book are devoted to what is called the "front end," or point of interaction between a firm engaged in Internet business and the world. In Chapter 5, "Languages of the Internet," we introduce the concept of a markup language and the tools at your disposal for creating a Web presence. We describe a new markup language (XML) that is critical for business communication because it facilitates the exchange of information between different computing platforms. In Chapter 6, "Web Site Design and Content," we explore designing Web pages and discuss how to create a Web site that won't turn customers away but will keep them coming back for more. We discuss major considerations when designing a Web page, such as purpose, target audience, clarity, and how to take advantage of the special nature of the Web. In Chapter 7, "Getting Your Business Online," we review a spectrum of options in selecting a Web hosting service that are available to your company, including basic networking and telecommunications technologies such as wireless and DSL.

5 Languages of the Internet

In this chapter ...

THE FACE OF INTERNET BUSINESS ....

Every business presents a face to the world. This face can be a storefront, letterhead, business card, advertisement, Web site, or packaging. In Internet business technology this face is known as the *presentation tier*. The presentation tier is part of any modern Internet business N-tier hardware and software architecture. The presentation tier is what the customer sees. It is the window that the Internet business company presents to the rest of the world. Part II of the book, which this chapter begins, is devoted to the presentation tier.

In Figure 4–4 in Chapter 4, "Internet and Web Technology," we illustrated the simple process of requesting a file from a server using HTTP. This server represents the presentation tier, but actually much more goes on. For example, assume you are a customer of Amazon and enter the URL www.amazon.com in your browser. You are served up the Web home page for Amazon. You may then "interact" with the site by searching for book titles and making purchases. This interaction is actually more sophisticated than what is illustrated in Figure 4–4. Indeed, it is more like what you see in the very generic N-tier Internet business system illustrated in Figure 5–1. (The Web server, business logic software, and database management software might all be on the same machine, or on separate machines. We look at this architecture in much more detail in Chapter 13, "Internet Business Architecture.")

In our Amazon example, when a customer makes a purchase using shopping cart technology, this uses the business logic software of the application tier. When the customer retrieves information from the database, this uses the database software and data in the data tier. The function of the Web server in the presentation tier is to provide a company's face to the world for doing business. In this chapter, and in Part II of the book as a whole, our emphasis is on the interaction between the client and the presentation tier. It is important to present a well-designed Web page to the customer or business partner that facilitates a business transaction. For now, we are not going to worry about what happens on the "back end." The back end of Internet business represented by the application server and database server is the topic of Part IV of the book.

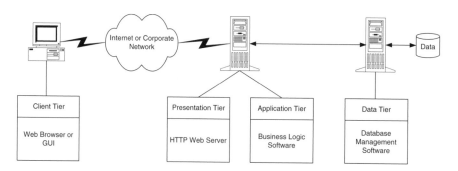

Figure 5–1 A generic N-tier architecture.

In Chapter 4 we saw that three components of the Web are HTTP, HTML, and URLs. We discussed HTTP and URLs. In this chapter we examine HTML in detail. In the next section, "Markup Languages and HTML," we introduce the concept of a markup language and contrast it with a "what you see is what you get" (WYSIWYG) language characteristic of most word processors such as Microsoft Word. We examine the syntax of HTML, explain the common structure of every Web page, and show how to construct a Web page using some simple HTML. What actually constitutes good Web page design is detailed in the next chapter on Web site design and content.

Web pages are created using HTML, but the average user will not want to create an entire Web site by typing in HTML text. In the section, "Tools for Creating a Fabulous Web Page," we describe tools that are available to an Internet business for creating a sophisticated Web site. Although HTML is a very powerful markup language for Web page presentation, there are problems with HTML. In the section "The Joy of X: XML, XSL, and XHTML," we introduce XML (extensible markup language). XML is an exciting development with immense importance for Internet business. XSL is a very important formatting language for XML. We also introduce XHTML here, which is used to segue from HTML to XML. Most Web sites, regardless of whether they are business-to-consumer or business-to-business, are dynamic. The user can interact with the site. In "Dynamic Web Pages" we show how this is done. We conclude the chapter with a section on "Future Trends and Implications."

MARKUP LANGUAGES AND HTML . . . .

HTML is an acronym for hypertext markup language. What is hypertext markup language? In order to understand a markup language, consider the two distinct approaches to word processing. One approach is *what you see is what you get* or *WYSIWYG*; the other is to use a markup language. With WYSIWYG, what you see displayed on the screen is a very accurate representation of what gets printed. An example of a WYSIWYG word processor is Microsoft Word. As an example of WYSIWYG, consider the following book title in boldface. What you are seeing on the printed page is what you would see on the screen using a WYSIWYG word processor.

The Essential Guide to Internet Business Technology

This title could be saved in ASCII text except for the boldface formatting. That is, there is no ASCII code for a boldface uppercase letter E or boldface for any other letter for that matter. If you were to write this title in, say, Microsoft Word 2000, and save the corresponding file, Word would save it as a .doc file, which is a binary file. Recall the discussion in Chapter 2, "What Do I Need to Know about Hardware?," on binary versus text files. In order to read the file you would need software capable of translating the Microsoft .doc coding scheme. If you were to send a .doc file to someone using the Unix or Linux operating system, she would not be able to read the file without a product such as StarOffice from Sun Microsystems. Or, if you sent the file to someone with Word 97, he could not read the file unless it was first translated to the Word 97 coding scheme.

Although the Windows operating system is the dominant operating system for desktop computers, the .doc binary encoding scheme is far from universal, and may well be less widely used in the future. Tim Berners-Lee, realizing how important it is for the Web to be universal, wrote in his book *Weaving the Web* [12]: "The least common denominator we could assume among all different types of computers was that they all had some sort of keyboard input device, and that they could all produce ASCII (plain text) characters." Hence, HTML, which Berners-Lee developed, is written in a text file format. This means that if we are to display formatting, and we want the HTML files to be text, we need a markup language. A *markup language* is a set of code words used to tell a browser (or other software) how to display the text. So, if we want to use HTML to boldface the book title illustrated earlier, we would write the text:

```
<b>The Essential Guide to Internet Business Technology</b>
```

The <b> and </b> are called *tags*. An HTML document consists of two things: tags and the actual text that gets displayed. All HTML tags have the format <tagname> and </tagname>. For example, to underline a word in HTML you type <underline> and </underline> on either side of the word. The <underline> is the start tag and the </underline> is the end tag. All text between the start and end tags is formatted as instructed by the tags. It is the job of the browser to read the tags and do the proper formatting. The browser assumes anything between the < and the > is a tag and does not display it. (If you need to actually display a < or > in HTML you would type in &< or &>.) Although HTML tag names are not case-sensitive, it is better to use lowercase for reasons described later. There are other markup languages such as RTF (rich text format), which is supported by most word processors, and TₑX, in which this book is written, but HTML is by far the most common. The basic structure of a Web page is:

```
<html>
    <head>
          Head content here
    </head>
    <body>
        Body content here
    </body>
</html>
```

The information in the head of an HTML document is not displayed by the browser. Typical information contained in the head consists of:

- A title—when you bookmark a Web page, the default name used for the bookmark is the text contained between the title tags

- Tags that index the document for search engines (more on this in the section "How to Get a High Ranking for Your Web Site" in Chapter 6, "Web Site Design and Content")

- Scripts (see the section "Dynamic Web Pages" in this chapter)
- Style sheets (see the section "The Joy of X" in this chapter)

The actual material that gets displayed by the browser is contained in the body of the HTML document. The HTML for a Web page is illustrated in Figure 5–2. The way that the browser displays the HTML in Figure 5–2 is given in Figure 5–3.

```html
<html>
<head>
<title>html sample page</title>
<link rel="stylesheet" type="text/css" href="book.css" />
<meta name="keywords" content="book, technology,
computing" />
</head>
<body>
<h1 align="center">The Essential Guide to Internet Business
Technology</h1>
<h2 align="center">By Gail Honda and Kipp Martin</h2>
<br />
<p>An important paradigm is the cycle of computing. It is
used throughout this book to place modern N-tier
architectures within an historical context. </p>
<table>
<tr>
<td>Cycle of computing</td>
<td> <img src="cycle.gif" alt="cycle of computing" /></td>
</tr>
</table>
<div class="shadow">
<p>Electronic business is expected to grow to $7 trillion
by 2005 and the top five fastest-growing occupations
through 2008 are computer-related.</p>
</div>
<p>This book is based on a course taught at <a
href="http://www.uchicago.edu">The University of Chicago.
</a></p>
</body>
</html>
```

Figure 5–2 HTML code for the Web page.

A markup language like HTML and a WYSIWYG-based word processing program such as Microsoft Word are fundamentally different in the way they work. Notice, for example, the tag pair <p> and </p>. These tags are used to start and end a paragraph. The browser will treat a stream of text between the tags `<p>` and `</p>` as the same paragraph regardless of the spacing used. Similarly, the amount of white space between two words in the HTML document is irrelevant, as the browser will display only one space unless specifically instructed to do otherwise via a tag. If you want to create vertical space between two lines of text using HTML, rather than hitting the return as you would with a WYSIWYG-based word processing program, you would use the `<br/>` tag.

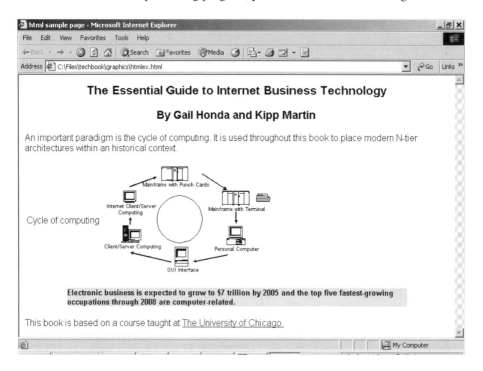

Figure 5–3 Web page for HTML code.

One of the most important tags is the anchor tag `<a>`. The anchor tag allows users to link from one Web page to another. It is a crucial feature of HTML. For example, the text `University of Chicago` that lies between the starting and ending anchor tags in Figure 5–2 is underlined and highlighted when it is displayed in the Web page (depending upon browser settings). The text between the anchor tags is hypertext. When viewers click on this hypertext they are taken to the server specified by the `href` attribute of the anchor tag. For example, in Figure 5–4, the text `href="http://www.uchicago.edu"` will take the viewer to the Web server with the domain name `www.uchicago.edu` when the viewer clicks on the hypertext `University of Chicago`. With appropriate multimedia plug-in tools for the browser, the hypertext can also link to sound or graphic files.

There is also an object-oriented programming aspect to a Web page. Notice, for example, the `<div>` tag in Figure 5–2. Associated with this `<div>` tag is an attribute `class=''shadow''`. The `<div>` and `</div>` tags are used to define a specific block

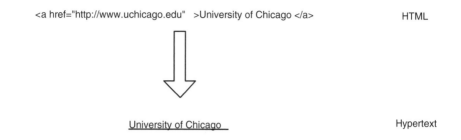

Figure 5–4 *A URL specified by an anchor tag.*

of the HTML document. By using the class attribute with the tags we can create distinct blocks of the HTML document, each with its own formatting properties. Note that the browser displays the text between the tags in the class "shadow" differently than it does the rest of the HTML document. The object-oriented aspect of a Web page is further illustrated in the Technical Appendix.

HTML is an open standard and anyone can use it. The HTML standard is maintained by the W3C (World Wide Web Consortium) headed by Tim Berners-Lee. The complete listing of the HTML standard is available at www.w3c.org. You can also download their free browser Amaya at the site. For those wishing to learn more about Web markup languages, and to keep up with the latest developments, we highly recommend the W3C Web site.

Cascading Style Sheets

Anyone who has worked with spreadsheets knows the value of separating the "data" from the model. For example, if an interest rate is used in many cell calculations in a spreadsheet, it is best to have a single separate cell that contains the interest rate rather than to hard code the actual value of the interest rate into every cell that uses the rate for a calculation. This concept applies to Web development as well—it's useful to separate the content from the format of the content. There are a number of reasons to do so.

- It should be possible to change the formatting of an entire Web site without editing each of the individual pages. By changing a style sheet, the entire Web site is reformatted.

- It should be possible to easily adapt a Web site so that it can be displayed on different devices, e.g., a Palm Pilot, cell phone browser, or desktop browser.

- It makes it easier to write Web pages if you do not have to worry about formatting and can concentrate on content.

- It makes it easier to give an entire Web site the same "look and feel." When new pages are added, they can use the style sheet of the pages already created.

These objectives are achieved in HTML by using *cascading style sheets* (CSS). Here is the style sheet used to create the Web page displayed in Figure 5–3.

```
h1 { font-family: arial; font-size: 16pt; color: black }
h2 { font-family: arial; font-size: 14pt; color: black }
body {font-family: arial; font-size:12pt; color:black;
      background-color:white}
a   { color: blue }
table    {font-family: arial; font-size:12pt; color:black;
      background-color:white}
div.shadow {font-family: arial; font-size:10pt; color:black;
         background-color:#99ffff;   font-weight:bold;
         margin-left:10 ;margin-right:10}
```

The style sheet is read by the Web page to which it applies. The Web page reads the style sheet when the following command is included in the head section.

```
<link rel="stylesheet" type="text/css" href="book.css" />
```

The name of the file that is the actual cascading style sheet is `book.css`. This file resides in the same directory as the HTML file used to create Figure 5–3. Of course, the style sheet can reside in any directory, as long as the path to the style sheet is specified by the `href` attribute.

Each line in the style sheet file is a formatting rule. This rule has two parts to it. It has a *selector* (the part of the HTML document like `h1`) and a *declaration*. The declaration is what you see between the { and the }. The declaration has a property and a value. For example, consider the first line of the style file:

```
h1  { font-family: arial; font-size: 16pt; color: black }
```

This formatting rule applies to any part of the HTML document that is set off by the heading element tag `h1`. There are actually three declarations in this formatting rule. The declarations are separated by semicolons. The first declaration states that the property `font-family` has value `arial`. The second declaration says that the property `font-size` has value `16pt`. Finally, the third declaration states that the property `color` has value `black`.

Cascading style sheets can also use the class attribute. Consider the format rule:

```
div.shadow {font-family: arial; font-size:10pt; color:black;
         background-color:#99ffff;   font-weight:bold;
         margin-left:10 ;margin-right:10}
```

This rule states that the HTML element `div` has class value `shadow`. This statement allows a Web developer to designate a section of the Web page content by using the tags

```
<div class="shadow">
    Web page content here ...
</div>
```

to format the content using the formatting definitions for the shadow class. For example, in this case the text in the shadow class will be 10 point, bold black arial with a light blue background color (designated by #99ffff). The left and right margins will be indented 10 percent. In 5–3 the shaded text that begins "Electronic business ... " just below the cycle of computing figure is formatted using this class. A class is obviously a very powerful feature of style sheets. We can define various classes of format styles, and easily format that area of the Web page using a <div> tag with the appropriate class name.

TOOLS FOR CREATING A FABULOUS WEB PAGE

After gaining a basic understanding of HTML, the next step is to understand how HTML pages are created. There are three ways to create HTML pages.

1. Use your favorite word processor such as Word Perfect, Microsoft Word, Notepad, whatever, to create a *text file* that is the HTML document, an example of which you see in Figure 5–2. (Note: Even if Microsoft Word automatically creates .doc files which are binary files, if you save a file specifically as a text file by selecting "Text Only (*.txt)" in the "Save as type" window using the "Save As" command, the file will be saved as a text file.) It is very important to save the file as a text file because an important feature of HTML files is that they are text and therefore platform independent! Whether you are using Windows 3.1, Windows 95, Windows 98, Windows 2000, Windows NT, a Unix or Linux workstation, or a Mac, it matters not. HTML is HTML is HTML. Of course, this first way to create an HTML page is very difficult and tedious—you have to know what the tags mean and have to type them all in. This is particularly true if there is a lot of formatting such as in building a table. People who are GUI-oriented, as opposed to command line-oriented, will rarely use this option. They prefer method 2.

2. At the other end of the spectrum from creating a text file with HTML tags is to use what is called Web authoring software. This is software that allows a user to click on icons, such as a table or a link, and the software automatically generates the underlying HTML. Most Web authoring software will also provide a window that displays the HTML source so that one can edit and directly enter HTML tags if necessary. The Web authoring software can be quite powerful and complex, often allowing developers to create Web pages that link to back end databases.

   Examples of commercial Web authoring software include Dreamweaver from Macromedia, FrontPage from Microsoft, GoLive from Adobe, Homesite from Allaire, and Web.Designer from Corel. A Web search will reveal many products in addition to these. These packages require little or no knowledge of HTML and make extensive use of visual tools. Some browsers such as Amaya and Netscape Communicator are equipped with HTML editors.

3. There is a third option, that lies somewhere in between the first and second options. This option is to use a converter program. A good example is Office 2000, in particular, Word 2000. With Word 2000 you can write a document as you normally would

and then simply save the document as an HTML file. This option is not as powerful as the second, and sometimes things get "lost in the translation," but it is a good way to get up and running quickly. As the Web becomes even more central to business, Word processors will probably simply morph into HTML editors.

In Chapter 4 we discussed the file URL that allows a user to view how a Web page looks without logging on to the Internet. This is very useful in the development of Web pages regardless of which of the three options just discussed is used. This allows a developer to see how the formatting will actually look using a browser.

THE JOY OF X: XML, XSL, AND XHTML . . . .

Bill Gates, in discussing software development, once said, "Today we're at another important inflection point, embracing XML in everything we do." Extensible markup language (XML) has created an enormous amount of interest in the Internet business community. In order to understand all of this excitement, consider the following four scenarios.

Scenario 1: The following is a question from a reader of the *Chicago Tribune* to Jim Coates, who writes a Q & A column on personal computing. (Copyrighted February 12, 2001, Chicago Tribune Company. All rights reserved. Used with permission.)

> Q: My wife has an old DOS recipe program called COOK by East Hampton Industries in New York. She has used this program since the late '80s and has upgraded it several times. When she inquired as to when they planned to put out a Windows version, they advised that they did not intend any more upgrades of the program.
>
> She uses the program almost daily and has over 700 recipes that she has tediously entered. I thought I might be able to convert the recipe data files and then import them into one of the better Windows cooking programs, but have not found any of them that will do the conversion. The data files use a .dt3 ending. I am concerned that she will eventually lose the ability to use the program with the continuing Windows upgrading. Are you aware of any way we might be able to convert these data files?
>
> Jimmy D. Wiggs @aol.com

This reader's problem is caused by the fact that the food recipes are stored in a proprietary binary format. If the recipes were stored as text files, they could be read by most word processors. What would be nice is to store the recipes as text files and have keywords in the files that give the text data some meaning so they could be easily organized. For example, it would be great to be able to organize the text files and find all French cooking recipes, or all recipes that use curry.

Scenario 2: Consider a large clothing retailer that publishes an extensive catalog in HTML on the Web. This company lists the price of all their items on the Web catalog, and some items may appear on more than one page. For example, polo shirts might be on a page devoted to shirts and another page devoted to casual clothing. This company is responsive to demand and in this industry there is considerable error in forecasting demand. Hence, the company frequently changes prices on its inventory to better reflect demand. If these prices were "hard coded" into (written directly on) each HTML page, going in and editing each page and making sure all the prices were consistent each time the prices changed would be a laborious task. It would be much easier to update the prices in a database and then have the Web pages automatically reflect these new prices.

Scenario 3: A company would like to create a Web service whereby, when an inventory level triggers a reorder, a purchase order document is automatically sent over the Web to a computer of the appropriate supplier where a shipping order is automatically created. In order for this to work, software on the supplier's computer has to "read" and understand the purchase order. There must be a set of keywords that give meaning to the text in order to identify the stock keeping unit, price, order quantity, etc., for this system to work. Clearly, this would be difficult if just HTML were used, since the HTML keywords (tags) are designed to describe formatting, not give meaning to elements in purchase orders.

Scenario 4: A software company wants to develop a tool that will surf the Web and locate the minimum cost item in a specific category. For example, a customer wants to buy the DVD of the movie, *The Man Who Shot Liberty Valance*. The software tool would take the product category of DVD, and the DVD title, and search the Web for the lowest price. Although the search tool could search for Web pages with the exact sequence of words "The Man Who Shot Liberty Valance," finding the price of the DVD on that page (this is called screen scraping) would be difficult because there is no `<price>` tag in HTML. The HTML only provides information on how text is displayed; it provides no information about what the text means. HTML lends formatting to text but no meaning. Somehow, the price would have to be extracted from the meaning of the text—a nontrivial and error-prone task for the software to perform.

There are three key problems in these scenarios: 1) we need to have data in a format that is easily exchanged and not proprietary, 2) we need to be able to give meaning to the data so the data file can be processed by software applications, and 3) all parties involved must agree on this meaning. XML addresses these problems. Like HTML, XML is a markup language. However, unlike HTML, with XML you can give meaning to your data. HTML is for formatting data; it is about syntax. XML gives meaning to the data; it is about semantics. HTML requires the use of a fixed set of tags, while with XML the user creates tags. In this sense, XML is a *meta language*. A meta language is a language used to define other languages. XML is object-oriented and can be used with scripting languages to greatly enhance the functionality of a Web page. Finally, with XML, a Web developer can easily separate the data from the formatting and content of a Web page.

Now let's see how XML eliminates the problems described in our four scenarios. This is best done through an example. This example is designed to illustrate the power of XML and is much simpler than what you will find in a real implementation. Consider a record company that sells Doo Wop 45 RPM records from the 1950s and 1960s. The company wants to display a listing of its records on a Web page based on the most recent information in its database. A part of the database (two out of the seven records in the XML file) in XML format appears in Figure 5–5.

The first line in the file states that the file contains XML data. Don't worry about the second line for now. Notice the tags. There are no HTML tags. For example, the XML *element tag* `<PRICE>` is not a valid HTML tag. These tags have nothing to do with formatting. The tags are designed to define the object RECORD. Each RECORD has a

```
<?xmlversion="1.0"?>
<!DOCTYPE CATALOG SYSTEM "doowop.dtd">
<CATALOG genre="Doo Wop">
    <RECORD>
        <TITLE>In The Still of the Night</TITLE>
        <GROUP>The Five Satins</GROUP>
        <YEAR>1956</YEAR>
        <PRICE>15.00</PRICE>
    </RECORD>
    <RECORD>
        <TITLE>The Duke of Earl</TITLE>
        <GROUP>Gene Chandler</GROUP>
        <YEAR>1962</YEAR>
        <PRICE>5.50</PRICE>
    </RECORD>
 ... other records ...
 </CATALOG>
```

Figure 5–5 Part of the `doowop.xml` file.

`TITLE`, a `GROUP`, a `YEAR`, and a `PRICE`. However, the syntax of the XML element tags is similar to HTML in that there is a start `<tag>` and end `</tag>`. The XML element tags can also have *attributes* that give them further meaning. For example, the `<CATALOG>` tag has an attribute `genre` which describes the type of music in the catalog. In this case, the `genre` attribute is equal to `Doo Wop`.

This XML file could be created from a database (more on this in Chapter 12, "The Power of Databases"), created using an XML editor, or created with any word processor that can save a file as ASCII text. It is important to understand that the tags are defined by the user and depend on how they are applied. For example, tags used to describe an option (as in finance) would be very different from tags used to describe car engine parts.

A key feature of XML data is a treelike structure. This is illustrated in Figure 5–6. The root node is `CATALOG`, which is the XML object defined by the `<CATALOG>` tags. Immediately below the root nodes are the `RECORD` nodes. There is a `RECORD` node for each of the seven distinct 45 RPM records in the database. Each `RECORD` node has four child nodes, a `TITLE` node, a `GROUP` node, a `YEAR` node, and a `PRICE` node. The actual values for the children of the first and seventh `RECORD` nodes are given in the figure.

This treelike structure is used by scripting languages such as JavaScript or VBScript to access parts of the XML object in the development of Web pages. For example, we could use JavaScript to select and display only those records that cost $5.00 or less. The display of the XML data file in the Internet Explorer browser is in Figure 5–7. The browser displays the XML file in a tree structure similar to that of Figure 5–6. Clicking on the "+" sign to the left of the `RECORD` element expands the element to show its children. Clicking on the hyphen ("-") sign to the left of the `RECORD` element hides the children elements

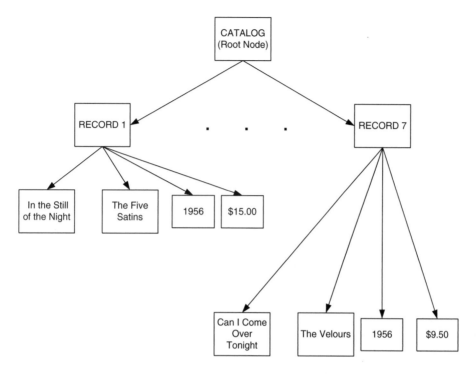

Figure 5–6 Tree structure of XML file `doowop.xml`.

from display. Of course, what is shown in Figure 5–7 is not what we want to display on our Web page; we want a record catalog in a more presentable form. But first, a few more details about XML.

It is important to understand that XML is a much stricter markup language than HTML. The following is true of XML, but not HTML:

- The tags are case-sensitive. For example, `<PRICE>` and `</price>` opening and closing tags will result in an error when the XML document is read.

- The tags must be properly nested. The following nesting will result in an error:

```
<PARENT>
    <CHILD1>
    <CHILD2>
    </CHILD1>
    </CHILD2>
</PARENT>
```

- Both opening and closing tags are required. For example, in HTML you may begin a paragraph with a `<p>` and do not need to end the paragraph with a `</p>` tag. In our XML example we could not open a `<RECORD>` tag without closing it.

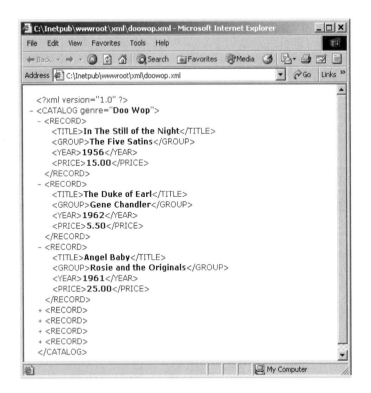

Figure 5–7 The XML file displayed in Internet Explorer.

There are other specifications for XML syntax. See the W3C Web site, or a book on XML such as Pardi [126]. An XML document that satisfies the basic XML syntax requirements is said to be *well formed*. An XML *parser* is used to read an XML file and construct an appropriate tree structure such as that shown in Figure 5–6. If there is a mistake in the XML syntax, the parser will give an error message. A number of parsers are available over the Web. Internet Explorer has a built-in parser. It will attempt to parse any file with an `.xml` extension.

Unfortunately, just having the correct syntax in an XML document is not enough. For example, there are numerous hedge funds actively trading financial options. Different funds might wish to exchange financial information concerning executed trades. One hedge fund might use the tag pair `<STRIKE>` and `</STRIKE>` to denote the strike price of an option. However, if another fund chooses to use the tag pair `<STRIKEPRICE>` and `</STRIKEPRICE>` there is a problem if the two funds wish to exchange XML data files. It is crucial that there exist an industry standard vocabulary, and that XML files be *validated* against the industry standard. One way to accomplish this is through the use of a document type definition (DTD) file. A very simple DTD file, `doowop.dtd`, for the `doowop.xml` file in Figure 5–5, is illustrated in Figure 5–8.

```
<!ELEMENT CATALOG (RECORD*) >
<!ATTLIST CATALOG genre CDATA #REQUIRED>
<!ELEMENT RECORD ( TITLE, GROUP, YEAR, PRICE)>
<!ELEMENT TITLE (#PCDATA)>
<!ELEMENT GROUP (#PCDATA)>
<!ELEMENT YEAR (#PCDATA)>
<!ELEMENT PRICE (#PCDATA)>
```

Figure 5–8 DTD file for `doowop.xml`.

Go back and examine the second line of Figure 5–5 and note that it references the file illustrated in Figure 5–8. The file in Figure 5–8 is the file that the browser reads and uses to validate the XML file in Figure 5–5. The details of the syntax of the DTD file in Figure 5–8 are not important. The important thing to understand is that the DTD gives meaning to the XML document because the XML document must be validated against the DTD. A valid XML document must conform to the DTD.

In our example this means that every tag used must correspond to one of the tags listed in the DTD. Furthermore, for each `<RECORD>`, `</RECORD>` pair there must be exactly one pair of tags for the `TITLE`, `GROUP`, `YEAR`, and `PRICE`, and they must appear in the exact order given in the DTD file. This means that although a document with a tag pair `<LEADSINGER>`, `</LEADSINGER>` is well formed, it is not valid because it does not conform to the DTD. This is a very rigid system, yet it is this rigidity that makes XML so powerful. In the options example, if there were a DTD for defining a financial option, there could be no conflict over exchanging XML data on the strike price of the option. Having an agreed upon industry standard for a DTD also addresses the problem raised in Scenarios 3 and 4. For example, a Web page displaying prices of DVDs based upon an XML industry standard will have tags that unambiguously define the selling price of the DVD.

There are some limitations to DTD files. For example, they do not use XML syntax and they do not permit different data types such as floating point numbers and integers. A more modern approach to validation is through *schemas*. Unfortunately, there are several schema standards available. More on this in the Technical Appendix. Suffice it to say that XML schemas are here to stay and are supported by all industry heavyweights. An important Web site for information on schemas in addition to the W3C Web site is `www.biztalk.org`. This Web site is devoted to providing information on using XML for B2B document exchange and enterprise software application integration. Biztalk.org also maintains a library of proposed schemas for a number of industries.

Using an agreed upon schema or DTD is important if companies wish to exchange documents. One can also use an XML *namespace* to further qualify the meaning of tags in an XML document. Using a namespace is akin to using an area code, which allows the same seven-digit telephone number to be used in different locations. In the XML world, the area code corresponds to a URI (Uniform Resource Identifier) in the root element. Take, for example,

```
<CATALOG xmlns:myname="http://www.myname.com" genre="Doo Wop">
```

In this example the URI is `http://www.myname.com`. The URI does not have to be a valid URL, but a URL is a good choice since it is unique. Then, whenever a tag pair like `<TITLE>` is used, it could be qualified by `<myname:TITLE>`. Using namespaces reduces the likelihood of confusion over tag meaning when companies exchange documents.

Ultimately, we want to use the XML data file to create a Web page that looks like the one in Figure 5–9. We have talked about how XML is about data and meaning, while HTML is about format and presentation. How did the data file in Figure 5–5 get displayed as Figure 5–9? The answer is through the use of extensible stylesheet language transformations (XSLT). We use the XSLT to *transform* the XML into HTML. The actual display in Figure 5–9 is the result of four files coming together. See Figure 5–10.

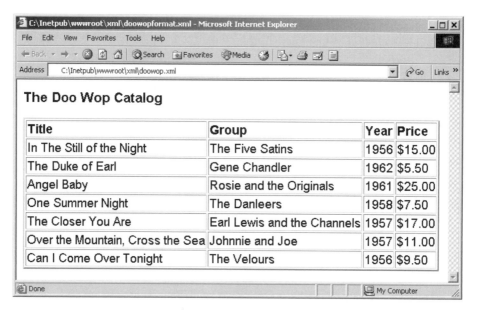

Figure 5–9 *The XML file displayed in Internet Explorer using XSLT.*

Tech Talk

XSL: This is the acronym for extensible stylesheet language, which is an open standard from the W3C. XSL is to XML what CSS is to HTML. There are three components to XSL. The first component is XSLT, which is a language used to transform XML documents into HTML. The second component is the XPath language used for accessing parts of the XML document. The third component is an XML formatting vocabulary.

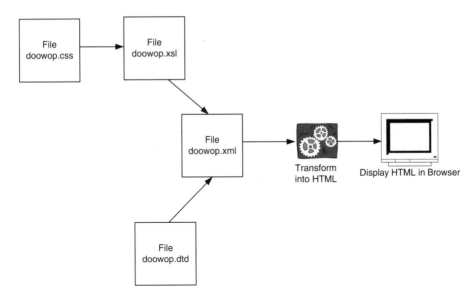

Figure 5-10 Files used to display `doowop.xml`.

In order to make this transformation, we add the following line to the `doowop.xml` file:

```
<?xml:stylesheet type = "text/xsl" href = "doowop.xsl"?>
```

This line references the file `doowop.xsl` which contains the XSLT commands and instructs the browser to use the markup instructions from the file `doowop.xsl`. It is this file, `doowop.xsl`, that tells the browser how to use the data from `doowop.xml`. The XSL file `doowop.xsl` uses formatting instructions in the file `doowop.css`. The file `doowop.xsl` not only provides formatting information, it also provides rules for transforming the XML into HTML so that it can be displayed in a browser. We are not going into the technical details of these commands. The technically inclined reader should consult the Technical Appendix.

Let's summarize by considering the four scenarios used to introduce this section. First, an XML file is plain ASCII text and XML is an open standard controlled by the W3C. The problem described in Scenario 1 goes away because XML data files will always be readable with simple text editors.

More significantly, if we alter, for example, a price of one or more records in the XML database (Figure 5–5), the change is automatically reflected on the Web page (Figure 5–9) when the file is reloaded in the browser. There is no need to change any HTML. We could also add or delete records in the XML database without ever having to change any HTML. We can also add or delete records, change the price, etc., without ever changing the markup XSL file. Not only that, but we could use the same XSL file for other record categories such as classical or jazz. There is nothing "hard coded" into the `doowop.xsl` file. For more on XSLT, see Pardi [126]. Thus, the problem described in Scenario 2 is eliminated. The problems described in scenarios 3 and 4 are eliminated by DTDs, schemas, and industry cooperation through organizations such as biztalk.org.

We hope you are not Xed out by now because there is one more important X to talk about—extensible hypertext markup language (XHTML). There are two problems with the current HTML standard. First, HTML is not valid or even well formed XML. This presents a problem because XML is quickly becoming a standard. Both Netscape Navigator and Internet Explorer version 5.0 and above have XML processors, but these processors cannot handle HTML. Conversely, an HTML processor does not handle XML. (Note: Your browser will try to process a file with an .xml extension as XML and a file with an .html extension as HTML.) As Web applications and services become XML centered, and software focuses on processing XML, the current version of HTML will cease to be supported. A second problem with HTML is that the document content has become too co-mingled with formatting commands regarding fonts, colors, etc. This issue was addressed in our discussions of CSS and XSL.

XHTML is the next generation of HTML, but unlike earlier generations, XHTML is written in XML. The DTD that defines the current 1.0 version of XHTML uses the tag set of HTML 4.01. Think of XHTML as a reformulation of HTML in XML combining the markup and formatting ability of HTML with the rigor of XML. As with XML, the concepts of valid (or strictly conforming) and well formed carry over into XHTML. For example, to be well formed, an XHTML document must satisfy the following:

- The tags must be nested properly.

- There are no optional end tags, e.g., if you start a paragraph with the paragraph tag `<p>` you must end it with `</p>`.

- Empty tags such as a line break `<br>` must be written as `<br />`.

The basic structure of a Web page written in XHTML does not change. The basic structure of any Web page in XHTML is:

```
<html>
    <head>
        <title>This is XHTML </title>
            Other head content here
    </head>
    <body>
        Body content here
    </body>
</html>
```

Since XHTML is written using XML, the validation concept applies. There are currently three levels of validation for XHTML. Each level of validation is checked against a different DTD. The details of each of the following DTDs is available at the W3C Web site.

- Strict XHTML: The strict DTD is pure "XHTML." The document must be well formed, all of the tags must be lowercase, and many older or "deprecated" tags such as `<center>` are not supported. Strict XHTML also does not support the use of frames.

- Transitional XHTML. This uses the transitional DTD. This still requires that the document be well formed and that tags be lowercase, but it supports deprecated tags such as `<center>`.

- Frameset XHTML. This is the DTD to use if your Web page has frames.

An important feature of XHTML is that it forces the Web developer to truly separate out the data, the content, and the formatting. For example, in XHTML if you want the heading `<h1>` to be the color red, you must put this information in a style sheet—it is not part of the body of the XHTML document.

DYNAMIC WEB PAGES ....

The HTML introduced earlier is considered static in the sense that it simply describes how a page is marked up. However, through the use of *scripts* Web pages become dynamic. Everyone has no doubt viewed Web pages with moving text, changing colors, popup windows, etc. These enhancements to Web pages are accomplished either through the use of Java Applets or through scripts. Java Applets are programs written in the Java programming language. Applets are downloaded over the Web and "plugged-in" to the Web page. The Java programming language was described in Chapter 3, "Software Is Everywhere." The most popular Web page scripting language is JavaScript, which was originally introduced by Netscape. There is an acronym, DHTML (dynamic hypertext markup language) that is frequently used. The DHTML acronym essentially refers to documents that combine HTML, style sheets, scripts, and Java Applets. There is no DHTML standard supported by the W3C.

Another client scripting language is VBScript from Microsoft. Although VBScript is an excellent scripting language, only Internet Explorer has a VBScript interpreter. Thus, if VBScript is used as a client language it is necessary that the client use Internet Explorer or obtain a special add-on for Netscape Navigator.

Java Applets and JavaScript are used for making very "glitzy" Web pages—pages with lots of moving text, pop-up windows, changing colors, etc. Most of these fancy features are not necessary and are a minor presentation enhancement without contributing to the business function of a page. If anything, they contribute to making the page download more slowly and are often distracting. However, Java Applets and JavaScript can contribute significantly to the business function of a Web page. For example, when a customer is filling out a purchase order form, JavaScript can be used to make sure that the data input is valid (e.g., a social security number has nine digits, a phone number includes the area code, etc.). It makes more sense to do this type of error checking at the client end, rather than at the server end. Later, in Chapter 13, we discuss client side versus server side computing and provide more detail about Java Applets and JavaScript.

FUTURE TRENDS AND IMPLICATIONS . . . .

It is clear that XML is going to play a critical role in many aspects of Internet business. It is supported by major players such as IBM, Microsoft, Oracle, and Sun. Your company should have an IT team planning how to incorporate the XML standard into your Internet business. We have also talked about the importance of open text formats versus closed binary formats. Develop a plan for migrating all mission-critical data into an XML format.

In order to capitalize on the power of XML, it is necessary to have industry agreed-upon DTDs and schemas. Be a leader or active participant in your industry in defining these schemas. Don't let your competitors define them exclusively to their benefit. Register as a contributor to `biztalk.org` and publish your schemas for others to evaluate and use.

Have a plan for making the transition from HTML to XHTML. Make sure your Web page developers are creating new content that is valid XHTML. The following rules should be followed when creating Web pages:

- Write HTML tags in lowercase.

- Close every start tag with an end tag.

- Close empty element tags properly; for example, the `<br>` tag should be written as `<br />`.

- Cease using deprecated tags (see w3c.org for a list).

- Make sure all attributes such as URLs in anchor tags are quoted.

- Include an XML declaration at the start of each document.

- Include a DTD reference in each document.

If you change the extension on an HTML file from `.html` to `.xml` the browser will read it as XML and test if it is well formed. You can also run your HTML pages through a validator at the W3C Web site. Taking current HTML pages and transforming them into valid XHTML may not be easy. A good Unix programmer can write a shell script to change all uppercase tags to lowercase. There is a program called Tidy available at the W3C site which is designed to convert HTML into well formed XML.

Another important trend in markup languages is the growing use of wireless markup language (WML). This is a markup language designed expressly to display content on wireless devices that do not have the viewing area or bandwidth of a desktop computer. Wireless communication is indeed an important trend in Internet business. A company will need to have the capability to display wireless content in the future because both employees and customers will want to obtain information from a company Web site using wireless devices.

WML is a markup language written in XML and is to wireless devices what XHTML (or HTML) is to the desktop browser. WML is made of decks instead of pages, and the decks are made up of cards. WML is a specification of wireless application protocol (WAP), a wireless protocol that is a product of the WAP Forum. The WAP Forum is an industry association of most of the major players in telecommunications, hardware, and software. For example, AT&T Wireless Services, Ericsson Mobile Communications AB, Motorola, and Nokia are all members of the WAP Forum. It is their objective to make WAP the worldwide de facto standard for providing Internet services to wireless devices. Other WAP specifications are WMLScript and wireless telephony application interface (WTAI). We refer the reader to the Technical Appendix for details on WAP and WML.

6   Web Site Design and Content

In this chapter ...

THE AGE OF INFORMATION OVERLOAD ....

In the Information Age, we are bombarded every day with thousands of messages from all media. Information of every kind clamors for our attention from every corner of our existence. Movies, clothing, gasoline pumps, menus, even restrooms are no longer free from advertisements beckoning to us. When you factor in the billions of Web pages in existence and the millions being produced every day, as well as the messages you receive every hour via voicemail, fax, PDA (personal digital assistant), mobile phone, pager, and email, you will conclude that we are in the Age of Information Overload. In the Information Age the supply of information far exceeds our demand for it: Our time and attention are limited and we must be selective in the information we gather and process.

. . . .

HOW TO BREAK THROUGH THE CLUTTER IN THE AGE OF INFORMATION OVERLOAD

A successful Web site MUST take advantage of the special nature of the Web, which is unlike other media.

So how are you going to get information about your company to current and potential customers in Internet business when your target audience is already experiencing information overload and effort is required to find your Web site and navigate around it? It won't be easy, but there are steps you can take to drive customers to your site, make it easy for them to get the information they need, and keep them coming back. This is what this chapter is all about. An informative, easily navigable, and up-to-date Web site can be a tremendous asset to any Internet business strategy. But establishing and maintaining an excellent site takes time, resources, and constant care. A poorly designed, out-of-date, or obviously neglected site is akin to negative advertising for your company, possibly turning potential customers away, never to return.

There are certain characteristics of a site that must be in place if it is to be successful. It must take advantage of the special nature of the Web, which is unlike other media. We discuss these characteristics in the next section, "The Nature of the Web." A site must be designed with a specific purpose in mind and must be targeted to a particular audience you want to reach. These topics are covered in the next two sections of the chapter, "What Is the Purpose of the Site?" and "Who Is Your Audience?" A site must provide pertinent information about the company, products, and services. It should be almost effortless for users to find the information on your site that they need. How to go about doing this is covered in the section, "What Content Will You Provide?" One problem that many online retailers face is abandonment by the user before completing the purchase. It is important that you know the "Don'ts" of Web pages that turn customers away, as well as the "Do's" of getting a high ranking for your Web page on search engines. These will be addressed in the sections on "Closing the Online Sale" and "How to Get a High Ranking for Your Web Page." To manage a large and complex Web site, we discuss your options in

"Managing Web Site Content." Two marketing and design experts then share their "Best Practices for Web Site Design and Content." We close the chapter with "Future Trends and Implications."

THE NATURE OF THE WEB ....

To fully exploit the possibilities of the Web it is important that you think of it as much more than just another advertising medium. It is truly a revolutionary medium with capabilities far exceeding those of print, radio, or video. First of all, it is *nonlinear*. This means that there is no straight-line path from beginning to end on the Web as there is with viewing a television program or listening to a song on the radio. Whenever users surf the Web, there is no telling beforehand which links they will click or which sites they will visit. This is a fundamental characteristic of *hypertext*, or links on the Web. Web sites are not meant to be viewed from "beginning" to "end," if a beginning and end can even be defined. Users will visit a site, search for the information they need, and move on to the next site, as quickly as possible. The design of a Web site should allow users to do this as efficiently as possible.

THE SPECIAL NATURE OF THE WEB

The Web is:

- Nonlinear
- Interactive
- Active on the part of the user
- Fast

Second, the Web is *interactive*. The best sites allow the user to take some kind of action, whether it be to get a credit check, compare prices, make a reservation, or order a product. This is very different from print, radio, and video, which can only serve up information. Of course, these other media can prompt the user for some action, like providing a toll-free number to call to make a purchase, but this requires another medium or tool and more effort on the user's part. It is this immediate, interactive nature of the Web that makes surfing fun, fast, and keeps users coming back for more.

Third, the Web user is an *active* participant in the experience. Web users control and direct the trajectory of their attention as well as the viewing and listening landscape before them. This active participation also *personalizes* the Web experience, since in all likelihood no two users' experiences on the Web are exactly alike, unlike the viewing of the same television program and commercials by millions at the same time. Moreover, users don't sit as close to their television screens as they do to their computer screens. Thus, the Web experience is up close and personal as opposed to distant and impersonal.

Fourth, the Web is a much *faster* medium than traditional forms. A lot of people watch television to relax, turn off their minds, and "veg." Television viewers typically will watch a program even if it isn't scintillating every single moment. This is not true of the Web user. On the Web, users' attention span are short. Long downloads, boring pages, or confusing sites will cause them to exit immediately. Expectations on the users' parts are also high that they will find what they need very quickly so Web sites must be easily navigable. Responses from the server must be immediate or they will lose interest. Translated into Web site design criteria, this means the simpler, the better. High-resolution photos, fancy graphics, and special effects take time to download, and you risk losing your audience if you include too many of these on your site. On the other hand, an all-text page is boring to view. Your site must achieve that delicate balance between speed and visual appeal. Web designers will want to showcase their talent and incorporate special effects into a site, but Web usability experts will tell you that speed should be the more important criterion.

Finally, although *usability* is not a characteristic of the Web, it is a very desirable characteristic of all Web sites. Web usability guru Jakob Nielsen, states in his book, *Designing Web Usability: The Practice of Simplicity* [123], that "the only real success criterion for a Web site is repeat traffic from loyal users." How do you get this repeat traffic? By using his "HOME RUN" formula for building a successful site. Nielsen claims there are seven main reasons users return to truly stellar sites. They are:

- **H**igh quality content
- **O**ften updated
- **M**inimum download time
- **E**ase of use
- **R**elevant to users' needs
- **U**nique to the online medium
- **N**et-centric corporate culture

We refer you to his book if you would like to know in more detail what each of these entails. However, you probably understand by now that establishing and maintaining a successful Web site is an all-consuming task. Please read further for more details on how to make the most of the Web for your Internet business.

WHAT IS THE PURPOSE OF THE SITE? . . . .

Once you understand the nature of the Web and how it differs from traditional forms of media, the next step is to determine the purpose of your site. Good Web sites require a lot of planning up front. Far in advance of meetings with your Web designer or before designing it yourself, you need to think hard about your purpose. Your purpose will drive many other considerations of your site, such as content and design. In the early days of the Web, it was enough for a company to establish a site and serve up information about the company and its products and services. Companies rushed to set up a Web presence in order to, if nothing else, prove that they were part of the "new economy." These days, users expect much more from visiting a site, including fast downloads, relevant information, and interactive experiences. You must consider not only how to drive traffic to your site, but how to keep it there once it arrives. This requires a deep understanding of the purpose of your Web site.

If, as Nielsen states, the goal of your Web site should be to attract repeat traffic from loyal users, then you might think of your site as the Web microcosm of your business itself. As a business you want to build a base of loyal repeat customers, so why not consider your site as a means to do this? If you think of your site in this way and focus on the word "repeat," you can begin to envision the shape your site must take. You see that your site must be constantly updated and refreshed in order to keep enticing customers coming back. You see that your site must provide new information, new products, or new entertainment to prevent it from becoming stale. If you want your loyal customers to visit your site daily, as a news site would, then you must refresh your content daily. If your company's product or service is needed on a weekly or monthly basis, then you must provide enough incentive for your customers to come back to your site in that interval by making available new offerings and promotions.

If this goal of attracting loyal customers for repeat visits to your site seems abstract right now, it will become more concrete as we delve into the specifics of your site, one by one, throughout this chapter. The goal is abstract, but the means to achieve it are not. To achieve this goal, your site must first of all have a purpose. Will it be to sell a product or service? Will it be to enhance your company's brand name or product image? Will it be to gather information from visitors? Will it be to provide information? Ideally, you would like your site to do all of these things, but one of the purposes should be primary and dominate the others.

Take, for example, *Nytimes.com*, the site for the newspaper *The New York Times*. While a purpose of the site may be to sign users up for subscriptions, the main purpose is to inform its users. The home page (the first page users see when they type in a site's address) of *Nytimes.com* is completely dominated by news stories that are constantly updated so that new content can be found daily, if not hourly. There are subtle links to a page where a user can sign up for a subscription, but these are clearly not the overriding purpose of the site. You can see, however, that by constantly updating its site with fresh news stories, *Nytimes.com* is building a customer base of repeat users who, if they like what they see on the site enough, may indeed sign up for a subscription. In fact, the strategy for this Web site is "classic" Internet economy, which entails giving away something free in the hope that users will purchase whatever it is the company is selling.

Giving something away free on the Web as an enticement for a purchase is a strategy that is in use on many sites, which is why we call it classic. *Hooversonline.com* is another excellent example. It offers the latest business news as well as information on companies, SEC filings, and IPOs to name a few topics. The site offers a lot for free, such as "capsules" on company profiles, but if you want the fuller, more in-depth look at companies including competitive reports, you have to have a paid subscription. At *Fodors.com*, site of the venerable travel guidebook company Fodor's, you can get lots of free and valuable travel information, from news about hijackings in Turkey to advice on tipping in Morocco to "How to Stay Dry and Warm in Paris." You can download travel bargains as well as learn traveling language essentials in French, German, Italian, and Spanish. If you want the complete travel guide to a destination from Fodor's, however, you must order it from an online bookseller who is listed in the book catalog. It's interesting that Fodor's doesn't ship the book itself; apparently, it's not in the direct Web order business. Nevertheless, whether it be *The New York Times*, Hoover's, Fodor's, or any one of a number of companies, the "something free" is a great Internet business strategy: enticement and partial information free; full information for a fee. If you can figure out a smart way to do this for your site while keeping the information fresh, you have a Web-savvy, winning strategy that's sure to keep customers coming back for more.

WHO IS YOUR AUDIENCE? . . . .

Once you understand the goal of your site and you've decided on its primary purpose, the next step is to determine who your target audience will be. There is a particular kind of person who will be interested in your company, and your site must be tailored to appeal to that person. Demographics have been the traditional way to segment a target audience for a particular product or service, or in our case, the site. Marketers for a company conduct research on the gender, age group, income level, level of education, and geographic location of the persons who would be most likely to purchase their product. They then conduct focus groups comprising members of the target audience to refine their product and advertisements.

Ideally, you would like to do the same for your site before launching it. If you have an existing customer base, you may wish to determine its demographics and then design your Web site for potential customers in the same demographic. If you do not have an existing customer base and your Web site is your first foray into the business world, it is important that you conduct market research to determine your target audience before you launch your site.

Once you have determined your target audience, you can take advantage of a new branch of market research arising from the proliferation of Web sites: screening a site's usability by watching how users from the target audience navigate it. In the same way that market researchers track the eye movements of viewers of a print or television advertisement, so do they track users' clicks on a site to see where the users go and what problems they encounter before the site is launched. This can be done in a traditional manner where focus group participants meet in a room with computer terminals and their clicks are followed by a moderator or are videotaped.

Once a site is established, market research companies can use new techniques to survey users online. One of these involves querying visitors to the site with pop-up windows as the visitors are logged on. Results from the research can be used to refine the site. One company that specializes in this kind of research is Vividence, recommended by *PC Magazine* [114]. Vividence bills itself as "the leading authority in Web experience evaluation" and boasts an impressive client list that includes Cisco Systems, Compaq, eBay, Hewlett-Packard, Microsoft, Nordstrom.com, Pfizer, SAP, and Wells Fargo. Let us stress that site refinement is an *ongoing* and *never-ending process*, just as building your company is ongoing and never ending.

In the previous section, we stated that your site may have many purposes. Similarly, it may have many target audiences. You may not only want to reach prospective customers through your site but also prospective investors and partners. Thus, in the same way that you design your site with your primary purpose in mind, but also taking into consideration your other purposes, so should you design your site with your primary target audience in mind, but also take into consideration other target audiences. This you can do by having pages on your site (and links on your home page to these pages) with information your secondary and tertiary audiences but not necessarily your prospective customers might be interested in. Just as *Nytimes.com*'s home page was mainly devoted to breaking news stories with a couple of discreet links for subscriptions, so can your home page be mainly devoted to your primary target audience, with subtle links for your other target audiences.

As an example of how a target audience will determine the design and content of a site, we describe the *Neimanmarcus.com* site for high-end retailer Neiman Marcus and contrast it with *Landsend.com*, site for Lands' End, the catalog and outlet retailer. The Neiman Marcus site is definitely tailored toward the upscale, fashion-forward customer. The home page immediately lets the user know the color of the season. Links to women's wear and the beauty page provide details on the color and style of clothing and makeup for the coming season. The design of the home page and all major links is spare and elegant with a monochromatic background in juicy designer colors like citrusy green, luscious violet, or camellia pink. Text is used sparingly and its color does not contrast conspicuously with the background. No prices are shown until a photograph is clicked on. The design of the site focuses on the photographs, beautifully shot and cropped.

The Lands' End home page (see Figure 6–1), on the other hand, exemplifies that of a catalog and outlet retailer. Text is abundant and the major points of focus showcase specially priced items and their prices. When a dress is clicked on, different fabric swatches that the dress is available in are also shown, which gives the user the feel of a made-to-order item of clothing. Styles and fabrics are mostly classic and timeless. As innovative pluses, the *Landsend.com* site has nifty features like giving you the ability to browse the site with a friend while sharing a shopping cart, as well as the fun of "trying" selected clothing on a virtual 3D model of yourself, the hairstyle, face shape, coloring, and body type of which are specified by you.

With these two sites there are two different target audiences and, correspondingly, two different designs and contents. Think about who your target audience is and design your site accordingly. Will your site look youthful and exuberant with hot trends in product offerings, or will it look classic and subdued, with timeless offerings that will last for years, if not decades? Will it be designed for technical people, with content loaded with jargon that only they can understand, or will it be for the average Web user, with everyday language as the *lingua franca*? You wouldn't roll out a product without test marketing it first with a target audience, so don't launch a site without doing the market research first.

Figure 6–1 The *Landsend.com* home page. Screen shot reprinted courtesy of Lands' End.

WHAT CONTENT WILL YOU PROVIDE?. . . . .

While design can make a site attractive, readable, and engaging, content is a site's *raison d'être*. Your customers will keep coming back for more only if your content is compelling, current, and relevant to their needs. To use a brick-and-mortar store analogy, site design corresponds to store layout, furnishings, signage, and display while site content is analogous to the merchandise, sales staff, and transaction processing; in other words, the total sales experience. While a store's layout and furnishings may make the shopping experience more pleasurable, we become loyal and repeat customers to a store because we like the merchandise and the prices, the salespeople are friendly and helpful, and transactions are smooth. Top notch content does the same for visitors to a site: It offers them high quality and current merchandise or services at reasonable prices, and it provides friendly and helpful service through prose that is clear, personable, and to-the-point. It processes transactions smoothly with as little effort as possible on the users' part. We discuss the important elements of content within the framework of the four characteristics of the nature of the Web we described earlier in the chapter.

Recall that the first key characteristic of the Web we mentioned is nonlinearity. Because of the way search engines work, it is likely that visitors will click to your site and arrive at a page other than the home page. This means that they will miss the nice introduction to your company which you have provided on the home page. What does this imply for content? This implies first of all that *every* page of your site must be identified with your company's name (and trademark if you have one), ideally in a visually consistent manner throughout your site. All pages on your site should have navigation links that can take visitors to the home and other pages. This is especially important because if visitors land on a page without identity and navigation links, even using the "Back button" will not take them to a more central location on the site, let alone to the home page. Thus they will be stuck on a single page with no identification and no way of finding out on whose site they landed.

. . . .

TIPS ON WEB SITE CONTENT BASED ON THE SPECIAL NATURE OF THE WEB

- **Nonlinearity**: Every page of your site should be identified with your company's name and trademark and have navigation buttons to other pages.

- **Interactivity**: The more you allow the user to interact with the product, the better your chances of closing the sale.

- **User Activity**: Direct users as quickly as possible to whatever it is they are looking for.

- **Fast Medium**: Use short pages, short blocks of text, and highlight keywords in colored or bold fonts.

The second characteristic of the Web we identified is interactivity. A good site is more than just words and pictures on a computer screen. It allows the user to click around for more information, especially on products and services, the equivalent of smelling the leather or fingering the fabric. Most sites allow the user to take closer looks at the merchandise by clicking on a thumbnail photo that shows or enlarges a detail. For some goods, like high-end clothing, this may be inadequate since much of the selling power of an item might be in the luxurious feel of a fabric or in the handsewn details that are too small for the screen to capture. Nevertheless, close-ups and pans of product photos help the user engage with the product, like picking it up in a store or trying it on, which is a step toward a sale. Some sites, like *Amazon.com*, allow users to read other users' reviews of a product as well as add their own. *Amazon.com* does an excellent job of engaging users in the review process by allowing them to vote on the usefulness of a review, letting them read reviewers' profiles, and even providing a ranking system of reviewers which gives points for number of reviews written and usefulness of reviews. This is truly a masterful stroke in allowing users to take ownership of the site and take full advantage of the Web's capabilities by having a voice in the company and its products. The more you allow users to interact with the product, the better your chances of closing the sale.

The third characteristic of the Web experience is that it is up-close and personal, as opposed to distant and impersonal. Users are in control and they are directing their experience to their needs and wishes. Some Web users browse sites leisurely, some out of curiosity, but most are searching for something in particular, like information or a certain product. Trained salespersons in brick-and-mortar stores can tell immediately when customers walk through the doorway whether they are browsing or are on a mission. They can tell by the gait of their steps and the look of determination on their faces.

Assume that most visitors to your site are on a mission. If they come in through a search engine they are definitely looking for something in particular. What does this mean for content? This means that you should direct the users as quickly as possible to whatever it is they are looking for. You can do this with clear, succinct prose to guide them around your site, and by paring product information to its essentials. The personalized experience users create is akin to having a brick-and-mortar salesperson who knows the users and will not waste too much time showing them items which he knows are not to their tastes. The advantage to users of shopping on the Web, of course, is that they are not pressured to buy as they would be by having a personal shopper select items for them face-to-face. The best site content strategy for turning the personalized experience into a sale is to enhance the personal touch for the users through the use of "cookies" (discussed in more detail in Chapter 11, "Marketing on the Internet") and to ensure your transactions process is smooth and glitch-free. We discuss transaction processing further in Chapter 10, "Internet Business Transactions."

Fourth, we characterized the Web as a medium much faster than traditional media. This means that a site's content must be eminently readable, presented in a form such that the message and the meaning can be digested in a glance. Reading on a computer screen is much different from reading on paper. Because most Web users are alert, active readers of content on the computer, content on a site should ideally present itself in small bites, as opposed to long, multipage, multiscreen text that taxes the user's attention. Long articles that would not be a problem on paper can be a major roadblock to engaging the customer on a Web site. Short blocks of text, no more than two to three sentences long, should replace rambling paragraphs which users will likely skim anyway. Bullet points followed by snippets of information or at most a sentence or two can be used effectively to communicate complicated information that would otherwise require several paragraphs. Fast is the keyword here. Users are clicking rapidly through search engines and sites to find what they want. Let keywords in your site stand out through shorter prose, bold or colored fonts, bullet points, and small blocks of text. And be sure your Web site has a "text only" option, which allows the user to download just the text of your site, without the time-consuming graphics. Many users are still using primitive browsers that would make your site easier to download if there were only text.

Finally, we introduced Nielsen's concept of usability and the goal of Web sites, which is to attract loyal customers through repeat traffic. Usability on the Web can be described as customer satisfaction in navigating your site. Will your site be annoying and frustrating or will it be pleasant and fun? Both design and content will determine the outcome of this experience. In addition to establishing guideposts throughout your site to allow the users to get their bearings and navigate smoothly around it and ensuring that the users can get the information they need quickly, you must provide for smooth transactions that are processed glitch-free. Many would-be customers bail out of a site and abandon their shopping carts just prior to the point of purchase, usually out of frustration at the difficulty of completing the transaction. To close more sales on your site, conduct market research on usability for your site, particularly at the transaction stage.

We would like to close this section on content by relating an experience a user had with a site, *Peets.com*. Headquartered in Berkeley, California, Peet's is a coffee and tea retailer founded in 1966. We relate this experience because we would like to provide an example of excellent content on a site, backed by customer service. First of all, all pages on *Peets.com* download quickly. The design of each page is simple with restful earth tone backgrounds. Most pages are about one screen size long; the few longer ones rarely require scrolling beyond two screens. Blocks of text are short, usually no longer than two or three sentences, so the user can view at a glance what information is being provided. In addition to offering the highest quality and freshest coffees and teas at reasonable prices, Peet's has an attractive company culture that is low-key and friendly.

The user in our narrative placed two different orders of green tea as gifts to friends in the Chicago area. *Peets.com* offered a tracking mechanism for shipments, which appeared to be a link to the U.S. Postal Service site for tracking packages. Presumably, Peet's added a USPS "delivery confirmation" label to its shipments, provided the package number to the user, and automatically linked the user to the USPS site so she could track her package.

Unfortunately at the time there was a glitch with the tracking mechanism (which was being ironed out, the user was informed by a Peet's representative) so when the user who ordered the green tea tried to track her packages, the USPS site indicated no record of the packages being shipped out. In the meantime, she had been informed through email by Peet's that the packages had been shipped. Because of the conflicting information, she decided to query Peet's through its customer service email link. She received an email response to her query from a Peet's representative within hours. The representative assured her that the packages were indeed shipped, that the tracking mechanism would indicate when the packages were delivered, and that, yes, there was a glitch which Peet's was working to eliminate.

When a week or two later the tracking mechanism still indicated that there was no record of shipment, the user contacted Peet's once again through the customer service email address and indicated she wanted some assurance that her packages were delivered but did not want to call the intended recipients herself. Again, within hours, the same representative sent a return email admitting that there had been problems with tracking the packages around the time the orders were placed. The representative wrote that she understood the user's reluctance to call and offered to call the intended recipients herself. Reassured, the user agreed.

Within a day or two, the representative left a telephone message that she had called both recipients and had succeeded in contacting one of them who did indeed receive the tea. The user then returned the representative's call through Peet's 800 number and left a message that she was satisfied that both packages had been received. Satisfied and amazed at the level of personal service that Peet's provided to help her find peace of mind regarding her packages, the user is sure to return to *Peets.com* as a loyal customer.

The even happier ending to this story is that a check back later to *Peets.com* indicates that Peet's has changed its tracking mechanism since this experience occurred. It is hoped that this has eliminated the problem and provides for a glitch-free ordering experience. The moral of the story is that even the best Web sites are *constantly* upgraded to provide a smooth, seamless experience for the customer. The content on *Peets.com* created a fast, easily navigable, eminently usable experience that was continuously being improved toward the elusive goal of customer satisfaction. This is the experience for your customer toward which you should be striving. In the "history" section on *Peets.com*, the company claims that, "Peet's endeavors to provide the best customer service of any coffee company in the world." We believe that Peet's is well on its way toward this goal.

. . . .

HIGHLIGHTS OF THE PEETS.COM EXPERIENCE

- Every Web page was short (no longer than one or two screen scrolls).
- Blocks of text were short, about one to two sentences each.
- Peet's offered great product quality and prices.
- Customers could use a tracking mechanism for orders placed.
- Customer service was backed by email and telephone (with 800 number).
- Email inquiries were responded to within hours.

CLOSING THE ONLINE SALE . . . .

An important feature on your Web site for getting customers to buy and not just surf is an accurate search engine. When customers land on your site, chances are they are looking for something specific. Does your site enable them to find exactly what they are looking for with a single entry into a search engine? According to a study by Jupiter Media Metrix, 80 percent of users will bail out of a site if the search engine doesn't function well. In fact, an efficient search engine can markedly increase sales. For example, on eBay, which logs about 30 million searches a day, bidding goes "way up" whenever a new capability is added to its search engine [76].

A really smart search engine like Amazon's can even make suggestions on other items to buy when users enter a specific product. Many are familiar with the list of books that appears with every inquiry about another book on Amazon's site. The list provides the names of other books purchased by those who purchased the book inquired about. The reasoning behind this is that users will also enjoy other books purchased by those who purchased the book in which they are interested. Thus, don't underestimate the power of the best search engine technology that can not only help users find exactly what they need instantaneously but also cross-sell and upsell.

Even if your site has easily navigable design, engaging, ever-changing content, and an efficient search engine, getting users to actually purchase something is a delicate business. Research reports have estimated that between 25 percent to 78 percent (depending on the study cited) of users who selected items online for purchase end up abandoning their virtual shopping carts before making a purchase [134]. This occurrence is so prevalent it even has a name: shopping cart abandonment syndrome. What is going on?

Ideally, in an online store purchasing scenario, users select items by clicking on a square next to the item's photograph, which places the item in a virtual shopping cart. When the users are done shopping, they proceed to checkout, where the costs of their items are totaled, shipping charges are added, and they are asked for credit card and shipping information. When they finish entering the information, they click to signify that the transaction is complete. Then they exit the site and wait for the order to be delivered. In reality, however, many users exit the site before completing the transaction or even before getting to checkout. This is costing online retailers billions of dollars annually. Why are shoppers abandoning the sites and what can online retailers do to help close the sale?

Reasons for abandonment range from the emotional to the rational. Emotionally, some shoppers need assurance that their purchases are valid. They exit prematurely because of the lack of human intervention, which would, in a brick-and-mortar store, be provided by the salesperson who assures the customers that the color and style look right on them, or that the PDA they are considering is really the most popular model in the store (how many times have we heard, "I just sold three of those"?). Retailing guru and author of *Why We Buy* [162], Paco Underhill, claims that the difference between the online and offline retailing experiences is that people go to the mall not just to shop but for entertainment and to be with and see other people. Also with offline retailing, whether it be a clothier, supermarket, or electronics superstore, there is a well-defined protocol of how we proceed from selecting our items to checkout, to making the purchase.

In the online world, Underhill claims, there is still much variation from site to site, which causes confusion and users to bail out. He believes that standardization of the online shopping process could go a long way toward helping Web retailers close their sales [42]. Because the day when online retailers will unite to provide a standardized shopping experience is still in the future, individual retailers can make the shopping experience on their sites more user-friendly by providing immediate human shopping assistance through either email, instant messaging, or the telephone. Immediate human intervention is expensive, but providing a comfortable shopping environment for your users is one of the most important steps you can take to create an emotionally safe shopping experience for your users and to attract loyal customers and repeat traffic.

On the rational side of Web selling, there are many steps retailers can take to ease the process of shopping for their users. One of these is to ensure that your customers do not become frustrated with the shopping cart technology on your site. Some of the major complaints among shopping cart users that researchers have unearthed are:

- Shoppers are not given the opportunity to monitor their selections and change, delete, or add items as they wish.

- Shoppers are not constantly updated on the items they have selected and are not given a running total.

- Shoppers are informed that a particular item they selected is not available only at the time of checkout instead of when they select it (which could encourage them to select a substitute).

- Shoppers are asked for too much information in order to complete the sale (some sites ask for as many as six pages).

- Shoppers run into software glitches that put them in an endless loop of providing the same information over and over without completing the sale.

- Shoppers have to fill out forms all over again whenever they make a single error in completing a form.

- Shoppers are shocked at the total of their order when tallied at checkout.

- Shoppers are not informed of the shipping prices until after they provide the necessary purchasing information.

- Shoppers feel shipping prices are too high, or at least too high of a percentage of the overall cost of goods.

Problems such as these can be eliminated through Web site design, a much easier (and generally less expensive) prospect to fix than fulfilling the customer's emotional side of buying. Purchasing and implementing the right shopping cart technology is key to closing the online sale. When inquiring about the technology with different vendors, be certain that the shopping cart you implement on your site will be easy to use. What are some of the necessary features? Bill Demas, VP of Marketing for the Web consulting firm Vividence, has compiled the following "Eight Steps to Boosting Online Sales," which appeared in an article by Stacy Perman in the December 2000 issue of *eCompany Now*. (The magazine is now known as *Business 2.0*). © 2000 Time Inc. All rights reserved. [134]:

1. **List all charges up front.** Sticker shock is a fast way to lose potential customers. Present product prices, shipping and handling, and taxes before you ask for billing and personal information.

2. **Let shoppers see what's in their carts.** Just as in a retail store, cybershoppers like to keep tabs on what they're buying. Give them a way to see a running tally of items and how much they've spent.

3. **Allow customers to change orders.** Users like to be able to remove items and modify quantities, especially after seeing the bill. In addition to "buy lists," add "wish lists" that let customers put items on hold while they decide what they want to purchase. Make it simple for customers to transfer items from the wish list to the buying list and vice versa.

4. **Save cart contents for return visits.** Research shows that Internet retail shoppers often put items in a cart and come back to the site later to make the purchase. Be sure to automatically save whatever was in the cart, even if there was no purchase. This is especially valuable at sites where the purchase is an expensive one.

5. **Make special promotions easy to use.** It can be difficult for a shopper to figure out how to apply a special promotion to a purchase. Make this an obvious and simple step, and do it early in the checkout process.

6. **Hold your customer's hand.** Let customers know when a purchase is on the way or held up. If it's the latter, explain why and keep the customer up to date via email. Provide a way for the customer to return to the site and check order status.

7. **Encourage shipping to multiple destinations.** If a shopper is buying gifts, make it easy to send those gifts to a variety of different addresses.

8. **Keep forms as short as possible.** Ask only for the information you need to process an order. Also, if shoppers need to go back a screen to correct an error, do not clear all the fields on the page and force them to fill out the form again.

HOW TO GET A HIGH RANKING FOR YOUR WEB SITE ....

Suppose you've worked hard to create a top notch Web site that is eminently usable with compelling content and provides an excellent shopping experience. Everything's set to go except for one small problem: Nobody can find you! How do you draw traffic to your site? There are traditional advertising methods you can use, either offline or online. In the late 1990s, when dot-coms were flush with venture capital, many of them spent millions on Superbowl and other television commercials as well as full-page advertisements in popular business publications to promote their company names. While tactics such as these may have worked in the short run to drive traffic to their Web sites, we can conclude from the dot-com fallout and the drying up of venture capital that there is a need for more sustainable and less expensive means of promoting a site.

If you don't have a generous advertising and public relations budget that will get your company's name and Web site address repeatedly in the popular press, one useful strategy to drive traffic to your site is to get a high ranking for your site on a search engine. Search engines such as Google, Yahoo!, Lycos, and Altavista help users find information, products, and services. Recall from Chapter 4, "Internet and Web Technology," that there are two basic ways a search engine works. In the first—the "index method" used by Google, Lycos, and Altavista—users enter one or more keywords into the search engine, click on the search button, and almost instantaneously will receive a list of Web sites that contain those keywords. In the second—the "table of contents" method used by Yahoo! and others—users "drill down" from a list of general topics to more and more specific topics until they finally find what they are looking for.

What you would like is for your Web site to appear as one of the first on the list when a relevant keyword or appropriate drill-down is entered. For example, if your company is selling French wine, you would like your Web site to be listed high up whenever a user enters keywords such as "wine," "champagne," "French wine," "Reims," "Burgundy," "Rhone," "Bordeaux," etc. Since returned lists often list thousands of entries, it is imperative that your Web site appear on one of the first few pages of entries. Few users have the time and patience to filter through much more than that, and generally speaking, entries become less relevant the further they are down the list.

How can you do this? Before we explain, it is necessary to demystify the search process. Once you understand how the search process works, you can better comprehend ways to see your site highly ranked on a search list. Search engines use what is known as a "spider," also known as a "crawler" or a "bot," which reads Web pages and creates entries for the search engine's index. A spider figuratively crawls all over the Web and searches many pages at a time. The entries it gathers for the search engine's index, as well as the addresses for the corresponding Web sites, are called up when matching keywords are entered. Since it is virtually impossible to catalog every single word on every single page on the entire World Wide Web, a spider will search a selected subset of the Web page. This selection depends on search criteria that differ among engines. Some actually will search all words on a Web page, some search on words in the title of a page, some search on the first words of a page, some search all words until a timeout limit is reached, and others search on keywords listed in "meta tags" of a Web document. Thus, you want to ensure that the keywords to your Web site are well-placed in the critical locations listed above.

A *meta tag* is part of the HTML document that constitutes the source of your Web page. Behind each Web page that you view through your browser is an HTML document that tells the browser how to display the words and graphics on the page. HTML is the language of the Web (see Chapter 5, "Languages of the Internet," for more on HTML). It is called a markup language because it uses "markup" or tags to dictate how elements on a page should look. One important set of tags of the HTML document of your Web page is called the meta tags. The content of the tags do not appear on the Web page itself, but contains a brief description of the page as well as its keywords. The meta tags for our French wine company's Web page might look something like:

```
<META name = "description"
content="We specialize in French wines.">
<META name = "keywords" content="wine, champagne,
French wine, Reims, Burgundy, Rhone, Bordeaux">
```

Therefore, a spider that searched on meta tags would index these keywords as well as keywords in the description so that when a user entered "Rhone" or "French wine" for example, this Web site would be listed. There are tales of those who abuse the meta tags so that their Web pages receive a high ranking, even if the keywords have nothing to do with their site. For example, one enterprising young man who wanted his resume floated all over the Web entered the keyword "sex" multiple times in his meta tag. It did appear highly ranked for many Web searches and he did eventually get a job, but we don't recommend this strategy and have to wonder where he ended up employed.

We have discussed how you can get a high ranking for your Web page by entering keywords into your Web page or its meta tags. These are completely free methods of increasing your chances that someone will be informed of your page through a search engine. Another method is to get a lot of other Web pages to provide links to yours. Google ranks the pages it displays in response to a keyword based on the number of links there are to a page (the more links there are to your page, the higher the ranking).

If you don't feel that these methods are sufficient for the kinds of rankings you would like to see, there are means of improving your rankings through paid methods, short of purchasing advertising. One method is to create a "doorway" or "gateway," which is an HTML page designed expressly to get a high ranking on search engines. This can be done by hiring a consultant to create one for you or by purchasing software, that enables you to create one yourself. One such software is Web Position Gold, sold at *Webposition.com*, which boasts a number of popular press and customer testimonials to its productivity. The software package also allows you to submit your doorway page to search engines, check on the rankings of your pages, and track the visitors to your site to see where they're coming from.

Another way to get a high ranking is to out-and-out pay for a ranking. *Goto.com* ranks Web sites on its lists based on how much a company has paid for a ranking (and even reveals how much each company is paying for a listing!). Thus you can bypass the search techniques completely and pay expressly for a ranking on *Goto.com*. The optimal strategy for driving traffic to your site is to use a combination of free and paid methods mentioned above. What's most important, however, is to have a Web site that's easy to use with interesting content that users will want to return to time and time again. If you have all of these ingredients, your site is on its way to success!

MANAGING WEB SITE CONTENT ....

While we're on the subject of tools you can use to create, optimize, and manage a Web site, let us not forget that increasingly necessary class of *content management tools*. Content management tools have become necessary because Web sites have become large and complex. It is not unusual for a company's Web site to double or triple in size to thousands of pages in a matter of months. The problem with Web sites such as these is getting the necessary site content (which can change within a matter of days, if not hours) produced, approved, published, and removed at the right place at the right time. This is a formidable task when the Web site has thousands of pages that need to be managed, and the workflow from content production to publication requires a chain of workers, perhaps all at different sites, to create, edit, approve, and publish a single piece of content.

Clearly, it is not practical for everyone providing content for the site, which can include someone from marketing personnel who determines prices for products to someone from human resources personnel who writes up job listings, to learn HTML or the intricacies of Web site creation. Content management tools can ease the process so that those providing content can create it in a user-friendly format like Microsoft Word. The content is automatically forwarded to an editor for proofreading and a manager for approval, and the final version sent to a member of the Web site crew who posts the content (or is even automatically posted) to the site. Some content may even require that a team of persons collaborate on a single piece; this process, too, can be provided by a content management product. Content management can also include integration of content to back end functions like database management.

Unfortunately, content management tools can be expensive, costing in the hundreds of thousands of dollars for high-end products. They may require the services of consultants to implement. One company offering a suite of content-related products is Vignette, which recently partnered with BEA Systems in a joint venture to sell and market its products. Vignette offers a number of products, including those designed to aggregate content, manage content, personalize content, syndicate content (distribute content to affiliates and customers proactively), and create content for wireless devices. BroadVision Inc. offers a product called BladeRunner, which accommodates both the casual user content provider and the more Web-savvy site crew. With BladeRunner casual users can create content using Microsoft Office, which is then automatically forwarded to management for approval. The content is then seamlessly directed and propagated to a variety of formats, including the Web, wireless devices, fax, and email. Once your Web site demands management beyond a Webmaster or small Web crew to manage, consider content management tools to help meet your Internet business needs.

BEST PRACTICES FOR WEB SITE DESIGN AND CONTENT ....

In this section we walk you through a step-by-step procedure on what you should consider when designing (or redesigning) your Web site. The information in this section is provided courtesy of Lin Sakai, principal of New York-based brand identity and design consultant LiDesign (www.lidesign.net), and Lesley Verdi, principal of Keane Verdi marketing consultants, also in New York. For Internet business conducted through Web sites, Sakai and Verdi advocate the following best practices in order to:

1. Turn surfers into visitors

2. Turn window shoppers into customers

3. Turn customers into customers for life

Turning surfers into visitors does not have to cost a fortune. Following are 10 ways to drive traffic to your site (some we have already mentioned), if you're on a shoestring budget:

1. Create a meta tag of keywords for all major search engines.

2. Barter link exchanges with sites that have strong affinity.

3. Barter banner advertising exchanges with sites that have strong affinity.

4. Provide content on community sites like Women.com, Motley Fool, etc.

5. Use opt-in emails (more about this in Chapter 11).

6. Advertise in chat rooms (if done very subtly).

7. Consider transit advertising (subways, buses, etc.).

8. Sponsor an event.

9. Use viral marketing (more about this in Chapter 11).

10. Develop a public relations program (press releases, article placement, etc.).

In order to turn window shoppers into customers, be sure you consider the following steps:

- **Download quickly**. Web surfers are impatient and want information instantaneously.

- **Cool is not always convenient**. The most up-to-date animation and cool effects mean nothing if the visitor can't get into the site easily.

- **Communicate the value of your brand instantly**. What value are you offering to your customers? Communicate this information quickly.

- **Communicate emotional benefits**. Visual metaphors help communicate important emotional benefits. Use graphics and photos wisely without greatly increasing your download time.

- **Avoid the "wallpaper trap."** While brick-and-mortar companies have the advantage of brand familiarity, dot-coms have to work harder to establish their brand image. Try to use distinctive graphics to communicate a clear brand identity. Avoid making the site look identical to others in the category.

- **Establish a unique presence**. Use interesting imagery and stylish graphics to establish a unique and polished brand personality.

- **Make it easy to browse**. Use simple icons and minimal copy to lead the customers into the site. Avoid pointing in too many directions at once. Do not use navigation bars on the top, side, middle, and bottom panels, that require more time to scan and understand.

- **Don't sacrifice convenience for cleverness**. Don't use unfamiliar terms or categories, even if they're creative, if your visitor can't figure them out in a matter of seconds.

- **Give them a reason to buy**. The need for change is a powerful buying incentive. You can showcase a new buying opportunity each season, month, or week in an easy-to-recognize format.

- **Maximize seasonal buying opportunities**. Seasonal promotions are a tried-and-true retailing tool.

- **Enable customization**. Conduct online surveys to customize selections and facilitate decision making.

- **Make it worth their while to buy**. Offer incentives such as special promotions, gifts with purchase, discounts for first-time buyers, free shipping, and free gift wrap.

- **Make checking out as simple as 1-2-3**. One-click shopping is a must. Consolidate customer information into a single, scroll-down page.

So how do you turn customers into customers for life? By engaging them, and keeping the communication with them flowing. You can do this when you:

- **Actively manage customer relationships**. Aim for a continuous dialog with targeted customers. Engaging in customer relationship management (CRM) requires a combination of technology and service that can be managed internally or outsourced.

- **Invite customers to register**. Let customers give you permission to "contact them." They won't come back to your site unless you remind them. This is like a magazine relying only on newsstand sales. Turn customers into subscribers.

- **Identify your best customers**. Use direct marketing techniques that allow you to identify and understand your customers. The return on marketing investment can be easily measured and course-corrected on the fly.

- **Connect with your customers via email**. Target your best customers with personal and relevant messages and information. Giving is more important than taking at the beginning of a relationship.

- **Give free information and advice**. Create pages they'll want to "bookmark" and return to regularly. Link to other sites. Always address the big picture—their life!

- **Exceed customer expectations**. Be proactive in anticipating customer needs and interests. Amazon (which we discuss in Chapter 11) uses collaborative filtering to cross-sell additional books to customers based on what others have already bought.

- **Reward your best customers**. Reward customer loyalty with special benefits and privileges.

- **Make customers a part of your team**. Engage them in your product development process so you can provide them with products and services they help create.

FUTURE TRENDS AND IMPLICATIONS ....

What lies ahead for Web design and content? It seems there are two major trends at odds with one another. The first is that the newest Web design technology allows developers to add greater and fancier features to their sites. These features include audio and video streaming media, interactive imaging, dynamic graphics, animation, and 3D imaging. One of the most popular development tools for adding pizzazz to sites is Macromedia's Flash. Flash's ease of use has contributed to its popularization and has enabled even nontechnical types to create splashy sites. Apple, which has always been strong in the graphics department, has developed a platform called Quicktime, which has sold over 100 million copies. Quicktime allows developers to add MP3 files, animation, video, and sound to their sites. Adobe Systems has come up with a direct competitor to Flash with its LiveMotion. LiveMotion adds animation to the well-known and popular family of Web design software at Adobe Systems.

The second trend is led by those who ardently support simplicity, ease of navigation, and quick downloads in Web site design. Proponents of this trend include Jakob Nielsen mentioned above and Vincent Flanders, coauthor of the book *Web Pages That Suck* [50] and developer of an irreverent Web site by the same name. As you can see, the two trends are completely at odds with one another because although fancy features are fun and exciting, they make sites more complicated, harder to navigate, and cause them to take longer to download. Despite the wisdom of usability, which states that a user is usually searching for something specific on the Web and will bail out of a site at a moment's notice if it is too complicated to navigate or takes too long to download, Web developers and their clients end up adding frills and thrills to a site because they like them or they want to create a certain cool image. Having a site loaded with animation, audio and video streaming, dynamic graphics and 3D imaging is like having your Superbowl commercial: It lends a certain status to the owner.

Which of these trends will win out in the end? It's difficult to say because of two more conflicting trends. The movement toward high speed Internet connections like cable and DSL, that allow for greater bandwidth capacities, may soon make the problem of slow downloads obsolete. If prices for these high-speed connections drop and their setup requirements become less inconvenient, more and more users may switch, thereby reducing the problem caused by bandwidth-hungry streaming media and animated graphics. Yet this scenario seems a long way off. Nielsen NetRatings reports that just slightly more than one in 10 U.S. households that have an Internet connection have access through a high-speed connection [98]. Users like to use POTS (plain old telephone service) for their Internet connection even if it's slower and cuts off telephone use because it's cheap, doesn't require a special modem, and doesn't require a service technician to come to the home to install special apparatus.

On the flip side of the trend toward high-speed connections, however, is the proliferation of wireless Web devices such as PDAs and mobile phones. These wireless devices with their four-inch and two-inch screens can display only the very simplest of Web pages. Only so much text can appear on a miniature screen at one time, and any graphics underlay or overlay will muddy the readability. Streaming media and dynamic graphics are practically out of the question given the current technology. Moreover, navigating the Web with one-finger clicks on a handheld device is much more tedious than navigating with a mouse on a desk. Thus, Web developers designing specifically for mobile computing devices (also called *m-computing*) will have to minimize the number of clicks necessary to navigate a site, which translates into simplicity. Yet m-computing has not caught on in the United States the way it has in Asia and in Europe. We are a nation of desktop and notebook lovers with our large screens and full keyboards, and this may hinder the trend toward simplicity in Web design.

The only true trend we can predict is that Web design and content are still relatively new concepts and determining what works best is still evolving. This is what makes Web site design and content so exciting. Standards in design such as home pages and navigation buttons are beginning to emerge, but as we saw with shopping carts, there is as yet no agreed-upon procedure in checkout service. Of course, no one wants total standardization of sites, just as we wouldn't want every brick-and-mortar store to be laid out in exactly the same way, since this would be boring and detract from the individuality of each store and site. Yet there is the sense that Internet business and commercial Web sites are evolving toward a shared goal: to develop sites and practices that will make Internet business viable and profitable. It is now clear that the cash-burning, born-to-IPO model is no longer sustainable. What will take its place? Business models with "old economy" values and "new economy" technology will make the Web a viable and profitable place to be.

The implications of this chapter are that we believe that simpler Web designs are, in the end, more profitable. Unless the user can easily navigate your site, easily examine all products and services you describe, and proceed to a glitch-free checkout experience, you will very likely lose the sale. One report states that 84 percent of users say they exit a site because of long download times [98]. Making a purchase on a site requires that users hang in there until the sale is closed. Why lose prospective customers because of unnecessary animation or fancy graphics? If it's within your budget to do so, conduct usability testing, either outsourced or in-house, so your company can see where users falter on your site. What is obvious to you is not necessarily obvious to a first-time visitor to your site. Many users are not only employing slow connections, but also primitive browsers, which do not capture fancy graphics, special effects, and 16 million colors. Keep them in mind as you develop your site. We come down on the side of the usability experts on Web site design: Less is more.

7 Getting Your Business Online

In this chapter ...

WHERE ARE YOU ON THE INTERNET BUSINESS TECHNOLOGY SPECTRUM? . . . .

Getting your business online is not an easy proposition. There is an entire spectrum of things you can do, from purchasing the hardware and software and doing it all yourself, to outsourcing *everything*, including computer hardware and software applications. In this chapter we introduce you to the entire spectrum of possibilities so you can see where your company wants to be. This decision will depend on your resources (financial and human), your time constraints (how quickly you want to be up and running), your need to scale your business, and your understanding of Internet business technology. Few companies will have the capacity to do everything themselves or the trust to outsource everything. Most firms will fall somewhere in between.

No matter which solution your company chooses, if you are involved in the decision, you will at some point have to work with outside technology vendors and service providers. Working with technology vendors and service providers used to be the purview of in-house tech support. But as the scope of Internet business expands, we are witnessing more and more nontechnically trained managers taking on these responsibilities. Finance and human resource personnel are using online databases. Marketers are working with Web developers. Sales forces are purchasing wireless devices with online capabilities to make them more effective in the field. Everyone in business is coming into contact with the front lines of technology providers.

. . . .

KEEPING INFORMED ON TECHNOLOGY

One way to be informed is to read a book like this to introduce you to the important concepts and terminology. To keep up in the field, you may wish to read the technology sections of *The Wall Street Journal*, *The New York Times*, and *Business Week*, or entire magazines and Web sites devoted to Internet business in the general interest, like *Business 2.0* and *Fast Company*. You may wish to take a short course on technology essentials. The more you understand about technology, the less daunting and more fun it becomes. As your knowledge grows, so will your company and your technology provider grow to appreciate you.

While working with technology vendors and service providers may not be as much fun and exciting as meeting with the creative people copywriting your next television commercial, working effectively with them is key to getting your business online as smoothly as possible. Perhaps the most important thing you can do to work effectively with them is to *be informed*. Technology providers like working with informed people because it makes their already difficult job easier and saves time and money for all involved.

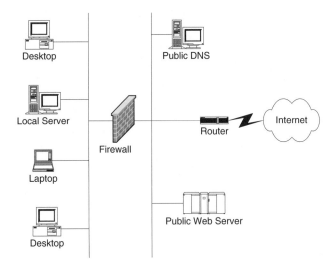

Figure 7–1 Connecting a LAN to the Internet.

In Figure 7–1 we present a very simple diagram of a corporate network connected to the Internet. (See the Tech Talk below for the explanation of the firewall. This concept is explored in greater detail in Chapter 9, "Security and Internet Business.") The complexity of a company's network will vary greatly depending on its Internet business needs. At one end of the spectrum a company may simply choose to have an online presence to educate potential customers and business partners about the company. At the other end of the spectrum a company may be fully engaged in electronic commerce and linking its e-commerce business with all its back end enterprise applications such as customer relationship management, enterprise resource planning, etc. In the next section, "The Hardware Decision," we discuss options available to a company for building a system such as that illustrated in Figure 7–1. There is an entire spectrum of hardware options available to the firm. One option is to buy and maintain all of the hardware. By hardware, we mean all of the desktop machines, servers, and networking equipment. Slightly further down the spectrum is to own all of the hardware but to turn some of it over, usually the Web servers, to a colocation service for its upkeep. Many firms are taking the next step down the spectrum, which is to outsource their hardware needs to a managed service provider (MSP). An even more radical solution that firms are now using is to outsource not only their hardware but their software. This increasingly popular solution is covered in the section "Never Buy Software Again."

Tech Talk

Firewall: a network device designed to filter traffic entering a LAN. It is designed to prevent an intruder from "attacking" computers on the LAN. Firewalls are discussed in greater detail in Chapter 9.

Because you may need outside help in deciding which way to go or if you want someone to make the decisions for you, we include the section on "How to Choose a Consulting Service." Regardless of how much outsourcing is done, a company engaged in Internet business will still need an Internet connection. This connection is represented by the "lightning bolt" into the "cloud" in Figure 7–1. This connection is often referred to as the "last mile" (or first mile) because it represents the last leg of the Internet connection between the Internet service provider (ISP) and the user. It is the connection between a company and a central office or point of presence (POP) of a telecommunications company/ISP. The options that are available for making this connection are discussed in the section "Getting Connected." Finally, we conclude the chapter with "Future Trends and Implications."

THE HARDWARE DECISION.......................

In this section on hardware, we discuss the hardware outsourcing decision in terms of the paradigm illustrated in Figure 7–2. This figure depicts a two-by-two matrix. The column dimension represents hardware ownership, i.e., whether the company owns the hardware in question. The row dimension represents hardware location, i.e., whether the hardware is located on the company premises or on the premises of a Web hosting service.

THE HARDWARE TECHNOLOGY MATRIX

In the row one column one position, the company owns its own hardware (for example the Web servers) and the hardware is on company premises. In this case, the only thing not owned by the company in Figure 7–1 is the last mile connection to the Internet. In order to get the Internet connection the company must contract with an *Internet service provider (ISP)*. In this scenario, the actual connection to the Internet is all that is provided by the ISP. The row two column one position represents the situation in which the company owns the hardware, but the hardware is not located on its premises. In this case the company makes use of a *colocation service*.

In the row two column two position, the company does not own the hardware and the hardware is not located on company premises. In this case, the company uses a *managed service provider (MSP)*. In the final position, row one column two, the hardware is on company premises, but it does not own the hardware; it *leases* it. We discuss these options in more detail, moving in a counterclockwise direction and starting with the "Total Control" option.

Total Control: One option for a company engaged in Internet business is to own and operate all of the servers necessary for the business on company premises. We are calling this the Total Control option because the only service the company needs to contract for is

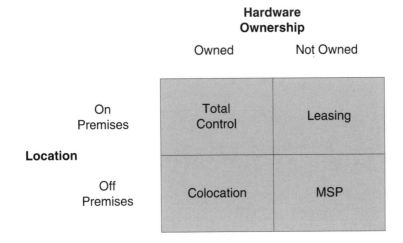

Figure 7–2 Hardware ownership and location matrix.

an Internet connection from an ISP. This option requires that the company own both server hardware and server software. The following are advantages of this option:

- You have complete control over the process from start to finish. If your own server crashes you can give it top priority, whereas if you contract out your hardware and your provider's server crashes you have no control over how quickly the problem is fixed.
- You have complete control over all hardware and software options. You can configure your Web front end "presentation layer" with your back end enterprise application software.
- You know exactly what the security features of your system are.
- It is easy to control and modify content because you have ready access to everything.

The following are disadvantages of this option:

- This is clearly the more expensive option. You need to provide both server hardware and software.
- You have to provide for a high-speed connection to the Internet from your company premises. See the section "Getting Connected" for more detail.
- You need a well-trained technical support staff to keep things up and running.

It is important to understand that with this option you are responsible for your Web site availability and scalability. In order to mitigate potential problems many firms turn to a company like Akamai to enhance the content delivery of their servers. Akamai has an extensive network of over 9,700 servers in 56 countries.

. . . .

Akamai Technology

Two products offered from Akamai are **FreeFlow** and **EdgeSuite**. These products are designed to take the load off your company's servers by having Akamai servers deliver some of the content. With FreeFlow, some of the content of your company's Web pages is served up by the Akamai server network. This specified content is usually high bandwidth material like sound, video, or graphics. In Chapter 2, "What Do I Need to Know about Hardware?," we discussed the high bandwidth needs of multimedia content. With FreeFlow, when a user requests a Web page from your server, your server delivers the Web page, while the Akamai specified content comes from the Akamai network. Akamai uses sophisticated mathematical algorithms developed by professors from MIT to determine which "optimal" server should deliver each request.

Akamai's EdgeSuite product offering is similar in philosophy. Some content of your Web site is stored with your company and some is stored with Akamai. The content is divided into static and dynamic content. Static content might be the product descriptions and photos of an online catalog, and the dynamic content might be the prices that are changed from week to week from your company's corporate database. With EdgeSuite the static content of your company's Web site can be hosted or "cached" on Akamai servers. When a Web page of the catalog is requested, the static content is automatically delivered from the Akamai servers and your company's servers provide the dynamic content. The dynamic content is delivered to the Akamai network, which then serves up both static and dynamic content.

Colocation: In this scenario you own your own hardware, but store it at another location. This may sound strange at first, but there are a number of good reasons for using this solution. Note that the colocation solution is mainly applicable to server computers, not desktop computers used for personal productivity.

The advantages for the colocation solution are as follows:

- The colocation service provides a high-speed connection to the Internet.

- The colocation service is responsible for climate control and typically provides power backup like diesel power generators.

- The colocation service is responsible for the physical security of the machines.

- The colocation service usually provides for redundant connections to an Internet service provider.

There are also several disadvantages to the colocation solution:

- This is still an expensive solution. Although the cost of providing your own high-speed network connection from company premises is eliminated, there is still the cost of purchasing all of the hardware.
- You can connect to your server only remotely, usually through Telnet.
- You may still need security expertise to prevent hackers from breaking into the system remotely.

Managed Service Provider: In the beginning, the only choice for a company that wanted to get online was to use an ISP. Over time the ISPs morphed into Web hosting services, which provided not only a fast Internet connection but also space on a server machine for a Web site. Then, as the Web hosting companies began to offer more and more services such as database access, shopping cart technology, etc., the ISPs morphed further into managed service providers (MSPs). The process of displaying a Web page through an MSP is illustrated in Figure 7–3. The Web page is often developed on a company computer and sent using FTP to the MSP server machine. The Web page is then served up by the MSP server machine via the Internet to client computers of those downloading the Web page.

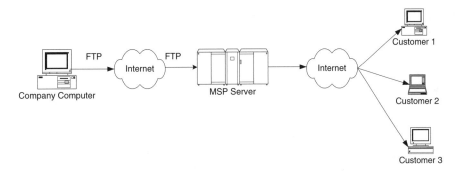

Figure 7–3 Using an MSP.

There are essentially two kinds of hosting services available from an MSP—*shared hosting* and *dedicated hosting*. With a shared hosting account your company is sharing the same server with other companies. This is the cheaper of the two options, but limits the kind and amount of Internet business your company can engage in. The dedicated hosting option is more expensive, but your company is the only user of the server.
The advantages of using an MSP include the following:

- This might well be a lower cost option relative to owning all the hardware yourself.
- No system maintenance is required.

- No knowledge of server software or hardware is required.

- A high-speed Internet connection from company premises may no longer be required.

Disadvantages of the MSP solution include the following:

- You depend on a provider for security and upkeep of your Web site.

- You must update and control the content remotely.

- Depending upon the service level contracted for, you may not be able to implement some of the more sophisticated aspects of having a Web site such as having your customers access a database using a form. This is not the best option if customers need to interact directly with a corporate database.

When choosing an MSP the following important factors should be considered.

- Cost—how are you going to be charged? There are least three kinds of charges: 1) a setup fee, 2) monthly rent that will depend upon how much space (measured in megabytes) you use, and 3) a traffic charge (how many people access your Web site).

- How much memory are you allocated?

- How much traffic are you allowed?

- What kind of access does your provider have for the outside world? You want the provider to have a high-speed connection so customers can easily access your Web site.

- Does your provider use load balancing (routing traffic to the least utilized server)?

- Does your provider have $24 \times 7 \times 365$ technical support?

- What is the level of security of your provider?

- What kinds of business continuity services are provided? Is your site "always" up and running? The guaranteed "uptime" of the server should be clearly spelled out in a *service level agreement* (SLA) along with penalties if the MSP fails to provide.

- What kind of log file reporting is provided?

- How do you alter the content of your Web pages? Does the provider give you a Telnet or an FTP connection to the server so you can alter your content at will? Or, can you use your browser to alter content?

- Can you carry out some of the more sophisticated aspects of Web business? For example, can your customers fill out a form and enter information in a database?

- Do you get your own domain name like www.yourcompany.com? This is very important. You want exclusive rights to your own name. You don't want to lease it. This way if you change the MSP, the links to your Web page remain the same and valid. Your Web address should look like http://www.yourcompany.com.

- How many email addresses do you get? Your email address should look like
  `yourname@yourcompany.com`.

- Does your provider support features like FrontPage extensions?

Leasing: According to the Equipment Leasing Association, computers are the most commonly leased piece of equipment in the United States. Significant cost savings are possible through leasing. Not only may this be cheaper than the purchase decision, but the problem of computer obsolescence is eliminated. For example, Nabisco leased more than $50 million in servers and estimated that it saved 20 percent by doing so [79].

Many companies are leasing more than just computer equipment. The leasing of software and services is also becoming an important part of IT strategy. A good illustration of this is the United States Navy. In October of 2000, Electronic Data Systems (EDS) was awarded a $6.9 billion contract over five years with the U.S. Navy. Under the contract, EDS is responsible for providing, operating, and maintaining all of the computers and servers used by the Navy [83]. We discuss the leasing of software and services in the next two sections.

NEVER BUY SOFTWARE AGAIN . . . .

Never buy software again for Internet business? How can this be? This scenario could take place if, as some visionaries predict, software becomes a utility like electricity and telephone that users rent or lease over the Internet and for which they pay only for usage. "The question is whether it takes five or seven or ten years, not whether it will happen," says Tim Chou, president of Oracle's Business OnLine application services, of software being offered as a service over a network [32]. This sounds futuristic but is already happening, thanks to a relatively new kind of Internet business company, the application service provider (ASP). The ASP is to software what the MSP is to hardware. Rather than purchasing software and all of the hardware necessary to run it, in addition to hiring IT personnel to manage the entire architecture, a company can simply pay a monthly fee to rent the software from an ASP that provides it remotely over the Internet. The ASP industry is still in a nascent stage, representing only about 2 percent of software revenues in 2000. Yet despite an expected shakeout among the hundreds of companies involved in Internet outsourcing, the ASP industry is expected to grow to $11 billion by 2003 [56].

The advantages of going with an ASP are numerous. A few of the more important ones are:

- There is a substantial cost savings in most cases. Software is a considerable expense for most companies if the cost of hardware, IT personnel, and constant upgrades are taken into consideration. Premiere Technologies based in Atlanta claimed to have saved $3 million over five years by outsourcing its PeopleSoft application to ASP TransChannel [117]. As a point of comparison, ASP Corio charges $795 a month per user for access to a single PeopleSoft accounting application, whereas it would cost in the neighborhood of $100,000 to purchase and install the same application on your own servers, not including maintenance [121].

- Time to get an application up and running can be sharply reduced. When Volvo's Relationship/Interactive Marketing Group wanted to deploy an application that could provide information to Volvo about its Web site visitors, the group asked Personify to build a pilot, then host the service. It took less than two months for Personify to have the application up and running. Kris Narayanan, database marketing manager for the Volvo Group, estimates that it would have taken four to six months to do it in-house [117].

- Since the data for the outsourced software are also housed with the ASP, business partners can access the data without putting at risk other data stored within a company's firewall. In the Volvo/Personify example, the Volvo group could allow Volvo's advertising agency and Volvo dealers access to the Web site visitor data without letting them inside Volvo's firewalls.

Yet for all the advantages ASPs have to offer, the industry as a whole has not taken off as was initially expected in the late 1990s when venture capitalists were plunking billions into the industry. This is not only due to inertia in adopting new technology, but also due to inherent disadvantages in the system. These include:

- Having data as well as software stored with the ASP can compromise the security of the data. Having data stored outside a company's firewall is not the ideal solution if the data are sensitive and confidential. Also, when ASP start-ups Pandesic and Red Gorilla suddenly shut down due to lack of funding, they left their customers in the lurch. Many found themselves not only without their software services, but also without their data, which were difficult to retrieve once the ASPs shuttered their doors.

- For large companies that already have a substantial hardware and IT personnel infrastructure in place, it may not be cost-effective to rent software. ASPs generally charge a monthly fee per user so if the number of users within a company is very high, it may not make sense to go the rental route.

- Many companies require complex, sophisticated, custom-built software, which some ASPs are unable to offer. Internet business software is as varied as the myriad business functions, and not all ASPs will be able to fulfill every software need. ASPs are beginning to segment themselves into niche players, with the largest ASPs like Usinternetworking and Qwest Cyber.Solutions going after the big business market.

If you are considering the trade-offs between purchasing software outright and renting it from an ASP, here are some things you should consider. The time may be right for you to begin investigating ASPs if you are considering deployment of a large, company-wide application and do not have the in-house expertise to do so. You may also consider an ASP if the demand for new applications is outstripping your company's ability to provide the necessary hardware and IT personnel. Furthermore, perhaps you would like to spread the costs of a new application over several years with a fixed monthly cost as opposed to paying a large up-front cost for acquiring software and hardware. Maybe you have to get an application up and running very quickly and lack the time to make purchase decisions on hardware and tinker with it to get the application running. It may be acceptable, if not desirable, for the data associated with the software you are considering to be outside your company's firewall. In these situations an ASP may be for you.

ASPs come in many different flavors so be sure to select the one that meets your needs. The ASP should also be able to scale up when your company does. A useful taxonomy is proposed by J. P. Vellotti and Sean Carroll of *PC Magazine* who classify ASPs into five main categories based on the type of software provided [165]. The categories are:

- **Collaboration**: email, scheduling, and meeting planning

- **Data Management**: warehousing, online storage, and colocation

- **Packaged Applications**: includes traditional applications such as Microsoft Office and Lotus Notes

- **MIS**: CRM, ERP, financial management, HR

- **Network and Telecommunications**: Networks, systems management and remote access via virtual private networks (VPN). See the section, "Getting Connected" later in this chapter.

See the online article with links to each category for lists of the leading ASPs in each category.

If your needs are broader than what can be offered by an ASP in a single category, you may consider going with an *ASP aggregator*. An ASP aggregator, or *aggregator* for short, offers many different kinds of software, from email to data management to CRM, and lets customers pick and choose the optimal combination for their needs. The aggregator then ideally goes one step further to integrate the different applications so that they work together seamlessly and are able to share data. In this way, companies can have a single monthly statement rather than many spread over many ASPs, as well as a single point of contact.

Perhaps the best known aggregator is Sunnyvale, CA-based Jamcracker, because of its well-known founder, K. B. Chandrasekhar, who also founded MSP Exodus Communications. The plan of the company is to make Jamcracker the one-stop shop to go to from any company device, wired or wireless, for seamlessly integrated software delivered over the Internet. Jamcracker is fanatical about customer service, paying above-market rates for highly trained personnel who can deliver to their clients a guaranteed uptime of 99.99 percent. In addition, software partners whose applications Jamcracker offers have to undergo a stringent evaluation process before Jamcracker places their offerings on its menu. While Jamcracker's business model sounds like a win-win proposition for company, customers, and software partners alike, the idea, like that of ASPs, may be ahead of its time. Founder Chandrasekhar doesn't see this as a problem: "We have made a habit of being ahead of the market," he says. "That's what we do." [32]

The difficulty with ASPs is selecting the right one, laying out in writing acceptable service and security levels, and continually working with the ASP to ensure that the standards set in the beginning are met. Do due diligence as you would with any outsourcing company or consultant. Check references, compare prices, and meet the prospective team who will be providing your software services. Ensure that the data that will be housed with your ASP along with the software will be as secure as necessary. Check into the customer support your ASP provides should there be a breakdown in services. How responsive is your ASP to your concerns about service? You need also to consider your future needs and how well the ASP can grow with you. Changing ASPs in midstream due to a scaling problem can result in costly downtime and search time to find a suitable replacement. Be certain that the ASP can provide the time-to-market you need to get your application up and running as quickly as you need it.

Once you have selected an ASP, be sure to get the service level agreement SLA in writing (sometimes as thick as a telephone book) that locks in your uptime and the penalties that will be assessed if your ASP doesn't deliver as contracted. Finally, be sure to have an exit strategy in writing that details guarantees on data recovery should the ASP suddenly go out of business (which is not uncommon). All in all, evaluate and treat your ASP as a trusted business partner and be sure that your ASP will work with you in the long term.

HOW TO CHOOSE A CONSULTING SERVICE . . . . .

If you've considered all the options for getting your business online, or want to get a Web site up and running or improve the one you have, or have decided that your business can't make the transition to Internet business without additional help, there is an army of consultants waiting to assist you. Web consultants, both large and small, have sprung up like wildflowers in the Texas springtime. There's one for every project and budget, whether you're a Fortune 100 company or a sole proprietorship. There was a time when you couldn't get the attention of some of the leading Web consulting firms, let alone a proposal for a project, because demand for their services was so high. This situation is changing as some of these firms' leading clients, Internet start-ups, have fallen by the wayside. Many of these consulting firms have hyped themselves to stardom, with names to match. The key is to be able to distinguish between consultants who can truly help you get online within your time constraints and budget, and those who offer too much or too little for your particular needs.

To help you distinguish among them, note that there is a definite hierarchy among the consultants with each firm occupying a certain niche. Each firm has its strengths and weaknesses and caters to projects within a certain price range. Traditional full-service consulting firms like McKinsey & Company, Boston Consulting Group, and Accenture (formerly Andersen Consulting) have had to quickly shore up their forces in order to compete in the Internet business arena. Newer upstarts that focus primarily on Internet business include "older new" firms like Sapient, Scient, and Razorfish and "newer new" firms like Fort Point Partners and Gen3 Partners.

How do you begin to make sense of all of these names? First, by reading an excellent series of *Business2.com* articles collectively called "A Confederacy of Consultants" [135], that analyzes over 20 major players in Internet business consulting from behemoth IBM Global Services to Method, that has 30 employees. The article provides information on each firm such as its founding date, headquarters, leadership, number of employees, 1999 revenue and net income, strengths and weaknesses, and clients.

If the firms analyzed in this article cater to clients with budgets bigger than yours, there's another good resource to turn to: *e-sourcers*. E-sourcers are online directories of Web consultants and service providers that allow you to search, research, and find companies that can meet your budget, timing, and location requirements. There are three leading e-sourcers, according to *Ecompany.com* (now *Business 2.0*): Itradar.com, BSource.com, and eConstructors.com [4]. The service is free for clients and is paid for by the companies the e-sourcers represent.

Once you've narrowed your search to a handful of seemingly compatible consulting firms, it's not enough to "RFP" (request for proposal) and select the cheapest. It's very important to do thorough background checks not only on the firm itself but on the actual consultants who will be working on your project. Follow up on past client lists and dig around to see if you can find other clients who are not on the firm's official list. Be as diligent as though you were researching a potential business partner (which in essence these consultants are) or business team member like an attorney or banker. Many of these Web consultants are hired to clean up after messes left by other consultants. Don't waste your precious resources of time and money on consultants who can't deliver the goods.

After you've selected your firm, someone in your company must be assigned to take an active role in working with the consultants throughout the project from beginning to end. This helps to ensure that the project will be completed on time and under budget. Schedule regular meetings with your consultants to discuss the progress of your project. Don't be afraid to ask hard questions or to speak up if it looks as though things are going awry. Chances are things will not go smoothly from time to time, and you must be vigilant to take care of problems quickly, before they turn into crises. Don't be intimidated by techno-speak. If you don't understand something, don't be afraid to ask questions. On the other hand, don't be too intrusive so that the consultants cannot get their work done. Deftly manage your relationship with your consultants as you would with your customers and your business partners. By doing so, you are protecting your investment in your company and helping to ensure that you are getting the best work from your consulting firm.

GETTING CONNECTED . . . .

Regardless of whether a company owns, leases, or uses an MSP to provide hardware, it still needs an Internet connection. Indeed, even if a company uses the services of an ASP it must still connect to the ASP using the Internet. In this section we address the available technologies for the "last mile" connection to the Internet. In deciding which kind of connection is best for your company, it is helpful to explicitly understand the business purpose of the network. In Chapter 4, "Internet and Web Technology," we defined the Internet as the public, worldwide network using the protocol TCP/IP. Related to this are the concepts of *intranet* and *extranet*. By intranet, we mean a network to be used only by company employees. It is a private company network that is not constrained geographically and could be worldwide. An intranet is not necessarily built upon TCP/IP, although this is becoming more common. By extranet, we mean a private network connecting a company with customers or business partners. Again, the extranet may or may not be based on TCP/IP.

In the first subsection below, "Internet Connections," we discuss the kinds of connections available to a company if it is simply trying to link a LAN (local area network) to the Internet. Recall in Chapter 4 that a LAN was defined as a communications network consisting of cables, computers, and network devices confined to a very small geographic area such as a building or single floor of a building. In the second subsection, "Intranet or Extranet Connection," we discuss possibilities for building an intranet or extranet.

Internet Connections

Refer to Figure 7–1. In this subsection we address the problem of how to make the last mile "lightning bolt" connection between the router and the "cloud" that represents the Internet. There are three kinds of connections available, depending on the size of your company and the speed of the link required:

- **Narrowband**—for simple Web browsing and email for a small number of employees (perhaps one megabit per second (Mbps) or less)

- **Midband**—for numerous employees using the Web simultaneously (perhaps 1–10 Mbps)

- **Broadband**—for multiple servers hosting Web pages and applications (over 10 Mbps)

By narrowband connection, we mean a standard dial-up connection using a modem and POTS (plain old telephone service). Our focus in this chapter is dedicated Internet access that may be either midband or broadband. As opposed to a dial-up connection, by dedicated we mean "always on." The details of a dedicated connection are illustrated in Figure 7–4 and are described below. In order to get a dedicated line, a company must first contract with an Internet service provider (ISP) that has a POP (point of presence) in the same city or nearby city. The large ISPs have numerous POPs throughout the world. In order to have a dedicated access connection a company needs a private line to the LEC (local exchange carrier) office (such as a local telephone company) as well as a private line from the LEC office to the ISP POP which the ISP provides. A large ISP will have its own high-speed fiber backbone linked to the public Internet at network access points (NAPs).

Dedicated connections using copper operate at speeds from 56 Kbps (kilobits per second) to 44.7 Mbps (megabits per second). Speeds over 2 Gbps (gigabits per second) are possible using fiber optic cable. The speed available at a dedicated access POP may vary greatly from city to city. The type of customer premise equipment (CPE) (the hardware necessary on your company premises for an Internet connection) depends on the speed and type of the connection. CPE for an Internet connection at each LAN would typically include a router, a CSU/DSU (channel services unit/data services unit), and a multiplexor. The function of a router was discussed in Chapter 4. A CSU/DSU is used to connect computers, video equipment, and multiplexors to digital phone lines. Multiplexors allow multiple devices to share the same dedicated line.

Typical midband and broadband speeds are given in Table 7–1. A very common connection is a T-carrier line, either T1 or T3. These were originally dedicated digital lines introduced by AT&T to carry voice, but are now used for data. If a full T1 line with a speed

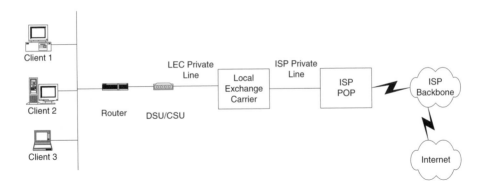

Figure 7–4 A dedicated Internet connection.

of 1.544 Mbps is not needed, fractional T1 connections can be purchased. If a T3 speed of 44.7 Mbps is not sufficient, say for a company wishing to host Web servers, there are large ISPs that provide SONET (synchronous optical network) technology. This technology uses fiber optic cable. Fiber optic speeds typically vary from OC1 (51.84 Mbps) to OC48 (2.488 Gbps).

Table 7–1 Wired Network Connection Speeds

Network Connection–Wires	Speed
xDSL	Download—384 Kbps to 1.544 Mbps
	Upload—128 Kbps to 640 Kbps
T1	1.544 Mbps
T3	44.7 Mbps
Frame Relay	56 Kbps to 1.544 Mbps
Ethernet	up to 100 Mbps
OC1	51.84 Mbps
OC3	155 Mbps
OC12	622 Mbps
OC48	2.488 Gbps

An alternative at the lower end of the spectrum that is becoming more popular is digital subscriber line service (DSL). This service comes in many variations and is often abbreviated xDSL, where "x" stands for a letter that denotes the kind of DSL service. One common variant is ADSL which is asymmetric DSL. A nice feature of ADSL is that it provides both POTS and an "always on" Internet connection over the same copper wire connection. This is illustrated in Figure 7–5. Note that there is a direct connection from the company to an ILEC (incumbent local exchange carrier). By the Telecommunications Act of 1996, the ILEC is required to open up its services to competitors who want to offer Internet access using DSL. The competitors are called competitive local exchange carriers

(CLEC). At the ILEC central office, the signal pulsing through the lines, whether voice or data, goes through a switching process. Voice goes through a PSTN (public switched telephone network) switch, whereas data go through digital switching equipment and are sent to the location of the ISP through an ISP backbone.

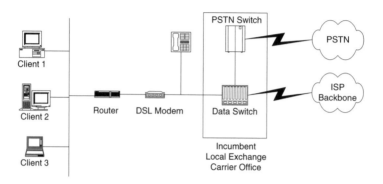

Figure 7–5 A DSL connection.

There are two important features of DSL that must be considered. First, if a company is to use DSL, company premises must be within approximately one to three miles of an ILEC central office. The potential speed of the service is affected by this distance. This also means that DSL is not a viable solution for businesses in a rural area. Second, as the word asymmetric implies, the upstream and downstream speeds are not equal. Typically, downloading speed is much faster than uploading speed. Refer back to Table 7–1. Consequently, asymmetric DSL is currently not a good solution for a company wishing to host Web servers.

There are some small businesses using Internet service over cable connections. However, cable-based Internet service is used mainly in the consumer market. A problem with Internet cable service is that as more customers use the service, connection speeds are reduced.

Finally, we come to wireless technology. We are primarily concerned with a company making the last mile connection from a LAN to the Internet. Also, the technologies we describe are *fixed point wireless* connections rather than *mobile wireless* connections. We do not discuss wireless networking within a corporate LAN, telephony solutions, or wireless Internet connections for handheld devices. We refer the reader to Dodd [39] for a good discussion of other wireless technologies.

Broadband wireless covers the frequency band from 2 to 42 GHz. See [148]. In general, the higher the frequency, the higher the bandwidth. However, there is a trade-off between high and low frequencies. The higher the frequency, the more rapidly the waves dissipate over distance. Also, the higher frequencies require a "line-of-sight" (a relatively clear straight line with few obstructions) between the transmitter and the receiver. We break the discussion of fixed point wireless into two parts: terrestrial and satellite-based.

Terrestrial Wireless: The generic terrestrial point-to-multipoint wireless network is illustrated in Figure 7–6. The basic idea is to have a broadcast tower mounted on a tall building. This tower broadcasts to multiple points in the metropolitan area. The transceiver for receiving the signal is often a small dish, perhaps 18 inches in diameter, mounted on the rooftop of the receiving building. The transceiver is connected to a modem that converts the radio or microwave frequency waves into a digital signal. The digital signal is sent to a router that is connected to the computers in the LAN in the building. The client computers and the router in the LAN use ethernet. From the perspective of the individual computers in the LAN, there is no difference between a wireless or a wired last mile connection.

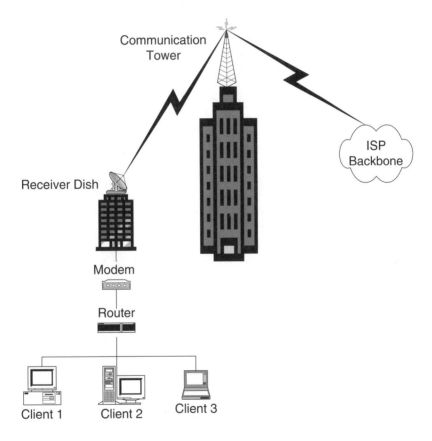

Figure 7–6 *Terrestrial wireless solution.*

A high-bandwidth terrestrial wireless option for corporations is local multipoint distribution system (LMDS), that broadcasts in microwave bandwidths centered at the 28GHz part of the spectrum. The broadcast spectrum is in the OC1 to OC12 range. This is a very good last mile solution from an ISP to a company's building or complex that is not wired and where it is very costly to lay cable. This is a line-of-sight technology from the transmitter of the ISP to a receiver on the rooftop of the company. Unfortunately, the range of the service is only two to four miles. Another wireless microwave technology is multichannel multipoint distribution service or microwave multipoint distribution service (MMDS). MMDS is broadcast in a lower frequency range of 2.2 to 2.4 GHz, but has a broader reach of up to 30 miles. This technology has a lower bandwidth and ranges from 128 Kbps to 3 Mbps.

Sprint recently has begun its Broadband Direct service. Data, in the form of radio waves, are sent to and from a transmission tower. Like LMDS, it is a line-of-sight technology, but has a radius of 30–35 miles from the transmission tower. Like ADSL, it is an asymmetric service. Typical download speeds are 512 Kbps to 1.5 Mbps and maximum download speed is 5 Mbps. Upload speed is a maximum of 256 Kbps.

A very new and exciting development is wireless optical. This is fiber optic technology without the fiber cable—i.e., the data are carried by light through the air. A good example of this technology is Fiberless Optics from Terabeam. This is a point-to-multipoint system similar to that illustrated in Figure 7–6 with speeds of up to 100 Mbps. With wireless optical, a company does not even need a rooftop transceiver. The connection is made through an office window.

Satellite Wireless: The satellite wireless connection is illustrated in Figure 7–7. The big advantage of satellite over terrestrial wireless is that it is essentially available anywhere. An example of a satellite-based wireless solution is the system developed by Tachyon, Inc. Tachyon offers a download bandwidth of up to 2 Mbps and upload bandwidth of 256 Kbps. A competing technology is StarBand Satellite Internet service from StarBand Communications Inc. This satellite-based technology with download speed of 500 Kbps and upload speeds of 40 to 60 Kbps is not as fast as terrestrial wireless, such as Sprint Broadband Direct, but because it is satellite-based, it is possible to get this service in remote areas. A disadvantage of the satellite system is latency (delay). The latency of a satellite system is about 500 milliseconds, more than twice that of the terrestrial wireless (see Table 7–2 for a rundown of connection speeds).

Related to the satellite wireless solution is a stratospheric solution. Often called HALO (High Altitude Long Operation), this solution is a communications platform flying in the stratosphere above cities. An example of this solution is Skystation International. Its platform is a blimp that hovers over metropolitan areas and can cover 7,500 square miles. It operates in the 47 GHz frequency band and offers transfer rates of up to 10 Mbps.

Although this subsection is devoted to wireless last mile connections, a very important LAN technology growing in popularity is wireless ethernet.

Tech Talk

Wireless LANs are growing in popularity. An important technology is the IEEE (Institute of Electrical and Electronic Engineers) 802.11b high-rate wireless standard. With an 802.11b card a notebook user can connect to an ethernet LAN at 11 Mbps.

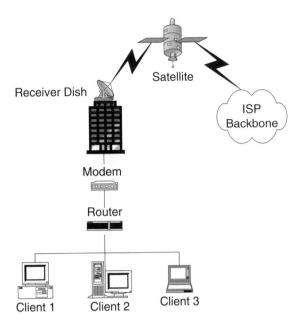

Figure 7–7 Satellite wireless solution.

Table 7–2 Wireless Network Connection Speeds

Network Connection–Wires	Download Speed
StarBand Satellite	500 Kbps
MMDS	128 Kbps - 3 Mbps
Tachyon Satellite	2 Mbps
Sprint Broadband	5 Mbps
HALO Skystation	10 Mbps
Wireless Ethernet	up to 11 Mbps
Terabeam	100 Mbps
LMDS	OC1–OC12

Intranet or Extranet Connections

In the previous subsection, we assumed that the "cloud" the company wished to connect to was the public Internet. One problem with the public Internet is security. Companies often elect to build private networks. This network might be an intranet–i.e., a network for the exclusive use of company employees, or it might be an extranet–i.e., a network for the exclusive use of a company and its business partners. Note that we do not capitalize the first letter of the words intranet and extranet because these networks are not necessarily built on the Internet protocol TCP/IP.

Consider the case in which a company would like to link corporate headquarters with several regional offices. One solution is to establish a set of *point-to-point connections* over *private* leased lines between the headquarters and the offices. This is illustrated in Figure 7–8. This solution is very similar to the one illustrated in Figure 7–4. With the point-to-point solution the corporation would typically contract with a major carrier capable of providing long distance "leased line" connections. Each of the LANs would then require a local access line to the carrier's POP in their respective cities. However, unlike the paradigm illustrated in Figure 7–4 in which each LAN uses the Internet as a connection, the carrier would provide dedicated private lines between each of the LANs. With this solution, the company has an "always on" intranet with a guaranteed bandwidth and good security. Typically, a company would use a T1 or T3 connection to the POP, however. Within metropolitan areas, wireless connections are becoming more popular. A drawback of the point-to-point solution is that it does not scale well. If there are n (the number of) sites to connect there are $n(n-1)/2$ leased lines to purchase, plus the associated customer premise equipment.

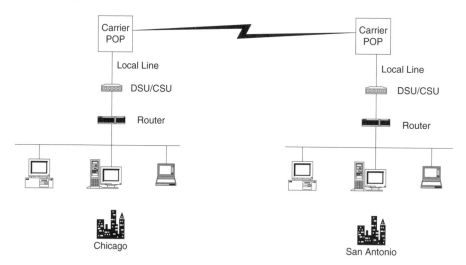

Figure 7–8 A point-to-point connection.

An alternative to the leased line approach is *packet switching technologies*. One of the most popular of these packet switching technologies is *frame relay*. This is illustrated in Figure 7–9. With a frame relay connection, each of the company LANs is required to have a dedicated line to the carrier's POP, but these are the only dedicated lines needed. Also with frame relay, additional CPE such as a FRAD (frame relay assembler/disassembler) is required. Once inside the carrier frame relay cloud, the company does not pay for a point-to-point dedicated connection between every pair of LANs. Rather, there is a permanent virtual circuit connecting the LANs that is programmed into the switches inside the carrier network. The switches know where to send packets based on the header information. Frame relay is usually a much cheaper option than point-to-point leased lines.

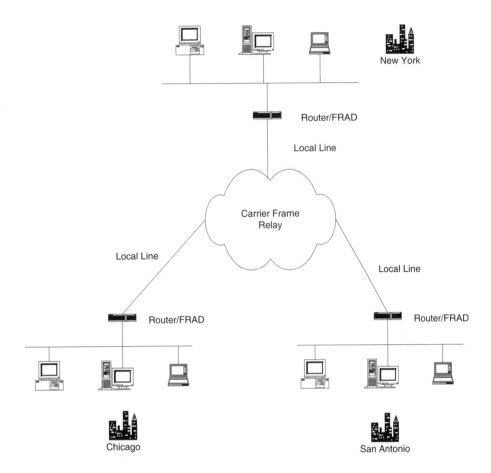

Figure 7–9 A frame relay connection.

Another option for building a private network is to use a *virtual private network* (VPN). A VPN is a private network that uses the public Internet. To insure privacy, a VPN makes use of encryption and authentication. Encryption and authentication are discussed in detail in Chapter 9, "Security and Internet Business." Thus, a VPN offers a company the ubiquity of the Internet but added security through encryption and authentication.

FUTURE TRENDS AND IMPLICATIONS............

At this point it is very difficult to predict what is going to happen to the outsourcing market. With regard to hardware, it seems that the trend toward outsourcing and colocation will continue into the future. One of the reasons for this is that demand for highly trained and skilled IT personnel will outstrip supply, leaving companies short of being able to provide for upkeep of their own hardware. Another reason is that as a company grows, it is easier and faster to scale its hardware infrastructure through outsourcing rather than ownership. A third reason is that as Internet business hardware requirements continue to grow and become ever more sophisticated, few companies will have the resources to provide the necessary climate control, backup power sources, and redundant connections to maintain the architecture. One consequence of all of this growth is the increasing demand for energy needed to power the Internet business infrastructure. We are already witnessing acute power shortages in California. It is only a matter of time before shortages become a national, if not international, problem, forcing the private and public sectors to seek new sources of energy.

In software, the ASP market was incredibly hot for a brief time, and now there are forecasts for considerable consolidation in this market. A number of firms have been burned badly by outsourcing. Consider poor eVineyard Inc. They had a contract for enterprise resource planning software (ERP) from the ASP Pandesic LLC. (ERP software is discussed in more detail in Chapter 14, "Enterprise Application Software.") eVineyard thought it was safe to go with Pandesic because Pandesic was a joint venture of two well-established firms, Intel and SAP AG. When Pandesic eventually folded, eVineyard was left scrambling to hire an IT staff to implement the software in-house. Shortly thereafter eVineyard was burned again when ShopTok Inc. failed and left eVineyard without an online chat operation [74].

We cannot emphasize enough that if you choose to go with an ASP make sure you *have a backup of your critical data*. Some visionaries are predicting that software or computer use in general will morph into a utility-like entity where people just pay for usage and everything is outsourced, like electricity or telephone service. We are still a long way from that situation. In the interim, most companies will resort to a hybrid solution that involves some ownership of software and some outsourcing. In this scenario, there are certain data and software that a company will want to retain ownership of, but there will invariably be some software it will want to outsource.

The Internet backbone is based on fiber optic cable. Fiber optic is a technology for both the present and future. However, the battle for the last mile, among competing technologies and competing companies within each technology, is very much up for grabs. In this market there is intense competition among DSL, direct leased lines, cable, and wireless. Having a dedicated high-speed broadband connection will become an essential part of doing business, especially if a company serves up Web pages on its own servers. There are numerous telecommunications firms, ISPs, MSPs, and cable companies seeking to fill this growing demand. We have only seen the tip of the iceberg in wireless connections, especially with regard to handheld devices. As Internet business becomes more mobile, the future of the wireless market will remain promising, particularly in satellite technology for reaching nonurban areas.

Finally, when considering whether to engage in Internet business through in-house means or through a colocation service, an MSP, or an ASP, it is crucial to make a decision that scales with your business. For example, an in-house solution may work well for your current level of Internet business activity, but may be totally inadequate for future levels. As more and more business functions become Internet-based, your need for more powerful connections and more sophisticated architecture will continue to grow. Don't make the mistake of limiting your company's growth by thinking only of your present needs. While you don't want to pay for unused excess capacity, you don't want to disrupt your Internet business when you need to scale. When selecting an ISP, MSP, or ASP, make sure that your provider will be able to grow with you and seamlessly scale your Internet business needs.

Part 3

Nuts and Bolts
of Internet Business

In the third part of the book we delve into different Internet business models as well as functions such as financial transactions and marketing. We also cover what no company doing business on the Internet can afford to be without—security. In Chapter 8, "Rethinking Internet Business Models," we explore the ingenious models that continue to transform the way people do business. We discuss what went right and what went wrong with the most prominent Internet business models. In Chapter 9, "Security and Internet Business," we describe the different means by which you and your company can protect yourselves. We include password safety, encryption, public and private key systems, digital signatures, and firewalls. In Chapter 10, "Internet Business Transactions," we discuss how to build a storefront, the different ways you can receive payment online, and how you can most efficiently fulfill orders. We cover B2C (business-to-consumer), B2B (business-to-business), and P2P (peer-to-peer) transactions. In Chapter 11, "Marketing on the Internet," we discuss Internet marketing strategies like branding, one-to-one marketing, permission marketing, viral marketing, partnering, and doing more with less. We cover tracking and measuring your customers' movements on your Web site, and the different media you can use to get your message across.

8 Rethinking Internet Business Models

In this chapter ...

WHAT IS AN INTERNET BUSINESS MODEL? . . . . . .

This chapter opens Part III of the book, "The Nuts and Bolts of Internet Business." This is where we get down to the nitty-gritty and present the necessary components for building an Internet business. Before engaging in Internet business it is necessary to have a business plan. A business plan is what an entrepreneur presents to a venture capitalist, a banker, or an investor to try to garner financial support. A business plan might include information on current or potential markets, prospective partners, competition, sales projections, and of course the big idea for a product or service. Since the days of the dot-com gold rush, thousands of Internet business plans have been written, sent, and presented to potential investors and lenders. Although thousands of plans have been written, most of them can be distilled down to a handful of fundamental ideas on how to do business using the Internet. These fundamental ideas are what we call Internet business models.

An Internet business model is an idea stripped down to its essentials, and an Internet business plan is a concrete, real-world implementation of the idea. There may be many plans for a single model. The Internet retailing model, for example, which we discuss in detail in a later section, is essentially about selling physical goods online, as a retail store would. But there can be many variations on this model, from selling hot sauce (Hothothot.com) to furniture (the now defunct Furniture.com). There may also be variations on payment plans, shipping options, frequent buyer points, affiliate programs, advertising on the site, etc., so there are countless different plans for a single model.

. . . .

THE DIFFERENCE BETWEEN AN INTERNET BUSINESS MODEL AND AN INTERNET BUSINESS PLAN

> An Internet business model is an idea stripped down to its essentials, and an Internet business plan is a concrete, real-world implementation of the idea.

Before we probe into the models, we discuss the dot-com fallout in the section, "The Myth of the Dot-Com Fallout," and why we think that despite the fallout, Internet business will be BIG. In the following section, "Is Internet Business Different?" we discuss whether models for Internet business are different from models for traditional business. Do the same principles apply? Is the Internet just another channel in traditional business, or does the Internet fundamentally change the nature of business? The dot-com fallout would have us believe that the models are similar. That is, it may be that in the dot-com gold rush a number of years ago, investors and entrepreneurs alike felt that different rules could apply to Internet business. They thought that simply maximizing the number of "hits" on a Web site and paying whatever it took to gather those hits, rather than focusing on business fundamentals like profitability, would be enough for Internet business success. This resulted in many dot-coms going under as they blew their funding on promoting their Web site rather than trying to build a feasible business that would bring in more money than it spent. The subsequent implosion showed us that business fundamentals are just as important to dot-coms as they are to traditional companies.

In the section, "What Works, What Doesn't," we discuss the basic Internet business models that have emerged over the years. These include B2C (business-to-consumer), B2B (business-to-business), and bricks-and-clicks, a combination of offline and online business. We don't mean to provide you with an exhaustive taxonomy of models, just enough to give you a sense of what can be done with the Internet, why some business plans for a model succeed, and why some fail. The reason we call this chapter "Rethinking Internet Business Models" is that many firms who used these models have failed—spectacularly. Why have they failed? Is a model inherently a failure, or is it just the implementation of the model, the business plan, a failure? What can be learned from these failures? Can we recast these models to bring about success? We track the future of these ideas in the closing section on "Future Trends and Implications."

THE MYTH OF THE DOT-COM FALLOUT . . . .

The Nasdaq is tanking. Technology companies are lowering their earnings expectations. Many once-high-flying Internet stocks have been delisted. Pets.com, Furniture.com, Toysmart.com, and Urbanfetch.com are among the better-known dot-coms that no longer exist. (If you want to track the demise of battered dot-coms and maybe even contribute to a Death Wish List for dot-coms you can't stand, there are several Web sites devoted entirely to dot-com failure, like www.thecompost.com.) Even the venerable Amazon hasn't shown a profit in seven years. What does all of this say about the future of Internet business? Is profitable Internet business an oxymoron? Is the path to profitability on the Internet just a pipe dream?

Our response is a resounding NO. On the contrary, we will go so far as to say that in ten years, the Internet will be as essential to business as electricity is now. Think about that. Think about pulling the electricity on your company. Your company's productivity would nosedive in seconds. We predict that this will be the scenario in your company in ten years if you shut down your Internet connection. Of course, if your company is an "Internet pure play" (another name for dot-com) this already holds true.

If your company's business is information-intensive, this may also be true. In the Information Age, the transmission of information via the Internet, whether it be among employees or with customers, suppliers, and business partners, will be vital to virtually all businesses. Even the writing of this book, for example, which is completely information-intensive, might have taken at least twice as long without the Internet. Without the Internet for sending many daily emails and attaching articles, chapters, and graphics between Chicago and Honolulu (where each author lives), as well as to our publisher and reviewers, we would have to be mailing diskettes or Zip drives and hard copy nearly every day, and wait at least two to three days to receive a package between the two cities. The coordination of keeping manuscript files current for both authors would have been extremely difficult without the Internet. With the Internet it's a snap. And of course, gathering up-to-the-minute information for research for this book without the Web would have been impossible.

Software, too, as we have seen in Chapter 7, "Getting Your Business Online," will be transmitted to a company through ASPs via the Internet much as a utility is. Software will be paid for on a per-usage basis, rather than purchased in shrink-wrap for individual desktop computers. Without software, how far can a company go? And how many businesses ten years from now will be without a Web site that provides instant global reach, a way to interact with customers, suppliers, and business partners, a channel for selling products and services, and a means to disseminate information about the company?

There are probably many more ways that the Internet will become essential to business that no one has even thought of yet. This is what makes Internet business so exciting. Companies and people like you are coming up with new ways that the Internet can be used to make businesses more efficient, more productive, and generate more revenue. Yes, the printing press, pony express, post office, telephone, radio, and television, and of course the computer, have all radically changed the way we do business. The Internet will no doubt be at least as, if not more, transforming than these inventions and institutions.

The Industrial Revolution has taken about a hundred years to mature, until the advent of a new age, the Information Age. Comparatively, the Information Age is at most twenty years old, so we still have a lot to learn. Many dot-coms failed miserably because they set aside the time-honored principles of basic business in favor of "maximizing eyeballs" or "instant branding." We have witnessed the shakeout and will learn from their mistakes. This is what this chapter is all about: rethinking Internet business models.

IS INTERNET BUSINESS DIFFERENT? . . . .

This brings us to the question as to whether Internet business is fundamentally different from "traditional" or offline business. Does the Internet change the rules about business, or is it just another medium like television? Is Internet business truly a revolution like the Industrial Revolution, which launched society out of the Agrarian Age, or is it just a blip in the ongoing evolution of business? Opinions about Internet business run the entire gamut, from viewing the Web as just another channel [145]: "The Web is only a tool. . .It's not a business model by itself," (Timothy Crown, President and CEO of Insight Enterprises, Inc.) to acknowledging the transforming power of the Internet [71]: "There is no limit to what the Internet can become over the next twenty years. . .The Internet eliminates barriers of distance, time and even politics," (Roger McNamee, general partner of Integral Capital Partners and Silver Lake Partners, two private investment firms that focus on technology companies).

In many cases, people's opinions will depend on the type of business they are in. Someone in catalog sales might view Internet business as just another channel to sell more merchandise. Orders had been coming in through the telephone, fax, and mail, and now through the Internet. On the other hand, someone who works for an Internet pure play will probably realize that the entire company could not exist without the Internet. Finally, there are the mom and pop who own the neighborhood candy store, for whom business hasn't changed one iota since the advent of the Internet and probably never will.

Within this spectrum of opinions, we are at the end with those who believe that society is on the verge of an Internet business revolution. The Internet is already revolutionizing business in the Information Age the way the steam engine and factory production revolutionized business during the Industrial Revolution. While the essence of business remains the same whether one is in Internet business or traditional business—the focus on profitability—the Internet has produced brand new business models that would not be possible without it. But Internet business is more than just new business models. It is radically altering the flow of information, arguably a company's most critical asset, in the same way that factories radically altered the means of production during the Industrial Revolution.

These new and rapid flows of information occur between parties who might otherwise not have the opportunity to communicate in the same way. This is why the Internet is radically altering relationships between companies and customers, between suppliers and purchasers, between companies and business partners, among employees within the same company, and is creating instant communities among those who share common interests. With the Internet, reaching out to customers in new ways through mass customization and one-to-one marketing is possible. B2B exchanges, like Covisint and Plasticsnet.com, are bringing together suppliers and purchasers in ways never before dreamed possible. Companies and their business partners, like advertising agencies or dealerships, can share data over the Internet instantaneously and in a secure fashion. Company-wide paper memos are no longer necessary thanks to instant email communication via an intranet. And fans of a particular product, like *Fast Company* magazine and Slimfast, are forming communities through the ease of communication and relationship building via the Internet.

Furthermore, just as the Industrial Revolution had the power not only to change the way people did business but to change the way people lived, so, too, does Internet business hold the potential to change the entire fabric of society. Indeed, the Industrial Revolution ushered in a whole new way of working and living. Whereas on farms during the Agrarian Age people worked and lived by the natural rhythms of the day, from sunrise to sunset, people in the factories during the Industrial Revolution worked in manmade shifts defined by the time clock and the whistle. Rather than work on farms to grow enough food to subsist, people flocked to the factories and earned wages that they used to purchase food. Work and life on the farm were inseparable; in the factories they were separate as night and day.

Internet business holds the power to reverse what the Industrial Revolution hath wrought. In the Information Age, where a company's most critical assets are ideas and information, the ease and rapidity of flows of information that the Internet provides can bond together people into a single entity, even if they are not in the same physical location. Many startups begin as "virtual companies" that consist of employees working out of their homes and communicating and sharing data via the Internet. Ease of communication and data sharing allow some employees to remain working for a company but to work, at least part time, out of their homes. Many workers are giving up corporate life altogether, and are moving back into their homes to work as free agents. Rather than earn wages at a company, they may get paid by the project, much as some farm families did piecework at home before the Industrial Revolution to supplement household incomes. Thanks to the Internet, people are moving back to their homes, and work and life are co-mingling once again. While we will probably never see the day when commutes to work are a relic of the past, the Internet is transforming the way we live as well as the way we do business.

WHAT WORKS, WHAT DOESN'T.................

In this section we *rethink* basic Internet business models. From the many examples we try to tease out what's been done that's right and what's been done that's wrong. If there's one Internet business strategy that had to be rethought, it's "first-mover advantage." The dot-com heyday was so frenzied because everyone thought that to be the first Internet retailer, the first auction, the first portal, or first whatever meant instant success in Internet business. Entrepreneurs scrambled to get funded, to build fast companies and fast brands, to lead explosive IPOs and create vast wealth, all the while forgetting about business fundamentals like profitability. Now that the dust has settled over the bombed-out dot-com landscape, people are talking about "second-mover advantage." With second-mover advantage, entrepreneurs can learn from the first mover's mistakes, and their successes. This is precisely what we intend to do in this section.

The Internet Retailing Model

The Internet retailing model, also known as the *virtual merchant* model, is an Internet business that sells merchandise exclusively through a virtual storefront, or Web site. Product photographs and descriptions are organized and displayed on the site along with their list prices. Virtual shopping cart technology is used, whereby a shopper can click on a box next to the product description, and the product, along with the price, will be "added" to the cart. Well-executed shopping carts will display a list of what has been added to the cart along with the prices and a running total so the shopper can keep track of his potential purchases. When the shopper is ready to check out, he clicks on the check-out option and is usually given the opportunity to change his mind on any of the items in the cart. Well-designed shopping carts will also provide the total of the items together with the shipping costs before the shopper proceeds to fill out the purchase forms.

When he is ready to purchase, he is presented with a form, which he completes, filling in his credit card (or other form of payment) information, billing and shipping addresses, and any other information the Internet retailer deems necessary. (Internet retailers must be careful not to overwhelm the shopper with too many forms, lest the shopper resort to "shopping cart abandonment syndrome." See Chapter 6, "Web Site Design and Content.") When all of the virtual paperwork is completed, the shopper clicks on a "complete purchase" button and—zap—the transaction is completed. Depending on the availability of the items ordered and the efficiency of the retailer, the items are delivered as soon as possible to the shipping address, commonly via the U.S. Postal Service, Federal Express, or UPS.

This is the basic Internet retailing model, though variations on the theme abound. Internet retailers have tried to sell everything from clothing to furniture, with mixed success. Some retailers provide additional customer service via a prominently displayed email address and a telephone number, and some provide none at all. Some retailers allow for tracking of packages, while others do not. Some retailers allow a shopper to cancel a shipment up until the day before it is shipped, and some hold that the transaction is final. Some have generous and easy return policies, while others have stringent and difficult policies. Some retailers are profitable and others are not. What sets them apart?

. . . .

SUCCESSFUL INTERNET RETAILING LESSONS

- Begin with the right product. An Internet retailing product has a better chance of succeeding if it is:

    1. Not readily available through physical stores
    2. More easily located through a search on the Web
    3. Relatively inexpensive
    4. Easily shipped

- Take advantage of the special nature of the Internet to give your online customers a value-added experience over that of competitors.

- Be sure your transaction and fulfillment infrastructures are firmly and profitably in place.

First, it is important to begin with the right product. Products most likely to sell well over the Web are those that cannot be found at a store on every street corner, are relatively inexpensive, and are easily shipped. Actually, the same could be said of items sold through catalogs (telephone and mail-order), though we shall discuss the value that having a Web site adds below. Outside of major metropolitan areas, there are many products that cannot be readily purchased. Specialty items like ethnic foods, customized products, and hard-to-find items without large retail distribution systems are good candidates for Internet retailers. If an item can be readily purchased in someone's neighborhood, it is unlikely that he will purchase it over the Web and incur delays and shipping costs. Ethnicgrocer.com sells over 20,000 ethnic food products through multiple Web sites and has received several rounds of multimillion dollar funding. Its products seem like good candidates for Internet retailing, though whether the company can stand on its own and achieve profitability remains to be seen. Its products are relatively inexpensive, too (under $20), which is attractive to Internet shoppers.

Companies selling high-end products find that expensive purchases (ranging from several hundred to several thousand dollars) often need to be made in person because they require handholding, gentle coaxing, and the reassurance of a live salesperson in order to complete the sale. At Neimanmarcus.com certain products displayed on the Web site will not even be sold online unless the shopper provides contact information (either email or telephone) so that a "personal shopper" can reach her and guide her through the purchase. There also seems to be a limit on the size of items that can easily be shipped. While Dell.com seems to have no problem shipping custom-made desktop computers around the country, the number one complaint from customers about Furniture.com had to do with delivery problems. Promised six- to eight-week delivery times turned into six-month waits, which caused one-third of all orders to be canceled (without penalty up until delivery day, promised the company) and resulted in astronomical storage costs. Product quality and bill disputes also led to the demise of Furniture.com, which closed its doors on November 6, 2000 [125].

Second, take advantage of the special nature of the Internet to give your customers a value-added experience over that of competitors. The quintessential Internet retailer, Amazon, provides the best example of how this can be done. As we mentioned above, the sought-after qualities of product offerings between an Internet retailer and a catalog company are not that different. Certain items will sell better than others if a live salesperson and physical storefront are not present. The value in selling a product online comes with the information a Web site can provide that a catalog company cannot.

Take books, for example. Books are relatively small, inexpensive, easily shipped, and many selections, especially specialized texts, cannot be bought in a brick-and-mortar bookstore. They could as readily be sold through a catalog (which they have been, on a small scale) as they could through the Web. However, what Amazon offers, first and foremost, is selection. Its original business model was to sell any book, anywhere, at any time. Anywhere and anytime can be taken care of through 365/24/7 catalog sales, but any book can only be sold through the Web. The cost of mailing out catalogs with descriptions of every book in print (they are the size of a telephone book), as well as those of out-of-print books and instant updates as soon as books become available, would be next to impossible. With the Web, virtually any book can be easily displayed, described, and sold. It is not inexpensive to maintain the necessary database and the presentation layer to do so, but it can be (and is being) done.

In addition, Amazon provides customer reviews of all books that have a willing reviewer, which in many cases turns customers into marketers. These reviews are dynamic and constantly being updated. Furthermore, users of the Web site are given the opportunity to rate the quality of the reviews. This form of marketing, again, would be prohibitively expensive with a catalog company. Also, customers can be notified via email, at essentially no cost, when a book they are anticipating becomes available. This could be done through the telephone or mail, but the cost of doing so for millions of customers would be a logistical and financial nightmare.

Perhaps most value-added of all Amazon features is the personalization of marketing through the use of cookies. Cookies allows Amazon to cross-sell to customers based on their past purchases and similar purchases made by other customers. (See Chapter 11, "Marketing on the Internet," for details on how cookies work.) These are the Web offerings that have launched Amazon into the premier retailing rank, even though it has yet to turn a profit. Other current and prospective retailers would do well to learn from Amazon's lessons.

Third, an Internet retailer's transaction and fulfillment infrastructure must be firmly and profitably in place. While you want to create a smooth transaction process, hassle-free return policy, and quick delivery system for your customers, you do not want to over-promise and underdeliver. Reconsider the case of Furniture.com. In addition to offering a difficult product to ship, it also offered free shipping, free returns, and a no-penalty cancellation policy until the day of delivery. This is in large part why it was able to attract a million users per month and $22 million in revenues for nine months in 2000. This is also why in large part it went under, because it could not fulfill the promises it made [125]. Many Internet retailers, because they can forego the cost of physical infrastructure, rent, and live salespersons, underestimate the cost of doing business online. Instead of rent, you have to purchase or lease servers to keep the Web site "always on" as well as warehouse space for inventory and equipment for fulfillment. Instead of salespersons, you have to hire order fulfillment workers, customer service representatives on the telephone and using email, and an IT group and Webmaster to keep the site fresh to support the offerings and purchases online. Finally, you have to assure the customer that his purchases are secure and that the value you add to the customer's experience outweighs the shipping costs associated with the purchase.

The Auction Model

One of the unique features of the Internet is that it allows buyers and sellers from around the world to virtually come together in a single marketplace and to transmit information to and from one another instantaneously. Because of this, dynamic pricing mechanisms are possible. A dynamic pricing mechanism (as opposed to fixed prices) allows the price of an item to slide up or down until it hits a point at which both buyer and seller are satisfied. Dynamic pricing dates back to the oldest marketplaces of civilization when buyer and seller haggled over the price of goods. When dynamic pricing is combined with competition—that is, multiple buyers competing to purchase an item from a single seller, or multiple sellers competing to sell to a single buyer—this is called an *auction*.

An auction is one of the oldest kinds of marketplaces. Live auctions are still commonly used to sell livestock, art, and antiques. But the special nature of the Internet has brought auctioning to a whole new level, allowing a seller to sell virtually any item to the highest bidder in a worldwide audience of prospective buyers. This was the insight of Pierre Omidyar when he founded Internet auction house eBay to auction off his wife's collection of Pez dispensers. With 27 percent ownership of eBay [77] and a net worth in the billions, Chairman Omidyar also prides himself on the fact that eBay is one of the few Internet pure plays that has been consistently profitable since its inception. EBay boasts some 8,000 categories of merchandise and more than 22 million registered users. It has a staggering Internet auction transaction market share (59 percent in 2000 [99]) despite competition from other Internet powerhouses Yahoo! and Amazon. Why has the auction model been so successful for eBay?

The essential eBay model is this: A seller posts a description and photograph of the item for sale along with a minimum bid and end-of-auction date and time on the Web site and pays a listing fee to eBay. Buyers bid on the item, and when time is up, the highest bidder purchases the item. The seller receives the payment and ships the item, and eBay receives a percentage of the sales price. The model's beauty is in its simplicity: eBay purchases no inventory, keeps no inventory, and pays no shipping. It simply acts as a broker. There are no fulfillment workers to hire and no Christmas deadlines to meet. In 2000 eBay earned $48.3 million on $431.4 million in sales, which represents a one-year net income growth of 347.2 percent [77]. eBay is truly one of the blockbuster successes of Internet business.

Not all Internet auctions are successful, however. B2C auction site Firstauction.com was founded to cater specifically to women. It specialized in dinnerware, jewelry, beauty supplies, women's apparel, and more. It unfortunately had to close its doors in May 2001, a sign that not every Internet auction will enjoy the success of eBay. It takes a tremendous marketing budget to attract enough buyers and sellers to an auction site in order to make it work. With eBay, having first-mover advantage was truly an advantage, as it was able to establish its name and get the concept out quickly and effectively. Even venerable Internet companies like Yahoo! and Amazon have not been able to compete with eBay on the auction turf. The rippling effect of eBay into society at large can be witnessed in eBay University, a traveling seminar program that teaches participants how to be more effective as buyers and sellers. Fervor at these seminars reaches a religious pitch, as many eBay loyalists claim that the auction site transformed their lives by allowing them to quit their jobs, sell items on eBay full time, and "find a purpose in life." [100]

There have been other business plans based on the auction model. B2B corporate liquidation firm DoveBid, whose history goes back to the Depression years, established an online arm for auctioning off corporate assets. Most of its several hundred auctions per year are Webcast live, which means they are broadcast over the Internet at the same time it is happening. This lowers the cost of bidding for most participants. Although in 1999 DoveBid lost $4 million on sales of $12 million due to investments in technology, marketing, and acquisitions, the company was on track to be profitable by the end of 2001 [44].

There are a number of business plans that are loosely based on the *reverse auction* model, in which sellers do the bidding. One of the better known examples is Priceline. With Priceline, the consumers name the price they are willing to pay for an item. In response, prospective sellers decide whether to accept that price; that is, to offer their wares at the price offered by the buyer. In general, if the price is met, the consumer is obligated to buy. It has worked well for items like airline tickets and hotel rooms, which are "perishable" and for which companies are willing to sell at a lower price when the sale date approaches the perish date. Priceline has had its share of trying times. It planned a reverse auction for gasoline and groceries, which it had to bow out of, due to financial difficulties. But as of 2000, it was selling 50,000 airline tickets and booking 10,000 hotel rooms per week, which brought in annual revenues of hundreds of millions of dollars [112]. The Priceline plan is not a strict reverse auction in that the sellers are not engaged in a competitive bidding process. Other plans loosely based on the reverse auction model include Ybag.com and MyGeek.com. These are both one buyer-multiple seller models, where the buyer submits a request, multiple sellers respond with a bid, and the buyer can accept the lowest bid.

The lesson to be learned from the auction model is that not all auctions can achieve the stunning success of eBay. It is a model seemingly custom made for the Internet, but execution seems to be key. Not all products are suitable for auction sale. Not everyone wants to bid or haggle on the price of groceries, for example. Also, eBay's success seems to have led to some customer dissatisfaction. According to a survey, because the number of items sold on eBay has grown tremendously, the average price of antiques and collectibles sold on eBay has fallen by 40 percent between the first five months of 2000 and the first five months of 2001. Moreover, because more people are scouring flea markets and garage sales for second-hand items to be sold on eBay, the prices at these sources have risen, squeezing the profit margin of dealers on eBay [178]. Nevertheless, eBay's success seems to depend a lot on smart branding and CEO Meg Whitman's ability to keep the site user-friendly with a reputation for being a fun and safe place to do business. eBay's execution is one few others seem to have matched.

....

WHY EBAY HAS SUCCEEDED WITH THE AUCTION MODEL

- Brilliant idea
- First-mover advantage (it worked in this case)
- Smart branding
- No inventory
- No fulfillment costs
- No shipping costs

The Portal Model

In 1998 many dot-coms wanted to be a *portal*. The formula seemed simple at the time: build a "gateway" site that users would log on to when they went online, sell advertising on the site based on the number of visitors, and watch the profits flow. The portal would attract users by offering at a single site a search engine, email, chat rooms, real-time news and stock updates, weather, virtual malls, and best of all, personalization. Generalized portals would be to the Internet what networks are to television and major brands to consumer products. In addition, there would be niche portals, targeted at groups based on ethnicity, sexual orientation, or interests such as health, sports, and pets.

Yahoo! was the first site to morph from a search engine to a generalized portal in 1997, followed closely by Altavista, Excite, Infoseek, and Lycos, all proclaiming to be a portal. In those early heady days of the dot-com frenzy, many of these portals succeeded initially because they were seen by investors as a sure thing and because many of their advertisers were other, well-funded dot-coms cutting multimillion dollar placement deals with them. As was the case with eBay and auctions, first-mover status seemed to work well for Yahoo!. In addition, its simple site design and smart moves like outsourcing its search engine to free up resources for features like chat rooms and clubs all contributed to its success. In the end, between January 1999 and January 2001, Yahoo!'s unique visitor count rose 79 percent, while others had slow or negative growth and traffic a fraction of Yahoo!'s. The end of the dot-com frenzy had also brought about a drying up of advertising revenues. The nail in the coffin for the portal craze was hammered in February 2001 when owner Disney announced portal Go.com would cease to exist [119].

The news got even grimmer when the following month Yahoo! announced that for the first quarter of 2001 revenues would fall to $170 million, or $60 million less than the company had predicted. Also, rather than bring in the $30 million in earnings expected by Wall Street, the company announced it would break even. The shortfall was attributed to declining advertising revenues from both dot-coms and traditional advertisers [158]. Yahoo!'s woes reflect not only a general decline in advertising revenues online, but an overall decline in advertising revenues in all media due to the slowing American economy. More to the point, however, is that many advertisers are beginning to doubt the efficacy of all online advertising, with click-through rates on banner ads of one to two percent or lower.

The problem is, without advertising revenues, portals are dead. They are very expensive to build, with prices ranging from $500,000 to several hundred million dollars, according to Giga Information Group [2]. They are costly to maintain because real-time news, stock quotes, and weather, as well as a useful search engine, all require constant updating. On the back end, the hardware infrastructure to handle millions of hits a day without crashing (Yahoo! reported one billion page views per day worldwide in March 2001 [158]) is also very costly. Upkeep and sales require a significant staff (Yahoo! had over 3,000 employees in 2000, up 63.6 percent from the year before, according to Hoover-sonline.com). Finally, marketing expenses can skyrocket in trying to attract users to the portal, and visitors are unlikely to return time and time again without some compelling reason. To cover these expenses, there was a time when portals could command tens of millions of dollars in a single placement deal (for $18.5 million CDNow became Lycos's exclusive music retailer in 1998 [119], and for $89 million Drkoop.com got placement on AOL's portal and access to its 20 million customers [171]), but these deals are now few and far between.

There are a couple of bright spots in the portal story, however. One is the morphing of a portal into what is called an *enterprise portal*. This is a portal designed specifically for a company, which all employees log on to before clicking into its offerings. These offerings might include human resources documents like vacation forms and employee directories, conference room reservation forms, calendars of events, videos of CEO speeches, newsletters, databases, and sales force tools. Although investment in an enterprise portal can be hefty—say, several hundred thousand dollars to start—if a company has tens or hundreds of thousands of employees, the savings on paper and legwork can be quite substantial. IBM's portal for its 325,000 employees saves an estimated $500 million a year through paper conservation and online purchasing [159].

Related to the enterprise portal is a *vortal*. A vortal is a portal designed to meet the disparate needs of a specific industry. An effective vortal contains relevant industry news, the latest technologies, newsgroups, a means for buying and selling industry-related products, etc. Examples of vortals include Plasticsnet.com and Ventro.com.

. . . .

WHY THE PORTAL MODEL IS HARD TO SUSTAIN

1. Building a portal is expensive.

2. Maintaining a portal is expensive.

3. Attracting users to a portal is expensive.

4. Getting users to return to a portal time and time again is difficult.

5. Advertising revenues are drying up.

The second bright spot is the morphing of portals into *affinity portals*. Affinity portals started as niche portals catering to special interest groups based on ethnicity, sexual orientation, or hobbies, but it was too expensive to market to prospective users, difficult to get them to keep coming back, and increasingly hard to secure advertising revenues. Subsequently, because it was too expensive to get users to come to portals, the portals began going out to the affinity groups. Portals were being built for groups already in place like labor unions and college alumni associations. At the AFL-CIO site built by iBelong, there are different sites for individual labor unions like the Teamsters and Communication Workers of America. The portal offers news, email, sports news, financial information, and shopping for products made by unionized manufacturers, much of it tailored to the specific individual labor unions it serves. Although the site receives some revenues from advertising, rather than being viewed as a revenue source, the portal is seen by the AFL-CIO as an effective means to communicate among and unify its members [156]. Thus, while the generalized portal of the Yahoo! genre may have already seen its best days, the portal as an Internet business model has found ways to serve a purpose and thrive.

The Content Model

There is probably no other Internet business model that has caused more CEOs to tear their hair out than the *content model*. The content model is simple: Offer top-notch content on a Web site in the form of news, articles, or entertainment, attract users, and make money by either charging users for the right to view the content (*subscription model*) or by attracting large numbers of viewers with free content and charging for advertising on the site (*advertising model*). In theory, the content model was supposed to work like a print publication but even better because there wouldn't be the cost of paper, printing, mailing, and distribution onto magazine racks. Instead, the bulk of expenses could go into paying first-rate content producers and most of the revenues would be gravy. Right?

Wrong. First, most dot-com content providers underestimated the cost of launching such a business model. Although there are no costs of printing and physical distribution, the technology costs to get a site up and running are high, and marketing costs to attract and build a loyal following are astronomical. The cost of marketing is so high because competition is fierce. Not anyone can produce a print magazine and distribute it nationwide, but just about anyone can produce a Web site and fill it with content. A person surfing the Web can visit far more sites than a person walking into a bookstore can view magazines on the rack. Moreover, with a Web site running 24/7, content is expected to change much more rapidly than with a weekly or monthly print publication. With many online publications, content changes daily, if not hourly. Thus, editorial costs also skyrocket relative to those for print publications.

Second, it is very hard to get users to pay for content online. The culture of the Web has been to give things away things free, and with so many sites offering free content, very few have been able to charge for content successfully. Two notable exceptions are *The Wall Street Journal* and *Consumer Reports*. Both offer first-rate content on a subscription basis, for which users happily pay. *The Wall Street Journal* offers an annual online subscription for $59 and an annual print subscription for $175. Presumably, since most *WSJ* subscriptions are paid for by one's company or are a business expense, it is easy to see how the venerable *WSJ* continues to be a subscription success, both offline and online. *Consumer Reports* charges $3.95 per month or $24 for an annual subscription to its online reports. In this case, the user is probably saving money well upwards of $3.95 or $24 in the purchases she is investigating in *Consumer Reports* (especially if the purchase is a major one such as an automobile), so the investment is worthwhile many times over.

Other content sites that have tried to be profitable off of subscriptions include the well-known Thestreet.com. When Thestreet.com launched in 1996, it was using the "give-away-something-for-free-charge-for-more" model used by well-known companies like Hooversonline.com discussed in Chapter 6. Four years later, Thestreet.com, well-respected in financial journalism, declared that it would move its star columnists to a separate site and charge more for subscription. Currently, it offers some financial news free on its home page, but charges for a subscription to its other sites, Realmoney.com ($19.95 per month or $199.95 per year) and Thestreetpros.com ($40.00 per month or $400.00 per year). Thestreet.com has seen its share of ups and downs but barely manages to survive in the face of other sites offering financial coverage free, including CBS's MarketWatch and The Motley Fool(fool.com). Which will endure remains to be seen.

Third, advertisers are becoming increasingly skeptical of the online medium, especially with click-through rates for banner ads languishing in the one to two percent range, if not lower. Similar to the portal model, it was thought that advertisements could pay for the launching and maintenance of a content site and then some. Unfortunately, this has not always been the case. Content site Channel A, catering to Asian-Americans, underwent several changes in business plans, all without success. It began as a typical content site, believing that its compelling content would attract a desirable demographic of users, namely wealthy, educated, and wired Asian-Americans. It planned to be profitable on advertising revenue. When advertising failed, it morphed into a site for an audience of "Asia watchers," or non-Asians interested in Asia. Its third incarnation revolved around the theme of "Modern Asian Living," which delved into Internet commerce, selling Asian-themed goods like rock gardens and origami sets. When all of these efforts failed, it closed its doors in July of 1998 [144]. Channel A was short-lived, but a testimony to the shortcomings of the advertising content model.

Yes, the content model is still in the experimental stage, as are many of the Internet business models. Profitable content models with subscription-based revenues are very difficult to sustain. Online advertising revenues are down, due to skepticism and the economy, which places into question the viability of funding a site based on the banner ads it can sell. Rethinking the content model, it seems that even with compelling content, only the special few are able to remain profitable either through subscriptions or advertising. `Salon.com` is a content site with critical and popular kudos that offers itself free, but is still struggling to remain alive. Internet business remains an expensive venture through launching and maintenance. Do not underestimate the cost of building and maintaining a site, whether it be for portals or content. The content model is an attractive but tough business to be in. Take heed.

. . . .

WHY THE CONTENT MODEL HAS FAILED WITH FEW EXCEPTIONS

1. Launching a content site is expensive.

   - Technology costs for a site are expensive.
   - Marketing costs for a site are expensive.
   - Providing fresh content for a 24/7 site is expensive.

2. It is hard to get users to pay for content.

3. Getting users to return to a content site time and time again is difficult.

4. Advertising revenues are drying up.

The B2B Exchange Model

Shortly following the B2C (business-to-consumer) dot-com explosion and sudden death in 1999 came the hype about B2B (business-to-business) exchanges. If B2C retailing took a nose dive in the IPO market and elsewhere, B2B would surely reign. B2B revenue projections were estimated to dwarf those of B2C revenues. B2B was the talk of the town. In the first half of 2000, venture capitalists invested $3.5 billion in 142 B2B firms. By the end of the year, enthusiasm had waned, leading to the total dot-com industry plunge in 2001 [183]. The B2B model was in dire need of rethinking.

What was the B2B model? Essentially, it was this: That through the Internet, many buyers and many sellers in an industry could come together and arrive at a market agreed-upon price that would benefit both sides. The transactions would be frictionless. Buyers would benefit because they could easily comparison shop among the many sellers as well as aggregate for volume discounts. Sellers would benefit thanks to the expanded marketplace, giving them an entrée to prospective buyers never before possible. Despite this optimistic outlook, the successful B2B exchange model was the exception rather than the rule. Many promising startup exchanges in industries that were ostensibly in need of such a market mechanism folded. Once again, the Internet appeared to promise more than it could deliver. What went wrong?

The biggest resistance to B2B exchanges resulted from resistance to change. Many buyers, after decades of relationships with suppliers, had negotiated favorable terms through long-term contracts that they were unwilling to relinquish. Favorable terms aside, many buyers did not want to end their personal relationships with suppliers, many of whom they had done business with over a lunch and a handshake. Many people are simply loathe to change their long-standing way of doing business and were certainly not going to switch to a new system which in many cases required special software and specially trained personnel.

From the suppliers' side, there were also very few who were willing to give up their personal relationships and terms with buyers in order to enter the exchange fray, bidding against many other suppliers for a single job. Furthermore, in order to participate in such an exchange, suppliers often had to give up three to five percent of the purchase price, whittling down the already narrow profit margins. Thus, many suppliers dug in their heels, and reconsidered joining an exchange just when many of their competitors had entered the ring.

Other problems that led to reluctance to join on the part of buyers and sellers had to do with limitations on the hardware and software necessary to enter such an exchange. The computer-related tools with which one could participate were often rudimentary, leading many prospective buyers and sellers to stick with their fax and telephone orders. Moreover, participating often required a complete retooling of hardware and software on the part of buyers and sellers in order for them to be compatible with the system in place. This also led to barriers to participation.

One example to illustrate the difficulty of establishing a B2B marketplace arises from the hotel industry. Traditionally, hotels work with a bevy of local suppliers to furnish their needs, from bedsheets to French fries. Deals and contracts are often sealed with a handshake over a meal, and hotel buyers are left to make numerous telephone calls and transmit numerous faxes to get an order delivered in the right quantity at a specific date and time. Computer expertise was appallingly lacking among both hotel buyers and suppliers, which is why they resorted to the telephone and fax already in place. B2B market enthusiasts like Zoho Corp., Avendra, and PurchasePro rushed in to make the entire hotel purchasing process more efficient, theoretically saving buyers billions of dollars annually.

Unfortunately, theory did not mesh with reality. What these B2B marketplaces faced were hotels and suppliers who refused to change with the times, often because they saw no overriding benefit to joining an exchange. In many cases, a buyer would have to surrender a long-standing relationship with a supplier and its accompanying favorable terms in order to participate in an exchange. Few were willing to yield such circumstances that had taken years to establish. In addition, both buyers and suppliers were woefully inadequate when it came to the hardware and software infrastructure and Internet connections necessary to participate. "We literally had to teach people to use a PC," says Chris Hjelm, president and CEO of Zoho. "We found extremely slow Internet connections or none at all—or PCs that some people would refer to as boat anchors." [14]

WHY B2B EXCHANGES HAVE NOT FULFILLED THEIR PROMISE

1. Buyers and suppliers are bound to tradition.

   - Relationships are built over decades and are hard to relinquish.
   - Many deals are still sealed with lunches and handshakes.
   - To join an exchange often means giving up the time-honored discounts.

2. Buyers and suppliers are not equipped with the proper hardware, software, and Internet connections for exchanges.

3. Early exchanges offered only rudimentary tools.

4. Many suppliers custom manufacture their products for buyers, for which exchanges are of little use.

5. Few suppliers wanted to surrender their long-standing contracts to enter into a bidding competition with other suppliers.

6. Few suppliers were willing to pay a percentage of sales to the B2B exchange middle person.

Nevertheless, B2B exchanges are making strides to improve their services and attract more participants. They are upgrading their tools so that buyers can select suppliers based not only on price, but on quality, delivery, and other features. Integration of different hardware and software configurations from different buyers and suppliers is becoming easier with the adoption of near-industry standards like XML, fast becoming the *lingua franca* of the B2B industry (see Chapter 5, "Languages of the Internet," for more detail). More suppliers are beginning to offer "direct" goods, or the parts necessary for manufacturing the end product, rather than simply offering "indirect" goods like office supplies. There are other hurdles still to overcome, like the fact that many suppliers offer customized products for their buyers, for which B2B marketplaces are of little use [157].

It looks like B2B exchanges have a future in the Internet business landscape, but a shakeout will occur before the survivors can remain confident in their mission. Eventually, B2B transactions will be a hybrid of those occurring over B2B exchanges and those occurring the old-fashioned way, with handshakes and golf games and telephone calls and faxes. But the former is steadily taking over the latter. Companies large and small alike will have to come to terms that at least part of their business will be done over the Internet, but perhaps not as rapidly as once projected. It may take another generation of buyers and suppliers to turn over before B2B exchanges become the predominant way of doing business. As of now, they're still perceived as ahead of their time.

Bricks and Clicks

Bricks and clicks, also known as *click and mortar*, refers to the Internet business model that combines both offline and online selling. It usually refers to the model adopted by once pure brick and mortar retailers like Sears, Kmart, and Barnes and Noble, who have added online channels for selling their goods. (Less frequently is the bricks and clicks model established in the other direction, as a dot-com first, then adding brick and mortar stores, though this, too, is changing.) Most brick and mortar retailers added an online arm in response to the pure play Internet retailers who were muscling in on their territory in the late 1990s. They also did not want to appear as dinosaurs in the new, fast-moving Information Age.

It wasn't easy for traditional retailers to begin selling online, and many of their sites are still in an experimental and growing stage. In the first place, launching and marketing a major Internet commerce site costs at minimum an estimated $25 million to $50 million, according to Mary Modahl, vice president of research at Forrester Research [153], a major undertaking for a company of any size. Barnes and Noble reportedly spent more than $100 million on its online answer to Amazon. Sears planned to spend between $75 million and $100 million on `Sears.com` in 2000 alone [149]. Secondly, it was initially difficult to integrate an online business with an offline business, oftentimes creating two separate and unrelated entities within the same company. This was the case with `Barnesandnoble.com`, which was established as a dot-com separate from the nationwide chain of bookstores, with little cross-selling and integration between the two [132]. In another example, Sears sells gift certificate cards through `Sears.com`, but the cards cannot be used for online purchases (though Sears is working on this) [149].

Yet bricks and clicks retailers remain optimistic. JCPenney.com, treated as a division of J.C. Penney's $4 billion catalog unit, projects sales of $1 billion by 2002, and expects to be profitable by that year. This may be possible since the company is banking on its catalog unit infrastructure, including customer service, to handle much of the online sales. Kmart's Bluelight.com, despite the devastating experiences of stock prices of other public dot-coms, expects a successful IPO when it is spun off from its parent company [149]. Kmart is working hard to integrate online sales with its brick and mortar stores. Not only is it accepting returns from online sales at its 2,300 stores, customers can order items in-store through Internet kiosks if something they want is not in stock. Moreover, Bluelight.com tracks purchasing patterns and offers personalized discounts both offline and online. [164]

Bricks and clicks retailers have a reason to be optimistic. A report by Giga Information Group predicts that multichannel retailers, which currently command only one-third of the total online retail market, will increase their share to two-thirds, or $92 billion by

2002. Online consumer sales as a whole are expected to mushroom to $152 billion in 2002 and $233 billion in 2004. Thus, grabbing a bigger share of an expanding pie is what click and mortar retailers hope to do in the coming years. Even so, the percentage of online sales to total consumer spending was still a miniscule 0.4 percent in 1999 and is expected to grow to only three percent in 2004 [47]. As a chilling contrast, for pure play retailers, it is predicted by Forrester Research that almost all pure Internet retailing will be dead by 2002 [104].

Originally, companies launched an online retailing arm thinking that this would reduce the cost of doing business. However, Saks Fifth Avenue recently announced that, instead of making a separate business unit out of Saks.com, it will roll Saks.com into its offline business. The logic for doing this is to take advantage of its offline logistical resources already in place. Kmart also announced a similar plan for its online and offline operations. The Gartner Group [46] believes that offline and online consolidation is an important trend in retailing.

LESSONS FROM THE FIRST WAVE OF BRICKS AND CLICKS

1. Establishing a major Internet commerce Web site for a brick and mortar retailer is expensive.

- At minimum, it costs $25 million to $50 million to launch and market a major site.
- Sears planned to spend between $75 million and $100 million on its site, Sears.com, in 2000 alone.

2. The offline and online shopping experiences should be seamless for the customer.

- Customers should be able to return merchandise through stores and via mail no matter where they purchased the item.
- Gift certificates should be valid both in stores and online.
- Customers should be able to do research on an item online and walk into a store and purchase it quickly and efficiently.
- Special loyalty offers (like buy-seven-get-one-free) should integrate both offline and online purchases for each customer.

Integration of offline and online sales is the ideal scenario: One seamless, integrated shopping experience, no matter which channel—brick and mortar store, telephone, fax, or online—is used by the customer. Easier said than done, at least one company has managed to come close to the ideal. Lids sells 10 million hats a year through its 370 retail stores in 42 states and through its online operation, Lids.com. Every purchase by a customer, whether offline or online, is tracked and recorded so customers can take easy advantage of the buy-seven-hats-get-one-free offer (called the Headfirst loyalty program). Gift certificates and coupons are good at both retail stores and on the Web site. Merchandise can be returned at stores or through the mail, no matter how or where it was purchased, which seems to be increasingly standard for all bricks and clicks operations. Stores can order hats that aren't in stock and can either hold them for customers to pick up or can have them shipped from the warehouse to customers. Lids' 50,000-square-foot warehouse doesn't distinguish between its retail outlets and individual online customers. An order is an order, and it fulfills them efficiently with a near-zero error rate [153]. In other words, Lids has managed to provide the customer with a seamless multichannel shopping experience so that the customer barely distinguishes between an offline and an online purchase. This is the service to which all bricks and clicks should aspire.

FUTURE TRENDS AND IMPLICATIONS. . . . .

In this chapter we reviewed the fundamental Internet business models and pointed out companies with business plans that have succeeded for each model, and those with plans that have failed. There are a few overarching lessons to be learned, lessons that hint at the future of Internet business and the viability of making these Internet business models and others yet to be developed, work. The first is that Internet business is still in a nascent stage, not even a decade old, and there are still many kinks to be worked out. The Industrial Revolution is well over a century old, and it took many decades before companies got the factory model right, especially with regard to working conditions. We shouldn't be too hasty in declaring the dot-com dead. It's just that in the initial years of Internet business, most of those who built Internet business—the entrepreneurs and the venture capitalists—were overzealous in their quest for fast wealth, which the IPO markets fed, at least in the beginning. There was a brand new medium, a brand new vocabulary consisting of words like hits and eyeballs, and a brand new optimism over how the Internet could change the fundamental nature of business. It has and it will, only it will take a little longer than initially expected because people's attitudes do not often change as rapidly as technological advances.

This brings us to our second lesson, which is that there is strong inertia to embracing change in the way people do business. B2B auctions and B2B exchanges are foundering because people are reluctant to relinquish person-to-person relationships in favor of a system that relies on the Internet, no matter how logical and efficient it may seem. There is a cost to adopting something new, a cost in time and effort to learn and reorganize, and a cost in equipment, which many are unwilling to pay, especially if the new system is untested and it is doubtful whether any benefits at all will be reaped. Business is still on the cusp between the Industrial Age and the Information Age. Most people currently in business grew up during the Industrial Age and are accustomed to doing things the traditional way. It may take a generation before those who came of age during the Information Age and who are completely comfortable with computers and the Internet—in fact who know little about doing things without them—are making decisions about how the Internet is used in business. Until then, Internet business models will continue to be perfected and slowly adopted as people's attitudes and the infrastructure change over time.

Third, advertising revenue has turned out to be much less than expected. The advertising model was in some cases initially sustainable because dot-coms had been injected with cash and were marketing themselves like crazy to establish a brand. When the cash dried up, so did the advertising revenue, and so did many of the portals and content sites that depended on it. Then people began to doubt the efficacy of online advertising as a whole, which further reduced the amount of advertising. Yahoo! was one of the few that could exist on advertising revenues, but even this success story is experiencing its share of woes. Due to the slowing American economy, advertising revenues in all media are declining and the Web is sure to be hit hard. Part of the reason is that click-through rates are so dismal, but perhaps they are an unfair gauge of online advertising. After all, if there were an equivalent of a click-through rate for print, radio, or television advertising, wouldn't rates be just as low?

The fourth lesson is that major Internet business is expensive. It was initially believed that a commerce site would be less expensive to run than a physical store because one could save on rent and labor. It was also believed that a content site would be less expensive than a print publication. People thought that because you didn't have to deal as much with the physical world there would be enormous cost savings. Unfortunately, this isn't true, and it's unlikely that the costs will decrease in the future. Nevertheless, despite the high cost, companies are savings billions of dollars by adopting Internet business. We saw that IBM's enterprise portal saves the company $500 million a year. Carrier Corporation has saved $100 million by uniting its retailers, dealers, and installers using the Web. Bricks and clicks with multichannel selling encourage their customers to use email or the Web rather than the telephone or fax because to do so can save many dollars per transaction. For some things, nothing will replace the human touch, but someday, much of business will be done over the Internet. It's just a matter of time.

9   Security and Internet Business

In this chapter ...

TRUST EVERYONE, BUT BRAND YOUR CATTLE ·······································

Hallie Stillwell, a famous West Texas Rancher, once said: "Trust everyone, but brand your cattle." In the heyday of West Texas ranching, you protected your most valuable asset—cattle—by branding them. In the era of the Internet, information is often a company's most valuable asset. In this chapter we talk about how to brand information. Every day there is a new headline related to computer security. If it is not about some computer virus infecting an email system it is about credit card numbers in a database being stolen, or a Web site like Yahoo! or Buy.com forced to close because of a flood of traffic launched against them. Clearly, the secure exchange of information over the Internet and the secure storage of confidential data are crucial for Internet business to prosper. This is becoming more true as companies outsource their software needs to application service providers (ASPs) and consumers store more and more data online. Here are some sobering statistics. The following facts are from the CSI (Computer Survey Institute) report conducted with the help of the San Francisco FBI, released March 12, 2001. There were 538 U.S. corporations responding to the survey.

- Eighty-five percent reported computer security breaches within the past 12 months.

- Of the companies reporting a breach, 186 were able to quantify the loss. The total was approximately $377 million.

- Seventy percent of the respondents reported their Internet connection as a frequent point of attack.

The research firm Computer Economics has estimated that virus related costs in the year 2001 through August exceed $10 billion [78]. Raphael Gray, a Welsh teenager, cracked numerous computer networks and posted 23,000 credit card numbers (including Bill Gates's) on a Web site. Gray then took his prank one step further and used Gates's credit card to send the Microsoft magnate a case of Viagra. In total, Gray's hacking led to $4 million in fraudulent credit card charges and caused two companies to close. Perhaps most sobering is a forecast from the Gartner Group [177] that U.S. enterprises will increase their spending on information security from the current level of 0.4 percent of revenues to four percent by the year 2011. This is a tenfold increase over the decade.

Computer security is a vast subject and there are many kinds of malicious acts. One of the most common is to place an executable file (i.e., program) onto the victim's computer. Three types of malicious programs are a *worm*, a *virus*, and a *trojan horse*. A worm is an independent program that makes copies of itself in different computers throughout a network. It is often a malicious application that damages or destroys files. According to the Microsoft Security Web site, on July 19, 2001, the Code Red worm infected 250,000 servers in nine hours. Once the worm infected a system, it scanned other vulnerable systems and then infected them. The uncontrolled growth in scanning severely affected a number of installations.

Unlike a worm, a virus is not an independent program that distributes itself. A virus is code attached to an existing program. When the infected program is executed, the virus code is activated and may attach itself (infect) other executable files on the hard disk network. A classic example of a virus is the Melissa virus unleashed in March, 1999. The Melissa virus was a macro (a sequence of commands, menu selections, and keystrokes) that was recorded within a Microsoft Word document. The document was sent as an email attachment with a subject heading that read, "Important message from Username," where Username was the name of the person from whose computer the email was sent. When the document was opened, the virus was activated and sent a copy of the attachment to everyone listed in the Microsoft Outlook address book on the host computer. Since the receiver would usually open an attachment sent by someone he knew, the virus spread like wildfire and shut down email servers around the world.

A trojan horse is a program that appears to perform one task but actually performs another (usually malicious) task. Thus, a trojan horse is similar to a virus, since it is attached to another program. However, a trojan horse does not necessarily replicate or attach itself to other programs on the computer. Nevertheless, it can do considerable damage, such as erase all of the files on the hard drive. It is becoming common practice to refer to all three parasites as a computer virus.

. . . .

ORGANIZED CRIME

Extortion has always been an important source of revenue for organized crime in the brick and mortar world. Not to be left out of the Internet revolution, organized crime is getting into Internet business. Organized crime rings in the former Soviet Union are recruiting top notch computer hackers to work for them. Many of these hackers are recruited by former KGB members. The objective is to break into Internet commerce sites, steal credit card numbers (or other valuable information), and threaten to release the information unless the Internet commerce company pays off the syndicate. The FBI estimates that more than 40 companies in 20 states are targets of Eastern European organized crime outfits, and that more than one million credit card numbers have been stolen. See [107].

Other examples of malicious acts are *denial-of-service attacks* and *break-ins*. In a denial-of-service attack the perpetrator floods a server with requests for authentication. The requests have false return addresses, which the server cannot find. The server then gets "hung" waiting for responses from the false addresses. A break-in is a security breach. One kind is a spoofing attack in which the perpetrator gains access to a system by sending packets with the IP addresses of trusted machines. Hackers routinely break into systems and steal confidential information. Once they have the confidential information they sometimes blackmail the owner of the information.

The primary focus of this chapter is the secure exchange and protection of confidential information using the Internet. This information might be email, a credit card number used to make a purchase, or a file exchange between business partners. In the next section, "Security Basics," we introduce the reader to the vernacular used in cryptography. We also discuss some broad issues related to security and protecting computer systems. In the section, "Tradition: Single Key Encryption," we present some of the most common methods for encrypting messages. This encryption is based upon a key which also must be used to decrypt the message. This means that somehow two parties must exchange this key. For thousands of years the only secure way to do this was manually. Unfortunately, for two parties connected only by a network, this does not work since there is no secure way to exchange the key. It was not until relatively recently that encryption systems were developed that did not require the exchange of a private key. These new systems, which are fundamental to Internet business, are the topic of the section, "Innovation: Public and Private Key Encryption."

Although a public and private key system allows two parties to exchange information securely, an important problem remains—namely, verification. If you receive a message, how do you verify that it really came from the party you think it came from? This is the topic of the section "Trust and Digital Signatures." Many people wonder if it is safe to send a credit card number out over the Internet. In the section, "Putting It All Together: Secure Socket Layers," we show how the technologies developed in the previous two sections are combined to provide for a very secure exchange of information using a browser such as Netscape Navigator or Internet Explorer. Throughout the book we talk about LANs and protecting computers in a LAN. We discuss how this is done in the section, "Firewalls and Proxy Servers." The ability to exchange information securely over the Internet is not the only security challenge in Internet business today. Another issue is the concern users have over the information companies are collecting about them. This is the topic of the section on "Privacy." We conclude the chapter with "Future Trends and Implications."

Before going further into the details of security, we leave the reader with an important analogy. Protecting a company network connected to the Internet from a break-in is like protecting a car from a car thief. With a car you can take reasonable measures such as locking your door, installing an alarm system, or buying The Club to protect yourself from the average-to-good car thief. However, if a great car thief really wants your car, you may as well kiss it goodbye. The same holds true for the Internet: There is little you can do to protect yourself from a great hacker who wants to get into your system.

PASSWORD BASICS ....

It is much easier to break into a computer system using nontechnical rather than technical means. Perhaps the easiest and most common way is to steal passwords using nontechnical means. A simple and common technique is to put a "plant" in a janitorial crew. This person copies passwords people write down on post-it notes next to their computers on their desks. Another common technique is for a thief, posing as a person from the company's information technology group, to call individuals within the company and ask them to verify their password. People will often give their password up without thinking. Also, people often use easily determined passwords like the name of a spouse or children. Here are some tips on password safety.

1. Don't keep the password that comes with your system.

2. Don't ever let anyone use your password.

3. Don't send your password out over email. Assume that your email is being intercepted.

4. Don't write your password down—especially next to your computer or on your desk.

5. Change your password frequently. Some systems require this.

6. Don't use passwords that are proper names or fictional characters, e.g., Bill, Mary, or Hamlet.

7. Don't use the name of a spouse, child, or pet.

8. Pick a mix of alphabetic (upper and lower case) and numeric characters.

9. Don't use the same password for multiple accounts.

10. Don't store the password on your computer unencrypted.

If you keep multiple passwords, pick odd mixes of alphabetic and numeric characters and don't write them down, how do you remember them? This is a nontrivial problem. First, think of a set of words that has some meaning to you, but to no one else. The longer the better. An example would be the maiden names of your mother, grandmother, and great-grandmother. This constitutes your *passphrase*, which is another word for long password. Next, put all of your passwords into a text file and secure this file using encryption methods described in the next section. Then protect the encrypted file with your passphrase. In other words, a passphrase, known only to you and written down nowhere, is used to secure your encrypted passwords.

TRADITION: SINGLE KEY ENCRYPTION . . . .

Before the information age, much of the interest in security was focused on *cryptography*, the study of encryption and decryption. This interest was motivated primarily by military security. Indeed, after the battle of Pearl Harbor in 1941 the United States Navy was in a very weak position. It did not know where the Japanese would strike next. Successfully cracking the Japanese code was critical to the United States' winning the battle of Midway in 1942. But more on this later.

In this section we introduce a few basic cryptography concepts. First, cryptography is the mathematics of codes and code breaking. The basic process is outlined in Figure 9–1. Assume Thelma wants to send a message to Louise. The original message is referred to as plaintext. An encryption algorithm or cipher is used to convert the plaintext into ciphertext. Most ciphers make use of a key. The key is used in conjunction with the cipher to produce the ciphertext. Different keys applied to the same cipher will produce different ciphertext. In this section we work with single key ciphers. Single keys are also called secret keys or symmetric keys. The term secret key is used because this key should be known to only the two parties (e.g., Thelma and Louise) exchanging the information. The term symmetric key is used because the same key is used for both encryption and decryption.

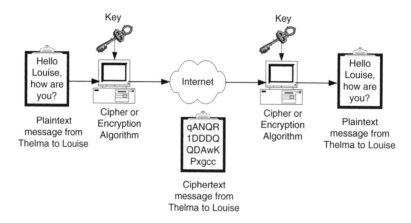

Figure 9–1 *A simple example of single key encryption.*

Two of the most common ciphers are *substitution* and *transposition*. A substitution cipher works by replacing each bit or character with a substitute bit or character. One of the earliest substitution ciphers is the Caesar cipher allegedly due to Julius Caesar. Supposedly, Caesar would encode a message by substituting a letter with the letter three places to the right in the alphabet. This substitution is illustrated in Table 9–1. In this example, the key for the Caesar cipher is the information to substitute a letter with one three places to the right.

Table 9–1 The Caesar Substitution

A	→	D
B	→	E
C	→	F
D	→	G
⋮	⋮	⋮

As an example of the Caesar shift, consider the plaintext `security is crucial`. Ignoring the spaces, the encryption of this plaintext into ciphertext is given below.

```
securityiscrucial → vhfxulwblvfuxfldo
```

Of course, in practice a substitution cipher is more complex than a single substitution. The famous German Enigma machine used during World War II was based on a substitution cipher. This machine looked like a complex typewriter. It had a series of rotors that moved as an operator typed in the message. The moving rotors changed the correspondence between the letters in the plaintext and the ciphertext.

A transposition cipher (also called a permutation cipher) rearranges the order of the bits or characters. A transposition cipher is based on a permutation matrix. A permutation matrix is illustrated in Figure 9–2. This permutation matrix is applied to each consecutive set of five characters in the plaintext. It says to transpose the first and second characters with each other, and transpose the fourth and fifth characters. In this case, the cipher is to do a transposition and the key is the permutation matrix. Again, we illustrate with the plaintext `security is crucial`. For convenience, we mark off each set of five characters with an | symbol.

$$\texttt{secur|ityis|cruci|al} \rightarrow \texttt{escru|tiysi|rcuic|la}$$

$$\pi = \begin{pmatrix} 1 & 2 & 3 & 4 & 5 \\ 2 & 1 & 3 & 5 & 4 \end{pmatrix}$$

Figure 9–2 A five character permutation matrix

There are many symmetric (single) key algorithms. Many of these algorithms use multiple rounds of both substitution and transposition. Symmetric key algorithms include CAST, DES, Triple-DES, and IDEA. The U.S. government has recently adopted the Advanced Encryption Standard (AES) which is based upon a very secure single key algorithm.

A good single key cipher is very secure. On a computer, a key is a string of 0s and 1s, each representing a bit. For someone trying to determine the key, the most effective direct mathematical attack is to enumerate all possible values of the bits in the key. This is not practical for a large key. For example, for a 56-bit key, one would have to enumerate 2^{56} or about 72,057,600,000,000,000 possibilities. We discuss breaking ciphers later in the chapter. Of course, the fundamental flaw with a single key system is that *both parties* must have the key. How do you exchange the key securely? This was a problem the Japanese had during World War II. They had a vast Pacific empire and they physically had to distribute the code books by destroyer and airplane. This was very time consuming. They were in the process of changing the code books throughout the empire when United States cryptographers in Hawaii broke their code. The United States was then able to obtain crucial information, leading to the defeat of the Japanese Navy at Midway.

THE EPIPHANY: PUBLIC KEY ENCRYPTION ....

The fundamental problem with single key encryption is exchanging the key securely. This problem existed for thousands of years. Then one day in 1975 a young mathematician named Whitfield Diffie had an epiphany. Instead of using a single key to both encrypt and decrypt, why not use two keys: one to encrypt and a second to decrypt. This system is called *public key cryptography*. Public key cryptography is based upon a public and private key. Beginning with the pioneering work of Diffie and his two colleagues, Martin Hellman and Ralph Merkle, a number of public key cryptosystems have been developed. One of the most widely used for Internet security is the *RSA algorithm*. It is named after its inventors from MIT: Ron Rivest, Adi Shamir, and Leonard Adleman.

. . . .

WHO WAS FIRST?

Documents released in December 1997 by the British security agency, the General Communication Headquarters (GCHQ), show that Diffie, Hellman, Merkle, Rivest, Shamir, and Adleman were actually not the first to develop public cryptography. A British cryptographer named James Ellis working at GCHQ wrote an internal paper, "The Possibility of Secure Non-Secret Encryption," in which he essentially described the idea of public key encryption. Two of Ellis's colleagues, Clifford Cocks and Malcolm Williamson, developed methods to implement Ellis's idea, which essentially corresponded to the RSA and Diffie-Hellman methods. These were published in internal memos in 1973 and 1974, respectively. The British let these ideas languish and did not take full advantage of their potential. An excellent write-up of this history is in *Crypto* by Steven Levy [103].

The encryption process is illustrated in Figure 9–3. Assume Thelma wants to send Louise an encrypted message. Thelma takes the plaintext and encrypts with Louise's public key. A critical feature of public key cryptography is that the public key is exactly as the name implies—public! Louise makes her public key known to the world (how this is done is described shortly). Anyone can have access to it. After using Louise's public key to encrypt the plaintext into ciphertext, Thelma sends it to Louise over the Internet. Louise then takes the ciphertext and decrypts it back into plaintext using her private key. It is crucial that Louise not share the private key with anyone. Although the public key is used to encrypt the plaintext into ciphertext, *only the private key* can decrypt the ciphertext back into the original plaintext. Indeed, this is the most critical aspect of the system.

Tech Talk

A prime number is an integer greater than 1 that is divisible only by 1 and the number itself. For example, 19 is a prime number, but 20 is not a prime number (it is divisible by prime numbers 2 and 5). There are an infinite number of prime numbers, so we will never run out of them and we can pick them as large as we like.

If plaintext is encrypted using a public key only the private key can decrypt the ciphertext. How is this asymmetry explained? Unfortunately, the mathematics involved here is beyond the scope of this book. However, most of the public key cryptography systems are based upon the branch of mathematics called number theory. In particular, most of the

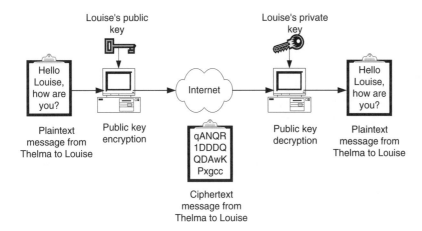

Figure 9–3 Public key cryptography.

public key systems use prime numbers. For example, the RSA algorithm uses a public key that is based upon the integer $n = pq$ where p and q are prime numbers. The private key is based on the prime number factors of n, namely p and q. The security is based on the fact that even if you know n, there is no known efficient way of figuring out p and q. The Diffie-Hellman method uses prime numbers and discrete logarithms in finite fields. Aren't you glad you asked? Just think of a public key as a very large integer.

A very popular piece of software that implements public key cryptography is PGP (Pretty Good Privacy). The PGP software generates a key pair (private and public). The private key is protected by a passphrase known only to the creator of the key pair. The public key is then published. There are several ways to "publish" the public key. One way is to send your public key via email to people you wish to communicate with securely. Although the public key is naturally stored as a binary file since it is an integer(s), public keys are usually transferred as text files. An example public key that has been converted to a text file is given in Figure 9–4. The recipient of this public key would simply add it to his or her key ring. The key ring is a list of public keys. There are also Web servers that list public keys and it is easy to submit a public key to these servers. PGP software also works as an add-on to popular email programs such as Eudora from Qualcomm and Outlook from Microsoft. With the PGP add-on, sending an encrypted email is only a mouse click away.

Public key encryption overcomes the fundamental problem of single key encryption, which is how to exchange the single key. There is a problem with public key encryption, however, and that is it is much slower than single key encryption. Depending upon the ciphers used, single key encryption may be 1,000 times faster than public key encryption. Fortunately, there is an easy solution to this problem. The solution is to use both public and single key encryption. First, a one-time only session (single) key is created. The session key is used to encrypt the plaintext into ciphertext. Next, the session key is encrypted using the public key of the recipient. Typically, the session key is much smaller than the

```
-----BEGIN PGP PUBLIC KEY BLOCK-----
Version: PGP for Personal Privacy 5.5.5

mQGiBDcEGN4RBADUeevule+dRmkrfQC/AvujEXuANMflhiiOaA7JuaHNMuxRkdVf
RuZAUe77u0PG7Cb0mw2D9upKk/1vQgdj3N6USwcg0Wj3p0xN6sa4h7081bauDB27
LIwQsa3b/aCtU0thU5VXVSe0IulKovQQ1WQArXefKVcCOXva7D6YGi1xwQCg/zA7
PqZADSBpUs9aByYGf/cWrHOD/RUp6URHNFP08Ej8mRINbUq3fV3QDHVZOF344k3I
rMbhm2KnAcUgBkDSZN70J5DgYUsjEyX5BT6/c+kvkfFjj6U1BZbU671yGc8Aoa+V
Q9+kRcu1UBjdv3inJQ6YqXAZP0pKL7as9xurgJZqRBsVCA/ySOimD5bC6oKRd9tE
xbpZA/4yW0N6y8Sol9U4pY2+5Ep9C81RfUnp+MndSEzxJNnvRYWW3pcQgyz+3e8I
zVhscXrOd2uqtDERz5KlFMBdFJsz3EbuZB8YhjifFaDdXcIF2P8Yk6K7hAl78g1H
P/pwSP0kmUDG6B89AiQ9H/zvjxPMtWiGqKcIUBs3gBynhI5O+bQqS21wcCBNYXJ0
aW4gPGtpcHHAubWFydGluQGdzb5Yi51Y2hppY2Fnby51ZHU+iQBLBBARAgALBQI3BBje
BAsDAgEACgkQRPZMZmpYZak/rACg5uFzLEZXnYjmOZe9iCox+ycroYQAn1I5fFy1
P5h9H5K2q2woKiZIEqaauQINBDcEGN4QCAD2Qle3CH8IF3KiutapQvMF6P1TET1P
tvFuuUs4INoBp1ajFOmPQFXz0AfGy0Op1K33TGSGSfgMg711l6RfUodNQ+PVZX9x2
Uk89PY3bzpnhV5JZzf24rnRPxfx2vIPFRzBhznzJZv8V+bv9kV7HAarTW56NoKVy
OtQa8L9GAFgr5fSI/VhOSdvNILSd5JEHNmszbDgNRR0PfIizHHxbLY7288kjwEPw
pVsYjY67VYy4XTjTNP18F1dDox0YbN4zISy1Kv884bEpQBgRjXyEpwpy1obEAxnI
By16ypUM2Zafq9AKUJsCRtMIPWakXUGfnHy9iUsiGSa6q6JewlXpMgs7AAICCADZ
tTvrIqrrMx0VG7qt/JakVw6vK2ayTfQYACjrXHhDBITd0Eaaq6oDWy4HUvC1zm7h
vl0ehATo0jJC6DR1Q7aHLUZeq/DMgdKBgaKOPCG3N4BTNxDfu8HctRAx58AcQaDi
ccuEPOpekwMXoeq4gcXrLSd4obe0VIJpdRuYfcc6aFW99XGuH49eJBR1jT1xYyMq
thzquGdDqprMCYZUP0wB8I79tLNvgAN2YzhLsj/f66VhKb7eE9a0sw1So7gNN8aY
fg71UtncDD3zNLnlJdSr6EeGGZC9T8N526vVUbdTfT3uRJP4HtpTXGa/JXhZ52m9
j1EzW6eWY13QkNSK2NuviQBFBBgRAgAGBQI3BBjeAAoJEET2TGZqWGWpaZIAmIuI
DQDnyJMQ4vBMxY0Ybyle1pQAn2xDU65bpjISf7HPWxg1pQyperqg
=Ln2y
-----END PGP PUBLIC KEY BLOCK-----
```

Figure 9–4 Public key for kipp.martin@gsb.uchicago.edu.

plaintext, so encrypting just the session key using a public key is not very time consuming. For example, even a 128-bit session key provides excellent security. Then, the ciphertext and encrypted session key are sent to the recipient. The process of Thelma sending Louise an encrypted message is illustrated in Figure 9–5.

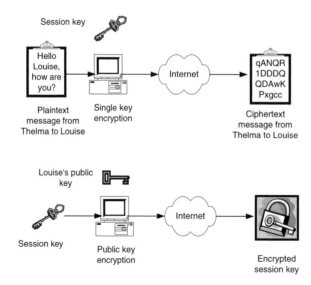

Figure 9–5 Using a session key and public key for encryption.

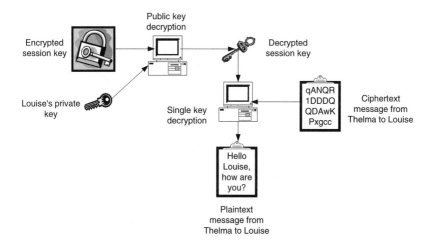

Figure 9–6 Using a session key and public key for decryption.

....

PRETTY GOOD PRIVACY

PGP was written by Phil Zimmermann. Version 1.0 was released in 1991. PGP has led a pretty controversial life since then. First, PGP used the RSA algorithm (it is now based on Diffie-Hellman). The patent for this algorithm was held by RSA Security. Jim Bidzos, then president of RSA Security, and Phil Zimmermann did not get along. Zimmermann was part of the crusade against the nuclear arms race and Bidzos was an ex-Marine. Bidzos and Zimmermann were at odds until 1994 when MIT stepped in and brokered a truce. However, the controversy over PGP did not end. Phil Zimmermann has been a target of a U.S. government investigation over illegally exporting encryption software. Both freeware (from MIT) and commercial versions (from Network Associates) of PGP are now available. Actually, the "G" in PGP should stand for Great and not Good.

Louise now has two encrypted files: the session key that was encrypted by Thelma using Louise's public key, and the ciphertext of the original plaintext message, which was encrypted using the session key and a single key cipher. The process that Louise follows to get the original plaintext message is illustrated in Figure 9–6. First, Louise uses her private key to decrypt the encrypted session key. Then, using the session key she decrypts the ciphertext that was created using the session key and a single key cipher.

TRUST AND DIGITAL SIGNATURES ....

In the last section we described how to send an encrypted message. Now, suppose you get an important email from a colleague. How can you verify 1) that the email was indeed from your colleague, and 2) that the email was not tampered with? It is possible to use the public key system for both authentication and message integrity. Perhaps the easiest way to implement a digital signature is to essentially flip the encryption process illustrated in Figure 9–3. The digital signature process is illustrated in 9–7. Assume Thelma now wants to send a digitally signed message to Louise. As illustrated in Figure 9–7, Thelma sends two files to Louise. The first file is the original plaintext. The second file is the plaintext encrypted using Thelma's private key. This second file constitutes the digital signature. Louise then uses Thelma's public key to decrypt the signed message and compare it with the original plaintext message. Note the asymmetry. We now encrypt with the private key and decrypt with the public key. An important feature of the public-private key pair is that the original plaintext message will agree with the decrypted signed message if and only if the unique public and private key pair was used. Thus, if the two messages do not agree one of two things happened. Either the plaintext message was not signed with the private key associated with the corresponding public key, or the original plaintext message was altered.

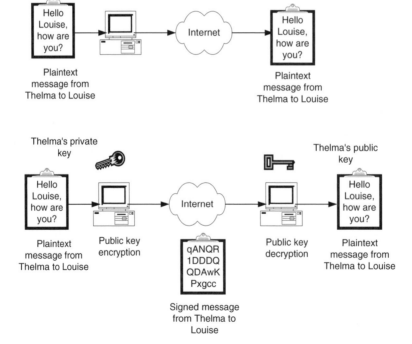

Figure 9–7 Signing a digital document.

The problem with the process illustrated in Figure 9–7 is the same one mentioned in the previous section, namely, that public key encryption is computationally cumbersome. An alternative to signing the entire plaintext document with a private key is to first create something called a *message digest.* Think of a message digest as a compact, fixed-length (usually 128-bit or 160-bit) "fingerprint" of the long, variable-length plaintext. It is created using a *hash function* in such a way that if the original plaintext is tampered with, applying the same hash function to the tampered plaintext would produce a different fingerprint, or message digest, from applying the hash function to the original plaintext. A message digest differs from ciphertext in that the hash function is one-way; that is, the plaintext cannot be recovered by decrypting the message digest. A message digest is simply used to determine whether the original plaintext was tampered with. The message digest is the same length regardless of the size of the plaintext message. The one-way hash function is a very powerful mathematical technique so that the chance of two different plaintext messages getting distilled into the same message digest is effectively zero. This process is illustrated in Figure 9–8.

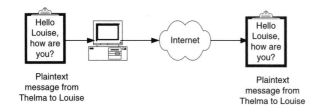

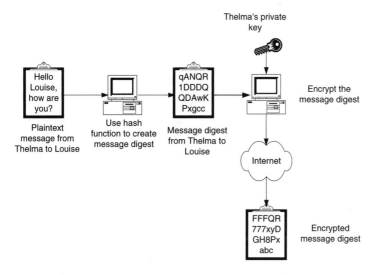

Figure 9–8 *Signing a digital document using a hash function.*

Tech Talk

Hash function: A one-way hash function takes a variable length input message and distills the message into a fixed length message digest. There is an extremely low probability that two distinct inputs will produce the same digest.

In Figure 9–9 we illustrate what a signed and hashed email actually looks like. Note that the email includes the type of hash function, SHA1, the original plaintext message, and the encrypted message digest that constitutes the signature. Now, what happens at the other end?

```
-----BEGIN PGP SIGNED MESSAGE-----
Hash: SHA1

Hello Louise, how are you?
-----BEGIN PGP SIGNATURE-----
Version: PGP for Personal Privacy 5.5.5

iQA/AwUBOyebrET2TGZqWGWpEQINCgCgubBIjWdX3L633
eCA+RI4a2/jOjIAn1QGZcpPEFLapgE8QgWlvAD22GTc
=vJMq
-----END PGP SIGNATURE-----
```

Figure 9–9 *Simple email and corresponding signed message digest.*

The digitally signed email is now processed as follows. First, Louise applies the hash function to the original plaintext message in order to create a message digest. Next, the encrypted message digest that is the digital signature is decrypted using Thelma's public key. This results in two message digests, which Louise compares. If they are not identical then either the plaintext message in the email was altered, or the digital signature was signed with a private key not corresponding to Thelma's public key. This process is illustrated in Figure 9–10.

The digital signature method we have described guarantees that the message has not been tampered with and that the private key that signed the document matches the public key that decrypted the message digest. However, there is no guarantee that an entity or person publishing a public key is really who he says he is. Indeed, the system we have described is subject to the man-in-the-middle attack. This works as follows. Assume Thelma wants to send Louise a digitally signed message. Louise requests that Thelma send her Thelma's public key. Thelma complies and sends Louise her public key. However, Joe, our man-in-the-middle, intercepts this document, poses as Thelma, and sends Louise his public key in place of Thelma's public key. Next, Thelma sends to Louise a digitally signed message. Joe also intercepts this, alters the text, and resends it to Louise signed using his private key. Unfortunately, in reality, Louise now has Joe's public key which she believes

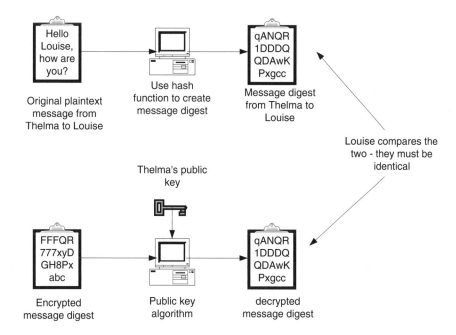

Figure 9–10 Verifying a digital signature.

to be Thelma's public key. Louise then verifies that the signature is valid and has an altered document she believes is from Thelma.

Clearly, a function similar to the one performed by a notary is required in the digital world. This function is performed by a *certificate authority*. It is the job of a certificate authority to validate a public key. This is done by issuing a digital certificate. A digital certificate contains the holder's name and public key. This is then digitally signed by the certificate authority.

PUTTING IT ALL TOGETHER: SECURE SOCKET LAYERS ....

Everything we have done so far in this chapter lays the foundation for this section. We now explain how secure transactions are done over the Internet. Recall from Chapter 4, "Internet and Web Technology," that the information contained in packets sent over the Internet is not encrypted. However, encryption is clearly required in many B2B and B2C transactions. One of the better known examples is a customer filling out credit card information on a form on a Web site and then submitting this information. The key technology used is SSL (secure socket layer). This technology was originally developed by Netscape Corporation for use in Netscape Navigator. This technology is now the universal standard for encrypting information exchanged between a Web browser and server. It is, for example, the technology used in Microsoft's Internet Explorer. The SSL technology is built upon the following:

- Public key encryption
- Single key encryption using a session key
- Digital signature
- Digital certificates

The process by which information is securely exchanged between a browser and Web server is illustrated in Figure 9–11. First the user with a browser selects a secure URL at a `.com`. A secure URL is one that begins with `https` rather than `http`. With Internet Explorer you will see a lock icon at the bottom of the browser window. Very quickly and unbeknownst to the user, the server sends an X.509 digital certificate to the browser running on the client machine. This digital certificate contains the `.com` public key and is signed by the private key of a certificate authority. Public keys for leading certificate authorities are part of browser software. The browser automatically uses the certificate authority's public key it has stored in memory to verify the signature. If the certificate is legitimate, the transaction proceeds. The browser randomly generates a session key and a single key encryption algorithm is used to encrypt the information the user will send to the `.com` server. Then the public key of the `.com` is used to encrypt the session key using public key encryption. The browser sends the encrypted user information and encrypted session key back over the Internet to the `.com` Web server. There the `.com` private key is used to decrypt the session key and the decrypted session key is used to decrypt the confidential user information.

Tech Talk

X.509 Certificate: This is a format for a digital certificate established by International Telecommunication Union-Telecommunication (ITU-T). This standard includes fields for items such as the public key, validity period, signature algorithm, etc. A secure Web server passes an X.509 certificate to the browser before the exchange of confidential information.

Tech Talk

Certificate authority: An organization that issues digital certificates, i.e., signs public keys. A good example is VeriSign. Your Internet browser contains a list of trusted certificate authorities.

SSL comes in two strengths, 40 bit and 128 bit. A single key size of 128 bits is very secure. It is approximately 3×10^{26} stronger than 40-bit encryption. The default size in the most recent releases of both Internet Explorer and Netscape Navigator is 128 bits. These sizes refer to the size of the session key generated, not the size of the public key. The size of the public key and the size of the session key are not related.

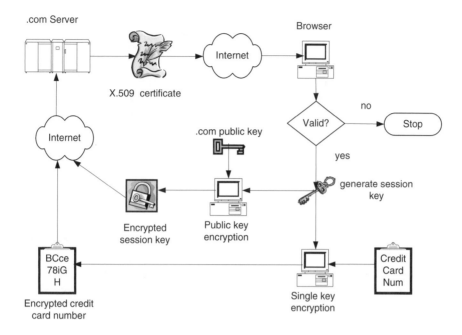

.com Server

Browser

X.509 certificate

no

Valid?

Stop

yes

.com public key

Internet

generate session
key

Encrypted
session key

Public key
encryption

BCce
78iG
H

Credit
Card
Num

Encrypted credit
card number

Single key
encryption

Figure 9–11 Secure socket layer technology.

Although volumes have been written about computer security and code-breaking, we briefly address the security of public key cryptography and SSL. We discuss three ways to defeat public key cryptography.

1. **Cryptanalysis:** This is the science of deciphering the ciphertext. It is a direct mathematical attack on the cryptosystem. For example, the RSA public key system can be broken by factoring into primes the integer n defined earlier that is part of the public key. This may seem easy, after all a number like 55 is easily factored as $55 = 5 \times 11$. The ease of factoring a small integer such as 55 is very misleading—the same is not true of large integers. In fact, the time required to factor large integers is measured in MIPS years. A MIPS year is the number of instructions a computer could perform in one year if it executed instructions at the rate of one million per second.

   The largest known integer to be factored is 512 bits. The effort required almost 300 computers and took approximately 8,000 MIPS years. For those with a strong competitive spirit and plenty of spare time, we recommend a visit to the RSA Security Web site. RSA Laboratories lists a 2048 bit integer with a $200,000 prize for factoring it. To put this in perspective, RSA Laboratories estimates that it would take approximately 342 million 500 MHz Pentium-based machines one year to factor a 1024 bit integer. In Chapter 2, "What Do I Need to Know About Hardware?" we talked about the impressive growth in computing power and the fact that this growth is likely to continue. Fortunately, though, there are an infinite number of prime numbers and as computers get faster we can simply pick larger integers for our public and private keys.

Public key encryption can also be broken by a cryptanalysis attack on the single key algorithm. However, as we mentioned earlier, the only known way to break the single key algorithms that are part of a public key encryption system is to do a complete enumeration of the possible values of the session key. This is currently not possible with a 128-bit session key.

2. **Reverse-Engineer the Implementation:** This is the process of figuring out how keys were generated and then duplicating the process. For example, many key generation systems are based on random number generators. Random number generators on a computer require an initial seed number to "get started." An example of reverse-engineering is figuring out what the seed is. An excellent example of this occurred in 1995 shortly after Netscape developed the SSL technology [103]. Dave Wagner and Ian Goldberg, two first-year graduate students at UC Berkeley, discovered that the seed used by the Netscape random number generator was calculated using the time of day, Process ID, and Parent ID. These numbers are fairly easy to get when multiple users share a server. Netscape was forced to admit a poor implementation of a great theory. A great cryptosystem is easily defeated by poor implementation.

3. **Passphrase attack:** The easiest thing to do is to steal or guess a passphrase. We have already discussed nontechnical means for doing so. There are a number of technical ways to steal a passphrase. Perhaps the most common is to infect a computer with a virus or worm in the form of a "sniffer program" that captures passphrases. Such a program can covertly record a passphrase sent over the network and then send the passphrase back to the virus's owner. Even more esoteric is a so-called "Tempest attack." By using sophisticated equipment it is possible to record electromagnetic signals from a computer. This makes it possible to record keystrokes and what is displayed on a video screen. It is possible to capture a passphrase as it is typed in. Tempest refers to a set of standards used to reduce electromagnetic emissions from electronic equipment. Tempest-shielding hardware is commercially available.

FIREWALLS AND PROXY SERVERS . . . .

The purpose of a *firewall* is to secure a network against attack. For example, a firewall might prevent an intruder from putting an executable file on the company computer that deletes files or it might prevent an intruder from defacing documents on a Web server. A firewall may be software or hardware, or both. Routers often act as a firewall in addition to routing packets. Packets must travel through the firewall to get from a LAN to a WAN, or vice versa. There are three main firewall technologies available: packet filtering, proxy servers, and stateful filtering.

Tech Talk

DMZ: The DMZ (DeMilitarized Zone) in a corporation is typically a network where the publicly available servers reside. It is protected by a firewall and is therefore more secure than an unprotected network. However, it is not as secure as the internal corporate network where important data is kept. The internal network is protected from the DMZ by an additional firewall.

1. **Packet filters**. A packet filtering firewall limits inbound or outbound packets based either on their IP address or port. We have already discussed IP addressing in Chapter 4. Think of a port as a phone line. Each application running on a Web server is assigned a port number. For example, HTTP connections are established through port 80 and FTP connections through port 21. A packet filter uses an ACL (access control list) to filter packets. Packets that do not have permission based on the list are not allowed in or out of the network. This function is usually performed by a screening router. For example, a screening router may not allow any traffic on port 21 or could block out all IP addresses that begin with 128. Unfortunately, this is not a fail-safe method. It is susceptible to the IP spoofing technique described earlier. An intruder could put acceptable IP addresses in her packets and get into the LAN.

2. **Proxy server**. A proxy server is used to prevent IP addresses on company computers from becoming known by an intruder on the Internet. Knowing the IP address of a computer allows an intruder to hack into the system. A proxy server sits between a client (an employee's computer) on a LAN and a server on the Internet. A request, for example, FTP or HTTP, comes from the client. Rather than go directly to the Web server on the Internet, the request first goes to the proxy server. The proxy server takes the request packets and repackages them into new packets that are sent onto the Web server. The proxy server often uses NAT (network address translation) and replaces the IP address in the request with the IP address of the proxy server when repackaging the packets. From the standpoint of the Web server, the request is coming from the proxy server, not the client machine behind the LAN. When the Web server responds with a file or Web page it sends it to the process on the proxy server. The proxy server then relays the file or Web page to the initiating client machine on the LAN. This prevents an intruder outside the LAN from knowing the IP address of the client and connecting directly with it. It is very safe. The downside is that this method does not scale well and performance is poor. Each client-Web server connection requires a separate process to run on the proxy server.

3. **Stateful filtering/inspection**. Unlike packet filtering described above, which is static, stateful filtering is dynamic. A problem with packet filtering is that it is an all-or-nothing solution. For example, if the filter allows a port to be open then that port is open to all traffic. This is a potentially dangerous situation. Stateful filtering dynamically builds a table and allows traffic in or out based on the table. For example, if a client behind the firewall requests a file through FTP, this request is maintained in a dynamic state table used for evaluating future traffic. When the server outside of the firewall responds to the file request, the packet information, such as IP address and port number, are checked to see

if there is a matching request in the state table. If not, the packet is not admitted past the firewall. When the FTP session ends, the port used by the session is closed.

The emphasis in this section is on corporate firewalls. However, home users with "always on" DSL or cable connections are also at risk. There are a number of personal firewall packages available such as BlackICE and ZoneAlarm.

PRIVACY

SSL technology is an excellent and secure way to encrypt confidential information that is sent from a consumer to an e-commerce Web site. However, what happens to this information once you send it to a company? What is its privacy policy? Companies such as Amazon and Buy.com have been the target of class action suits for privacy violations. There has been considerable backlash and negative publicity for companies such as DoubleClick that provide third-party banner ads and track customers.

The W3C is making an important contribution to help protect privacy with its privacy preferences project (P3P) initiative. The P3P initiative is an attempt to establish an industry standard for Web users to gain more control over how a Web site uses information about them. The basic idea is that a Web site owner uses a P3P policy generator and fills out a form about its privacy policy. The policy generator then generates an XML file that contains the Web site's privacy policy. This XML file is read by a P3P enabled browser when the user visits the Web site. Prior to visiting the Web site, the user of the browser sets the level of privacy she wants enforced. For example, a user may choose to accept all cookies. Or, she might choose to reject cookies written by a third party that do not comply with the P3P standard and have an "opt-out" mechanism on the Web site. When the Web site is visited the browser compares the user's preference with the current policy of the Web site. If the Web site does not meet the level of privacy required by the user, the user is alerted. An additional important feature of P3P is that it requires a Web site to provide a method for users to access the personal data that the site has collected about them.

Privacy policing solutions are also available from companies in the public sector. For example, TrustE has established a set of privacy standards, verification methods, and a consumer resolutions process. If a company follows the TrustE standards it is given a "seal of approval." A visitor to a Web site can click on the site's privacy policy and see if it has a TrustE seal of approval.

If you are concerned about the *privacy* of your Internet browsing you may wish to use services that allow you to surf anonymously. At a minimum, these services provide proxy services. With the proxy service your URL request goes to the proxy server, which in turn makes the request to the remote site without revealing your identity. Some of these services are quite complete. For example, SafeWeb uses 128-bit SSL technology to encrypt the data on a Web page and sends it to your browser. Your Internet service provider or network administrator cannot track your surfing activity. Similar products include IDzap, Anonymizer.com, and IDsecure.

In Chapter 11, "Marketing on the Internet," we discuss the use of cookies to track users. By default most browsers automatically allow all cookies to be written to a user's machine. It is fairly simple to configure a browser to accept no cookies, or prompt before accepting a cookie. However, "all-or-nothing" solutions are not sufficient for many people. You may wish to allow cookies from some sites and disallow others. There are a number of "cookie manager" applications available that allow a user more sophisticated cookie-filtering options. For example, with cookie managers it is usually possible to specify URLs of companies that the user wishes to allow to write cookies. Cookie managers are available from companies such as McAfee Software and Symantec.

For a good survey of privacy-related software see the article "Leave Me Alone" by Matthew Graven [62]. You may wish to visit the site dedicated to preventing sites from following your every move on the Internet and eliminating junk you're subjected to during your forays on the Internet. Log on to the site `www.junkbusters.com` for more information.

Finally, with regard to privacy, there is the question of whether to "opt in" or "opt out." With the opt in policy a site will not collect or use data you provide unless you specifically give permission ahead of time. With the opt out policy, unless you specifically indicate you are not willing to allow the dissemination of the information you provide, it will use the information you provide at will. A study by the Federal Trade Commission in early 2000 indicated that 75 percent of sites were opt out sites. Be aware of your status at each site. While this can be a bother, keeping close watch can prevent you from having personal information sold without your knowledge.

FUTURE TRENDS AND IMPLICATIONS . . . .

Perhaps the most important trend is the increasing cost of security. The more networked an organization becomes, the more important security issues become. According to a recent Gartner Group study, organizations currently dedicate only .4 percent of their revenue to information security. This figure is expected to increase by an order of magnitude to four percent by 2011.

Consumers are becoming much more concerned and educated about their online privacy. There are some simple actions a company can take in order to enhance consumers' confidence that their privacy is not being violated.

- Comply with the new P3P standard from the W3C.

- Have a clearly stated privacy policy. Make it easy to find on your site.

- If you choose to track customers using cookies, make it easy for them to "opt-out" of this tracking.

- Get certified by well-known privacy organizations such as TrustE or BBBOnLine.

Make use of organizations devoted to providing information about security. The Computer Security Division of the National Institute of Standards and Technology (NIST) is a U.S. federal organization devoted to improving information systems security and evaluating and establishing standards. CERT.org is a particularly valuable resource. It has a listing of current security threats and fixes. The SANS (System Administration, Networking, and Security) Institute is an organization for computer and networking professionals.

It also provides up-to-date alerts on security risks and viruses. The CSI (Computer Security Institute) is another valuable professional organization devoted to training and educating computer and networking professionals.

We have discussed the problems with passwords and passphrases. As people have more accounts and work more online it becomes impossible to remember them all. There is a clear trend to move away from passwords. Two alternatives to passwords/passphrases are *authenticators* and *biometrics*. A good example of a two-factor user authenticator is the SecureID authenticator from RSA Security. The idea is to identify a user through two things: Something she has and something she knows. The SecureID authenticator is either a card, like an ATM card, or a key fob that has a hardware token embedded in it. The SecureID authenticator has a timer that is synchronized with an RSA ACE/Server. The timer and the server are synchronized to generate the same authentication code every 60 seconds. This code, which appears on the authenticator (something the user has), is combined with the user's PIN number (something the user knows) to generate a one-time unique code. If this unique code is validated by the RSA ACE/Server, the user is permitted access to the requested secure service. RSA also provides authentication code generation software for handheld devices from Ericsson, Nokia, and Palm. In this case, the handheld device is essentially the token used for authentication.

Tech Talk

Token: A device to authenticate a user by something she has. An example is an RSA SecureID smart card or key fob.

One of the hottest areas in security is biometrics—a methodology for identifying people based on physical characteristics. These characteristics include iris patterns, retina patterns, voice, fingerprints, and handwriting. A good example of a biometric device is the U-Match Mouse from Biolink Technologies. The mouse works by associating a user name and password with a thumbprint. The mouse contains an internal scanner that reads the user's thumbprint. If the thumbprint does not match the user name/password, the user cannot log on to the computer.

The trend towards telecommuting has important implications for security. With numerous mobile users such as salespeople and field service technicians connecting to a network and accessing potentially sensitive information, encryption and authentication become crucial. Because of the expense of setting up private networks with leased lines, many companies are making use of VPNs, which we introduced in Chapter 7, "Getting Your Business Online." Recall that a VPN is a private network that uses the public Internet. It is private in the sense that the packets sent out over the Internet are encrypted. In order to manage such a network securely, it is necessary to have a server where public keys are stored, and which can be accessed by anyone, along with a key management system. Key management includes issuing keys, a key certification system, and revoking keys. The server along with the key management system is called a PKI (public key infrastructure). An effective PKI is a crucial part of a VPN. The SecureID authenticator from RSA Security described above is designed to authenticate users of a VPN.

There is also a trend to issue digital certificates to individual users. This way both merchant and consumer can verify themselves. There is a protocol from MasterCard and Visa called secure electronic transaction (SET). This technology involves the customer, the merchant, and the bank. It makes SSL even more secure because the customer gets a digital certificate from a participating credit card company. The merchant then verifies the customer, checks his or her credit at the participating bank and carries out the transaction. In Chapter 10, "Internet Business Transactions," we discuss transaction methods which do not require a credit number to be sent over the Internet.

We conclude this chapter by pointing out that the development, and in particular the publishing, of public key cryptography technology has been very controversial. The U.S. government fought, without success, the dissemination of this information. Its logic is based, in part, on not wanting criminals and terrorist organizations to have this information. Indeed, Osama bin Laden has used cryptography in messages to his cohorts. The counterargument is "if cryptography is outlawed, only outlaws will have cryptography." The book *Crypto* [103] by Steven Levy is a fascinating read about this controversy.

10 Internet Business Transactions

In this chapter ...

MINIMIZING TRANSACTION COSTS WITH INTERNET BUSINESS ....

The difference between information economy *b-webs*, a new type of business structure, and industrial economy corporations, according to Don Tapscott, David Ticoll, and Alex Lowy [155], lies in the transaction costs. The reason industrial economy corporations like Ford and General Motors grew to be so large is that transaction costs were so high, it was cheaper for a firm to perform a transaction itself rather than outsource or partner with another company. For example, one kind of transaction cost, the cost of seeking a reliable parts supplier, was very high in the days when even telephone service was in a rudimentary state. So, instead of going through the time and expense of locating a steel supplier, Ford would manufacture its own steel and generate its own power for producing the steel using coal. Thus, corporations in the industrial age grew to enormous size, following what has come to be known as *Coase's Law*, named after Ronald Coase, which states that a firm should grow until the cost of performing a transaction inside the firm exceeds that of performing it outside the firm.

The insight of Tapscott, Ticoll, and Lowy extends Coase's Law to the information economy. The three main kinds of transaction costs—search costs, contracting costs, and coordination costs—have been greatly reduced in the information economy, thanks especially to the Internet, which provides virtually free and instantaneous information that used to be very expensive and time-consuming to obtain. Coase's Law still holds, claim the trio, but, for the information economy, makes more sense stated backward: that firms should shrink in size by spinning off transactions to third-party firms or business partners until the cost of performing a transaction outside the firm exceeds the cost of performing it inside. The resulting business entity is what they call a b-web, a network of businesses and parties that come together via the Internet. An example is Amazon, which comprises a b-web that includes not only Jeff Bezos and his 7,500 employees, but authors, publishers, customers, reviewers, affiliates, companies which sell their wares on Amazon's site, and delivery companies. A general b-web is diagrammed in Figure 10–1.

....

COASE'S LAW FOR THE INFORMATION ECONOMY

Firms should shrink in size by spinning off transactions to third-party firms or business partners until the cost of performing a transaction outside the firm exceeds the cost of performing it inside.

Tapscott, Ticoll, and Lowy claim that their research has shown that the b-web has replaced the corporation as the primary unit of business in the information economy. Accordingly, there is a new primary business activity that replaces the corporation's primary

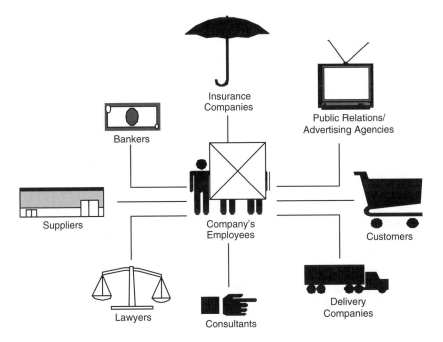

Figure 10–1 A hypothetical b-web.

function of production. This new activity is *fulfillment*, which goes beyond merely filling a customer's order. In fulfillment, a company creates and nourishes a relationship with a customer and provides an overall deeper sense of satisfaction. Through the Internet a customer becomes part of a company's b-web and a member of the company's team. A customer can become a marketer for a company (as we will see with viral marketing in Chapter 11, "Marketing on the Internet," a product tester like Amazon's book reviewers, and even a product designer like those who customize their own makeup on Reflect.com. A company that simply manufactures products and pushes them onto prospective customers will find itself left behind in a world where, through the Internet, a company can get to know its customers and their desires, and create products or services that fill their needs.

In this chapter we analyze the different transactions a company performs when doing business over the Internet. The chapter is divided into three main sections which describe different scenarios: B2C, B2B, and P2P (peer-to-peer computing). In the section on B2C systems, we begin with the building of an online store using "storefront" or "store-building" software. We then describe the different kinds of payment systems available for B2C transactions: everything from credit card systems to smart cards and micropayment systems. A discussion of how companies use third parties and logistics tools to fulfill orders completes the section on B2C transactions. In the B2B scenario, electronic exchange of data in transactions had been around even before the introduction of the Internet, primarily over private networks. Known as EDI, or electronic data interchange, this system has been used typically by larger companies because of the expense involved in establishing an EDI infrastructure. We discuss EDI and XML, a newer form of intercompany data exchange, in the section on B2B systems. This is followed by an introduction to B2B payment systems. The section on P2P systems focuses on payment systems that can be used between two parties, neither of which is a business that can accept credit cards (P2P payment systems are used on eBay, for example). The chapter concludes with a section on "Future Trends and Implications."

B2C SYSTEMS ....

In this section, we discuss different aspects of B2C Internet business, from building a storefront on the Web to taking credit card payments.

Building an Online Store

Principles for creating an online store are very much like those for creating a brick-and-mortar store. You want to present an attractive storefront that invites customers to enter. Once the customer is in the store, you want to present the merchandise in such a way that the offerings are appealing and easy to find. You want to provide sales help if the customer needs assistance. You want to make it easy for the customer to select items, change his mind if necessary, and proceed smoothly to checkout. The checkout process should be quick and gracious so that the customer wants to return to your store. The product return policy should be clearly stated and the return process simple and convenient. You want to maintain a relationship with the customer even when he is not in your store, informing him of special offerings he might be interested in, and making him feel valued and special to be your customer. Sound simple?

It isn't. It isn't easy for an offline store, and that goes double for an online store. That's because you can't control the environment in which your customer is shopping online. He may be at work, at home amidst the chaos of a big family and multiple pets, or on the road surfing on a notebook. A customer's environment will determine the amount of attention he can pay to his computer screen and how much patience he has in navigating your site. We discussed at some length the basic principles of good site design in Chapter 6, "Web Site Design and Content." These apply here also, but we'd like to go further in this section to introduce storefront software and services and point out what to look for when considering this growing technology.

There are essentially two ways to create an online store. One, you can purchase store-building software and install it on your server, or two, you can contract with a service that will create and maintain the store site for you. It used to be the case that a store-owner would purchase the store-building software in components—the storefront display, the shopping cart technology, the payment system, the customer relationship management software, etc.—but the current trend is to purchase complete store-building software with all parts integrated, or to contract the services that can create the online store and integrate it with your back end infrastructure, like accounting, purchasing, and fulfillment. Indeed, with the rise of b-webs and use of third-party services for everything from storefronts to fulfillment, it seems the nucleus of a b-web needn't be anything more than a person with an idea.

Prices for store-building software that you install on your server (or a hosted server) range from "free" to hundreds of thousands of dollars. An example of "free" software is Red Hat's Interchange, which is billed as "the most widely distributed open source e-business application available today" on `interchange.redhat.com/cgi-bin/ic/index.html`. Interchange is licensed under GPL, the general public license, which was explained in Chapter 3, "Software Is Everywhere." Indeed, the software is free, but for technical support and related services like implementation, systems integration, or training classes, the user is charged a fee. Interchange differs from most other store-building software in that it is open source, which according to the site allows for many of the features a standard packaged solution offers with the added advantages of customization capabilities and a price that can't be beat.

A leading, relatively inexpensive store-building software is ShopSite, which can be found at `www.shopsite.com`. Currently, ShopSite comes in three levels: Starter for the home or very small business that has under 15 products to offer, Manager for the small-to-medium-sized business, and Pro, which can accommodate up to hundreds of thousands of products. ShopSite allows you to create an electronic storefront and catalog, and process orders securely using credit card services from VeriSign and others. ShopSite is sold through resellers and exact pricing depends on the ShopSite's partners, like ISPs. ShopSite products and services may incur a monthly fee or an upfront cost, but expect to pay about $500 for Manager and $1,300 for Pro. The storefront is accessible through most major browsers and the software runs on servers that support all major variations of Unix and Windows NT or Windows 2000.

If you want to get your storefront up and running easily, some of the major portals offer you space and services on their sites. You can get a storefront running with either Amazon at `www.amazon.com/zshops` or Yahoo at `store.yahoo.com`. Yahoo charges $100 per month for offering up to 50 items, $300 per month for up to 1,000 items, and above that, $100 per month per additional 1,000 items. Amazon offers a different payment scheme through its Pro Merchant Subscription Services. A merchant pays both a register fee and a closing fee. Register fees ring up at $39.99 per month for up to 40,000 items and $.10 per item thereafter. Closing fees include a flat fee from $1.25 per order and a percentage of the sale, ranging from 1.25 percent to 5 percent. Optional merchandising fees to promote your goods on the site are also available. It is advisable to check out the respective sites to see which of the sites better suits your needs and merchandise. For additional storefront services vendors see [60] or [137].

To see whether the store-building software meets your needs, test it (most of the companies have demo sites) to see whether the storefront makes purchasing easy and convenient for your customers. For example, put yourself in the place of your customer to see:

- Is the store's home page attractive and make you want to continue browsing?

- Is it easy for you to find what you are looking for?

- Does the site offer a search engine?

- Is online help available?

- Does the shopping cart technology make it easy for you to order items you're interested in, then change your mind later?

- Does the shopping cart technology provide product availability and shipping time?

- Does the shopping cart technology provide a running total of items you entered so you can see how much you're spending?

- Does the shopping cart technology total the prices of your items along with the shipping charges before you enter a credit card number or other information on payment systems?

- Is checkout easy and fast? For example, is 1-Click service available or can you use an electronic wallet?

- Is tracking of an order available?

- Is there a prominent, easy-to-understand return policy?

As an online store owner you should also find out the following before purchasing:

- Does the software/service allow you to display pictures of your wares?

- Is it easy for you to change offerings, prices, and sale items on your storefront?

- Are payments secure and transacted in real-time?

- Is your storefront technology built in to your back end infrastructure so you can seamlessly connect with your accounting, database, purchasing, customer relationship management, and supply chain management software?

- Can the software/service handle international orders in different currencies?

- Does the software/service automatically calculate sales tax if applicable?

- How will the customer know his purchase is confirmed? Is it easy to send an email notification?

Accepting Payments
Credit Card Systems

Of all the payment systems available in Internet business, credit cards are still by far the most widely used. In fact, 90 percent of all online payments are transacted via credit cards [45]. While there is a lot of controversy over the security of using credit cards online, and while many different payment systems have been developed, credit cards remain the payment means of choice for the majority of online shoppers. But how can you make credit card services available to your customers in the first place? Does an online business differ from an offline business in its ability to offer credit card payment? What are some of the pitfalls you should be aware of in contracting for credit card services?

Establishing a Merchant Account for Credit Card Sales: Unfortunately, merchants engaged in electronic commerce are viewed differently than brick-and-mortar merchants by charge card services providers. Many Internet businesses are tagged as risky by credit card companies and banks. They are therefore either denied credit card services or are subject to higher fees and fines relative to their offline counterparts. This distinction probably stems back to the proliferation of online pornography sites, which may have *chargeback* rates of up to 30 percent of transactions. A chargeback occurs when a cardholder refuses to pay for a charge on his statement because he claims he either didn't make the charge or the merchandise was defective, and thereby refuses to pay. As a point of comparison, most brick-and-mortar companies generate chargeback rates of less than one-tenth of one percent. One entrepreneur had to pull the plug on his plans for an online dating service, into which he had already invested $10,000, because the credit-card issuers were going to penalize him up to $75,000 per month if he couldn't keep his chargeback rates to one percent of transactions or 2.5 percent of monthly revenue. The entrepreneur said that kind of penalty would have bankrupted the company and consequently backed out [10].

When investigating prospective credit card services providers, some terms you should know are *MAP* (merchant account provider), *MSP* (merchant service provider), and *ISO* (independent sales organization). These terms are often used interchangeably and can refer to banks, providers of merchant accounts, or providers of online credit card processing. These organizations can differ greatly in the fees and penalties they charge, so it is wise to exercise due diligence before signing on with one.

TERMS TO KNOW FOR CREDIT CARD PROCESSING

- MAP (merchant account provider) – Provides merchant accounts, which is the account into which revenues from credit card sales are deposited by the cardholder's bank. A merchant account provider can be a bank or an ISO.

- ISO (independent sales organization) – Provides merchant accounts and credit card services, usually at higher rates than banks because they bear a higher level of risk. Merchants who are unable to get credit card services from banks usually turn to ISOs. ISOs have had a shady reputation but there are reputable ones available if you search thoroughly.

- MSP (merchant service provider) – Offers more than merchant accounts in most cases. MSP is a general term that covers MAPs and ISOs, and the terms are often used interchangeably.

Banks are generally the most reliable and trustworthy of the service providers, but they also are the most selective in deciding to whom they will offer merchant accounts. A merchant account is necessary in order to process cards because it is into the merchant account that credit card revenues are deposited. MAP is the general term for companies offering merchant accounts, which can include banks and ISOs. MSP is the general term for companies offering merchant accounts and more. Banks are held to higher standards than many other kinds of credit card processors because the risk they are allowed to bear by law is limited. Thus, they must limit the number of "high risk" businesses to which they can offer merchant accounts and services. Many banks will flat out refuse to provide services to online companies because of perceived higher risk. Others will charge steep penalties for chargebacks, as we saw above. If you are turned down by bank after bank, your next option is to turn to an ISO.

ISOs have a checkered past that dates back to the early 1990s. Businesses usually turn to an ISO when they cannot set up a merchant account with a bank, and are in a vulnerable position. Some ISOs took advantage of this situation. ISOs developed a shady reputation when some of their group collected application fees from businesses and mysteriously disappeared. Others charged low discount rates but astronomical maintenance and transaction fees, which were often hidden in the contract. Still others used buried clauses or loose terminology to lock merchants into unfavorable positions for extended periods of time. There are reputable ISOs, but you must do the necessary homework and legwork, including *careful* reading of the contract, checking with companies who do business with them, and making sure there are trustworthy persons standing behind a Web site or advertisement. Don't let them prey on your vulnerabilities as an online merchant.

Protecting Your Business Against Credit Card Fraud: Once you have a credit card system in place, be sure to protect your business against fraud. This is especially true for online businesses when orders and credit card numbers are coming through the Internet, void of any physical proof of verification like the actual card or a signature. Use SSL described in Chapter 9, "Security and Internet Business," and SET described below to prevent your transactions from being tampered with or misrepresented.

Some businesses refuse to send merchandise if the billing address is different from the shipping address, although this is impractical if much of a company's business is in gifts. Some MSPs will verify a cardholder through the use of a billing address. Indeed, in many cases, the thief of a credit card will not know the billing address of the cardholder. One owner of an online computer and computer accessories store said his biggest problem was customers who repudiated their credit card purchases because they claimed the merchandise was defective when they received it. In most instances, the online merchant will be responsible for paying the chargeback to the cardholder's bank.

Another means of preventing fraud that is growing in popularity is the use of one-time use disposable credit card numbers. A pioneer in the software technology is Orbiscom, which was founded by Irish brothers-in-law Ian Flitcroft, an eye surgeon, and Graham O'Donnell, an electronics engineer. Customers wishing to make a purchase download software to create an O-card, which includes a randomly generated credit card number. With an O-card, the customer can set limits on spending, number of uses, and an expiration date. The merchant verifies the number with the O-cardholder's bank and is unaware that the number is only temporary. In this way, the customer is protected because the number cannot be used by credit card thieves for future purchases, the merchant is protected from fraudulent uses of numbers, and Orbiscom makes money from the software and per-transaction fees. American Express, MBNA, and Discover are some of the first credit-card issuers to use this new technology [6].

SET Online Credit Card Technology: In Chapter 9 we wrote about SSL which encrypts and decrypts HTTP data between client and server. The client and server in the online business world are the customer and merchant respectively. In this section we discuss a stronger form of security for bank card payments called *SET* or secure electronic transaction. You may be thinking, "Isn't SSL enough with its public and private keys, single key encryption, and hash functions?" We shall see how SET takes security for payments on the Internet one step further by providing trusted third-party authentication for clients (customers).

SSL was designed to provide secure communication between a client and a server. This is a very effective way to securely transmit credit card data for online payments. Not to get paranoid, but what happens to that credit card number once it's sitting on the merchants's server? How can you be sure that it's securely transferred to the merchant's bank for verification? What happens if a hacker breaks in to the merchant's server while your credit card number is sitting there? Also, how does the merchant know that you are whom you claim to be? In the offline world, a customer's identity is verified through confirming a signature and in some cases a photograph on a credit card, and a merchant's reliability is confirmed through the Better Business Bureau, credit card signage or decal in a store, and company history. But how can this authentication be realized online?

SET, created by a joint effort between Visa International and MasterCard, works through a system of *digital certificates* and *digital signatures* of trusted third parties. When the customer is ready to send his credit card information, he first sends his digital certificate, which includes his public key, signed by his bank. The customer bank's public key in the signature is in turn signed by an additional trusted third party, the SET certificate authority. The merchant then knows that the customer has been validated by trusted third parties. Similarly, the merchant sends to the customer her digital certificate containing her public key signed by the merchant bank, and the merchant bank's public key signed by the SET certificate authority. In this way, the customer knows the merchant has been validated by trusted third parties. This series of authorizations is illustrated in Figure 10–2. The transactions then proceed using the technology described in Chapter 9.

An additional benefit with SET is that SET protocol is not limited to communication between the merchant and the customer. In fact, the merchant's bank is involved. The bank card information from the customer is sent encrypted, using the merchant bank's public key, from the customer to the merchant to the merchant bank. The merchant does not store the customer's unencrypted credit card information. Once the merchant bank receives the customer's bank card information, it decrypts it using its private key and requests authorization from the customer bank, just as is done with offline bank card transactions. Once the merchant receives authorization of the customer's payment, she can confirm the completion of the transaction to the customer. These transactions are illustrated in Figure 10–3.

An added bonus of SET is enhancement of *nonrepudiation*. Nonrepudiation means that a customer cannot renege on a transaction that he later regrets. Repudiation, or rejection of a charge, is a major cause of credit card chargebacks, whereby a customer insists

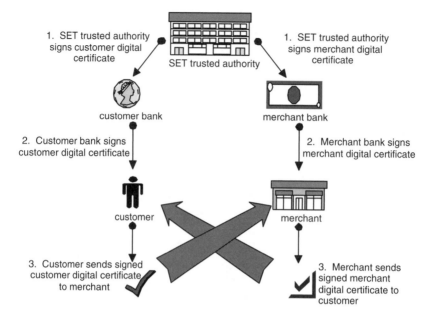

Figure 10–2 Customer and merchant verification using SET.

to his issuing bank that he did not charge an item on his bill or that the merchandise was defective. Current credit card regulations favor the customer's word, so the merchant has to swallow the cost of the lost sale in case of a chargeback. With SET the customer cannot deny a charge since his digital certificate, verified by his bank and the SET authority, and credit card information, encrypted with the merchant bank's public key, are on record. Thus, SET helps protect the merchant from customers suffering from buyer's remorse and from credit card fraud.

Also, while digital certificates are used in transactions involving SSL, there is no singular trusted international source as there is with SET. Instead, there is a plethora of certificate authorities, most of whose public keys are stored on standard browsers. With SET, the singular authority originates from Visa and MasterCard, in collaboration with IBM, Microsoft, Terisa Systems, GTE, VeriSign, and SAIC.

In sum, SET provides two additional benefits over SSL. First, we saw how SSL provides for secure communication between the merchant and the customer. It allows the customer to confirm the identity of the merchant through authentication provided by a certificate authority. In contrast, SET adds a level of security for the merchant by providing for authentication of the customer and verification of the customer's order. SET also helps to prevent repudiation by the customer and chargebacks.

Second, with SET the customer's credit card number is never seen by nor stored with the merchant. In Chapter 9 we discussed how hackers break into merchant's servers and steal credit card numbers. This cannot happen with SET. SET has not been as widely

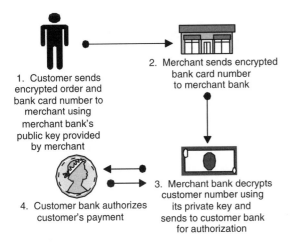

1. Customer sends encrypted order and bank card number to merchant using merchant bank's public key provided by merchant

2. Merchant sends encrypted bank card number to merchant bank

3. Merchant bank decrypts customer number using its private key and sends to customer bank for authorization

4. Customer bank authorizes customer's payment

Figure 10–3 Payment authorization using SET.

adopted as SSL, probably because few customers are willing to make the effort to become authenticated.

Electronic Wallets: If you've ever tried to purchase anything online using a credit card, you know that it can be a hassle to fill out numerous forms at checkout. Amazon has simplified this process with its 1-Click shopping. Another attempt to minimize the hassle is the creation of the *electronic wallet*. Similar to its physical world counterpart, an electronic wallet holds a person's ID and means to pay, usually credit card information. It also holds information like billing and shipping addresses. Using an electronic wallet at participating sites, a customer can transfer payment, billing, and shipping information directly into a merchant's forms rather than manually enter the same information each time he wants to make a purchase.

The problem with electronic wallets was the number of companies offering them. A merchant had to accommodate the different wallets on her Web site if she wanted to be compliant with all of them. To solve this problem, a standard was developed in June 1999, which the major companies offering electronic wallets hoped to adopt. It was called ECML, or electronic commerce modeling language. ECML's founding members included AOL Time Warner, American Express, Compaq, Discover, IBM, MasterCard, Microsoft, Novell, Sun Microsystems, and Visa. Despite ECML's auspicious beginnings, it appears the standard was never widely adopted. Rather, some of the leading companies offering services in electronic commerce have come up with competing versions of the wallet, including Microsoft's Passport, NextCard's Concierge, and Qpass's PowerWallet.

In fact, the heat on the electronic wallet wars was turned up with AOL Time Warner's $100 million infusion into Amazon in July 2001. An AOL-TW source leaked that part of the reason for the infusion was that AOL-TW wanted to exploit Amazon's Internet commerce technology to strengthen its electronic wallet program. This would enable it to go head-to-head with Microsoft's Passport, which currently boasts two billion authentications per month. Because electronic wallets can provide ease of entrée to shopping online for the holder and reams of consumer data for the provider, the stakes in this arena are high. Only time will tell whether the electronic wallet will become as ubiquitous as its physical counterpart, and who will emerge the victor [72].

Digital Currency

Credit cards are by far the most common payment system used online. But what about the millions of people who don't have credit cards? What about those who have a credit card but for whatever reason do not want to use a credit card to make a purchase (a surprise gift for a spouse, for example)? Are they barred from enjoying the ease and convenience of online shopping? Fortunately, the answer is no. A number of non-credit card-based systems have been developed, although few have been widely adopted. Many are still in the experimental stage, and it remains to be seen whether one will ever topple the credit card in popularity.

One interesting and challenging solution is *digital currency*. How great it would be if there were a true online equivalent of cash, whereby purchases could be made easily and anonymously, with no possibility of being traced. Even if you are not making illicit or illegal purchases, there are times when you may not wish to have a record of your purchase kept by a third party, or when you may wish to shop anonymously. Concerns over privacy also call for the development of digital currency.

One of the leading developers of digital currency is eCash Technologies. Founded in 1994, eCash, originally called DigiCash, has come up with a means by which customers can make purchases online from participating merchants more simply than they can using credit cards. There are no long forms to fill out, and no credit card numbers to enter. A customer first signs up for an eCash account with a participating bank. When he is ready to make the purchase, he requests eCash currency from the bank. Through a series of secure transactions, the bank approves the request, creates the eCash currency, and sends it back to the customer. When the customer is ready to check out at a participating merchant's site, he clicks on the eCash button, and a virtual eCash bank card appears and asks for a password. The customer enters the password, the merchant verifies the sale, and the transaction is complete. For a demo of eCash, visit www.ecash.net/demo.

In theory, the technology behind a digital currency system works as follows. The customer must first open an account with a bank and deposit money into it using traditional means, such as cash, a check, or a credit card. When the customer is ready to use digital currency, he first creates a randomly generated serial number and digitally signs it. This signed serial number, along with the amount desired, is transmitted to the bank. The bank then debits the customer's account and signs the serial number with one of its public keys, which depends on the amount of the withdrawal. The bank-signed serial number, sometimes called a *digital coin* is sent back to the customer. The customer uses this digital coin when making a purchase at a merchant participating in this digital currency system. The merchant confirms the amount with the bank's signature and submits the currency to the customer's bank. The bank verifies the serial number and credits the merchant's account for the amount it signed for [108]. This process is illustrated in Figure 10–4.

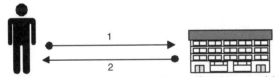

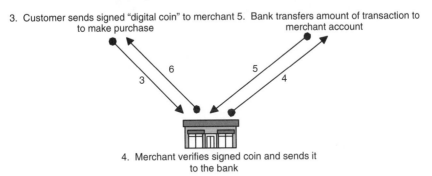

1. Customer generates a random serial number, digitally signs it, and sends it to the bank with the amount desired

2. Bank verifies signature, debits customer account, digitally signs serial number, depending on amount of transaction

3. Customer sends signed "digital coin" to merchant to make purchase

5. Bank transfers amount of transaction to merchant account

4. Merchant verifies signed coin and sends it to the bank

6. Merchant relays approval to customer and purchase is completed

Figure 10–4 How digital currency is transacted.

Even with this theoretical system, the transactions are not anonymous because the bank must know whose account to debit when it receives the customer-signed serial number. If it wanted to, the bank could keep track of all of the customer's purchases. For truly anonymous transactions, even to the bank itself, the technology becomes quite complex. In order for transactions to be truly anonymous, there must be a way the bank can certify the serial number it receives from the customer and approve the serial number it receives from the merchant without knowing the identity of the customer. This is done by using what is called a *blinding factor*. With a blinding factor the number received from the customer is different from the one received from the merchant.

This is done is by multiplying the serial number randomly generated by the customer by a large number (the blinding factor). The result is a very large number which cannot be easily factored. This huge number is sent to the bank, digitally signed by the bank (with the appropriate account debited), and sent back to the customer. The customer then divides the huge number by the blinding factor, which he alone knows. The result is the original serial number, still signed by the bank. When this digital coin is sent to the merchant, the transaction proceeds as usual, with the merchant sending the digital coin to the bank, and the bank crediting the merchant's account with the appropriate amount. The bank knows the request is legitimate because it is signed with its own signature. Only the bank cannot match the large number signed by the customer with the digital coin serial number submitted by the merchant [108]. This system gives rise to anonymous digital cash, illustrated in Figure 10–5. As you can see, digital currency can become very complicated to use, which is why most people prefer to stick to their credit cards, despite the security risk.

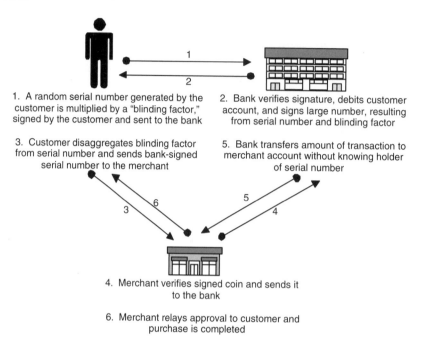

1. A random serial number generated by the customer is multiplied by a "blinding factor," signed by the customer and sent to the bank

2. Bank verifies signature, debits customer account, and signs large number, resulting from serial number and blinding factor

3. Customer disaggregates blinding factor from serial number and sends bank-signed serial number to the merchant

5. Bank transfers amount of transaction to merchant account without knowing holder of serial number

4. Merchant verifies signed coin and sends it to the bank

6. Merchant relays approval to customer and purchase is completed

Figure 10–5 How anonymous digital currency is transacted.

Micropayments

A growing segment of online commerce is called *microcommerce*, whereby the price of each transaction ranges from one cent to roughly $10. Typical products and services in microcommerce include downloads of a single article or of a single song, and participation in online games. Because of the relatively high fees charged to merchants for each credit card transaction, and because many consumers don't want to see charges for under $10 on their credit card statements, alternative forms of payment for microcommerce were developed.

One solution is to aggregate these *micropayments* and bill the consumer monthly on his telephone bill. This solution is provided by eCharge with its eCharge Phone payment system. eCharge even provides an instant line of credit for qualifying consumers wishing to sign on to eCharge Phone. eCharge also offers a Net Account payment system that authenticates both consumer and merchant before approving a transaction. It is designed especially for Internet payments and promises 100 percent protection against fraud for the consumer and reduced chargebacks for the merchant.

Another solution is to aggregate the micropayments and present the monthly total on a credit card statement. Qpass offers this convenience for the consumer and the merchant. For consumers, purchases are stored on their Qpass account until their monthly statement is tallied. For merchants, their merchant account is credited accordingly. Some leading publication companies using Qpass are *The New York Times* on the Web, which uses Qpass for single article access and crossword puzzle downloads, and *Consumer Reports* Online, which uses Qpass for single article sales, pay-per-view transactions, and individual product ratings reports.

Some micropayment system providers are claiming that companies can charge for access to content on their sites. Even a penny per page view for some sites garnering hundreds of millions of page views per month could add up to substantial revenue. Many companies remain skeptical, however, as to whether consumers will pay for content, with a few notable exceptions. The Internet culture, as described in Chapter 11, is still that information should be free. If charging for content on a pay-per-view or pay-per-click basis ever becomes widespread, only micropayment systems will make sense. As it stands, micropayments are still in the nascent stage and have not been widely adopted.

Smart Cards

Another alternative to credit card-free online payments is the use of *smart cards*. Smart cards were introduced in Chapter 9 as a device for security. In this chapter, they are presented as a means to make anonymous payments online. In the smart card there is an embedded chip that holds the amount the consumer has available to him. The chip is loaded with monetary value either by phone or at a brick-and-mortar store. Thus, the consumer has to be slightly inconvenienced and interrupt his purchase if the smart card is not already loaded with an adequate amount. Nevertheless, the smart card is convenient for those who do not have credit cards, the youth market, or those who for whatever reason do not wish to use their credit cards. Moreover, there is no need to provide personal information when using a smart card.

Smart cards are advantageous to the merchant as well. The merchant can serve those markets inadequately served by credit cards, especially for micropayments. There are no third-party payment authorizations, which reduces the time necessary for each transaction. The number of chargebacks is reduced because the cards are prepaid. The Smart Card Industry Association (SCIA) has as its goal that every PC will have a smart card reader shipped with it by 2005. Indeed, the SCIA claims that Microsoft is supporting smart cards with Windows 2000 and that IBM, Compaq, and Hewlett-Packard have PCs with a smart card reader as standard equipment [143].

One of the leading providers of smart cards is Mondex. Mondex is billed as the "direct electronic equivalent of cash" and is available not only on the Internet, but on digital television and mobile phones. Indeed, the electronic chip itself need not be embedded on a card *per se* but may be in a mobile phone, PC, or TV set-top box. Mondex is also equipped to handle multiple currencies. See www.mondex.com for more details. In July 2001 Visa International introduced its version of the smart card, which will reduce the cost of a card for issuing banks to $.99 from the typical $3 to $5 [141].

B2C Order Fulfillment and Logistics

Fulfillment may appear on the surface to be one of the least glamorous aspects of doing business online, but it is one of the most important ways by which a customer decides whether to give a company repeat business. In fact, fulfillment is so powerful, it can become a competitive tool with which you can drive your competitors into the dust. Many of the dot-coms that eventually folded simply could not deliver product as promised or expected. Stories abound about companies who could not fulfill orders in time for the 1999 and 2000 Christmas seasons, which gave rise to legions of irate customers who vowed never to return.

Thanks to the convenience and speed of the Internet, the bar on fulfillment has been raised to meet customers' expectations of quick, efficient, and trackable delivery. Not only is information expected to be at a customer's fingertips instantly via the Internet, goods ordered online are expected to be shipped within 24 hours of clicking the buy button. Additionally, customers assume they will receive email notification indicating when and by what means the merchandise left the warehouse as well as the expected date of delivery. How well a company handles fulfillment can make the difference between profitability and unprofitability.

Fulfillment is both difficult and expensive to do right. It is difficult because increasingly fulfillment is not only about moving goods, but about moving information in tandem with goods. That is, customers expect that they will be informed when an order is shipped and that they can track a package any time of day or night as it moves toward its destination. Customers expect to be able to change an order before it is shipped and return an order easily with a refund. Of course it goes without saying that the order must be correct, well packaged to avoid damage to the merchandise, and accompanied by the appropriate packing slips. It also helps if the packaging is attractive and reinforces the company's identity. It's easy to see how a top-notch fulfillment operation can be quite expensive. It has been estimated that product delivery can account for 10 percent of a product's cost [27].

There are essentially two ways to handle fulfillment: outsourcing and in-house. Both have their advantages and disadvantages. With outsourcing, as is usually the case, you have quicker time to market, and it allows you to focus on the "fundamentals" of your business. If your business is seasonal and you probably can't keep a warehouse running at near capacity all year round, you're probably better off outsourcing. But an increasing reliance on outsourcing can result in a decline in your customer service. How closely aligned is your outsourcing with your ordering and follow-up procedures? Does your outsourcing party send email to your customers informing them of when their orders were shipped? Does it allow your customers to track their packages? How well can your outsourcing party scale with your needs as your business grows?

If you outsource your fulfillment, you may spend less time filling orders but a lot more time coordinating with and managing communications with your outsourcer. Moreover, fulfillment is so closely tied with customer service that loss of control over this key transaction in Internet business can cause your entire business to slip. In the next section we examine how some companies manage to outsource their fulfillment, either by going to a third party or by drop-shipping.

THINGS TO CONSIDER WHEN DECIDING BETWEEN OUTSOURCING AND IN-HOUSE FULFILLMENT

- Time to market (usually quicker with outsourcing)
- Availability of fulfillment and logistics talent
- Cost of managing your own warehouse
- Seasonality and spikes of your business
- Ability to scale operations as your business grows
- Time to fill orders versus time to manage communications with third party
- Alignment of fulfillment with front end ordering and back end functions like accounting and inventory
- Communication with customer
- Tracking of packages
- Alignment with customer service

Outsourcing Fulfillment

Because of the difficulty of properly executing fulfillment and the capital outlays involved with doing it in-house, the industry of *e-logistics* has become a hot new area. Not only have third-party logistics (3PL) providers sprung up in recent years, logistics and transportation exchanges have also emerged, which provide a resource for logistics managers seeking services and talent. Collaboration is a buzzword in logistics, as companies seek to reduce transportation costs by sharing a truck's capacity, for example. Industry stalwarts like Federal Express and UPS, as well as upstarts like Manhattanassociates.com and iFulfill.com, are scrambling for a piece of the nearly one trillion dollar fulfillment and shipping industry.

If you are a small- to mid-sized company you may want to consider iFulfill.com, which can take care of everything for you from shopping cart technology and credit card processing to order picking and packing, shipping, and tracking. iFulfill.com claims on its Web site to provide "everything a Web merchant needs after the 'buy' button is clicked." Once your customer clicks on a link to purchase a product, he clicks into the iFulfill.com system, which takes care of the rest of the order. iFulfill.com provides you with the HTML code you add to your Web site to make the transition from your product offerings to iFulfill.com's pages. The customer's order appears on his credit card statement as iFulfill.com.

iFulfill.com charges a card processing fee (if you elect to use this service) as well as a fulfillment fee. Merchants get paid on the 25th of every month when iFulfill issues checks for 80 percent of the money due from the previous month. Twenty percent is held in reserve until the following month, as required by iFulfill's agreement with its credit card companies. This reserve amount allows iFulfill to offer low third-party credit card processing rates. iFulfill.com also handles returns within a thirty-day period from the time the customer receives his order. SSL and SET are used to ensure privacy of the customer and merchant data.

If you are a larger company, you may wish to engage the services of a provider like UPS e-Logistics. UPS e-Logistics can manage everything from complex order taking (like future shipments or back-ordered product), inventory, customer service, transportation, call center services, and returns—essentially everything in your supply chain operation. On its Web site UPS e-Logistics claims it can help get a company up and running in as little as eight weeks. Thus, it offers fulfillment solutions to everyone from start-ups to Fortune 500 companies.

An alternative to turning to a 3PL is to use a *drop shipper*, whereby inventory is not sent either by you or by a 3PL but is shipped directly from the manufacturer. One of the companies that managed to use drop shipping effectively (but was taken over by Burpee in 2001) is Garden.com. Garden.com managed a small warehouse operation in Austin, Texas, but the bulk of its offerings, like seeds, plants, tools, shrubs, and snails, were shipped directly from suppliers. It used proprietary software to manage communication with its more than 70 suppliers. The gardening industry is a huge $47 billion a year industry but is very fragmented and made up primarily of catalog businesses. It took the founders of Garden.com to build a software system from scratch that could shoot orders to suppliers, track suppliers' inventory and prices, and plan for future inventory. Suppliers received the orders, printed them out, and gave them to the order pickers. Orders in the garden business, because plants are living and perishable, can be tricky. Often a customer will order a plant but will not want it shipped for several months. Thus, inventory tracking was critical to Garden.com and the supplier. At some of the technically advanced suppliers, plants were bar-coded so pickers did not have to identify a difficult Latin name with a plant. Pickers would also often package the plant, and the plant was shipped directly to the customer. The value Garden.com added was giving customers a wide selection of plants and related products from a single site. When investigating the industry, Garden.com's founders discovered that gardening had no dominant national retailers, a niche they subsequently tried to fill [168].

In-house Fulfillment

In-house fulfillment is a major feat of coordination, teamwork, timing, and integration. While outsourcing might work well if you have a small number of products, as your company and product offerings grow, lack of control over fulfillment operations can mean costly breakdowns in customer service in general. "If I have one piece of advice on fulfillment to share with other businesses, it's not to skimp on fulfillment," says Selina Yoon, President of Master Communications, which provides educational products and services to multilingual and multicultural customers around the world. "Many companies when starting out will be primarily concerned with front end processes like getting traffic to their Web site or getting people to try their products. But they should also think about back end processes like how they will service their customers through fulfillment. Customers return because of fulfillment and excellent customer service."

"If I have one piece of advice on fulfillment to share with other businesses, it's not to skimp on fulfillment."—Selina Yoon, President of Master Communications.

Master Communications sells products through two Web sites, Asiaforkids.com, which is also a catalog business, and Familiesoftheworld.com, which showcases a video series focusing on lives of families in different countries. Since its founding in 1994, Asia for Kids has grown to become an award-winning business offering bilingual materials in 23 languages and resource materials for 52 countries. It has satisfied customers in all 50 states in the United States and over 35 countries in Asia, Europe, Australia, and South America.

The growth of the company has been accompanied by a growth in its fulfillment processes. When the company first started, Yoon considered outsourcing fulfillment and investigated several 3PLs. But because Asia for Kids' products were of different sizes and shapes (merchandise includes books, videos, software, crafts, dolls, stamps, cards, and seals), it was difficult to find a 3PL that could accommodate orders, large and small, at a cost-effective rate. Yoon said that 3PLs tried to limit the number of box sizes for shipping, which wouldn't work for Asia for Kids because it sells to both institutions and individuals. Thus, it has always fulfilled orders in-house and has made a sequence of additions and upgrades to its hardware and software to accommodate the growing business.

Asia for Kids' current fulfillment system is close to being fully automated. When an order comes in from the Web site, a program checks to ensure that the data fields are entered properly. A person also reviews orders to confirm that address information typed in by customers meets the postal standardization. Payment is taken care of electronically. Then an invoice is printed and transmitted electronically to the warehouse. At the warehouse, the order is picked from slots where merchandise is placed according to its turnover level and packed. Asia for Kids' computers are networked with UPS's system so that information on shipment (weight, destination, and speed of delivery) is transmitted electronically to the delivery company. The tracking number is communicated back to the Asia for Kids system. It is currently working on providing automatic email notification of tracking numbers to the customer. UPS delivers and retrieves shipments from Asia for Kids' warehouse twice a day.

When products come into the warehouse, they must be properly recorded and placed into their designated slots. If the product has a barcode, it is scanned so fulfillment personnel know exactly where to shelve it. If it does not, as is the case with many products from foreign countries, Asia for Kids turns to its specially trained personnel to read the labels off the packaging and place the products in their proper slots. Indeed, because the company works with items in many different languages, it is necessary to hire multilingual, college-educated personnel. Sometimes being able to read the label on a product in a foreign language is the only way to properly shelve it in the warehouse.

Product inventory as it comes in is entered into a database that links to the Web site, which in turn informs customers of availability of merchandise. Asia for Kids strives to minimize the number of times it must contact a customer to inform her that a product is back-ordered. Yoon said that her company's inventory philosophy is just-in-time management. She warns against blindly buying in large quantities simply for the cents-off discount. "When you have large stocks of a product in inventory you have cash tied up and must also pay for space in which it is being held," she said. "Take into consideration the total cost of product, which includes availability of cash and inventory costs." Yoon pointed out that her company carefully manages its inventory so it does not have to resort regularly to discount sales to reduce inventory overstock.

· ·

BEST PRACTICES FOR IN-HOUSE FULFILLMENT

- Remember that fulfillment is an integral part of customer service and key to generating return business
- Do not skimp on fulfillment
- As much as possible, integrate your front end business with back end fulfillment and customer service
- Consider your total cost of product when ordering wholesale; keep in mind tied up cash and inventory costs
- Manage your inventory carefully to reduce the number of discount sales you must have for overstock
- Build teamwork among your fulfillment personnel so the process works effectively and seamlessly

Yoon emphasizes that fulfillment is an integral part of customer service. She makes sure that her team is working together to provide the highest levels of service. She is working on ways in which special offers or gifts can be inserted into order shipments. A trained staff member is hired to respond quickly to email requests, which keeps response times short. She regularly holds company lunches to build teamwork and to ensure that everyone is on the same page. When problems do arise, they are nipped in the bud through careful monitoring of the fulfillment process and through information sharing, which results in staff members knowing what others are doing at all times. Executing in-house fulfillment properly and in a timely fashion is complex, but with the right hardware, software, management, and personnel, it can be turned into a powerful customer service tool. The

Internet has raised consumers' expectations about customer service, and companies must take great care to deliver.

Even the best fulfillment operations need tweaking from time to time. Yoon recalled the time she had an operations expert examine her ordering system. Asia for Kids was ordering approximately every two weeks in keeping with its just-in-time philosophy. But every order required four to five people from purchasing, receiving, warehousing, and finance to process it. The operations expert analyzed the situation and recommended that ordering be done every six to eight weeks instead. The costs of carrying a larger inventory, he asserted, would be more than offset by the decrease in total systems costs, which includes handling invoices, payments, and warehouse receiving.

The venerable Amazon is also making full-fledged efforts to examine its operations to cut costs in its "march to profitability." It has hired top-flight engineers to analyze the company's entire operation to flush out inefficiencies and unprofitable products. It has tinkered with the idea of outsourcing some of its fulfillment, once considered anathema to the company, but it has held back due to fear of losing control over customer service. It has considered holding only bestselling books in stock and ordering lower turnover books only when a customer orders one, but there is trepidation that too many books showing a greater than 24-hour shipping promise would result in decreased customer satisfaction. There are some products that are simply too costly to ship, like the glass candle holder that broke in four successive shipments to the same customer, and the patio chair that required 15 minutes to pack properly [70]. Fulfillment is a never-ending effort of improvement, but those who learn to master it will emerge winners in the arena of online commerce.

B2B SYSTEMS . . . .

In this section we cover the evolution of electronic B2B payment systems, from EDI and XML to efforts to develop a universal payment system for companies around the world.

Electronic Data Exchange with EDI and XML

Beginning about three decades ago, there has been a way for companies to exchange data electronically. The initial impetus for electronic data exchange arose from the need to replace paper purchase orders (P.O.) and invoices between buyer and seller. Paper P.O.s and invoices could take days to reach their destination via postal service, and then information had to be manually entered into a company's computers to be processed. Thus, not only were companies losing time in receiving orders and payments, but human error could easily enter the process when the information was keyed in by hand. The traditional type of electronic data exchange was called EDI or electronic data interchange.

While the benefits of EDI were obvious, there were tremendous disadvantages that restricted the use of EDI to only the largest of companies. The primary disadvantage was cost. When EDI was first introduced, expensive mainframes were the main source of computing power for businesses. On top of that, EDI required a computer network between trading partners (companies exchanging data with EDI), which in the early days meant point-to-point proprietary networks. This resulted in a very low adoption rate. Indeed, even three decades later, only about 125,000 organizations around the world use EDI. Some 80,000 of these organizations are in the United States, fewer than two percent of the 6.2 million registered U.S. businesses [180].

With the introduction of the PC and cheaper computing power in the 1980s and the introduction of the Internet in the 1990s, many of the drawbacks of early EDI were eliminated. At the same time, EDI has been further developed to do much more than replace P.O.s and invoices. In its current state, it is possible for, say, a retail company to be linked to its suppliers in such a way that point-of-sale inventory balances can be transmitted into the retail company's EDI system, which automatically transmits replenishment needs to suppliers. The suppliers can then adjust their production schedules accordingly and inform the retail company of upcoming shipments with all of the necessary documents transmitted electronically.

Despite the improvements, most small- to medium-sized businesses still have not adopted EDI, primarily because of cost and use of private networks. As late as 1998, Giga Information Group estimated that more than 95 percent of EDI transactions occurred over traditional value added networks (VANs), which are "third-party" private communications networks, rather than the Internet. Although Internet use for EDI will increase, VANs will still remain in use because of security concerns in transmitting critical data over the public Internet. VAN providers also use their own communications infrastructures to lower costs in order to compete with Internet solutions [167].

One very important development in electronic data exchange is the adoption of XML (see Chapter 5, "Languages of the Internet"). XML can eliminate many of the problems of cost and inflexibility of traditional EDI because XML will no doubt become a standard language of Web browsers. Thus, small- and mid-sized businesses can easily adopt XML-based technology rather than having to adhere to an inflexible traditional EDI infrastructure. XML doesn't have a fixed format and allows trading partners to create their own tags for information exchange. In addition, a single EDI transaction can cost between $25 and $50, whereas an XML-based transaction will cost around $5. According to Laura Walker, executive director of the Organization for the Advancement of Structured Information Standards (OASIS) [127], "Today, big companies may be using EDI, but they aren't using it with all of their suppliers because their smaller suppliers can't afford the equipment. But in the future, when everyone is using XML, they'll all be able to use it, big and small. By benefiting the small companies, we also benefit the big companies."

For a while XML was pitted against EDI, with proponents of the former claiming that it was going to wipe EDI out forever. In reality, though, EDI has been around for a while, is well integrated into many systems, and will remain so as companies have enormous capital invested in it. What is occurring is the development of a hybrid system called XML/EDI. XML/EDI translation software allows traditional EDI documents to be converted to XML-based dialects, including xCBL, cXML, ebXML, and BizTalk. In addition, EDI vendors will include XML translation capabilities as part of their systems [166]. This allows for the best of the XML world to be incorporated into legacy EDI systems.

While XML/EDI may provide an excellent hybrid solution, many are touting XML as "The Next Big Thing." According to Zona Research, the percentage of XML-based Internet commerce transactions was a paltry 0.5 percent in 2000 but will rise to 40 percent by the end of 2003. Upstream Consulting predicts that sales of XML-based products and services will jump to $2.4 billion in 2004, an enormous leap from $90 million in 2000. Because of flexibility and the relatively low cost of XML-based systems, it is being adopted by large and small companies alike for use in supply chain management, communications applications, and enterprise application integration. A registry for companies to connect with each other using XML, called the Universal Description, Discovery and Integration (UDDI) effort, has over 200 participants, including tech heavyweights IBM, Microsoft, Oracle, and Sun Microsystems [127]. If and when XML will replace EDI remains to be seen. In the meantime, XML/EDI is offering many companies a satisfactory hybrid solution.

B2B Payment Systems

B2B payments are much more complicated than B2C payments. If you think authenticating and verifying the ability to pay for a secure $20 transaction using a credit card is complicated online, think of how much more is involved in authentication and verification between two companies wanting to close a multimillion dollar deal via the Internet. With B2B payments, there are not only payments to consider, but in many cases also invoicing, shipping, financing, insurance, escrow, letters of credit, and a host of other commercial transactions, especially when working in global commerce.

It all comes down to one word: trust. How can two companies who have "met" only via the Internet trust each other enough to complete all of the financial transactions necessary for business online? Each will be skeptical as to the other's ability to pay or deliver the goods as ordered. This is why companies have been slow to participate in B2B marketplaces. It's difficult to transact business when you don't know anything about your prospective trading partner. Companies are reluctant to forego their long-established relationships with partners whom they trust and who more likely than not have given them special deals for many years.

As you can imagine, the arena of B2B payments has been slow to develop because of the complexity involved. There have been a proliferation of B2B marketplaces, but few have been able to offer participating companies the ease and cost effectiveness of electronic payment systems. This is unfortunate, as the security of assured payment and fulfillment would be a major draw to participation in B2B marketplaces. One online payment solution is the use of purchasing or procurement cards, also called *P-cards*, which are essentially credit cards for businesses. They are used primarily for transactions of $5,000 or less, though some credit card issuers are looking to raise the limits. There are also companies like Actrade which will handle the uncertainty of payments, by paying suppliers immediately and allowing buyers to determine when they want to pay, say, in 30 or 90 days. Actrade charges about one percent to 1.5 percent of the total transaction for its services, which is usually covered by the supplier since the supplier often offers a 1.5 percent to 2.5 percent discount for immediate payment [170].

Other companies offer a more full-service solution to B2B transactions. Aceva Technologies, which is backed by industry heavyweights AOL Time Warner and Oracle, offers to overcome the B2B financial problems of missed business opportunities, inefficient credit account management, and ineffective financial transaction problems with its suite of products and services. Aceva offers electronic invoice presentment, electronic payment, credit assessment, dispute handling, and integration with manufacturing systems [170].

Another company that tackles the problems of identity and trust online is aptly named Identrus. It was founded by a consortium of some of the world's largest banks, including ABN AMRO, Bank of America, Barclays, Chase Manhattan, Citigroup, Deutsche Bank, and HypoVereinsbank. Essentially what Identrus does is certify the identities of its customers who receive Identrus Global IDs and thereby create a network of trusted trading partners. Identrus is a leading provider of PKI (public key infrastructure) technology, which was defined in Chapter 9. Through Identrus, it is claimed that any company in its network can do business with any other company in the network online in complete confidence. This allows for savings in time and money in all business transactions. In this way, Identrus acts as a third-party authority that verifies identities and guarantees payment between banks of trading partners. In July 2001 Royal Bank of Scotland, Sanwa Bank of Japan, and Wells Fargo joined ABN AMRO, Bank of America, Deutsche Bank, and HypoVereinsbank as financial institutions offering Identrus Global ID digital certificates. Still, adoption is slow and it remains to be seen whether Global IDs will replace the SSL-based user ID and password systems [181].

In the same way that the development of a universal payment standard for B2C transactions largely failed, so, too, is the effort to come up with a single payment standard for B2B transactions giving way to competing standards. One major standard, called Project Eleanor, is being developed by the same banks that formed the Identrus alliance, in conjunction with iPlanet, a Sun-Netscape company. The other, called E-Payment Plus, is being initiated by SWIFT, an industry owned cooperative supplying secure messaging services and interface software to over 7,000 financial institutions in 193 countries. Project Eleanor will let any user with an Identrus Global ID click on a button and make an online payment using public key technology. E-Payment Plus will allow buyers to initiate a payment request with their bank that will allow the bank to create a record of the payment, thereby reducing the problems associated with purchase orders, invoices, and payment receipts. There is hope that a single payment standard will emerge, linking the strengths of each. Until then, many banks are waiting before deciding which standard to adopt [182].

P2P SYSTEMS . . . .

If Identrus won't authenticate you, and neither your bank nor an ISO will give you a merchant account, don't despair. There's always a P2P (peer-to-peer) system to turn to. P2P business transactions occur most frequently with online auctions, where a person selling an item often doesn't offer credit card payment options. P2P transactions are also used to send non-business-related payments from one person to another via email. For the most part, all you need for payment is a bank account, possibly a credit card, and an Internet connection with an email address. To receive payment, you need an email address and usually registration with the payment system provider.

There are a number of P2P systems on the market. If you are an eBay regular, you have most likely signed up with Billpoint. To use Billpoint you must register with eBay.

With Billpoint you can send money to and from your checking account. Although Billpoint is convenient for eBay sales and purchases, it is not recommended for non-eBay payments. One of the most popular and best-known P2P payment systems is PayPal, which has about 8.5 million users. Registration with PayPal is instantaneous, and the company offers different kinds of accounts, including a Personal Account, a Premier Account, and a Business Account. Each different kind of account has its own limitations on payments and transactions costs. A third system is eMoneyMail, which charges a flat $1 fee for every transaction. Registration takes a week or so as the company wants to verify not only your email address but your postal address. eMoneyMail sends you a special code via the postal service, which you then enter into a form on the eMoneyMail site. Thus, it is not useful for urgent transactions [91]. As all of the P2P systems have different registration processes, transaction fees, percentage fees, and payment limits, be sure to investigate each before signing on.

FUTURE TRENDS AND IMPLICATIONS ....

Transactions, including payment and fulfillment, are hardly the more glamorous aspects of Internet business. Yet they are the bread and butter of business, and in the case of fulfillment, the reason why customers return with repeat business. Thus, as much attention must be paid to transactions as to front end processes like Web design and marketing. Because transactions costs are being slashed with the Internet, more and more businesses are turning to third-party providers. Use of third-party providers as a whole, gets your business up and running more quickly, but you also lose control over your business processes. In some cases, the efforts required to manage the third-party provider is equal to or more than the efforts that would be required doing a task yourself.

Credit cards are still by far the most widely used means of payment on the Internet. It's a shame that online businesses are scrutinized more closely by credit card services providers than offline businesses, but this is the case. If you can't get credit card services from a bank, be sure to carefully investigate any ISO before signing on with one. In the future it may well be that credit cards will be replaced by forms of digital cash, which allows the customer to shop anonymously and the merchant to reduce the number of chargebacks. In the meantime, however, secure forms of digital cash appear to be more trouble than they're worth. A promising form of anonymous payment is the use of smart cards. The use of electronic wallets will probably propagate also as users find that the convenience of using one outweighs the trouble of establishing one.

With regard to fulfillment, it seems third-party providers may be the way to go when you're first starting up a business and have a small number of products to offer. However, when your business grows and becomes more complicated, it seems in-house fulfillment results in better customer service and better integration with other aspects of your business. With in-house fulfillment you can tinker with promotions and other enticements for customers more easily than you can with third-party providers. With in-house fulfillment you have better control over how goods are packed and shipped, which could mean the difference between repeat business or not. Whatever the case may be, don't skimp on fulfillment, or you may find yourself without returning customers.

B2B transactions are much more complicated than B2C transactions. B2B transactions between unknown parties not only involve authentication of identity and secure payments, but also electronically transmitted invoices, payment verifications, shipping documents, insurance, and escrow. Thus, B2B transactions have been slower to be adopted than B2C transactions. Right now, two competing B2B standards, Identrus and SWIFT, are gaining credibility, but it is hoped that in the future one standard will emerge that will make adoption of electronically certified B2B transactions much more widespread. In the area of general electronic data exchange, EDI has been the reigning technology for several decades, but XML offers a less expensive, more easily adoptable alternative. Whether XML will completely replace EDI remains to be seen, but in the meantime a hybrid technology called XML/EDI is offering the best of both worlds.

11 Marketing on the Internet

In this chapter ...

THE SECOND WAVE OF INTERNET MARKETING

In the first wave of Internet marketing, when dot-coms were flush with venture capital, the overriding strategy was to build a brand and build it fast. In some cases, this entailed throwing an amazing 75 percent of cash reserves toward marketing and advertising, particularly into high-profile television commercials [96]. Dot-coms wanted to reach as wide an audience as possible, so they plunked millions into TV spots, the wackier the better. The belief was that this TV audience represented millions of viewers who would log onto the Web site and purchase whatever it was the site was selling. This represented the fastest transfer of wealth from venture capitalists to advertising agencies in the history of Internet business.

This strategy proved ineffective and capital fled the Internet economy—a form of capital punishment for the sins of excess. Marketing was only one of the excesses, which also included expensive real estate, credit cards for all employees, workout rooms, foosball tables, and lavish parties. The "burn rate" for cash was considered the most important metric of a dot-com's success, and dot-com executives were more concerned about the next round of venture capital than they were about business basics. But marketing was the linchpin of the early dot-com strategy of "build to flip" rather than "build to last." Build to flip meant founders would build the company to the point they could sell it for hundreds of millions or take it to an IPO worth billions, sell their stake, and retire at the age of 30. Since a dot-com's worth in those days was based on hype rather than profitability, it's no wonder dot-com CEOs threw so much cash into marketing.

. . . .

THE NEW ROLE OF MARKETING IN INTERNET BUSINESS

In the aftermath of the dot-com carnage, marketing in Internet business has taken on a different role. In this second wave, marketing, advertising, and branding are all very important, but companies are retrenching. Doing more with less has become the new mantra. Smart, rather than all-out, marketing is the keyword of the day. Advertisements have become less outrageous and more subdued. Brick-and-mortar companies have also discovered the virtues of marketing on the Internet, so it is not just about building a dot-com brand, but about combining offline and online strategies and making the most of the special characteristics of the medium.

A number of new forms of marketing could not have gained in popularity and become prevalent without the unique medium of the Internet. One-to-one marketing, permission marketing, and viral marketing, while undergoing metamorphoses since they were first introduced, have become possible because the Internet is a relatively inexpensive, efficient, and personalizable medium. Transactions on the Internet are also trackable and measurable, which takes data gathering and market research to new levels. The medium also gives rise to new ways to annoy the prospective customer, with things such as spam and pop-up and pop-under windows. The combination of personalization and data gathering allows the Web to cull and record information about the customer that he might not want kept. Even the securest strongholds of data are prone to hacker attacks, which further heightens concerns about privacy.

While the Internet has affected all disciplines of business, it has had its biggest effect on marketing. The changes occurring in marketing due to the Internet are the fascinating subject of this chapter. In the first section, "Internet Marketing Strategies," we introduce branding on the Web, partnering, one-to-one marketing, permission marketing, viral marketing, doing more with less, and what not to do. In the second section, "One of the Greatest Things about the Web: Measurement," we show how tracking and data gathering occur on both the client and server sides of the Web. The third section, "Internet Marketing Media," is devoted to the different ways you can market using the Internet. Finally, we conclude the chapter with a section on "Future Trends and Implications," which will look at the ways Internet marketing is evolving.

INTERNET MARKETING STRATEGIES ....

Various online marketing strategies have been tried and tested. In this section we see what works and what doesn't.

The Death of Marketing?

Regis McKenna, chairman of Palo Alto high-tech marketing firm the McKenna Group, who helped guide some of today's computer giants, including AOL, Apple Computer, Compaq Computer, Microsoft, and 3Com, views marketing as, "becoming an integrated part of the whole organization, rather than a specific function. . . More and more, it's the CEO who's becoming the chief marketer. . . I don't think we can tell the difference any more between a corporate strategy and a marketing strategy. That's just vanished" [95]. If this is the case, marketing is increasingly responsible for setting the direction for the entire company. Marketing has traditionally been responsible for product development, pricing, promotion, and distribution. But in today's world, some of these responsibilities have been taken over by the CEO or CIO, or have been put in the hands of the customer. Thanks to the Web, Nike customers contribute to product development by custom-designing their own shoes. Pricing is also becoming the purview of the customer with firms like eBay and Priceline. CEOs today are rarely given ten to twenty years to lead a company in a new direction. In many cases, they are given less than a year to turn the company around. Many of them are chosen based on the instant "buzz" they can generate, putting the responsibility of promotion in the hands of the CEO. The decision to enter, promote, and distribute a company's products over the Web is no longer that of the marketing director alone, but a decision shared by the CEO and CIO.

Does this mean the end of marketing as we know it? Hardly. This means that marketing is in the process of transforming itself into something less compartmentalized and more powerful with respect to determining the company's growth and profitability. This is in no small part due to the power of the Internet. Suddenly, marketing is personal. Historically, marketing has been intended for the masses, all those watching a television program or listening to a radio program or reading a newspaper or magazine. The same message was served to everyone engaged in the shared activity with little concern for who that person was with the exception of that person belonging to a certain demographic. The Internet is changing all of that. Now, companies can track a customer's movements on the Web instantaneously. Consequently, the company can tailor its message to her based on this information. It's now possible to move beyond blanket advertisements toward personalized advertisements.

But does Internet marketing work? Should there be a difference between offline and online marketing? How can the two be integrated for an optimal marketing strategy? There has been a rethinking of the kinds of marketing that the Internet has spawned, such as one-to-one marketing, permission marketing, and viral marketing. Do these really work as presented in the books that introduced them, or do they have to be modified to contend with the realities of the marketplace? We address all of these issues in this section.

Building a Successful Brand

Some claim the Internet is unsuited for branding because it cannot evoke the kind of emotion that, say, a 30-second television spot can. While this opinion is changing with the use of rich media like video, many marketers firmly believe that the Internet, even without rich media, is extremely capable of evoking an emotional experience. At www. adiamondisforever.com, for example, a couple can design their own engagement ring, which creates a highly emotional experience and deepens their relationship with diamonds, according to Richard Lennox, director in charge of the Diamond Trading Company account for J. Walter Thompson. Holly Higgins, Internet advertising business development manager at Hewlett-Packard, agrees. She defines branding as the customer's experience every time she's touched, whether the customer is purchasing a printer cartridge at a reseller or having a creative, inventive experience with one of Hewlett-Packard's banner ads [22].

Branding is all about developing relationships and trust between the customer and the company, according to Lin Sakai, principal at brand identity and design consultant LiDesign (www.lidesign.net) in New York. The product or service, at some level, she said, satisfies some kind of emotional benefit. Unfortunately, in the early days of the dot-coms, these all-important aspects of branding were often left by the wayside. Duncan Ralph, Director of Brand Development Consulting at LiDesign, said that all too often branding and marketing are internally focused, politically influenced, or driven by single-minded "agency mentalities." Time and again, he sees the tremendous cost involved with creating a "traditional advertising campaign" completely overshadowing the true role of marketing and branding, which is satisfying customer needs and exceeding expectations.

"Branding is all about developing relationships and trust between the customer and the company." – Lin Sakai, principal at brand identity and design consultant LiDesign.

Ironically, given the early dot-com branding fiascoes, the Internet is ideally suited to developing relationships with customers, if not the greatest direct marketing medium ever invented. What this means, explained Lesley Verdi, principal of New York-based Keane Verdi marketing consultants, is that the marketer is able to market one-to-one with the customer over the Internet, as opposed to mass marketing. With the Internet, said Verdi, the marketer can know with whom she is communicating, get information and feedback from the customer, cross-sell, and upsell.

As an example of how branding can take place over the Internet, Sakai pointed to the Web site for InVite Health (`www.invitehealth.com`) created by LiDesign. InVite Health is a nutritional products company that develops pharmaceutical grade natural products for health professionals and their patients. The company's formulas reflect the most current scientific data from peer-reviewed professional journals wherever possible and are regularly modified to reflect advances in nutritional science. In addition to displaying the company's nutritional products, the Web site was created to provide a responsible online forum to explore new ideas in health and nutrition, an interactive platform with designated sections for professionals and consumers. See Figure 11–1 for a view of InVite Health's home page (screen shot reprinted courtesy of InVite Health).

Sakai said of the site: "Because their target audience includes medical professionals as well as consumers, their brand image calls for an authoritative, yet friendly look. When designing the Web site (since pictures connect with people more quickly and emotionally than words), we used photos and colors that would involve and draw visitors into the site. Beyond its look and feel, it's how the brand behaves that's important. The Web site provides a wonderful venue for InVite Health's advisory board (comprised of the nation's leading integrative medical specialists) to evaluate and provide guidance on the latest, often contradictory and confusing, health and nutrition news. It will offer Continuing Medical Education courses to professionals and hosted chat rooms for both professionals and consumers on such topics as diabetes."

Steven Kornblatt, President of InVite Health, said of the Web site that the company wanted a look and feel that was authoritative and scientific, yet friendly and accessible: "How we look, what we say, and how we say it must insure that visitors (both health professionals and consumers) feel we are credible and trustworthy." The goals of the Web site, which Kornblatt views as more of a public relations tool than a sales tool, were to:

- Raise awareness of the company and its nutritional supplement products
- Create a competitive advantage by communicating the company's unique benefits
- Develop customer trust and confidence by providing useful, reliable information about nutritional supplements and nutrition in general
- Sustain customer loyalty by offering membership benefits and incentive programs.

InVite Health's brand essence is good health, which Kornblatt feels is carried through via the Web site by meeting the goals above. "We are very pleased thus far with the response from the medical community," he said. "InVite Health is filling the need for a scientifically sound, professionally designed, and easy-to-navigate site that says 'of the highest quality'."

Figure 11–1 Home page for InViteHealth.com.

Branding on the Internet can result in other benefits. "Being on the Internet is being on the bleeding edge of technology and business," said Verdi. "It makes a brand contemporary and savvy and technologically advanced. Brand images are formed one customer at a time and this can be done very effectively online where you can provide interactivity and multimedia experiences. And, the great thing about the Internet is that it is regarded as a communication channel that all types of brands use." As more companies establish sites, being on the Internet is becoming a necessary part of doing business. But just because you establish your brand on the Internet, be aware of the difference between brand awareness and brand equity. "Just because a brand is known doesn't mean that it has any equity, any value to the customer," continued Verdi. "Companies lose customers when they don't deliver on the value proposition, when they don't satisfy customers, and when they don't pay attention to customer service."

The problem with dot-coms was that they believed building brand awareness was enough. They not only missed the mark by trying to do it too quickly in the wrong media, they also lacked a strong business model. A brand is only as strong as the company that it represents. Nor should it be one of the highest priorities in the initial stages of building a company. A start-up should focus instead on building a solid business model and providing value to its customers. Internet business is evolving, and we now know that the strategy of building a brand quickly is not sustainable. But the Internet has most certainly proved to be an excellent branding medium, as many marketers will attest. It's just necessary to make the most of the special nature of the Internet, as this chapter will show how.

Rethinking One-to-One Marketing

Before the days of mass production, all marketing, if you could call it that, was one-to-one. A proprietor knew all his customers, their tastes, what they purchased in the past, and worked to maintain good relationships with each of them. He may have tried to recommend a purchase to a customer based on the customer's past purchases. He focused more on selling additional items to his existing customers than he did on trying to acquire new customers. The extent of his advertising might have been a sign on the front of his store.

All of this changed with mass production. Products like Henry Ford's automobiles rolled off the assembly lines, and every effort was made to find new customers for these products. As factories churned out thousands of products in a day, it became impossible to keep track of all customers' preferences and past purchases. As retail distribution developed, there was little a manufacturer could do to find out who was buying the products. Mass production created mass markets and mass marketing. The first advertisements that appeared in newspapers, and later on radio and television, were designed to appeal to as many people as possible. When marketing became more sophisticated, the idea of marketing to a target audience in a particular demographic replaced mass advertising. Marketing became more segmented, but it was hardly one-to-one.

With the advent of computers and databases, information on customers could be kept more efficiently, but little was done with this information in marketing because it was too expensive to customize advertising for each customer. Catalog retailers, for example, had information on what their customers had purchased in the past, but all they could do to market their wares was to send yet another catalog. Manufacturers and service providers relied on traditional media such as print, radio, and television to get their messages across, but with little customization. In retail, a salesperson might have kept a database on repeat customers and may have called when an item his customer had purchased was going on sale. This level of personalization was rare, however, and generally restricted to high-end retailers.

With the Internet, marketing has transformed itself once again. It is now possible to take advantage of one-to-one marketing techniques. While the Internet didn't really take off in the mass market until 1996-1997, a book published in 1993 foreshadowed the changes the Internet would bring. *The One to One Future* [131], written by Don Peppers and Martha Rogers, launched the concept of *one-to-one marketing*, which at that time was a radical idea. Remember that the early 1990s was still a time when mass, or at least target, marketing ruled. Peppers and Rogers contended that a firm would do well to sell more to its existing customers than try to acquire new customers. They proposed that a firm should concentrate on deepening its relationships with current customers, rather than spending inordinate amounts of money trying to acquire new ones. In 1993, the Internet was still a new medium, used primarily by government officials and academics.

Ironically, the idea of one-to-one marketing really took off when the Internet became a mass medium. The interactivity of the Internet allowed customers to submit information about themselves, which could be immediately stored in a database. The database could be used to personalize, cheaply and efficiently, targeted advertisements to each individual customer. A customized advertisement could either be emailed to the customer or presented to the customer whenever the customer logged on to the company's Web site. The theory behind customized marketing is that the more information you have about a customer, the more personalized a message or advertisement can be, and the more likely the customer will purchase again because the advertisement will zero in on specific needs and preferences.

But the reality of one-to-one Internet marketing doesn't always mesh with the theory. While in theory it's possible to keep a database on a customer and send personalized advertisements, in reality it's very difficult to do it on a large scale and do it right. One problem is that some "personalized" advertisements turn out to be irrelevant to the customer's needs. Just because a customer purchased a red sweater in the past doesn't necessarily mean she's interested in a blue sweater of the same type if it goes on sale. Or just because a customer is a frequent flyer of an airline doesn't mean she's interested in information about all discounted flights if they're not for routes she travels.

Marketers try to use logic to figure out what a customer might be interested in based on past behavior and purchases, but the truth of the matter is that customers aren't always logical. In fact, human beings can be downright quirky in their purchasing behavior. Just because people want to name their price for airline fares and hotel rooms doesn't mean they want to do it for gasoline and groceries, as Priceline discovered. And while it may seem logical that busy urban professionals would want videos and Chunky Monkey ice cream delivered to their doorstep by placing an order on the Web, in reality it is difficult to build a profitable business model around this idea, as former delivery dot-coms Kozmo.com and Urbanfetch.com will attest.

A second problem with one-to-one Internet marketing is that it is difficult for even the most sophisticated software to supplant the human touch. Most one-to-one marketing software uses machine learning algorithms that search for patterns in databases [64]. When all is said and done, though, is an advertisement or purchase recommendation based on patterns and algorithms more effective than a telephone call from a personal shopper or live interaction with a salesperson at the mall? Maybe not, but if all of these methods are combined into an integrated offline and online marketing strategy, the synergy created will enhance the results of each method used alone. Indeed, the most successful one-to-one Internet marketers are companies like Omaha Steaks and The Sharper Image, who have well-developed offline marketing strategies and are using email marketing as another channel in the mix. "They have multiple touch points for dealing with customers," says Lynne Harvey, a senior analyst and consultant with Boston's Patricia Seybold Group. "They have call centers, catalogs, physical stores. You can get information in lots of different ways. There's always a person you can call who will help you. Email marketing is just the tip of the iceberg for these companies [97]."

The third problem with one-to-one Internet marketing is that it is expensive. In general, when one thinks of automation versus human intervention, automation is considered the less expensive option. But in the case of the sophisticated one-to-one marketing software, this is not necessarily so. The complexity and scale required for a successful implementation necessitates an investment of about $500,000 and a commitment of six months for installation and training. Moreover, it is a big challenge to train marketers to use the software effectively [97]. Thus implementation is not for the fainthearted or the small-budgeted. It is easy to see why the bloom is off the rose for one-to-one Internet marketing, yet its promise and technology keep its interest high. Personalized advertising based on past behavior *is* a marketer's dream. And dreams are what carry many of us through the day. Even if one-to-one Internet marketing is still in development, the possibilities continue to light the fires of many a marketer. In the spring of 2000, marketing columnist Jeffrey Graham addressed a group of traditional marketers who wanted to know more about Internet marketing and possibly make the switch into the new field. A year later he addressed the same group, many of whom had found jobs in Internet marketing but were subsequently laid off in the dot-com carnage. Graham wrote about this group: "Yet despite the lack of security, shifting organizational structures, inexperienced and chaotic management, and long, grueling hours, nobody wanted to return to traditional marketing. There is just too much opportunity in e-marketing to ever want to go back" [61]. As it now stands, successful one-to-one Internet marketing is a goal and a challenge. It is ever-evolving, as is everything else on the Web. The only conclusion that can be made about it is that to be successful it is best combined with other marketing channels.

. . . .

THE REALITY OF ONE-TO-ONE INTERNET MARKETING

- It's difficult to execute personalized Internet marketing on a large scale
- It's difficult for even the most sophisticated software to supplant the human touch
- Sophisticated one-to-one Internet marketing is expensive

Does Permission Marketing Work?

Permission marketing was a groundbreaking concept introduced by Internet marketing pioneer Seth Godin. In 1999 he published a book, *Permission Marketing* [58], in which he introduced the terms "interruption marketing" and "permission marketing." Interruption marketing was the traditional form of marketing such as television, radio, and print advertising which "interrupted" what you really wanted to see, listen to, or read. The most striking example of interruption marketing is the telemarketer who interrupts your dinner to tell you about the latest long distance service plan.

In the Age of Information Overload, however, your time and attention may be the most precious resources you have. Thus, to interrupt your attention with unwanted messages is to commit an egregious act. In fact, with the bombardment of advertising messages that you receive every day, the effectiveness of a single advertisement is close to zero.

The solution to this, according to Godin, is permission marketing. That is, a marketer asks for and receives permission from the customer to send information about the company's products and services. That way, advertising messages are actually requested. Is this possible? Are there people who would actually grant permission to be bombarded with even more marketing information? Sure there are, as long as the messages are relevant to the person's needs and interests, or, as is the case in many instances, the person is compensated for receiving the advertisements. Even if the person is not intrinsically interested in the product or service, he may be enticed into receiving information about it through the use of sweepstakes, coupons, or cash. The point is to come up with a cost-effective way to generate a lot of eyes and ears for messages about your company. You are no longer interrupting or bothering people to convey information, but they are actually anticipating, if not looking forward to it.

One of the first, best-known, and premier examples of permission marketing is the InCircle Rewards Program of Neiman Marcus. The concept is simple; the rewards are fabulous. First of all, a customer must sign up for a Neiman Marcus credit card. Usually, customers can sign up instantly in stores. When customers use their Neiman Marcus credit card, the company gathers information on every purchase made. For every dollar charged on the Neiman Marcus credit card, customers receive an InCircle point. Once a customer tallies up 3,000 points, she becomes an InCircle member.

Being an InCircle member has its privileges, including being invited to special shopping events at which shoppers can eat, drink, and earn double points, and receiving advance notice of sales, complimentary gift packaging, quarterly newsletters, and glossy issues of fashion-forward Neiman Marcus publications. Once she accrues 5,000 points, she is eligible for any number of gifts, which increase in value and rarity through 5,000,000 points (at which point she receives a pair of Lexus automobiles). Thus, by becoming an InCircle member, the Neiman Marcus customer gains entrée into an exclusive club and grants permission to receive lush publications on the latest Neiman Marcus offerings, keeping her current on up-to-the-minute fashions and accessories.

Does permission marketing work? If executed properly, there is nothing better than an audience waiting for more information about the products and services you are offering. Although this may not necessarily translate into sales, breaking through the clutter is a step in the right direction. Permission marketing is based on trust, trust that you will deliver to the customer no more and no less than promised. You will send her information, but you will not sell her contact information to other companies. You will also not try to "trick" her into agreeing to receive the advertisements. This is done by a simple "opt in" and "opt out" box on a Web site, which allows a visitor to a site to decide whether to receive the information ("opt in") or decline ("opt out").

The "trickery" works in this way: Many sites will have the opt in box automatically checked so that in order to opt out, the visitor has to deliberately click on the opt in box in order to change the configuration. Many times, these boxes are hidden deeply within the site so the customer does not encounter them. This means that the company has tacit permission to send the customer whatever advertising it wishes. Using this tactic, a company can boast a certain percentage of opt in customers. Tactics such as these can undermine the legitimacy and prove the downfall of permission marketing [163]. All in all, permission marketing is a concept whose time has come. However, it must be executed properly in order to work.

We have discussed how difficult it is to execute Internet marketing that is personal and relevant to a large number of people. If it's anticipated, a huge hurdle is overcome. Nevertheless, once the prospective customer's attention is directed to the advertisement, if it is not personal and relevant, the effort is lost. Thus, it is not practical to go about gathering as many "permission customers" as possible if they are not intrinsically interested in what you have to offer. The moral of the permission marketing story is that it can work if and only if you have executed the strategy properly without jeopardizing the trust of your site visitors. To understand how to get a visitor's permission in the first place, read on to the next section on "viral marketing."

DESIRED QUALITIES OF PERMISSION MARKETING

According to Godin, permission marketing must be [58]:

- Anticipated—people look forward to hearing from you
- Personal—the messages are directly related to the individual
- Relevant—the marketing is about something of interest to the prospect

Let Your Customers Do the (Viral) Marketing

Viruses are usually an undesirable thing to catch, whether physical or digital. But Seth Godin (yes, the same Seth Godin) has conceived of a new kind of virus—the ideavirus—and turned it into a positive force. An ideavirus, or the special case of *viral marketing*, relies on customers to disseminate a message quickly and widely. The vector of marketing is customer-to-customer, rather than business-to-customer. Aptly named, viral marketing was introduced in Godin's book, *Unleashing the Ideavirus*, published in 2000 [59], and also available through free download from www.ideavirus.com. The basic premise is that an ideavirus is word-of-mouth marketing on steroids. What makes the concept of an ideavirus work particularly well is—you guessed it, the special medium of the Internet. An idea can be transmitted much more rapidly, smoothly, and persistently from customer-to-customer using email and the Web than it can through mere word-of-mouth.

One of the examples of an ideavirus Godin uses is Hotmail, the free email service now owned by Microsoft. It took Hotmail less than a year to get 10 million users because of the power of the ideavirus. Here's how it worked: When a user sent an email using Hotmail, there was a small trailer at the bottom of every message that read, "Get Your Private, Free Email from Hotmail at www.hotmail.com." Of course, the URL was clickable so all the recipient had to do was click once to access the site, and click a few more times to have her own free email. It worked incredibly well because the advertisement was rapidly disseminated millions of times a day to the perfect target audience (other email users), and adopting Hotmail was just a few clicks away (smooth, in Godin's terms). In fact, Hotmail is that special case of the ideavirus called viral marketing, in which the medium of the virus is the product.

Godin contends that companies can create the infrastructure to pave the way for an ideavirus's propagation. In other words, ideaviruses can be made, and are not purely haphazard. He provides many techniques for unleashing an ideavirus, which we'll leave to you to investigate (after all, the advice is free!). This is yet another form of marketing which could only really take full effect thanks to the power of the Internet. Because of the casual nature of the ideavirus medium (usually email), the product or service marketed through ideaviruses is generally youth-oriented and more fun than serious. Examples in the book include Napster, GeoCities, Volkswagen, Polaroid, Blue Mountain Arts, and *Fast Company*. Therefore, unleashing an ideavirus isn't meant for every product or service. Nevertheless, an ideavirus is another channel to consider.

The Pros and Cons of Partnering

Partnering is another keyword that has been frequently applied to companies engaged in Internet business. AOL Time Warner is the greatest partnering initiative in the history of Internet business to date where the whole is greater than the sum of its parts. Partnering as a marketing strategy for Internet business works well when synergies are created, especially when it occurs between an offline and online company. Many brick-and-mortar companies, eager to get a foothold into Internet business, have partnered with companies with a strong Internet presence. Partnering can be as simple as agreeing to advertise each other's Web sites on one's own or as complicated as, well, AOL Time Warner.

Partnering became popular because of the open culture of the Internet. We mentioned the open source movement of software development in Chapter 3, "Software Is Everywhere," and the classic Internet strategy of giving away something free in Chapter 6, "Web Site Design and Content." Consequently, it is only fitting that the Internet would give rise to the concept of partnering, whereby a company could provide a service in exchange for a service from another company, without incurring additional costs. After all, the origins of the Internet indicate that it should be used collaboratively (as in research) to benefit many. The Massachusetts Institute of Technology (MIT) has decided to offer nearly all of its course materials, including lecture notes, course outlines, reading lists, and assignments, free on the Internet. This is an extension of the culture of the Internet [7]. Whether this can work in the for-profit world remains to be seen.

Some evidence suggests that partnering, despite its noble intentions, does not always work. Witness the partnership between Kellogg's and now defunct Toysmart.com in 2000, backed by Disney. The deal required Kellogg's to advertise on boxes of Froot Loops ® and Frosted Flakes an online loyalty program called Eet and Ern, which promoted Toysmart.com. However, Disney backed out on Toysmart.com only three weeks after the cereal boxes hit the shelves, which left Kellogg's hanging in the wind with its promotional boxes. While Kellogg's claims the retreat by Disney did not hurt its own offline sales, some analysts say that a move like this by Disney definitely hurt the product. "Brand equity cannot be bought," says Laura Mitrovich, a program manager with The Yankee Group. "Brand equity can only be built. . .Co-marketing deals are invitations for consumers to interact with brands. So when the dot-com partner fails, the offline marketer takes a punch as well. That's the crux of the risk" [55]. As is the case with one-to-one marketing and permission marketing, trust is the keyword. Be sure you know with whom you're dealing before entering into a partnering contract with the company and have alternate recourse written up in the contract in case one partner decides to bail out.

Doing More with Less

With the days of big-budget advertising over, the new marketing mantra is doing more with less. Unless you've got a marketing budget like Procter & Gamble's, it's time to search for creative alternatives. In Chapter 6, we described free ways to promote your Web site. These include putting appropriate keywords in the body of your Web pages and in the meta tags and registering your site with the major search engines. Other cost-effective techniques described in the chapter are creating a gateway page for your site and purchasing software like Web Position Gold. Viral marketing is another relatively inexpensive way to propagate your message. Other media like email marketing will be discussed later in the chapter.

If you've got a little bigger budget to work with and want to promote your site outside of cyberspace, there are less costly alternatives. One strategy is to seek out unconventional media for ad placement. We've all heard of passing out flyers to pedestrians or persons wearing sandwich boards, but some companies are using paper bags, bananas, coffee cup jackets, and automobiles to get their message across. Bag Media in Port Chester, NY, can put your message on paper bags for about five cents a bag and distribute them to doughnut and other shops. Askjeeves.com launched a nationwide campaign in which stickers that promoted the site were placed on bananas, apples, and oranges sold in supermarkets. The cost was less than $150,000. Java Jacket, the Portland, OR manufacturer of brown paper coffee cup jackets that prevent fingers from getting too hot, can put your message on a jacket for about $150 per case (1,300). Autowraps of San Francisco will place vinyl ads on vehicles, ranging from Volkswagen Beetles to 18-wheelers, to the tune of about $33,000 for the first month for 100 back-window ads and $20,000 per month thereafter. Companies that have purchased these unusual media are Hotjobs.com and Bizrate.com (Bag Media), Warner Bros., and *The Wall Street Journal* (Java Jacket) [54].

As was the case with viral marketing, however, it is important to consider whether these kinds of unconventional media are appropriate for your message. Like email, media like doughnuts bags, fruit, java jackets, and automobiles are casual, so they are most appropriate for hip, irreverent, or youth-oriented products and services. One must consider the market that would be purchasing the doughnuts, coffee, and fruit, or driving in the urban areas viewing the ads on automobiles. These media would probably not be appropriate to promote a hospital's site or certain luxury items, for example. Thus, while doing more with less is the catch phrase of the current marketing climate, be sure that less expensive media do not project an improper image for your company. With unconventional media, the medium is often the message.

. . . .

ON USING UNCONVENTIONAL MEDIA

While doing more with less is the catch phrase of the current marketing climate, be sure that less expensive media do not project an improper image for your company. With unconventional media, the medium is often the message.

What Not to Do

We have described the culture of the Internet as open, free, and collaborative. While there are some aspects of it that are proprietary, expensive, and competitive, many of the original visionaries of the Internet and their followers hold fast to the ideal that the Internet is a place of sharing. Tim Berners-Lee created the World Wide Web because he wanted to enable scientists with different computers and operating systems to be able to easily share research results. The first Mosaic browser, the predecessor to the Netscape browser created by Marc Andreesen, was freely downloaded and shared. Yahoo!'s founders originally created the search engine as a means to show others cool sites they had found and to help others navigate the Web. Amazon's first business model was to sell deeply discounted books over the Web. These pioneers' ideal is still much in evidence with the plethora of free information, free software downloads, and free trials of products and services available through the Internet.

There is another equally important and related characteristic of Internet culture which you must keep in mind when creating your Internet marketing strategy. That is the etiquette of respecting other people's time and bandwidth. This is especially true of advertisements. The Internet is a fast medium, and in this Age of Information Overload users' time is precious. It takes time to download email and navigate Web sites, so one should keep email short and Web sites usable. This means keeping unwanted advertisements out of others' email inboxes and shunning tricks to keep the user on your site (more on this later).

Closely related to time on the Internet is bandwidth, because anything that takes up bandwidth on the Internet takes time to download. Some people even dislike email sent in colorful text because color takes up more bits than plain text. Because the Internet was originally developed for government and research purposes rather than commercial use, there is a definite stigma attached to advertisements in inappropriate spaces. Inappropriate places include email inboxes, newsgroups, and chat rooms, although attitudes are changing as the Internet becomes more commercial.

The classic marketing example of not respecting other users' time and bandwidth is spam. Spam is unwanted email advertisements. Spam usually consists of get-rich-quick-schemes and ads for porn sites, but it now encompasses advertisements from a wide range of organizations. Spam is prevalent because email is an inexpensive and effective way to disseminate a message. It used to be that spammers got "flamed," sent back an angry email expressing outrage at receiving such a message. But flaming the spammer only confirms that your email address is a working one (as does asking to be removed from the list), which is likely to increase the amount of spam you receive.

There are measures being taken to fight spam. Some Internet service providers (ISPs) will cut off your service if they discover you are sending spam. Another daring measure is Microsoft's attempt to filter spam from its Hotmail accounts by unilaterally discarding email sent to and from sites hosted by Internet service providers suspected of propagating spam. There is also an organization called Mail Abuse Prevention System (MAPS), which maintains the Realtime Blackhole List (RBL), a list of ISPs that are known to host some spammers. When a company such as Hotmail signs on with MAPS, it can choose from several blocking options to control spam [18]. Thus, you may be tempted to resort to spam because it is cost-efficient, but we discourage you from doing so because it can have a lasting negative effect on your company.

Another unseemly form of Internet marketing is the use of devices to keep users on a Web site longer than they want to be. The objective behind using these devices is to improve site traffic numbers by forcibly boosting time users spend on a site or increasing the number of impressions per visit. One of these devices is called "multiple window launching" or "exiting." Multiple window launching works by a site taking control of the user's browser when the user indicates he wants to leave the site by typing in a new address. When he does this, the site launches more windows that the user must shut down in order to leave the site. Some of these windows cannot be shut down without shutting down the computer. The end result of using these windows is that the time the user spends on the site is increased, and with each window the user views, another "impression" can be added to the site's traffic numbers. Increased traffic numbers and increased times spent at a site means the site's company can charge more for advertising on the site.

Closely related to multiple window launching is the use of pop-under windows which open up "underneath" the main browser window as you're browsing and then remain on the screen even after you shut your browser down. This is akin to having an advertisement appear on your television screen after you've turned the television off. With increased time spent at a site and boosted site traffic numbers, more can be charged for advertisers on the site. Another related means of keeping users on a site against their will is "mousetrapping." With mousetrapping, the URLs of the browser's back and forward buttons are programmed to redirect the user back to the page he was on instead of backward or forward. Thus, the user is trapped on the site and must shut down the entire browser and sometimes his computer in order to exit [124].

Users are also fighting back against these forms of advertising. Many simply refuse to return to a site that engages in these practices. Others are taking the offensive by purchasing software or reconfiguring their browsers to quash the advertisements before they can appear. Software like Pop-Up Stopper from Panicware prevents pop-up windows and allows the user to choose which ads she views. Another program called Banner Catcher from Softica Solutions lets users control ad windows and eliminate ones they don't wish to see. In the end, devices to keep a user on a site beyond his will are shunned and attacked by many users and are generally associated with porn sites. If you want to maintain a clean and Internet culture-friendly image for your company, we suggest avoiding these techniques.

ONE OF THE GREATEST THINGS ABOUT THE WEB: MEASUREMENT.......................

One of the great promises of the Web for companies that established sites was that every movement of every visitor to the site could be tracked, collected, and organized. This would produce reams of data that could be analyzed for a more precise and scientific approach to marketing. The same promise held for scanner data in supermarkets, which so far has turned out to be largely a disappointment. Many supermarkets find the amount of data collected from scanners overwhelming and are not sure how to exploit the data to their advantage. Will the promise of Web site data turn out the same way? In this section, we look at server-side tracking and client-side tracking to see what data you can collect on your customers.

Marketing Vocabulary for Measurement

Before we discuss measurement, it is necessary to have some vocabulary to help you better understand what can be done with site traffic data.

- **Hit**: the number of times each page or *element* in a page is retrieved. A page with a lot of pictures will result in many hits to the server

- **Gross exposures or impressions**: the total number of times an ad was actually seen

- **Banner ad**: small rectangular graphics that appear usually at the top and along the right-hand side of Web pages

- **Ad views (or download)**: number of times an ad is delivered from the server

- **Click-through**: when a user clicks on a banner ad and goes to a company site (this is usually a very small number, about one or two percent or less of total number of views)

- **CPM (cost per thousand impressions)**: price a company pays for having 1,000 impressions delivered by a Web site

- **Unique users**: number of unique individuals who visit a site during a specified time period

- **Reach**: the percentage of possible audience you touch with your advertising

- **Conversion**: the moment when customers buy, whether the purchase is for a product or service, subscribing to a newsletter, or joining a discussion

- **Conversion cost**: advertising and other promotional costs divided by the number of sales

- **Retention**: getting customers to return to your site time and time again

For more on the language of data-based marketing on the Web, see the article by Jim Sterne, marketing consultant for Santa Barbara firm Target Marketing, and author of a number of books on Internet marketing [152]. Also, the Web sites of Ipro and WebMethods provide a nice glossary of terms.

Server-Side Tracking

To better understand their customers, companies would like to track visitors at their site and record as much information as possible. There are essentially two ways to track visitors at a Web site. One way is through *server-side tracking* and the other is through *client-side tracking*. Server-side tracking is based on the analysis of *server log files*, while client-side tracking is conducted, for the most part, through the use of *cookie files*. Cookies are discussed in the next subsection. The following illuminates the difference between the two and which might be more helpful to you and your company.

For tracking purposes, Web servers keep log files. Some of the items typically recorded in a log file are:

1. **Date**: the date when the URL request was made

2. **Time**: the time when the URL request was made

3. **Result**: the result of the request: was there an error or was there a successful transfer of data?

4. **Client IP Address**: the IP number of the client machine

5. **Bytes sent**: the number of bytes transferred by the request

6. **Method:** the type of action the client was requesting, for example the GET method

7. **User Agent:** the browser used by the client, e.g., Netscape Navigator or Internet Explorer

8. **URL Stem:** the target URL requested by the client

9. **Referrer:** the previous site visited by the user

These log files are text files and most servers at least support the W3C Extended Log File Format.

Tech Talk

W3C Extended Log File Format: a W3C standard format for HTTP server log files. This file format includes the time, client IP address, the method, the URL, and the result of the request. Other options are available. The log file for these basic options appears in Table 11–1.

In Table 11–1 we see a very small sample of a log file from Microsoft Internet Information Server. In its raw state, the information is not terribly revealing. It provides data on when a user logged on to the site, the user IP address, and the file requested. Other than that, it's not very insightful. Since many top-rated Web sites log millions of hits per day, it's easy to see how log files become very cumbersome to view.

To aid you in making sense of these mountains of data, there are companies that specialize in turning raw data of a log file into useful marketing information. Two examples of companies that do this are Ipro and Webtrends. They can provide analyses of server log data that can help you better understand the visitors to your site and help you market to them. For example, companies like these can track usage on your site at various times during the day so you can see when your site receives the most hits. They can also determine which pages of your site receive the most visitors, and how long the visitors spent on each page. In addition, their analysis can provide for a *reverse DNS lookup*. Recall that the DNS lookup is a process whereby a domain name is resolved into an IP address that is used for packet addressing. The reverse process takes the IP address and looks up the domain name. Log files record the IP address of a visitor. By applying a reverse DNS lookup to the log files it is possible to find out which industries are visiting your Web site. Information like this can help you make decisions about where to allocate your resources.

We also note that companies like Ipro and Webtrends provide independent verification on the number of times an ad is served up from a Web site. This is obviously crucial in determining ad revenue based upon CPM rates.

Table 11–1 Log File on Web Site Server

Time	Client IP Address	Method	URL	Status
00:37:39	128.135.93.86	GET	/htmls/b372/b372.html	200
00:37:39	128.135.93.86	GET	/htmls/b372/B372.h1.gif	200
00:37:39	128.135.93.86	GET	/htmls/b372/372.css	200
00:37:42	128.135.93.86	GET	/htmls/b372/handouts.html	200

Server-side tracking is very accurate in measuring hits. However, it is difficult to measure unique visitors to a Web site based on log file analysis. The best approximation of unique visitors based on the log file is to count distinct IP addresses. This may either overestimate or underestimate the true number of unique visitors. Consider the overestimation problem. A user may visit the same site from home and from work. Thus, the same user would register different IP addresses in the log file for the two distinct machines.

This problem is compounded by the dynamic assignment of IP addresses. In many organizations a machine is not assigned a unique IP address. Rather, the IP number is randomly selected from a pool of IP addresses when the machine connects to the network. This means that the same user may visit a Web site using the same machine, but with different IP addresses. This dynamic assignment of IP numbers is also done by many Internet service providers such as AOL Time Warner. Estimating unique users by counting distinct IP addresses in a log file may also underestimate the number of unique users. This may be the case when a Web site is viewed by different users in a PC lab such as that in a school or library or Internet cafe. In these examples, many people share the same PC. This leads to a number of distinct users with the same IP address.

Although a log file gives a very accurate measure of how many times a file was sent to the user, this number may underestimate the true number of times the file was actually viewed by a user. There are least two reasons for this. The first is caused by proxy servers. We discussed the use of proxy servers in Chapter 9, "Security and Internet Business," as a means of protecting computers on a LAN from hackers. However, proxy servers may also be used to cache frequently viewed Web pages. This allows these popular Web pages to be downloaded locally rather than over the Internet and thus provides more rapid response time. Similarly, files are cached by the browser on the user's machine. When the user hits the "back" button on her browser, the page comes from the cache, it is not downloaded again over the Internet. Both client and server caching result in the log file analysis underestimating the number of times pages were actually viewed. Thus, the number of ad views may underestimate the number of gross exposures of the ad. This can cause a problem if ad revenues are based on pages actually viewed.

On a positive note, the log file gives a very accurate account of which pages were served and which files were viewed by each user (IP address). Also, log file analysis does not suffer from the sample bias we describe in the next section. All IP addresses are counted regardless of whether they are from schools, government facilities, or from foreign countries.

Client-Side Tracking

There are two ways to track visitors from the client side. One is through "audience measurement" and the other is through the use of a little file called a "cookie." The first requires installing software on client machines to see where users are going when they surf the Internet. This is basically the "Nielsen approach." A representative sample of users agrees to have special software installed on their computers which will track the sites they visit every time they turn on their computers.

Media Metrix is a good example of a company using sampling in its Nielsen approach. Media Metrix first gathers a potential set of users using a random-digit-dial (RDD) sample frame. If the selected phone number has a mailing address, the prospective respondent is sent a mailing package directing her to a Media Metrix Web site. Selected individuals without mailing addresses are contacted by telephone.

At the Web site the respondent downloads special software to load on her computer and fills out a demographic profile. The client software provides accurate tracking of Web site visits. This software also tracks visits to "cached" pages, which server-side tracking does not do. With reports from companies such as Media Metrix, a company can get a sense of the demographics of visitors to the most-visited Web sites. There are, however, problems with the audience measurement methodology:

- Sample sizes are small, making it difficult to accurately track usage past several hundred top sites.

- Samples do not include K-12 schoolchildren, public libraries, or Internet cafes.

- Because many firms are reluctant to allow tracking software on their machines, there is potential bias against Web sites that are visited frequently while people are at work, but not at home.

- The sample does not include many important foreign countries with many Internet users such as China and Korea. Indeed, as much as 40 percent of an average Web site's traffic originates from outside the United States. [82] Thus, you could be missing some valuable international information if you adhered to information gathered from client-side tracking alone.

Other companies who do this type of work include Nielsen NetRatings and Predictive Networks Inc. The latter company has a particularly interesting business model [23]. It has developed software to analyze keyboard and mouse use. Just as men and women have different behavior patterns with a television remote control, so do they have different behavior patterns with the mouse and keyboard. Predictive's software is designed to create user silhouettes based on the user's distinct usage of the mouse, keyboard, and the Web sites they regularly visit. ISP subscribers agree to use Predictive software for reduced Web access charges. The ISP in turn uses Predictive software to deliver targeted ads.

A second way to track Web visitors from the client side is through the use of *cookies*. Cookies are a creation of Netscape and have caused quite a bit of controversy. Netscape was initially slow to publicize this technology and make users aware of this product. Cookies are designed to gather information from the client machine when a user visits a site. The reason cookies are controversial is that a corporation, government agency, or other institution can use cookies to both store and retrieve information from the client, in many cases unbeknownst to the user of the client machine.

There is a growing use of third-party ad servers which use cookie technology. A third-party ad server provides banner ads for other companies to display on their Web pages. The banner ads that are placed use cookie technology. A good example of this is DoubleClick. Its DART ad serving technology works as follows:

- A user clicks on a link to a company in the DoubleClick network; for example, Yahoo! or United Media.

- The companies in the network have banner ads, but the banner ad is actually a link back to DoubleClick.

- If you currently have a cookie placed on your machine from DoubleClick, the company reads your cookie and identifies you. Then it looks up information about you in its database. For example, if you used Yahoo!, DoubleClick might record what words and topics you have searched for in the past. If you do not currently have a cookie, they write one on your machine in order to keep track of you in the future.

- Given the available information about you, DoubleClick selects the most appropriate banner ad to send you from its inventory. For example, if you have frequently been checking out recipe or food-related items, you may see a banner ad from a food company as opposed to one from a sporting goods company.

A cookie is written on the client machine the first time a user visits a site. A cookie is a text file stored on the client machine. This text file will typically contain a unique identification number. The next time you visit the same Web site your cookie file is obtained and your user identification number is read. This process allows the company writing your cookie to keep track of links you are following and which products you are buying. This information is stored in a database and allows the company to deliver a more personalized Web experience. Refer to Figure 11–2. This is the Web page delivered to one of the authors (Martin) when he types in the URL www.amazon.com. Note how customized the Web page is. First, the author is greeted by name. More importantly, note the product recommendations based on past purchase behavior. For example, Martin had previously purchased a number of books on XML and the first book recommended to him is *XML: A Manager's Guide*. The first DVD recommendation is the John Wayne film *Rio Bravo*. Again, Martin had previously purchased several John Wayne DVD western movies from Amazon.

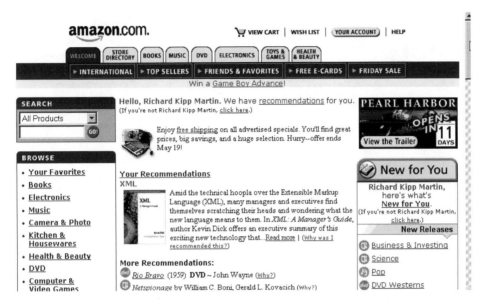

Figure 11–2 Amazon Web page with cookie customization. ©2001 Amazon.com, Inc. All Rights Reserved.

Next, view Figure 11–3. This figure is the Web page delivered by Amazon for the same URL as before, www.amazon.com. However, in this case, the author deleted the Amazon cookie file before entering the URL. Note the generic nature of the page and complete lack of customization. It is an interesting exercise to see the cookies that accumulate on your machine. If you have a Windows-based operating system, do a "file find" on the word cookie. You will find a cookies folder with all of your cookie files.

Cookies may provide a more accurate count of unique visitors than IP addresses in a server log file. A cookie is unique to a machine. This means that if the machine is assigned a different IP address, the unique cookie is still read. This helps eliminate the problem of dynamically assigned IP addresses. However, the cookie methodology does not overcome the problem of multiple users sharing a machine. If these users are logged in under the same account, they will all have the same cookie. Also, people delete their cookie files. This means that the same user may get assigned multiple cookie identification numbers at the same Web site. Users may also use software to block cookies. This software is discussed in Chapter 9.

Figure 11–3 Amazon Web page without cookie customization. ©2001 Amazon.com, Inc. All Rights Reserved.

INTERNET MARKETING MEDIA ....

Now that you understand the various strategies of Internet marketing (one-to-one, permission, viral, partnering, doing less with more, what not to do) and the measurement and data analysis behind Internet marketing, it's time to go forward with the how-tos of the different Internet marketing media.

Channel Bundling

Each medium can offer its own kind of benefits—if you know how to capitalize on it. If you can afford to do so, the ultimate strategy is to market on all fronts, online as well as offline, so that the different media reinforce one another in one seamless, integrated marketing campaign. This is called *channel bundling* and requires conscious effort on the parts of different departments of your company to work together toward a single goal. Too often the Internet marketing department is separate from the traditional marketing departments so that there is little coordination between the two. This is an inefficient use of resources that not even the biggest marketers can afford to sustain.

Don Peppers and Martha Rogers of one-to-one marketing fame have discovered that nearly 50 percent of the most sophisticated shoppers are doing their shopping online and offline; that is, they research the product online and purchase it offline [133]. They do this with high-end items like automobiles and electronics as well as with lower-end items purchased from Wal-mart and Kmart. Peppers and Rogers claim that the goal of a channel bundler is to establish a relationship with customers across all channels. They write that the relationship is built by tracking each contact with and purchase by the customer, whether online or offline, and tailoring marketing (products offered and communications) according to the responses of the customers.

Many brick-and-mortar companies are finding that extending their marketing beyond traditional media of television, radio, print, and billboards into the Internet is reinforcing their messages offline and online in a positive way. Marketers are finding that traditional media provide breadth in reaching larger audiences, while the Internet provides depth in allowing them to get to know their customers one-to-one. Television, for example, allows marketers to reach millions of prospective customers before they are even thinking of making a purchase, say, for a new car. A television commercial can tout the latest features on a new product or reinforce the brand before the prospective customer is even considering a purchase. Once the prospective customer is interested and logs on to the marketers' Web site, marketers can provide more in-depth information on a product through video streaming or allow the visitor to opt in to more information on the product via email. All in all, the latest marketing news indicates that channel bundling affords the most effective and complete way to market to an audience.

....

CHANNEL BUNDLING STRATEGY

> The ultimate strategy is to market on all fronts, online as well as offline, so that the different media reinforce one another in one seamless, integrated marketing campaign. Marketers are finding that traditional media provide breadth in reaching larger audiences, while the Internet provides depth in allowing them to get to know their customers one-to-one.

Banner Ads

The first thing to realize about *banner ads* is that they are still very much in an experimental stage. The typical banner ad, a horizontal, rectangular ad that appears at the top of a Web site, has morphed into different shapes bearing different names. A banner ad may be called a *skyscraper* if it is tall, skinny, and vertical, as opposed to horizontal, and usually placed on the right-hand side of a Web page. Banner ads can also be large and square and set in the middle of a page amidst content text. If so, they may be called *bulky boxes*. If a banner ad is business-card sized and set off to the upper-right-hand corner of a page, it may be called a *big impression*.

The first banner ad is purported to be one posted on HotWired in October 1994. Thus, in comparison to traditional media like television, radio, print, and billboards, banner ads are very new and marketers are still trying to figure out how to make best use of them. In the early days of the dot-com frenzy, it was thought that all Web sites could be self-financed through banner advertising. Dot-coms flush with venture capital threw millions of dollars at banner ads because of their ability to be narrowly targeted and because of their click-through ability. Click-through rates, however, were dismal, sinking from a little more than one percent in 1997 to 0.4 percent in 2000 [28]. Companies pulled their ads, sites lost a major source of revenue, and the banner ad was scorned for not delivering as promised, and even blamed for many a dot-com's demise.

The second thing to realize about banner ads is that despite their disappointing debut, they are still projected to be an important medium for both brick-and-mortar and dot-com advertising. Jupiter Research projects that online ad spending will total $16.5 billion worldwide by 2005; investment banking firm Lehman Brothers predicts an even healthier picture: $32.3 billion in online ad spending by 2005 [28]. Many online marketers remain optimistic about the banner ad because they feel the potential of the ad hasn't yet been realized. In the first phase of banner advertising, marketers thought that just because they placed an ad on a popular site visited by millions, that those same millions would see the ad, click on it, and complete the desired transaction. They are now realizing that like any other form of advertising, it must be targeted and of high creative quality in order to be effective.

The third thing to realize about banner ads is that the click-through rate (CTR) is not the ultimate metric by which they should be judged. Many banner ads work well as branding tools, even if they are not clicked on. Some of the best known online brands like Amazon and eBay are also among the top online advertisers. In December 2000 alone, Amazon spent $61.8 million and eBay $11.1 million on online advertising [49]. Banner ads were initially thought to be ineffective as a branding mechanism because of their static and rectangular nature, relative to television, which was thought to be much more capable of evoking emotions associated with branding. This is now not considered true, especially as richer forms of media like video and audio streaming are becoming available for banner ads. A metric that many marketers are using to gauge the effectiveness of banner ads is the conversion rate: how many users who saw the ad visited a site and completed the desired transaction, whether for making a purchase, signing up for a newsletter, or providing information?

Given all this rethinking about banner ads, what is the best way to proceed when advertising online? The latest thinking from online marketers is presented below in the following recommendations:

- **Understand the purpose of your banner ads.** As it was important to understand the purpose of your Web site before designing it, so it is important to understand what you are trying to achieve with your banner ad. Are you trying to increase brand awareness? Drive traffic to your site? Get visitors to make a purchase? All of these decisions will impact the design of your ad and determine on which sites you want to place your ad.

- **Be brief.** As visitors to a site are usually searching for something specific, their eyes will be sweeping the screen rapidly and your advertisement will only be in their line of sight for a very short time. Animation and sound are often used to attract users' attention, but some users have trained their eyes to avoid anything that looks like a flashing ad, and some are annoyed by a blast of noise. Use the short time you have to get your message across in a straightforward manner—busy visitors to a site don't have time to figure out esoteric messages.

- **Try to negotiate cost per action (CPA) rates rather than cost per 1,000 impression (CPM) rates.** When you pay only when a particular action such as a purchase or a signup is completed, you are making the most of your advertising dollars. While ad rates have traditionally been based on CPM, the trend has been moving toward CPA as the Internet allows for direct tracking of actions and marketers become more demanding.

- **Direct your customer to the right place on your site.** If you are marketing a promotion through your banner ad, make sure that when the prospective customer clicks on your ad to find out more about the promotion, he is directed to the appropriate page on your site. Many times a banner ad touting a promotion will lead to a site's home page that does not provide further information about the promotion. This will result in quick abandonment of your site and a waste of your customer's time and your ad placement.

- **Measure and analyze the results.** As we mentioned in the previous section, precise and instantaneous measurement is one of the most promising features of marketing on the Internet. Constantly monitor the effectiveness of your banner ads and constantly reconfigure your ads to reflect new information. The Internet is conducive to instant feedback and constant revision. Take advantage of the special nature of the medium.

Email Marketing

Email marketing, once considered the scourge of marketing because of the Internet culture described earlier in this chapter, has experienced a rebirth of sorts, followed by the beginnings of a second backlash. Before the days of permission marketing, email marketing was given one name only: spam. Spam was associated with those trying to hawk pornography or get-rich-quick schemes, unscrupulous sorts who would comb around for email addresses and send unsolicited advertisements. Then with the birth of permission marketing, it became permissible, if not smart, to send email messages about a product or service or promotion, as long as the recipient had granted permission in advance to receive such information. Email marketing had response rates much higher than direct mail or banner ads, and was a very inexpensive way to disseminate a message. This was the dawning of the era of email marketing, which spawned numerous companies to whom email marketing could be outsourced, oftentimes with great success. Many firms rode high on the boom of email advertisements, which could be targeted, personal, and relevant.

Recently, however, there has been a reconsideration of email marketing that forces online marketers to revamp their email marketing strategies. Email inboxes are becoming increasingly cluttered with advertisements, permitted or not, and marketers have to find a way to break through that clutter. Both Yahoo! and Microsoft's Hotmail offer users an email inbox filtering system that delegates junk email to a junk-mail box and allows all other email to enter a "premium inbox," which ostensibly holds only those email messages of primary importance to the user [48]. The result is that some marketers pay a premium to be able to deliver their ads into the premium inbox. Whether this is just a ploy that allows Yahoo! and Hotmail to charge more for certain kinds of advertising or whether it is a sincere attempt to protect their customers remains to be seen. Nevertheless, it is clear that even the most astute email marketers have to retailor their ads to break through the clutter.

Email marketing is decreasingly being viewed as spam, and increasingly being used by well-established, even high-end retailers. If email marketing is accepted by the recipient, it can be an effective and cost-effective means of getting a company's message across, keeping customers informed of new and special offerings, and strengthening the relationship between customers and the company. The key idea is to have the customers' permission to send it. Be sure customers opt in for the email and have a means by which customers can opt out in every email message.

FUTURE TRENDS AND IMPLICATIONS . . . .

Throughout this chapter we have emphasized the evolving nature of Internet marketing. The marketing mantras that held true in the heyday of the dot-coms are no longer valid. In those days the mantra was to build a brand and build it fast. Marketers now realize that building a brand takes time and the brand must be backed by a solid business model, true value proposition, and profitability. Marketers also found that it is not enough to advertise widely and wackily to drive traffic to a Web site. Internet marketing, like traditional marketing, must be targeted, thoughtful, and creative. In fact, what we have witnessed is a merging of Internet marketing and traditional marketing in which each has taken on characteristics of the other. As it now stands, Internet marketing is still considered separate from traditional marketing in many companies. Someday, when the two are truly integrated, there will just be marketing.

New forms of marketing have sprouted thanks to the special nature of the Internet medium. One-to-one marketing, permission marketing, and viral marketing, while in existence in one form or another since the earliest days of marketing, have taken off thanks to the Internet's special qualities. The Internet is a personalizable, relatively inexpensive, and fast medium that enhances the proliferation of these forms of marketing. Nevertheless, to execute these forms of marketing effectively requires a lot of know-how and professional experience. If you lack these, you can always outsource, but outsourcing can be expensive. Be prudent with your marketing dollars; a botched email campaign can cause irreparable damage to your company's image.

Since the dot-com fallout, the necessity to do more with less has given rise to different, less expensive media, compared with prime time television or full-page ads in national publications. These include media like doughnut bags, coffee cup jackets, popcorn bags, and fresh fruit, which are all more seamlessly integrated into our everyday lives than traditional forms of interruption marketing. If you think creatively, you might even come up with a few new media yourself. Email is another relatively new and inexpensive marketing medium that is evolving. Marketers are talking about adding rich media like video and audio to email messages, though most users' browsers at this point in time cannot support rich media. With these unconventional media, it is important to keep in mind their casual and somewhat edgy feel. Be sure that the medium is appropriate for your company and that you are targeting the right audience.

Partnering is seen as a strength in Internet marketing, whether for hosting links to each other's sites or complementing the strengths of online and offline companies. In the early days of the dot-coms, pure-play Internet companies did not want to partner with brick-and-mortar companies because the latter were viewed as dinosaurs of the old economy and would detract from the cutting edge image the former wanted to project. Since the fallout, however, partnering with an established brick-and-mortar company is seen as a strength because the traditional company lends credibility and substance to the young Internet start-up. Conversely, the traditional company must be sure that the Internet company has a solid business model and will be long-lived in order to avoid some of the partnering fiascoes we mentioned earlier in this chapter.

All in all, because Internet marketing is in flux, it is a very exciting time to be an Internet marketer. This is a time of novelty and experimentation, to see what works for your company and what doesn't. Because of the fast nature of the Internet, it's very easy to switch gears and modify in midstream if something isn't working. Don't be afraid to try new media and strategies. Integrate your online and offline marketing so you communicate a consistent message to your audience. Be mindful of the culture of the Internet so you don't abuse the medium or turn off current and prospective customers. Take advantage of the measurement available on the Internet to get to know your customers better, but respect their privacy. Above all, have fun.

ment available on the Internet to get to know your customers better, but respect their privacy. Above all, have fun.

Part 4

Back End: Support

In the fourth part of the book, we help you understand how the less visible aspects of Internet business take place. These functions, invisible to the customer, take place in the "middle tier" and "back end" of Internet business architecture. In Chapter 12, "The Power of Databases," we describe how to get information you need in and out of a database, how to design databases for optimum efficiency, and how to create and mine data warehouses. We discuss the importance of a relational database, and walk you through an example to show you how an efficient database should be designed. In Chapter 13, "Internet Business Architecture," we present the latest N-tier architectures that provide the backbone for large-scale Internet business applications. Included are the different paradigms for understanding architecture technologies, and how to manage the problems of scaling an Internet business system. In Chapter 14, "Enterprise Application Software," we provide introductions to the various software used to integrate and manage customer relationships, sales force, manufacturing, accounting, and a host of other functions. We discuss a number of important software technologies for "gluing" together different software applications in a distributed environment.

12 The Power of Databases

In this chapter ...

DATABASE TECHNOLOGY IS CRUCIAL . . . .

This chapter is about data—how to store them and how to use them. Pretty boring stuff, you might think, until you realize just how important data are to running a company. Accounts payable, accounts receivable, production planning, customer relationship management, supply chains, human resources/payroll, data mining—nothing works without data. Along with the explosion of computer power and networking capacity there has been an explosion in the use of corporate databases. Think of a *database* as a set of related files used by different departments and software applications within the firm. For example, an inventory database might be used by a purchasing staff to help manage a firm's supply chain. The inventory database might also be used by the sales force when filling orders.

In Chapter 2, "What Do I Need to Know About Hardware?" we introduced Say's Law, which states that supply creates demand. The supply of fast computers and database software has created a huge demand for database applications. Consider SPAR Handles AG, a strictly brick-and-mortar company. SPAR controls Germany's largest chain of supermarkets. It must manage data related to 400,000 items flowing through its system of 10,000 suppliers, 17 warehouses, and 5,000 independent franchise stores [116]. Or, consider MSN, one of the largest consumer portals, second only to AOL Time Warner's. Its messenger service experienced a severe disruption of service in the first week of July, 2001. The reason was that a disk controller of one of its database servers failed. What about a company like eBay? Its entire "product" is data. We are in the information economy and information is based on data!

Figure 12–1 illustrates a modern software architecture. This architecture illustrates the way a user, i.e., client, within the firm would interact with a corporate database using a corporate network or the Web. In Part IV of the book, which this chapter begins, we concentrate on the technology that goes into the application and data tiers. In this chapter we focus on the data tier. Whenever a user in either a B2B or B2C environment uses an HTML form and clicks on the submit button, she is implementing the process illustrated in this figure. In particular, the user is either getting information out of the database, or putting information into the database.

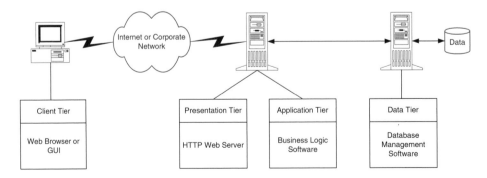

Figure 12–1 A generic N-tier architecture.

In the next section, "Database Management Systems," we introduce the concept of a database management system, describe what these systems can do, and mention the leading vendors. The leading vendors all sell relational database systems, and this is the topic of the section, "The Relational Database Model." For the database to be useful, end users must be able to get information from it, i.e., query the database, and put information into the database. Query processing is the focus of the section "SQL: Getting Information In and Out of the Database." Due to the explosion of computing power and the Internet, corporations are building huge databases. These databases must be harnessed to be useful. In the sections, "Building a Data Warehouse" and "Data Mining Basics," we describe how this is done. The chapter concludes with the section, "Future Trends and Implications."

DATABASE MANAGEMENT SYSTEMS ....

Databases are critical to most Internet commerce and Internet business applications. In most cases, the database is created and manipulated by software called a database management system, or DBMS. A user may interact directly with a DBMS, although, more typically in our N-tier architecture, it is the middle-tier business logic software that interacts with the DBMS. For example, a user with a desktop machine and Microsoft Office might use the Access DBMS to create a database of personal contacts. In this example, the user interacts directly with the DBMS. In another scenario a user goes to an Internet commerce site to purchase clothing using shopping cart software. This shopping cart software might interact with IBM's DB2 DBMS and a database that contains prices and availability of items selected for the shopping cart. Before describing the components of a DBMS, we introduce a simple example and some important vocabulary used throughout the rest of the chapter.

Figure 12–2 illustrates a very simple but typical database that a purchasing agent might use to place orders. In this example, all of the data are lumped into a single file, which is a table. This type of database is often called a *flat file* database. Each column in the table is called a *field* or *attribute*. In this example, the fields are the supplier's identification (sup_id), the supplier's street address (street), the supplier's city (city), the email address of a sales representative at a supplier (rep_e_mail), a stock keeping unit (SKU) number of an item to purchase (sku_num), the color of the SKU (color), and the price (price) of the SKU. Each row of the table is called a *record*. Think of a record as a collection of related fields. In this example, each record gives the price of an SKU if it is ordered from a particular representative at a particular supplier. In an actual database for a retail store, there might be hundreds of thousands of records in the table representing thousands of SKUs and hundreds of suppliers. In database vernacular a table is also called a *relation*. A relation that contains all of the attributes and records in the database is called the *universal relation*.

Associated with each table or relation is a *primary key*. The primary key is used to uniquely identify each record in the database. For example, a social security number is used to uniquely identify each person in the social security system. The primary key may consist of a single attribute or several attributes. In the relation illustrated in Figure 12–2, the primary key is the pair of attributes rep_e_mail and sku_num. This means there cannot be two distinct records (by distinct we mean they differ in value for at least one attribute, e.g., `price`) that have the same value for both `rep_e_mail` and `sku_num`. In other words, a particular `rep_e_mail` and `sku_num` combination is associated with one and only one record. This makes sense since a representative would not offer the same SKU at different prices. Note, however, that a single sales representative might supply more than one SKU (`tjr@s45.com` supplies SKUs 441 and 577), hence the `rep_e_mail` cannot be a primary key by itself. Also, an SKU might have multiple suppliers (SKU 577 is supplied by s45 and s55); hence, the `sku_num` by itself cannot be a primary key.

sup_id	street	city	rep_e_mail	sku_num	color	price
s45	78 State	Plano	tjr@s45.com	441	green	$53
s45	78 State	Plano	tjr@s45.com	577	blue	$55
s55	64 Dole	Lajitas	teg@s55.com	643	green	$63
s55	64 Dole	Lajitas	sne@s55.com	577	blue	$57
s57	72 Vine	Uvalde	arn@s57.com	342	red	$89
s99	15 Lake	Hondo	prm@s99.com	667	red	$56

Figure 12–2 A flat file database.

A DBMS typically has four important components. They are:

1. A *data definition language (DDL)*. This is the part of the DBMS that is used to create and clearly define each attribute in the database. The DDL is used to name attributes and specify the properties of the attributes. Some of the properties of an attribute include:

- Type of data, e.g., text, number, currency, date/time

- Whether null values (blank entries) are allowed

- An initial default value

- Constraints on the value of the attribute

- Whether or not it is indexed

We illustrate the graphical user interface (GUI) version of a DDL for Microsoft SQL Server in Figure 12–3. Note from this figure that we are setting the data type for the attribute, the number of characters (length) in the attribute, whether or not nulls are allowed, and we are also putting a constraint on the attribute `sku_num` that it be greater than 50. The most universal DDL is based on structured query language (SQL).

2. A *data manipulation language*. A data manipulation language is used to get information in and out of the database. An individual with a desktop machine will typically use a GUI with the database. For example, Microsoft Access has an easy-to-use Query Wizard for constructing database queries. In an Internet business or Internet commerce application the end user will often interact with the database using a Web form. This Web form eventually gets "translated" into SQL. SQL is by far the most popular data manipulation language.

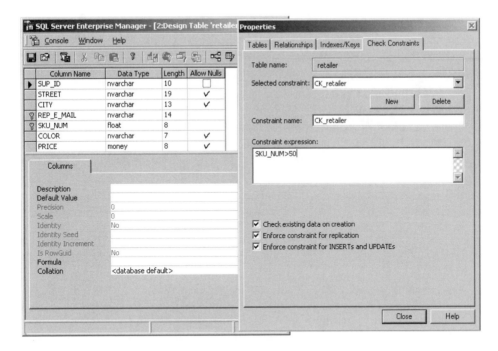

Figure 12–3 The DDL graphical user interface for SQL Server.

3. A *system catalog* or *data dictionary*. Think of the system catalog as a meta-database that contains information about a database. For example, a sophisticated DBMS will have a system catalog that contains tables listing all of the tables in the database, all of the attributes in the database, all of the keys and indices, etc. The system catalog is a set of tables just like any other database.

4. *Utility programs*. These are used for managing the files. Example tasks performed by utility programs include:

- Scheduled backups and data restoration

- Log file maintenance

- User account management

- Report generation

- Data import and export from/to other applications

    A good DBMS will also have the following features:

- A facility for allowing programmers to create SQL-based procedures and provide an interface to programming languages such as C, Java, or Visual Basic. A procedure is like a macro or program—a set of statements used to execute a task.

- A locking mechanism by which the DBMS handles simultaneous users of the same records. At the desktop level, generally only one person interacts with the database. However, in a corporate setting, many users will interact with the DBMS and *locking* features are required.

- A means by which transactions are executed. A transaction is a set of SQL statements treated as a single operation. For example, you might go to the Web site for the company managing your mutual funds and withdraw $10,000 from a bond fund and invest it in a stock fund. These are two separate operations that need to be treated as a single transaction. The DBMS must be sophisticated enough to execute either both of these operations or neither.

- Trigger execution. A trigger is an object that is associated with a table and is automatically executed when certain actions such as an insert or update are taken with the table. For example, a trigger can validate new data as they are entered.

- The ability to transform data into a data warehouse and mine the resulting data. This is covered later in this chapter.

- Transaction logging and failover capability. If the server running the DBMS goes down, failover capability allows the application and data to migrate to a backup server. Failover is discussed in more detail in Chapter 13, "Internet Business Architecture." If the primary storage device fails, an up-to-date copy of the database can be created by applying the recent transactions to the most recent backup.

In the next section we show why large corporate databases are never stored as one large flat file. Other models are required. Two early models for organizing data were the hierarchical model and the network model. Both models proved insufficient for easily manipulating large corporate databases. Retrieving information from a hierarchical database is much like finding a file on the hard drive of your computer. You start from the top and "drill down" until you find the file. How much drilling is necessary depends upon the file you are after and how the folders on the hard drive are organized. Similarly for hierarchical databases, how the database is structured initially has a big effect on how efficiently the user can extract information. Thus, the designer of the hierarchical database needs to know the kinds of queries the end user will have.

A network-based database is more flexible but requires a more complicated indexing scheme. Both the hierarchical and network database models are good for large systems when there is a predefined set of queries and transactions. However, in many settings, it is difficult to anticipate the types of transactions and queries required by the end user. The major DBMSs used today for Internet business are based on the *relational model*. The relational database model is based on organizing data into a set of relations or tables and then getting information by joining the tables together. This is illustrated in detail in the next section.

The development of the relational database was a major breakthrough. The relational database is the brainchild of Ted Codd [30]. Codd developed the relational model in 1970 while working at IBM. Companies producing database software, including IBM, did not quickly grasp the commercial value of Codd's work. Fast forward to 1977 when

Larry Ellison founded a new company called Software Development Labs. One of Ellison's co-founders, Ed Oates, realized the potential of relational databases, and Software Developments Labs programmed a minicomputer relational DBMS called Oracle. Software Development Labs changed the company name to Oracle, the name of its product, and went on to become the number one DBMS software company in the world.

. . . .

THE MAJOR PLAYERS

Oracle9*i* from Oracle, DB2 from IBM, and SQL Server from Microsoft are the top three relational DBMSs. According to a May 2001 study by Gartner Dataquest, Oracle has 33.8 percent market share, DB2 30.1 percent, and SQL Server 14.9 percent. In the Linux world two open source DBMSs are MySQL and PostgreSQL. Both Oracle9*i* and DB2 are multiplatform and work on both the Windows operating system and Unix/Linux. SQL Server is written for only the Windows operating system.

Although IBM developed the relational technology, it is still playing catch-up in the $8 billion-plus market. Initially, Oracle was the DBMS of choice for companies like SAP, PeopleSoft, and Siebel Systems, which produce enterprise application software (more on this software in Chapter 14, "Enterprise Application Software"). Now, however, Oracle is trying to become a completely integrated Internet business software shop and is competing directly and aggressively against companies that use its database systems. This has led these companies to be more receptive to products that compete with the Oracle DBMS. This is a window of opportunity for both IBM and Microsoft to gain market share in the DBMS software industry. Microsoft, which has long dominated the desktop market, is using SQL Server, along with other server products, to get into the enterprise application market.

THE RELATIONAL DATABASE MODEL . . . .

In the previous section we introduced the concept of a flat file database, which was illustrated in Figure 12–2. The flat file is a very easy structure to understand. However, there are serious problems with a flat file database.

- First, there is a tremendous amount of redundancy. For example, the supplier s45 supplies two SKUs, which results in the supplier address being stored twice. Imagine a realistic size application where the same supplier might supply thousands of SKUs. This would result in an enormous amount of redundant data. Similarly, the same SKU, for example, 577, may have many suppliers. This results in the same product information (in our small example, the product color) being repeated for each supplier of the product. In this example, there are two obvious *entities*—an SKU and a supplier. Think of an entity as person, place, thing, or object about which information is stored. There is in our example, in database vernacular, a *many-to-many relationship* between suppliers and products. That is, each supplier may have many products and each product may have many suppliers. Putting entities with a many-to-many relationship together in the same table causes redundancy.

- A flat file is subject to *deletion anomalies*. With all of the data in one file, it may be difficult to delete some unwanted information without deleting other important information. For example, what if we dropped SKU 342 from our product family? Deleting this record also deletes information about supplier s57, which we might not want to lose.

- A flat file is subject to *insertion anomalies*. If the same information, such as an address in Figure 12–2, appears in multiple places, then when a change is made it is necessary to make the change everywhere.

- There is a problem with null values. Often a flat file will contain many fields that are null. This leads to problems, if, for example, averages are being computed and a zero is used for a null value instead of a blank.

How can we reorganize the database in Figure 12–2 to eliminate these problems? Clearly, it contains a lot of redundant data. One approach is to reorganize the database as illustrated in Figure 12–4. In this figure there is only one row for each supplier and we have created new fields to represent different orders. For example, order 1 for supplier s45 is for product number 577, which is blue, at a price of $55, which is handled by sales rep tjr@s45.com. Since there is only one row for each supplier we have eliminated considerable redundancy because each supplier's street address and city are stored only once.

However, there are two big problems with the way we have chosen to reorganize the database. First, an order column is a *composite attribute*, i.e., it is made up of the attributes rep_e_mail, sku_num, color, and price. This makes it very difficult to sort the database by price. The second problem is that each of the order attributes is a repeating field or *multivalued attribute*. That is, there is an attribute, order, which can take on multiple values, i.e., order 1, order 2, etc. This is poor planning, because when we are initially constructing the database we are forced to predict ahead of time the maximum number of orders that each supplier can have. If we predict too small a number, we must alter the database by adding columns. If, on the other hand, we pick a value that is too large, this is not a good solution either, because this leads to many null fields. Indeed, the relation illustrated in Figure 12–4 violates *first normal form*. First normal form requires that a relation not have composite or multivalued attributes.

Rather than take the approach illustrated in the relation of Figure 12–4, we break the original relation in Figure 12–2 into two new relations. The two relations are suggested by the relation in 12–4. Rather than have a composite, multivalued attribute orders, we treat this as a new entity and create a new orders relation. We also create a supplier relation for the supplier entity. This is illustrated in Figures 12–5 and 12–6. Do not be confused with the use of the term orders in the orders relation. The orders relation is not a database of actual orders in the sense that there is an invoice and order quantity for

sup_id	street	city	order 1	order 2
s45	78 State	Plano	tjr@s45.com, 577, blue, $55	tjr@s45.com, 441, green, $63
s55	64 Dole	Lajitas	teg@s45.com, 643, green, $63	sne@s55.com, 577, blue, $57
s57	72 Vine	Uvalde	arn@s57.com, 342, red, $89	NULL
s99	15 Lake	Hondo	prm@s99.com, 667, red, $56	NULL

Figure 12–4 An alternative representation.

each record in the relation. Rather, the `orders` relation is used to provide information to a purchasing agent wanting to find a supplier (perhaps the lowest cost supplier) or suppliers for an SKU that needs to be ordered.

sup_id	street	city
s45	78 State	Plano
s55	64 Dole	Lajitas
s57	72 Vine	Uvalde
s99	15 Lake	Hondo

Figure 12–5 The `supplier` relation.

The two relations in Figures 12–5 and 12–6 contain all of the data in the original flat file relation, but the amount of redundancy is reduced considerably. However, information is "spread" across the relations. For example, if we wanted the street address and city of all suppliers for SKU 577 we would need information from both the `orders` and `supplier` relations. In order to get information like this it is necessary to *join* these relations. The join operation is of fundamental importance in relational databases.

sup_id	rep_e_mail	sku_num	price	color
s45	tjr@s45.com	441	$53	green
s45	tjr@s45.com	577	$55	blue
s55	teg@s45.com	643	$63	green
s55	sne@s55.com	577	$57	blue
s57	arn@s57.com	342	$89	red
s99	prm@s99.com	667	$56	red

Figure 12–6 The `orders` relation.

The key of the relation `supplier` is `sup_id`. The key of the relation `orders` is the attribute pair `rep_e_mail`, `sku_num`. In relational database terminology the primary key `sup_id` in the `supplier` relation is a *foreign key* in the `orders` relation. To join the relations, each unique record in the `supplier` relation identified by `sup_id` is matched with the set of records in the `orders` relation that have the identical value in the `sup_id` field. We say there is a *one-to-many relationship* between the `supplier` and `orders` relations. To illustrate, the record with `sup_id = s45` in the `supplier` relation matches with the first two records in the `orders` relation. See Figure 12–7.

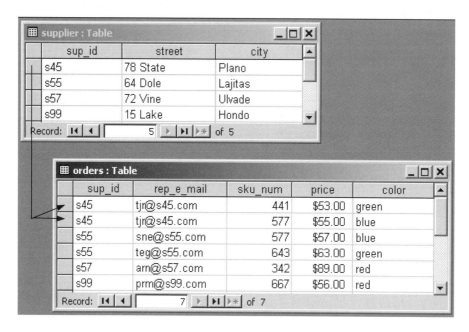

Figure 12–7 Joining the `supplier` and `orders` relations.

When all of the records in the `supplier` table are matched with all of the records in the `orders` table based on equal values of `sup_id`, we get the relation illustrated in Figure 12–8. The relation illustrated in Figure 12–8 is the join (also called inner join) of the `supplier` and `orders` relation. Joining relations allows a user to obtain information from both relations. For example, by joining `supplier` and `orders` we can find the street address and city of all suppliers for SKU 577. We do this by querying. How a database is queried is the topic of the next section.

sup_id	street	city	rep_e_mail	sku_num	price	color
s45	78 State	Plano	tjr@s45.com	441	$53.00	green
s45	78 State	Plano	tjr@s45.com	577	$55.00	blue
s55	64 Dole	Lajitas	sne@s55.com	577	$57.00	blue
s55	64 Dole	Lajitas	teg@s55.com	643	$63.00	green
s57	72 Vine	Ulvade	arn@s57.com	342	$89.00	red
s99	15 Lake	Hondo	prm@s99.com	667	$56.00	red

Figure 12–8 The join of the `supplier` and `orders` relations.

Tech Talk

Foreign key: an attribute in a relation that is the primary key in another relation. For example, in the `supplier` **relation** `sup_id` **is the primary key. The** `sup_id` **also appears in the** `orders` **relation. However, in the** `orders` **relation** `rep_e_mail` **and** `sku_num` **constitute the primary key. In the** `orders` **relation** `sup_id` **is a foreign key.**

The relational scheme illustrated in Figures 12–5 and 12–6 eliminates most of the redundancy and other problems associated with the relation in Figure 12–2. However, the new scheme is not quite perfect. In the `orders` relation, there is a one-to-many relationship between SKUs and supplier representatives (`rep_e_mail`). That is, a given SKU may be supplied by many sales representatives. This means that we store the color of the SKU for each representative of the SKU. This leads to unnecessary redundancy. In this small example, this is not a problem, but could be for a very large database where there is a lot of product information for many SKUs and many representatives. This redundancy is caused by the fact that the color attribute only depends upon the SKU and not the representative (unlike the price, which depends on both). That is, the `color` attribute depends on part, but not all, of the key for the `orders` relation. Recall that the primary key for the relation `orders` comprises `rep_e_mail` and `sku_num`. For the `orders` relation example, the redundancy problem is corrected by creating a third relation based on the SKU entity. The `orders` relation of Figure 12–6 is therefore broken further into the two relations illustrated in Figures 12–9 and 12–10.

sup_id	rep_e_mail	sku_num	price
s45	tjr@s45.com	441	$53
s45	tjr@s45.com	577	$55
s55	teg@s45.com	643	$63
s55	sne@s55.com	577	$57
s57	arn@s57.com	342	$89
s99	prm@s99.com	667	$56

Figure 12–9 The `orders` relation after normalization.

sku_num	color
441	green
643	green
577	blue
342	red
667	red

Figure 12–10 The `sku` relation after normalization.

This process of breaking up a relation into a series of smaller tables in order to remove redundancy is called *normalization*. We have already defined first normal form. There is also a *second normal form*, a *third normal form*, and a *Boyce-Codd normal form*. These other normal forms are beyond the scope of this book. For readers wishing to pursue this topic further we recommend Ullman [161]. Actually, one might "normalize" this database even further by breaking up the `orders` relation in Figure 12–9 into two new tables: a table with the attributes `rep_e_mail` and `sup_id`, and a second table with the attributes `rep_e_mail`, `sku_num`, and `price`. This removes some redundancy in 12–9 if there are suppliers that supply numerous SKUs, since we repeat the same `sup_id` for each SKU. However, breaking the new `orders` relation up in this fashion will require making two joins across three tables whenever it is necessary to find the address of a supplier associated with a `sku_num`. Indeed, one can normalize a database too much.

Our database now has three relations, `supplier`, `orders`, and `sku`. There is a one-to-many relationship between `supplier` and `orders` (entries in the primary key of `supplier`, `sup_id`, appear once in `supplier` but can appear many times in `orders`), and a one-to-many relationship between `sku` and `orders` (entries in the primary key of `sku`, `sku_num`, appear once in `sku` but can appear many times in `orders`). The `orders` relation is the linking relation between the `supplier` and `sku` relations that have a many-to-many relationship—for each SKU there are multiple suppliers and for each supplier there are multiple SKUs.

The one-to-many relationship in our example is the most common one found in relational databases. In general, you want to have a one-to-many relationship between two relations in a relational database. Indeed, when constructing a relational database it is best to avoid joining two relations that have a many-to-many relationship. Ideally, try to join one relation with another such that the attributes that constitute the primary key of the first appear as a foreign key in the second. In our example, the primary key of `supplier`, `sup_id`, is a foreign key in `orders`, and the primary key of `sku`, `sku_num`, is a foreign key in `orders`.

Creating too many tables is a common database design problem. For example, one could break the `supplier` relation into two separate relations. The first relation, call it `street`, would contain the attributes `sup_id` and `street`, and the second relation, call it `city`, would contain the attributes `sup_id` and `city`. There is a one-to-one relationship between these two tables and nothing is gained by breaking the `supplier` relation further into two separate relations. In general, it is not good relational database design to have two relations with a one-to-one relationship.

When constructing a database it helps to think of the naturally occurring distinct entities about which information is stored. In our example, there are three natural entities—a supplier, an order, and an SKU. Indeed, we have a relation for each one of these entities. Problems generally arise if there is a relation containing at least two distinct entities and there is a one-to-many or many-to-many relationship between the entities. Also, you don't want to break up an entity unnecessarily into relations as we just illustrated by breaking up the supplier relation into a street relation and city relation. Database designers create *entity-relationship* diagrams when constructing databases to aid in the process of determining what the relations should be. There is much literature on database design, entity-relationship diagrams, relational databases, and normalization. Readers wishing to pursue database theory and design in more detail should consult the books by Date [36] and Ullman [161].

The final database design illustrated in Figure 12–11 is a logical view of the database as opposed to a physical view of the database. This is how the relations appear to the database manager or application programmer. The physical view of the database is where and how the files are actually stored on the physical storage media. The end user of the database may well see neither of these views. A large corporate database often serves many functional areas within the firm and should provide different views for each area. A good DBMS is capable of creating different *views* of the database. Think of a view as a virtual table. It does not contain any data, but rather is a "mapping" to actual tables stored in the database. It is important to create these views because what an end user in accounting needs to see is very different from what an end user in marketing needs to see.

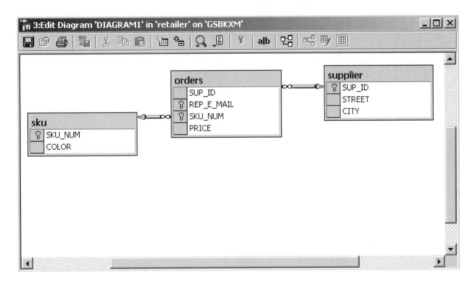

Figure 12–11 Logical view of a normalized database.

We have illustrated a relational database, discussed design issues, and shown how tables are joined together. In the next section we show how to actually use the database—how to get information in and out of the database.

SQL: GETTING INFORMATION IN AND OUT OF THE DATABASE ....

In this section we focus on data manipulation languages used by relational DBMSs. Fortunately, there is a standard data manipulation language that all of the major systems use. That language is *structured query language (SQL)*. SQL is to databases what HTML is to the Web. SQL was originally developed by IBM and is truly a *lingua franca* for the database world.

To illustrate the use of SQL, consider the relation in Figure 12–6. Let's say we want to know all of the email addresses of the sales reps that supply sku 577. The SQL query for this and the result are illustrated in Figure 12–12. The SQL query is in the upper window and the result of the query is in the lower window. As expected, the query found two sales reps for sku 577. These two reps have emails sne@s55.com and tjr@s45.com. Now, let's look at the syntax of the query in more detail. The SQL is:

```
SELECT orders.rep_e_mail, orders.sku_num
FROM orders
WHERE orders.sku_num=577
```

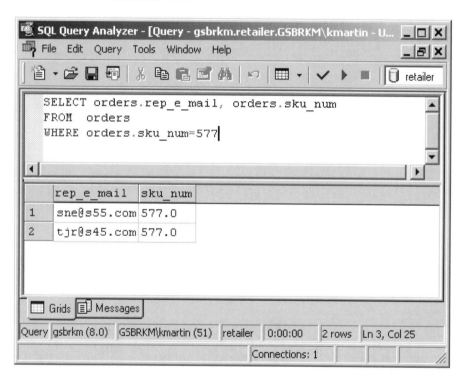

Figure 12–12 An example SQL query.

Note that SQL is a fourth generation language. Refer back to Chapter 3, "Software Is Everywhere," for details on fourth generation languages. The SQL states what we *want* to accomplish. It does not provide any programming details on how to actually search the relation retailer. There are three keywords in this statement.

SELECT: This keyword tells which attributes we want. In this example they are rep_e_mail and sku_num. We are also selecting from the relation orders. Note the "dot" notation used in SQL. For example, orders.sku_num refers to the attribute sku_num in the relation orders.

FROM: This keyword tells which relation to use. In this case it is relation orders.

WHERE: This keyword is used to describe the constraints that define the query. In this example there is only one constraint, which is that sku_num be 577.

Although SQL is a fourth generation language and one does not have to worry about programming logic as with a language like Java or C++, it still has a very precise syntax that the average user often finds cumbersome. There are two ways an end user will typically interact with a database in a corporate setting. The first is through a GUI that builds SQL queries. This is illustrated in Figure 12–13 for the personal database Microsoft Access. Note the Expression Builder on the right. It can be used to generate constraints for the SQL query. Using a GUI, the query is constructed graphically using the mouse and no SQL is required.

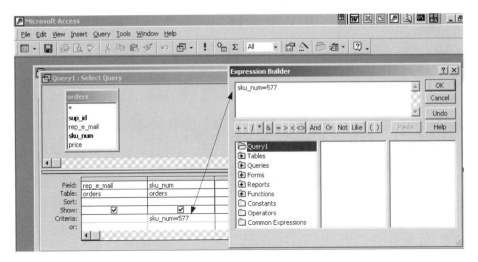

Figure 12–13 Building a query with a graphical user interface.

Another (perhaps the most common) way a user interacts with the corporate database is through client software. Refer back to Figure 12–1. The client software might be a Web browser or some other application that is based on a GUI. For the sake of discussion, let's assume it is a Web browser and that the user interface is an HTML form. The Web browser talks to the Web server and requests the form. The user fills out the form, hits the submit button, and sends it back to the Web server. The Web server then passes the information in the form back to the application tier. It is in the application tier where the "business logic" software resides. This is where a corporation can spend a lot of money on software development.

. . . .

THE APPLICATION TIER

A major function of application tier software (refer to Figure 12–1) is to take information from the client and construct the appropriate SQL statements using this information. All of the major database vendors support SQL. Application tier software is responsible for establishing a connection with the DBMS software and passing the SQL statements to the DBMS. This software is also responsible for getting the results of the query back from the DBMS and sending it on to the client.

The business logic software performs two basic tasks (at least). First, the business logic software takes the information from the Web form and incorporates it into the necessary SQL statements. Once the necessary SQL statements are constructed, they are passed to additional application tier software that is capable of establishing a connection and exchanging data with the DBMS software in the data tier. Finally, the information from the Web form, now incorporated into SQL statements, is passed to the DBMS where it is processed. This process then reverses itself and the results from the Web form query are passed back to the client. Sound complicated? It really isn't so bad. This process will be clarified and illustrated in further detail in the next chapter.

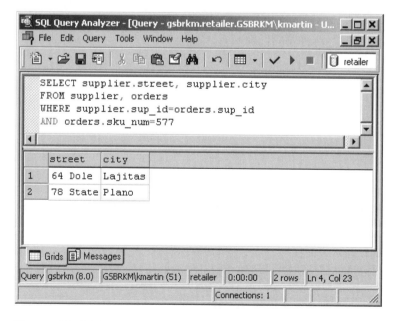

Figure 12–14 SQL query with relational join.

Before going to the next section, we construct one more SQL query—this time one that requires a join. Assume we need the street address and city of all suppliers for SKU 577. To get this information we first join the `supplier` relation from Figure 12–5 and the `orders` relation from Figure 12–9. The SQL and the result of the SQL are illustrated in Figure 12–14. Notice how simple it is to join two relations. In the FROM clause we include the two tables we wish to join, namely, `supplier` and `orders`. In the WHERE clause we indicate which attributes are used for the join. In this case, the common attribute is `sup_id`. There is also an AND clause to enforce the restriction that the `sku_num` is 577.

BUILDING A DATA WAREHOUSE ·················

You want to make a reservation for a coach fare on American Airlines flight 73 from Chicago to Honolulu on a specific date. Regardless of whether you are using a travel agent or a Web-based service like Expedia or Travelocity, information regarding seat availability and price must be quickly pulled from a database. Similarly, if you are trying to track a package sent using UPS or Federal Express, information must be extracted quickly from a database.

These are good examples of OLTP (online transaction processing). Clearly, the price and seat availability, or package location, must be accurate and up-to-the-moment. If you visit the Web site of your mutual fund company and transfer money from your money market to a stock fund, this transaction should occur as quickly as possible and the balance in both your money market and stock funds should be updated as quickly as possible. In these examples, data are being used for *operational* purposes. These examples of transaction processing illustrate that in many corporate settings there are database users who require up-to-the-moment records, and need to add, delete, and modify these records. A highly normalized, relational database is best suited for this purpose, and these are the kinds of databases we have discussed so far.

···

VARIATIONS ON A THEME

MOLAP, ROLAP, and HOLAP are all categories of OLAP. MOLAP stands for multidimensional OLAP. A MOLAP cube contains all of the possible aggregations based on the fact table and stores them for future use. This is illustrated in Figure 12–16. All queries to a MOLAP are answered from data stored in the cube, not the warehouse. ROLAP stands for relational OLAP. With ROLAP, the OLAP queries can be made directly to the warehouse using SQL without forming a cube. HOLAP is a hybrid approach, and stands for hybrid OLAP (hybrid online analytical processing). For example, you might cache the result of common OLAP queries for future use and quick access, but new queries would go back to the data warehouse.

However, data may also be used for *analytical* purposes. Consider our airline example. All airlines are actively involved with revenue management (often called yield management), i.e., filling as many seats as possible at the highest possible fares. Revenue management programs require historical data in aggregated form. For example, American Airlines would want to know, on average, the number of unfilled seats in each fare category, by day of week, for the last year. The revenue management system requires an online analytical processing (OLAP) system. In this case, a relational database is not necessarily optimal for analytical purposes. In fact, the very structure of relational databases—two dimensional tables—is not well suited to OLAP.

A multidimensional presentation is best suited to analytical processing. For example, a large grocery chain would be interested in analyzing purchase data along the dimensions of time, location, product, and customer demographics (which in turn has dimensions such as income, education, gender, etc.). Not only would the grocery chain want multidimensional data, they would also want aggregate data, e.g., total sales by year or quarter. A *data warehouse* is used to meet the needs of OLAP. The concept of a data warehouse is often attributed to Bill Inmon of IBM (IBM has unquestionably contributed more to the database field than any other company). Think of a data warehouse as a repository of historical, multidimensional, aggregated data. The data mart is a related concept. A data mart is a data warehouse that is subject-specific and normally used by a single department or group of users within a company.

There is a fast-growing literature on data warehousing, and we are going to focus on only a few key aspects. From the standpoint of a manager, one of the most important data warehouse concepts is the data cube. A cube is analogous to a pivot table (understanding what a pivot table is is not necessary to the following discussion) in Excel, only much more powerful and able to handle much larger data sets. We illustrate building a data warehouse and use of a cube through an example. The example is based on the FoodMart 2000 database that is a sample application in SQL Server. FoodMart is a fictitious multinational grocery chain.

The first step is to actually build a data warehouse from a relational database. The data warehouse is based on multidimensional data. Each relation or set of relations in the relational database contributes to a dimension. Consider Figure 12–15. In this figure the dimensions of interest are (clockwise from upper right-hand corner) product, time_by_day, store, and customer (under customer we also consider the affiliated dimensions of gender, marital status, yearly income, and education as noted in the column to the left). They are represented by the tables pictured. (The product table is joined to an auxiliary table, product_class.) These tables are called *dimension tables*.

In the center of the figure is the relation sales_fact_1998. This is not a relation in the original database, but is used to construct the data warehouse. It consists essentially of two sets of attributes. One set of attributes is made up of foreign keys which are the primary keys in the dimension tables. The second set of attributes is the *facts* which are the numerical values of interest. In this case, the facts correspond to sales figures (store_sales, store_cost, and unit_sales). Hence this table in the center is called a *fact table*.

The schema in Figure 12–15 is known as a *star schema*. It is a star schema when the dimension tables are directly linked to the fact table. (Actually, our schema is also partly a *snowflake schema* since the product dimension is defined by two tables, not one.)

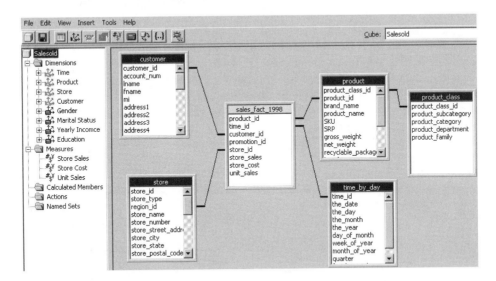

Figure 12–15 Data warehouse schema.

MeasuresLevel	+ Product Category				
		Store Sales			
+ Store Country	All Product	+ Baking Goods	+ Bathroom Products	+ Beer and Wine	+ Bread
All Store	355,712.69	9,988.47	8,615.68	9,073.47	10,835
+ Canada	52,172.79	1,548.32	1,237.02	1,386.70	1,509
+ Mexico	105,832.72	3,169.19	2,308.95	2,635.12	3,189
+ USA	197,707.18	5,270.96	5,069.71	5,051.65	6,141

Figure 12–16 An Example Data Cube.

Figure 12–16 is the data cube based on the schema in 12–15. A data cube presents data of a warehouse in a much more accessible form. There are two distinct sets of dimensions (also called attributes) that appear in the cube. In the lower window are the dimensions of store_country, product_category, and store_sales. In the upper window are the dimensions which do not explicitly appear in the lower window, like `education` and `marital_status`. For each dimension not in the lower window, we are aggregating or adding across all possible values. For example, `all_education` adds the `store_country`, `product_category`, and `store_sales` data for all education classes. Similarly, `all_marital_status` adds the same data for all marital status categories.

An important feature of the data cube is the ability to *drill down*—that is, get a more detailed view of the data by clicking on the various dimensions. This is illustrated in Figure 12–17. In the lower window, we have drilled down on `store_country` to state and city location. In the product category of baked goods we have drilled down to cooking oil. In the upper window we have narrowed the focus on education to `graduate_degree` and on gender to `female`. By drilling down, we can see what females with graduate degrees spent on cooking oil in San Francisco, CA.

Education	Graduate Degree	▼		Gender	F	▼
Marital Status	All Marital Status	▼		Time	All Time	▼
Yearly Incomce	All Yearly Incomce	▼		Customer	All Customer	▼

			MeasuresLevel	- Product Category	+ Product Subcategory
				Store Sales	
			All Product	- Baking Goods	
- Store Country	- Store State	+ Store City	All Product Total	Baking Goods Total	+ Cooking Oil
All Store	All Store Total		9,235.72	248.11	9:
+ Canada	Canada Total		1,084.11	45.62	2:
+ Mexico	Mexico Total		2,543.73	78.60	2ε
	USA Total		5,607.88	123.89	4ξ
		CA Total	4,642.12	109.72	3²
		+ Alameda			
- USA	- CA	+ Beverly Hills			
		+ Los Angeles	2,245.26	41.84	1:
		+ San Diego	1,305.03	43.62	1ε
		+ San Francisco	1,091.83	24.26	ε
	+ OR	OR Total	556.98	3.04	
	+ WA	WA Total	408.78	11.13	1:

Figure 12–17 Drilling down in a data cube.

The reader should realize that constructing a data warehouse is not easy. A data warehouse generally brings together in one location data from various departments within a company. It is not easy to make all the data compatible with all the others. Culling data from various databases and departments (or even companies after an acquisition or merger) may be difficult. Seemingly trivial things such as one database storing gender as M, F and another as `Male`, `Female` causes problems. The data must go through a data scrubbing process. Readers interested in pursuing data warehouse construction in more detail can consult Dyché [41].

DATA MINING BASICS ....

In the previous section we illustrated OLAP by drilling down through a data cube. This was a top-down process in the sense that the query originates with the user. The user manually guides the drilling process and has some idea of what she is looking for. For example, you could drill down in the cube to find the total sales of baked goods in Alameda in the last quarter of 1998. OLAP is great if you know what you are looking for. But what if you don't know what you are looking for? Your data could be full of hidden gems of information to help your business. The focus of *data mining* is finding patterns in the data. It is a "bottom-up procedure" concerned with finding hidden patterns without knowing exactly what you are looking for.

Tech Talk

Algorithm: a precise, step-by-step numerical procedure for solving a problem. Statistical algorithms, genetic algorithms, association rules, collaborative filters, cluster analysis, and decision trees have all been applied to data mining problems. Many of the data mining methods can be traced directly to the field of artificial intelligence.

A simple example of data mining based on a clustering algorithm is illustrated in Figure 12–18. The idea behind clustering is to take a heterogeneous (diverse) population and find homogeneous (similar) clusters or groups within that population. The data and the clustering algorithm determine the groups, not the intuition of the user. When homogeneous clusters are found, marketing efforts can be made toward that particular group. When using this kind of algorithm, the user does need to specify the number of groups to create, which demographic variables to look at, and which measure to use in organizing the cluster.

In our example, the user has asked the algorithm to create three groups. The measure used to create the clusters is `store sales`. The demographic variables used in the algorithm are `gender`, `annual income`, `marital status`, and `education`. Once the algorithm has created the clusters, the user can examine values of the demographic variables within each cluster. In this example, there is a cluster of high income and well educated people, a cluster of low income people with very little education, and a "middle class" cluster. One piece of interesting information revealed by the clusters is that the middle unit sales to the middle class far outweigh that to the upper and lower class. Thus, in this example, marketing dollars are most efficiently spent targeting the middle class.

Discovering clusters of homogeneous customers is important for targeting purposes. For example, DigiMine, a data mining company, helped boost readership of MSNBC.com by discovering a cluster of 22 percent of MSNBC readers who did not fit into the standard categories of sports fans, political news enthusiasts, etc. It turns out this large category was essentially interested in gossip tabloid kinds of articles. In response, MSNBC decided to feature at least one such story per day on its home page. See [94].

Another good example of data mining is our Amazon cookie example illustrated in Figure 11–2 in Chapter 11, "Marketing on the Internet." Recall that when entering the

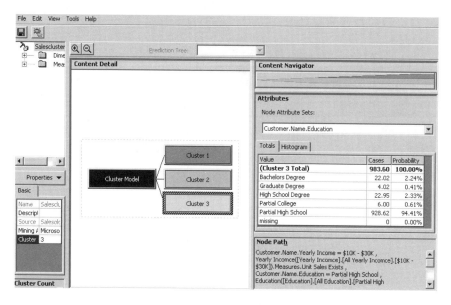

Figure 12–18 Data mining using clustering.

Amazon site, Amazon reads your cookie and gets your ID. This ID acts as a primary key in its customer database. It has mined this database using collaborative filters. The basic idea is to find people "like you" in terms of purchase behavior. This way, it can recommend books and videos based on what people "like you" have purchased. For example, it can determine from the database that you have purchased numerous books on XML. Other people who have purchased books on XML are therefore like you. It can then use the purchase patterns of other XML book purchasers to make recommendations to you. All of the leading DBMS vendors, Oracle, IBM, and Microsoft offer warehousing, OLAP, and data mining software modules. In its most recent release of Oracle9*i*, Oracle offers "in-database mining" capability. That is, mining is done on the original database and extraction of the data from a warehouse is not necessary. At this point it is good for the reader to step back and reflect on the fundamental difference among a query to a relational database, OLAP, and data mining. We illustrate with our Amazon example.

- **Relational Database Query:** "How many copies of *Professional XML Databases* by Kevin Williams, et al., are in stock?"

- **Data Warehouse OLAP:** "How many XML books by Wrox Press did we sell in the first quarter of 2001?"

- **Data Warehouse Mining:** "Which movie DVDs should we recommend to buyers of XML books?"

Two areas of data mining are currently hot. In Chapter 11 we discussed Web-based server and client-side tracking. A number of companies are now offering products to mine useful information from the reams of data in server log files, cookies, and registration databases. The other area is in customer relationship management, or CRM. This topic is discussed further in Chapter 14, "Enterprise Application Softare."

FUTURE TRENDS AND IMPLICATIONS ....

This chapter was about data. One of the most important trends in Internet business is the growing use of XML. Back in Chapter 5, "Languages of the Internet" we said XML was about giving meaning to data. So how do XML and databases relate? The major DBMS vendors store their data files as proprietary binary files, not as XML files. However, due to the overwhelming importance of XML, all of the major vendors have added modules to their products for reading and writing data in XML format. To illustrate, consider the SQL query in Figure 12–14. Recall that the query joins the `orders` and `supplier` relations and finds the attributes `street` and `city` for all records where the `sku_num` is 577. Let's see how this query is made using the Web and XML.

The user wants to make the query described above. She fills out an HTML form which is translated into what is represented in Figure 12–19. This is an XML document stored as a file named `retailer.xml`. The essential element in this document is the `sql:query` element. The `sql:query` element tag is used to define the SQL statement. The SQL statement is the same one that appears in Figure 12–14 with one exception. There is an additional part of the command, `FOR XML AUTO, elements`. This tells the DBMS, in this case Microsoft SQL Server, to return the result of the query as XML data. The SQL statement in Figure 12–19 is sent to SQL Server via the Web. The URL in this example is:

```
http://gsbrkm/retailer/templates/retailer.xml
```

The SQL Server in this example is running on the server gsbkxm. Don't worry about the details of how the file actually gets passed to SQL Server. SQL Server then executes the query and returns an XML file to the user's browser. The XML file returned by SQL Server is what you see in Figure 12–20. Using data in XML format with a DBMS will soon become very common.

We have just illustrated getting the query results from a DBMS as an XML file. This was done by sending SQL inside an XML file. However, SQL is really designed for relational databases. As more and more data are stored in native XML format, it makes more sense to have a query language designed specifically for XML. The W3C is working on developing a query language for XML. Currently, there is a working draft of XQuery, an XML Query Language.

In this chapter we talked about relational databases. Given the interest in object-oriented programming (recall Chapter 3) it is not surprising that there has been an interest in object-oriented databases where the fundamental unit of storage is an object (with classes, inheritance, etc.) rather than a relation. However, pure object-oriented database systems have not won out. Instead, the relational systems have become more object-oriented by allowing user-defined data types and multimedia data. Indeed, many mod-

```
<?xml version="1.0"?>
<?xml-stylesheet type="text/xsl" href="retailer.xsl"?>
<ROOT xmlns:sql="urn:schemas-microsoft-com:xml-sql">
<sql:query>
SELECT supplier.street, supplier.city
FROM supplier, orders
WHERE supplier.sup_id=orders.sup_id
AND orders.sku_num=577
FOR XML AUTO, elements
</sql:query>
</ROOT>
```

Figure 12–19 XML input to SQL Server.

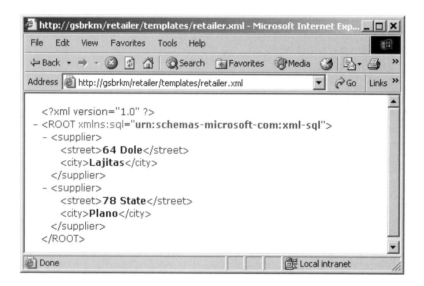

Figure 12–20 XML returned by SQL Server.

ern DBMSs allow BLOB (Binary Large Objects) fields. A BLOB field may include text, images, audio, and video.

Mobile computing is an important trend. There is often a need for remote users and road warriors to have a relational database tool on their handheld device. For example, a sales rep might want to query a copy of the customer database while flying between cities. This is now possible with IBM's DB2 Everyplace which supports the Palm OS, Symbian Epoc, and Windows CE operating systems (see Chapter 3). Microsoft's SQL Server Windows CE Edition works on handheld devices using the Windows CE operation system. Both of these products have file synchronization features.

So far, we have looked at databases only from the software perspective. We now turn to an important hardware issue. The explosion in the use of relational databases has led to a corresponding explosion in data storage. Where to store all of the data is now a very important problem for many companies. If you need more disk space for your desktop machine, you can always buy an external hard drive and attach it to the machine using an SCSI or USB cable connection. In the corporate world, servers and large databases are a bit more complicated. Two important storage technologies to know about are NAS (network attached storage) and SAN (storage area network). These are illustrated in Figures 12–21 and 12–22, respectively.

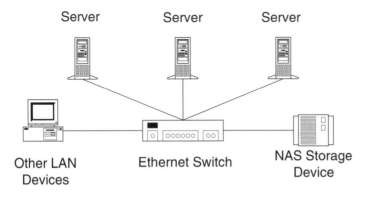

Figure 12–21 NAS (Network Attached Storage) architecture.

An NAS device is typically attached directly to an Ethernet LAN and assigned an IP address. The NAS device may be a server appliance that performs duties in addition to storage, or it could be a dedicated storage device with RAID (redundant array of independent disks) support. An SAN solution is a separate network that is attached to the LAN using a high-speed transport technology called Fibre Channel. Fibre Channel is a very high-speed technology that allows for communication between servers, desktop machines, and storage devices. Fibre Channel may use either copper or fiber optic cables. Think of SAN as having multiple hard drives directly attached to the server or servers.

Tech Talk

RAID (redundant array of independent disks): A RAID drive appears as one drive, but data is written across two or more drives. The data is divided among the multiple drives using a process called stripping.

Finally, a third option that many firms are choosing is to let a third party store the data. We have talked about MSPs and ASPs. A related service is SSP (storage service provider). This is a relatively new service, but many companies like IBM and EDS are trying to get into this market along with upstarts like Scale Eight. However, unlike an ASP or MSP, the SSP often locates the storage equipment on a company site, rather than

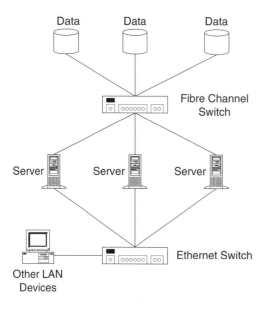

Figure 12–22 SAN (Storage Area Network) architecture.

at its own location. This is the leasing solution we discussed in Chapter 7, "Getting Your Business Online." (See Figure 7–2.) With leasing, the outsourcing company provides the storage hardware, installs it, and provides maintenance and monitoring.

This option of letting a third party store data has become increasingly important in light of the September 11, 2001 terrorist attacks, which destroyed not only many companies' computer systems, but also their data. Many firms are now turning to specialized data storage companies to store backup data in secure disaster-proof vaults off company premises. One such data protection firm is Boston-based Iron Mountain. Iron Mountain picks up tapes or other data storage devices from clients, stores them in high-tech vaults, and returns them to clients when needed. Prices start at about $150 a month. September 11 has brought renewed focus on disaster recovery plans for companies. Disaster can prove lethal for a company. According to the National Fire Protection Agency, 43 percent of companies directly hit by a disaster never reopen, and 29 percent close after three years. Even the 1993 World Trade Center bombing, the damage of which was far more contained than that of the September 11 attacks, caused many companies to go under because they were restricted from the building and couldn't access their data [90]. Don't get caught flat-footed in the face of disaster. Take precaution to back up and securely store mission-critical data.

13 Internet Business Architecture

In this chapter ...

THE EVOLUTION OF COMPUTING: COMING FULL CIRCLE ....

W e start this chapter by revisiting the cycle of computing paradigm introduced in Chapter 2, "What Do I Need to Know About Hardware?" This paradigm is illustrated in Figure 13–1. Recall that in the early days of computing there was the mainframe. All of the computing was done by mainframe and it was very difficult to interact with the mainframe. You had to know how to program. Then, the personal computer came along and put the power of a mainframe on a person's desktop. With the development of GUI-based operating systems like Mac OS and Windows 3.1 it was easy to communicate with the desktop computer. Throughout the 80s and into the 90s, there were remarkable improvements in chip speed and memory capacity. The trend was clearly bigger and more powerful desktop machines. An important parallel trend was the networking of computers. The ability of the desktop machine to handle word processing and perform spreadsheet analysis made it an *important* business tool; networking and sharing files across corporate networks made it a *crucial* business tool.

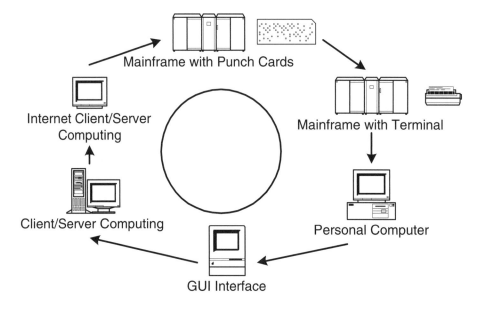

Figure 13–1 The cycle of computing.

In the twenty-first century we are coming full circle in the cycle and back to the the twelve o'clock position. Because of the Internet, the mainframe, now called an enterprise server, is more important than ever to a corporation. We are in the era of Internet client/server computing. The client is a machine with a Web browser interacting over the Internet with a server. However, there are big differences between client/server computing of today and mainframe computing of yesteryear, as outlined here.

- We have a GUI as opposed to command line interface, or worse yet, punch cards and a card reader.

- We have a universal interface in the browser. The browser is ubiquitous. Virtually everyone can use a browser.

- We have a universal and open networking protocol in TCP/IP. It is easy for computers to communicate with each other within a corporate network or across different corporate networks. Users are easily linked to the corporate network via the Internet. This was virtually impossible before the Internet.

- We are operating system-independent. Individuals working on computers with different operating systems can easily communicate with each other. Again, the Internet made this possible.

. . . .

A WORD ON TERMINOLOGY

The term client/server was used in the 80s and early 90s and is now somewhat outdated. A more common and general term used today is N-tier architecture. We study N-tier architectures in the section, "Server Technologies." Other popular terms include multi-tier architecture, Internet computing, and distributed computing. It all comes down to the same thing—an application (the client) using another application or data somewhere else (the server) on the network.

Although new and improved microprocessors are still being developed with breathtaking speed (so far so good for Moore's Law), access to a high-speed Internet connection and server reduces the need for a powerful desktop machine. In the next section, "Client/Server Paradigms," we look at the effect of the Internet on desktop computing. We develop three paradigms of computing in a modern corporate/consumer setting. Following the development of these computing paradigms, we look at client-side technologies that are important for Internet business in the section, "Client Technologies." Following the client-side technologies, we look at the important technologies on the server side of Internet business in the section, "Server Technologies." We study three tiers of server architecture: a presentation tier, an application tier, and a database tier. In the world of Internet server architecture there is a growing dichotomy between a Microsoft solution versus a non-Microsoft solution. Every company involved with Internet business will have to make a decision on which way to go. We play the role of an agnostic and present both solution technologies with a discussion of the advantages and disadvantages of each solution.

An important aspect of any use of the Internet for business is the ability to *scale.* What happens to your server architecture as you grow? This question is addressed and answered in the section, "Scaling and Web Farms." We conclude the chapter with a section on "Future Trends and Implications." In this section, we introduce the concept of a *Web service*. For now, think of a Web service as software that can be accessed and executed over the Internet. Web services provide a natural segue into Chapter 14, "Enterprise Application Software," in which we study business-to-business integration. A Web service will make sense to you by the end of the book.

CLIENT/SERVER PARADIGMS ....

We have now come full circle with Internet client/server computing and mainframes are more important than ever. What does this say about the future of the PC? There are numerous possibilities. First, consider the diagram in Figure 13–2. For reference, we call this Paradigm 1. This represents one end of the spectrum with a very *weak or thin client*. Basically, the client is a display, keyboard, and mouse connected to a server over the network. In fact, the icon we have used for the client in Figure 13–2 is just a monitor, not a PC. In this paradigm the server stores all of the data, and all of the applications execute on the server. The user of the client terminal sees a "desktop" display just as on a regular PC, but the software is actually running on the server and sending a graphical image to the client terminal. The client's only task is to display sets of colored pixels on the monitor. A good example of this paradigm is a company renting accounting software hosted on the server of an ASP. The company need only remotely log on to the ASP server machine and use the software. Nothing is required on company premises except the monitor and network connection. One might call this paradigm "server computing."

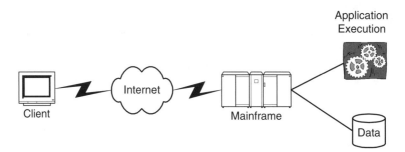

Figure 13–2 Paradigm 1: Weak client, strong server

The opposite end of the spectrum, Paradigm 2, is illustrated in Figure 13–3. This paradigm comprises the *strong* or *fat client* model and no server. Note in the diagram we have broken the link between the client and server. In this paradigm all of the data reside on the client and all of the computing is done on the client machine. In this paradigm the client is a reasonably powerful desktop PC, or perhaps even a workstation—hence, the term fat. This was the initial PC computing model before networking became feasible and popular. A good example of this style of computing is a small business owner using Quickbooks from Intuit to manage the payroll. One might call this paradigm "client computing."

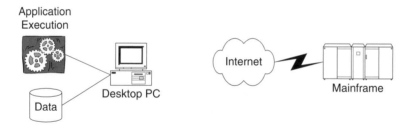

Figure 13–3 Paradigm 2: Strong client, weak server.

Most computing done today in a business setting is neither the pure weak client of Paradigm 1 nor the pure fat client of Paradigm 2. Rather, it is a mixture of the two models. We call this mixture Paradigm 3. Consider Figure 13–4. This is an example of client/server computing in which the server plays a relatively weak role (that is, we are closer to Paradigm 2 than Paradigm 1). In this figure, the server is providing the data but all of the computing is done on the client. In this paradigm the client is a PC. A simple example of this client/server model is a professor posting homework assignments or old exams on a server for students to download and read at their convenience. Another example of client/server computing at this end of the spectrum is print serving. The server is used to schedule and manage jobs submitted to a printer, but the computing is done on the client machine.

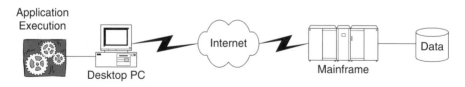

Figure 13–4 Paradigm 3: Client/Server computing–file serving.

Figure 13–5 is also an illustration of Paradigm 3, but is closer to Paradigm 1 than our previous example. Again, the client machine is a PC. In this illustration of Paradigm 3, computing is being done on both the client and server computers. Also, data often reside on both the client and server computers. In this variation of Paradigm 3, the desktop may be fairly thin. An example of this variation is a customer using shopping cart software interacting with an Internet retailing site. Some computing is typically done at the client end. For example, the client's browser might run a script program (this is discussed in the next section) ensuring that the form is properly filled out, e.g., an expiration date on the credit card is entered prior to submission. However, computing is also done on the server, e.g., calculation of a shipping charge or checking to see if the selected items are in stock. In this example some of the data reside with the client (the information the customer provides on the form), and some of the data reside on the server (prices, item availability, shipping costs, etc.).

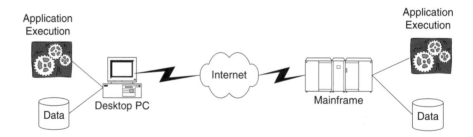

Figure 13–5 *Paradigm 3: Client/Server computing–a mixed solution.*

In Chapter 2, "What Do I Need to Know about Hardware," we quoted Larry Ellison calling the PC a "silly device" in 1995. He, along with many others, forecasted the demise of the PC at the hands of the network computer (NC). The NC model of computing envisioned by Ellison and others is the model illustrated in Figure 13–2. This obviously did not happen, and although sales are down, the PC made it to its 20th birthday party (for the IBM PC) in August of 2001 in pretty good shape. Proponents of the NC argued that the NC failed because it was too powerful–it was not thin enough. Executing applications on the NC required a reasonably powerful chip, main memory, and a hard drive. Since PC prices were dropping so rapidly in the mid to late 90s, the anticipated cost savings of the NC never materialized. The NC proponents now argue that a thinner client is needed, i.e., Paradigm 1. The most powerful argument typically advanced for Paradigm 1 is based on the total cost of ownership (TCO). In particular:

- The true thin client is a less expensive piece of hardware than a desktop PC. Most of the cost is the display.

- With a thin client it is not necessary to manage, debug, and update all of the different software configurations on individual desktop machines. Software is maintained and upgraded at only one point–the server.

- All users in the thin client model see the same interface and configuration. Training and help desk costs are significantly reduced.

- It is easy to control software access with a thin client. This can reduce the amount of wasted time devoted to playing games or using software for personal purposes. For example, consider employees working in a call center. If they have a weak client and access to only specific job-related software, they cannot waste company time surfing the Web.

Despite these strong arguments for the thin client, a February 2001 survey of CIOs by *CIO Magazine* [11] revealed that the Windows OS/Intel PC or clone accounted for 95 percent of desktop systems. Furthermore, only 24 percent of CIOs surveyed expected the desktop system to be replaced by other devices in the next five years. Why is this so?

- The TCO argument for thin clients does not account for all of the true cost associated with this model. TCO should stand for "Thinclient Cost Oversimplified" [11]. If the thin client model is used, the server must be up 100 percent of the time. If the server in the pure thin client model goes down, nothing gets done. This adds to network infrastructure costs and backup/redundancy costs.

- The PC model is the most flexible solution. This is perhaps the strongest argument in favor of the PC. The PC can always act as a thin client, but it can also run applications independently of the server. This allows the greatest flexibility in planning for corporate software and networking changes.

- With PC prices constantly going down, there are not big cost savings associated with thin client purchases over PCs.

In the short run, we believe it is very unlikely that the Paradigm 1 thin client model will eliminate the desktop PC. This may change as wireless technologies become more advanced. An important advantage of the fat client over the thin client is that you can run applications without being connected to the network. If you remove "the wire" from the equation, then the thin client may become more prevalent. The most likely scenario for now is that various forms of Paradigm 3 will dominate, in particular the model illustrated in Figure 13–5. The browser is the most important and universal piece of client software. In the next section we look at browser-based technologies that are important for Internet business.

CLIENT TECHNOLOGIES ....

Before the Internet, companies were forced to write specialized client software for their client/server applications. This software was typically not very generic and often depended heavily on the specific application, type of computer network, operating system, DBMS, etc. This has changed with the Internet. The Web browser is rapidly becoming the client software of choice. This makes software development at the client end far easier. It also makes training and support far easier since all of the client software has the same look and feel. In this section we discuss the technologies available for developing Web browser client applications. Although these technologies are often used to make "glitzy" Web pages—moving text, pop-up windows, changing colors, etc., we focus on business use rather than presentation.

JavaScript is one of the most frequently used languages for developing Web browser applications. JavaScript was developed by Netscape and first implemented in its Navigator browser. Microsoft followed suit and Internet Explorer supports JavaScript. JavaScript is a scripting language. JavaScript is quite different from the Java programming language. JavaScript is object-based and a programmer can reuse and extend objects that are part of the JavaScript programming language. However, JavaScript is not truly object-oriented because programmers cannot create their own classes and subclasses and make use of inheritance and polymorphism. Also, JavaScript is an interpreted language, which means the source code is not compiled into byte code as it is with the Java programming language. See the discussion about classes, objects, inheritance, polymorphism, compilers, and interpreters in Chapter 3,"Software Is Everywhere." JavaScript is not as complicated as Java.

Recall that HTML is used for formatting a Web page. It does this through a set of predefined tags that the browser understands. For example, there is a `<b>` tag to denote the start of text that should be in boldface. The `</b>` tag tells the browser where to stop using a boldface font. Similarly, JavaScript is added to an HTML document by a pair of `<script>` and `</script>` tags. Both Internet Explorer and Netscape Navigator have a built-in interpreter that executes the script between the tags. Thus, is not necessary to have a compiler to write JavaScript applications. An obviously nice feature of using JavaScript is that it is platform independent. The only requirement is that the user have a Web browser.

JavaScript makes heavy use of its "prepackaged" objects. The idea is to treat an HTML document as an object consisting of other objects such as a form, table, or paragraph. Using JavaScript you can manipulate attributes of the form object such as text boxes and radio buttons where data are entered. For example, JavaScript can make sure that the expiration date field for a credit card number hasn't been left blank on an order form.

Tech Talk

API (application program interface): Programs need to communicate with operating systems and other programs. An API is not a program or software. An API is a specification for a program that describes how another program or an operating system can communicate with it by accessing its data and methods. For example, all of the major database vendors provide drivers for their software that adhere to standard APIs (JDBC and OLE DB are two such standards discussed later in the chapter). This allows programmers to write vendor neutral software for accessing the data in the database.

Tech Talk

DOM (document object model): DOM is an API for accessing HTML and XML documents from a Web browser. The DOM for HTML is a specification of the W3C. Using the DOM, programmers can access the objects and their attributes of an HTML page being displayed in a Web browser.

JavaScript also makes use of *events*. Events include loading the Web page, clicking a mouse, moving a mouse over a link, submitting a form, etc. Each of these events can trigger the execution of JavaScript. For example, the event of loading the Web page could trigger JavaScript that would request data from the user through a pop-up window. The event of submitting a form could trigger a JavaScript routine to validate the data in the form.

To illustrate how useful this is, consider what happens when a customer fills out a form on a Web page in order to make a purchase. Typically, there are required fields in the form that must be filled in. For example, a name, credit card number, or an expiration date. One solution to checking the validity of the form is to have the user submit the form and then check the validity on the server. If the form is not valid, the server can send a message back to the user indicating this fact. However, in order to minimize the amount of information that must be exchanged over the network, this bit of *business logic* is easily and best done on the client end. (Business logic refers to any computing necessary to enact a business transaction; for example, calculation of a shipping cost, determining if an item is in stock, validating a Web form, etc. Business logic is often done by both the client and server computers.) When the user hits the submit button this event can trigger a JavaScript routine on the client that checks over the fields in the form and makes sure the necessary data are entered. For the more technically inclined, we illustrate this process and the HTML DOM with several examples in the "JavaScript and Client Programming" section in the Appendix.

There is also a DOM for XML. Recall our development of XML in Chapter 5, "Languages of the Internet." An XML document has a tree structure. There is always a root node for the document. The root node has children nodes, who may also have children, etc. The tree structure for the simple file we worked with is reproduced in Figure 13–6 for the sake of continuity. The XML DOM allows a JavaScript programmer to:

- Traverse the tree from the root node to any desired child node.

- Access the data in any node. For example, we could start at the root node CATALOG, move to Record 1, then to the PRICE node and get the price of $15 for the record.

- Insert or delete nodes in the tree.

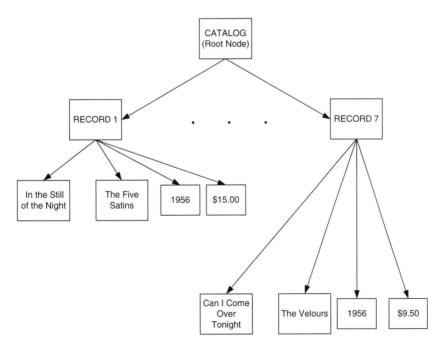

Figure 13–6 Tree structure of XML file doowop.xml.

The DOMs for HTML and XML along with a scripting language are very important for Internet business Web sites. A simple example is a retailer with an online catalog trying to keep the prices listed online up-to-date. The retailer could query a database for pricing information and store the query result as XML data. Then, using the DOMs for HTML and XML in conjunction with JavaScript, the retailer could locate the appropriate prices in the XML file and put them into the appropriate places on the Web page catalog.

Visual Basic Script (VBScript is another client-side scripting language. It is similar to JavaScript in both syntax and functionality. However, VBScript is a Microsoft technology and native to only the Internet Explorer browser. Other browsers such as Netscape Navigator require a special add-on piece of software. Since both JavaScript and VBScript are so similar in functionality, we recommend using JavaScript in order to maximize user compatibility.

Java is an important alternative to client scripting languages. Java is much more powerful than JavaScript. It is truly an object-oriented language, and Java programmers can create their own classes and subclasses through inheritance and polymorphism. Java is compiled into bytecode, and a Java program will execute more quickly than JavaScript. Java programs that run on browsers are called *Java Applets*.

The process for distributing Applets over the Internet is illustrated in Figure 13–7. Note that two files are downloaded. First, the Web page with the HTML is downloaded. Within the Web page are tags (just like for JavaScript) that tell the browser to run the Java Applet. In this case the tags are <object> and </object>. The object tag has attributes that include the name of the Java byte code file that the server downloads. This differs from JavaScript. With JavaScript, the script itself is part of the file that constitutes the Web page.

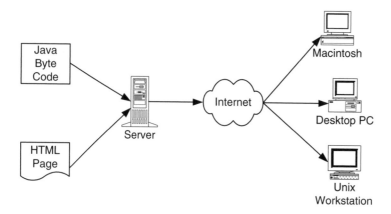

Figure 13–7 Downloading a Java Applet.

With a Java Applet there is reference in the Web page to the Java bytecode that the server sends to the browser as a file separate from the file that contains the HTML. The browser has a built-in Java virtual machine that takes the low-level bytecode instructions and converts it "just-in-time" into the machine code used by the client machine. Note also in Figure 13–7 that the server is sending the same two files to a Macintosh, a PC, and a Unix workstation. This is possible since the byte code is machine independent. It is only necessary that the browser have a virtual machine for the hardware and operating system that the browser is running on.

Like JavaScript, Applets are used for both presentation and executing business logic. Java Applets have an important advantage over JavaScript when it comes to executing business logic. In addition to being able to access the DOM, an Applet can interact directly with a server. The client machine cannot interact directly with a server using JavaScript.

Let's go back to our online shopping example. We were using JavaScript to verify the validity of the contents of a form. The Java Applet can do this and even more. For example, when a customer provides the Applet with his zip code, the Java Applet could pass this information directly to a server that would calculate the shipping cost and return this cost to the Applet. Although it is an executable piece of code, a Java Applet cannot run on its own (in technical terms it needs another processor space to run in). The browser provides a container for the Applet to run in. However, Java Applets can be cached on the client machine and do not need to be downloaded over the Internet each time they are run.

. . . .

MICROSOFT AND JAVA

There has always been considerable animosity between Sun and Microsoft over Java, even to the extent of litigation. Obviously, Microsoft is not enthusiastic about the "write-once, run-anywhere" philosophy since the Windows operating system is crucial to Microsoft. This animosity is coming to a head with the release of the new Microsoft XP operating system. The version of Internet Explorer integrated within the new XP operating system does not have a Java virtual machine. Without a Java virtual machine, users of Internet Explorer and XP will not be able to run Java Applets. In order to do so they will have to download a Java virtual machine. Sun has taken out ads in major newspapers calling on Microsoft customers to demand that the company support Java.

An alternative to Java Applets is the Microsoft technology called ActiveX controls. Think of an ActiveX control as an object that adds functionality to Internet Explorer (or another Windows based program). As with Java, the browser is made aware of the ActiveX control by an object tag. The ActiveX control may be automatically downloaded over the Internet when you click on a Web page, or it may be previously installed on your computer. A simple example of an ActiveX control is illustrated in Figure 13–8. The ActiveX control in this figure is a calendar. By using the controls in the upper right-hand corner of the calendar you can select any month of any year. This is obviously a nice bit of functionality to add to a Web page. The calendar application is not coded in HTML; rather, it is an object that is inserted into the page just like a Java Applet.

There are two problems with ActiveX control. First, this technology is specific to Microsoft. These controls require the Windows operating system in conjunction with Internet Explorer. Second, they are a security risk. Java Applets run within the confines of the browser. However, ActiveX controls have access to operating system resources outside the confines of the browser! If you download and install a hostile ActiveX control from a rogue Web site it could destroy and/or modify files on your system. Thus, it is important to download only digitally signed controls. You can set your browser's security level so that only digitally signed ActiveX controls are downloaded. Because ActiveX constrains the client to a Microsoft operating system, we recommend against this technology.

Figure 13–8 *Example of the calendar ActiveX control.*

Of course, not all of the business logic should be performed at the client end. For example, if it is necessary to query a large database, then it is not efficient to download the database to the client and perform the query on the client end. It is more efficient to perform the query on the server end and then pass the result of the query to the client. When you use the tracking facility at the Web site for UPS or Federal Express, the business logic of locating your package is done on the server. It is our intent in this chapter to present you with the various client and server technologies and enough technical detail so that you can carry on an intelligent discussion with a CIO about what kinds of computing tasks a browser and server can perform. We now focus on server computing technology.

SERVER TECHNOLOGIES . . . .

Now for the fun part—what happens behind the scenes. When corporate networking blossomed in the late 1980s and early 1990s, so did client/server computing. The typical client/server model used throughout the 1980s and 1990s was, in modern vernacular, a *two-tier architecture.* A typical two-tier architecture is illustrated in Figure 13–9. In this figure, the client is running a database application (for example, IBM's DB2 Personal Edition) that interacts through a company LAN with the server that is running a DBMS (for example IBM's DB2 UDB). In this two-tier scenario the client could download files from the DBMS and then make the query locally, or make the query on the server and download the result of the query. In either case, the client software in this scenario is not very generic; it is written to interact with a specific DBMS.

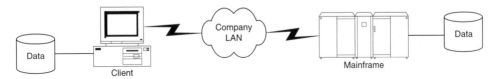

Figure 13–9 Traditional two-tier architecture.

Then, in the mid-nineties, the Web-based two-tier architecture became popular. This is illustrated in Figure 13–10. In this example the client is using a browser (for example, Netscape Navigator) and requesting Web pages from the Web server (for example, Apache running on Linux). There is an important difference in the scenarios illustrated by Figures 13–9 and Figure 13–10. In Figure 13–9 the server is strictly a database server and serving up the results of a query. In Figure 13–10 the server is strictly a presentation server providing Web pages. Remember a Web server is really nothing more than a "file broker" providing files that contain HTML using the HTTP protocol.

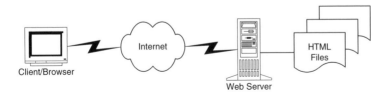

Figure 13–10 Web two-tier architecture.

Now, let's combine Figure 13–9 and Figure 13–10. Assume that the client software in our new scenario is a browser. With this combination we have a browser, a Web server, and a DBMS. How can the client communicate with a DBMS through the Web server if all the Web server can do is provide HTML files? It is certainly not efficient to write Web server software capable of interacting with all of the different DBMSs available. Neither is it efficient to build shopping cart technology, credit card verification technology, content management, etc., into the Web server. Instead, it makes sense to separate the business logic from the presentation (serving up Web pages) and let another software application take care of the business logic.

The business logic application has to "talk to" the Web server—they must exchange data. For example, the data in a form filled out by the user needs to be passed to the business logic application. The common gateway interface (CGI) is an interface for formatting the data used in the exchange. A CGI application is an application for executing business logic that uses CGI for exchanging data. Virtually all Web servers support CGI.

Figure 13–11 Using a CGI application with a database.

An example of how this works is illustrated in Figure 13–11. Assume that the end user (the client) submits a form requesting information from a database. The HTML in the form will contain the name of a CGI application to execute. This CGI application will have a .cgi suffix. When the Web server sees the .cgi suffix, it knows to exchange the information contained in the form submitted by the client browser with the CGI application using the CGI interface rules. The CGI application then makes the request to the database and constructs the Web page for the response that contains the result of the query. The response Web page—data and HTML—is passed back to the Web server following CGI interface rules. The Web server then passes the response Web page back to the user. Popular languages for writing CGI applications include Perl and C.

WHAT IS YOUR STATE?

A Web server fills requests for files. Once it fills the client request for a file, it maintains no history of the request. The relationship between the client and the server is *stateless*. This is why a Web server can handle so many simultaneous requests. It is not looking up information and keeping track of information associated with each file request. This has important consequences for Internet business. For example, consider shopping cart software. Most shopping cart software allows the customer to continue shopping after adding an item to the shopping cart. Once the consumer clicks on the link to continue shopping, the Web server has no memory of what is in the shopping cart. The shopping cart is part of a previous transaction. Additional software is required to maintain the state between the client and the server and record what is in the shopping cart.

There are a number of problems with the procedure we have just described. First, each request of a CGI application requires the start of a new process. Recall from Chapter 3, "Software Is Everywhere," that a process is a set of resources allocated to running a program that is being executed. This does not scale well when there are numerous requests for a CGI application, since each process will consume a nontrivial amount of system resources. Second, the CGI application is responsible for not only getting the data from the database, but also for returning the HTML that constitutes the Web page that the user sees as the result of the query. This means that presentation (i.e., HTML creation) is mixed in with the business logic. Finally, the third problem with CGI applications is that it is difficult for them to maintain "state" with the user. (See the shaded box "What Is Your State?" for the concept of state.) There is a technology called Fast CGI which allows a CGI program to remain running rather than starting it from scratch each time. This improves efficiency, but there is still a separate process for each CGI application which causes scaling problems. Although CGI remains a popular technology, CGI is being replaced by application servers.

. . . .

APPLICATION SERVER

An application server is a program designed to extend the functionality of a Web server. At a minimum, an application server allows the Web server to run software components written in Java, VBScript, C++, or other programming languages. Notice the number of Web pages that end with an `.asp` or `.jsp` suffix. When the Web server sees a request for a file with these extensions it passes off the request to the application server to process. The Web server is essentially acting as a broker between the client and the software components that constitute the application server. Many application servers come with a set of preconfigured components for customizing shopping carts and online catalogs; authenticating, analyzing, and tracking visitors; and processing orders. The name application server is somewhat of a misnomer since an application server is often not a stand-alone server and may depend on a Web server to initially process requests from the client. An application server is also called an app server.

Think of an *application server* or *app server* as a set of business logic software components that are all running in the same process space. In other words, the application server is a *container* for a set of business logic software components. For example, there might be a component for a shopping cart, a component for contacting a supplier, a component for querying a database, a component for processing a credit card. This is illustrated in Figure 13–12. Because all of the business logic components are running in the same process space, namely, the process space of the application server, this greatly conserves resources on the server and allows the system to scale. Furthermore, there may be multiple sessions associated with each component. For example, there might be a component for credit card processing, and each user simultaneously making a credit card purchase would constitute a session for this application.

....

COMPONENTS FOR NONTECHIES

Think of a component as an application that interfaces with another application through an API rather than with a person using a GUI. For example, assume you fill out a Web form with information (i.e., data) that must get entered into a database. These data must eventually become part of SQL command to get into the database. Component software would work behind the scenes to incorporate the data from the Web form into SQL commands and submit these commands to a database.

....

COMPONENTS FOR TECHIES

The term component is ambiguous and means different things to different people. The key idea is to reuse building blocks of code, i.e., classes, that have already been debugged and tested. Recall our definition of classes from Chapter 3, "Software Is Everywhere." A class is like a blueprint or pattern. Classes are made up of data (e.g., numbers or text) and methods that operate on the data.

One way to use a class is to "cut and paste" the source code for the class into the new source code under development. Another possibility is to take the new source code, compile it, and then link it with other previously developed classes, thereby creating an application with both new and old classes combined. A simpler approach is to have the new source code make calls to the classes that are needed on a "just-in-time" basis.

In this book we use the term component to refer to a class or set of classes that have been compiled (they are in binary format) and make their interface available to other applications. If an application knows the API for the component, then the application can interface with the component and use its methods and data. In this chapter we focus on components designed to add functionality to Web servers. In this setting the word object is often used interchangeably with the word component.

In Figure 13–12 we have the Web server and the application server on the same physical machine. Indeed, it could be the case that the application server components actually run in the same process space as the Web server. However, it is also common (especially for heavily trafficked sites) for the application server components to run on a machine that is physically separate from the machine that the Web server is running on. We discuss this issue further in the section "Scaling and Web Farms."

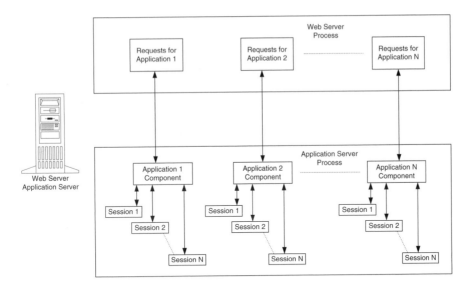

Figure 13–12 *An application server.*

The following are important properties for an application server:

- Speed is of the essence. When a user hits a submit button or uses a credit card to finalize a purchase and check out, things should happen quickly. Starting the application, initializing variables, opening database connections, etc., take time. Ideally, if a user initiates a process that executes a piece of business logic you want to keep the process running for the next user.

- It should consume a minimal amount of resources. Each time a user requests an application, e.g., connection to database, you don't want to start a new process. Recall our example from Chapter 3 and consider a Web-based retailer selling thousands of products online. Product information is contained in a database that users can access from the retailer's site in order to find out more about a product before purchasing it. The number of simultaneous users for a busy site can be quite large. If a new *process* were required every time a user accessed the database, the memory requirement in the retailer's servers would figuratively blow up, since every process requires its own memory space. For this model to be practical, a new *thread* (see Chapter 3), rather than a new process, must be created each time a new user wants to access the database. Because threads share memory, considerable memory is saved.

- Presentation should be separate from the logic. Most Web page designers are not programmers and most programmers are not Web page designers. It is a good practice to separate the Web page content (HTML, XML, and graphics) from the programming logic that makes the page work. This way, if the programming logic changes, the Web page design need not change. Similarly, you would prefer not to make changes to the business software if the Web page design changes.

- It should be stateful. A Web server is stateless. This means that as soon as it sends you the file you request, it forgets who you are. If you make a request for a new file, it knows nothing about your previous request. The application server should be stateful with the browser.

The addition of an application tier leads to the generic four-tier (or N-tier) architecture in Figure 13–13. The four tiers are 1) client, 2) presentation, 3) application/business logic, and 4) data. Breaking up the tiers improves scalability and stability. The presentation, application, and data tiers may be implemented (and often are for small sites) on the same machine/server. However, for sites with a large amount of traffic, the application server and database server often reside on separate machines. The application and database servers are often protected from the DMZ (see Chapter 7, "Getting Your Business Online") by an additional firewall. In fact, for a large application there may be multiple presentation, application, and database servers. This is discussed more fully in the next section, "Scaling and Web Farms."

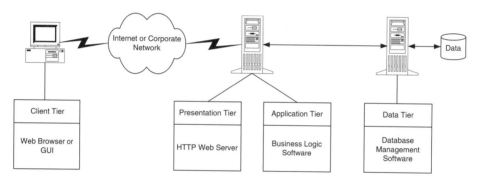

Figure 13–13 A generic N-tier architecture.

Microsoft Solutions

Microsoft dominates the desktop market with its Windows family of operating systems and its Office suite of applications. However, Microsoft is making a big push to get into the server software market. In this section, we give a brief overview of Microsoft server software and related technologies.

Microsoft Server Architecture Technologies

Operating System: A Windows Server operating system. There are several varieties. They are Windows 2000 Server, Windows 2000 Advanced Server, and Windows 2000 Datacenter. These operating systems differ in their ability to support symmetric multiprocessing and network load balancing (discussed in the section, "Scaling and Web Farms.").

Presentation Server: IIS (Internet Information Server). This is a Web server and ships with all versions of the Windows 2000 Server family.

Application Server: Microsoft has several application servers. The primary Microsoft application server is a software component that processes active server pages (ASP). When IIS gets a request for a page with an `.asp` extension, it automatically passes the request off to the component software specifically designed to handle `.asp` pages for processing. The name of this component is `asp.dll` and it is discussed in greater detail below. See also Figure 13–14. Another important Microsoft application server is Commerce Server 2000. This product is designed to get Internet commerce sites up and running quickly. It has customizable shopping carts, user profiling and authentication, catalogs, business analytics, order processing, and many other features. BizTalk Server is also an application server designed to help with B2B integration. BizTalk is discussed in Chapter 14, "Enterprise Application Software."

Database Server: The Microsoft DBMS is SQL Server.

Programming Languages: The programming languages used for Microsoft solutions are Visual C++, C#, and Visual Basic.

Component Software: COM+ is the Microsoft technology that provides the necessary "plumbing" so that components can talk to each other. COM is an acronym for component object model. Microsoft components often have a `.dll` extension which stands for dynamic link library. The `asp.dll` allows IIS to correctly process Web pages with an `.asp` extension.

Database Connectivity: ADO (ActiveX data object) and OLE DB (object linking and embedding database) are the primary technologies for connecting Web applications to the database tier. They are discussed shortly.

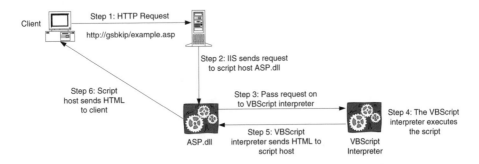

Figure 13–14 How active server pages work.

The ASP technology is illustrated in Figure 13–14. Note the sequence of events.

Step 1. The client browser submits a request for an an active server page, say, `example.asp`.

Step 2. The Web server, IIS, sees the `.asp` extension and passes the request off to an application server component (in this case, the application server is the software component `asp.dll`) for further processing. This component is often called a script host.

Step 3. The script host (`asp.dll`) determines which script interpreter to use (JScript or VBScript) and farms the script out to the appropriate interpreter. In Figure 13–14 we assume VBScript.

Step 4. The script interpreter executes the script.

Step 5. The script interpreter sends the result of the script execution as a stream of HTML back to the script host.

Step 6. The script host sends the HTML back to the client.

. . . .

ACTIVE SERVER PAGES

Active server pages (ASP) is a technology developed by Microsoft for adding functionality to a Web page. Recall from our discussion of JavaScript and VBScript in the section, "Client Technologies," that it is possible to add scripts to a Web page. These scripts are executed by the browser on the client machine.

The philosophy behind ASP is similar except that the scripts are executed on the server machine. Since ASP is a server-side technology, the browser may run on any operating system/hardware. This process is illustrated in Figure 13–14. The ASP technology is very flexible and is used for both presentation and business logic. Many Web sites are using ASP technology. Notice how many Web pages now have an `.asp` extension instead of an `.html` extension. For an example of ASP code and how it works, see the Technical Appendix.

Tech Talk

CLR: Common Language Runtime. The CLR manages the execution of the code compiled by the .NET languages (VB.NET, C#, JScript.NET, and managed C++). The .NET compilers take the source code and compile it into MSIL (Microsoft intermediate language). The MSIL is both operating system and hardware-independent. It is the job of the CLR to execute this code on the various Windows operating systems. The CLR is thus similar to the JRE (Java runtime environment).

Tech Talk

Middleware: Software that allows one application to communicate with another application over a network. For example, middleware is used to facilitate communication between a DBMS and an application server. Middleware is discussed more fully in Chapter 14.

. . . .

MICROSOFT .NET

Microsoft .NET is a comprehensive platform of software and services centered on the Internet. Microsoft .NET is Microsoft's approach to distributed computing based on the open XML standard. The .NET platform family of software products includes future versions of Windows operating systems, Web servers, and development tools (e.g., programming languages). ASP.NET is the .NET version of ASP. It represents a significant step forward. ASP.NET makes it easy to separate code from the HTML. This is very important because it separates the two distinct functions of presentation (HTML) and business logic (code).

Page presentation and business logic are often created by different individuals and departments. Separating these two functions makes it much easier to manage and update the HTML and code independently. Another significant improvement in ASP.NET is that it no longer relies on a scripting language. The code in ASP.NET is based on C#, C++, and Visual Basic. The application server for ASP.NET compiles the code into a DLL component; this component runs much more quickly than interpreted code such as VBScript. Like ASP, ASP.NET runs on any client.

One of the most common tasks performed in the application tier is processing client tier queries to the database tier. The client query must eventually end up in SQL format and the result of the query sent back to the client in the form of a Web page. The application server is responsible for this task. From a development standpoint, the application server software should be as independent of the DBMS as possible. For example, if a Web site is using Microsoft Access as the database, which is designed for intra-office use, scaling up to SQL Server or DB2, which are designed for full-blown Internet commerce use, should involve a minimum amount of application tier code rewriting. Two important Microsoft technologies make this possible. They are ADO and OLE DB data providers. Both ADO and OLE DB are good examples of middleware components. An OLE DB data provider is a software component that provides an API or interface for communicating with a data source. For example, there are OLE DB data providers for SQL Server, Oracle, and Access. ADO is a set of components used by a programmer to communicate with an OLE DB provider. ADO is independent of the data source.

Consider the diagram in Figure 13–15 which illustrates an N-tier architecture based on Microsoft technologies. Assume that the end user (the client) submits a form requesting information from an SQL Server database. What software is involved on the server side? First, in the presentation tier, there is the Web server (IIS) that initially serves up the Web page form. This form contains a link to a page with an `.asp` extension. When the form is submitted, IIS passes the page with the `.asp` extension to the `asp.dll` component. The ASP application uses ADO and OLE DB middleware to get the data from SQL Server and then send it back to the browser.

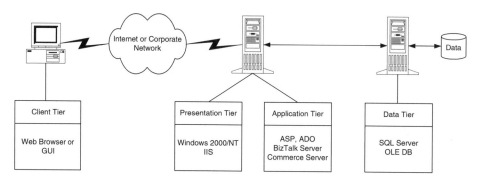

Figure 13–15 A Microsoft N-tier solution.

Non-Microsoft Solutions

Much of the initial excitement over Java centered around making fancy Web pages. This excitement has petered out. Java has yet to catch on as the primary development language for desktop applications. Where Java has really hit it big is in the application server market. More and more, the key battle shaping up is Microsoft versus Linux and Java. In this section we look at non-Microsoft N-tier architecture software.

Recall that a Java Applet is an application written in Java to extend the functionality of a browser. A *Java Servlet* is a program written in Java designed to extend the functionality of a Web server. A Java Servlet does not have a GUI and is similar to a CGI program. One can think of a Java application server as a process container for running Java Servlets. For example, a Java Servlet might be used to write a cookie on the client machine in order to track a visitor to a Web site. An important feature of Servlets is that they do not run as separate applications but as part of the application server and therefore help to conserve resources.

The desirability of separating the business logic from presentation was discussed earlier in the material on active server pages. Fortunately, in the Java world, it is also easy to separate presentation from business logic. The technology for doing so is *Java server pages* (JSP). The JSP technology is very similar to the ASP technology. With JSP technology it is not necessary to encode the HTML inside the Java source code. A JSP file can contain HTML, Java code, and tags that reference JavaBean components. When a JSP file is requested, the application server compiles the JSP into a Java Servlet and runs the Servlet. The JSP technology is analogous to the new ASP.NET technology from Microsoft. With both technologies, a page containing HTML, code, and references to components is compiled into an executable component. In the Java world this component is a Servlet; in the Microsoft .NET world it is a DLL.

Tech Talk

JavaBean: A Java class that has been compiled into an independent component. This component can be called from within a JavaServer page. For example, the Bean could be used to query a database. The use of JavaBeans is good for separating the presentation part of a JavaServer page (the HTML) from the business logic.

Tech Talk

J2EE (Java 2 Platform Enterprise Edition): A suite from Sun Microsystems of Java API specifications for Servlets, server pages, Enterprise JavaBeans, database connectivity, etc. These are the rules the middle tier and database tier applications and components must follow in order to talk to each other.

Tech Talk

EJB (Enterprise JavaBean): This is an API specification from Sun Microsystems for Java-based server components. Unlike the more generic JavaBean, an EJB must deliver a very specific interface that can be used by any application server conforming to the J2EE standard.

Java/Unix Server Architecture Technologies

Operating System: Unix and its variants are the most popular operating systems for Web servers. Among the Unix variants, Linux is the most popular operating system for Web servers.

Presentation Server: The most popular Web server is the open source product Apache. According to an August, 2001 survey (www.netcraft.com/survey), Apache has 58 percent of the market for Web servers. The next most popular Web server is IIS with approximately 26 percent of the market.

Application Server: The pioneering company in this area is BEA Systems with its WebLogic application server. BEA is led by Bill Coleman, a former Sun executive, who realized the importance of an operating system for Internet business. In addition to Microsoft, IBM, Oracle, and Sun are hot on the tail of BEA. All of the major non-Microsoft application servers are Java based. BEA remains the leader with approximately 18 percent of market share. IBM is next with approximately 15 percent (see www.idc.com/software/press/PR/GSW070901pr.stm).

Database Server: The two biggest players in the the database tier market are IBM with DB2 and Oracle with Oracle9*i*. MySQL and PostgreSQL are two popular open source databases.

Programming Languages: Java is easily the most widely used language for developing application tier software.

Component Software: The components used are Java Servlets and JavaBeans.

Database Connectivity: The key Java technology for database connectivity is JDBC (Java database connectivity). The logic behind JDBC is the same as the logic behind ADO and OLE DB—make the application tier independent of the database tier. The major database vendors (e.g., IBM and Oracle) provide JDBC drivers for their databases. The driver "buries" vendor-specific database implementation details (such as data structures) behind the JDBC API. The driver understands queries to the database made using vendor-neutral Java queries contained in the Java class `java.sql`.

In Figure 13–16 we show a complete N-tier architecture solution based on open source software. The open source application server is the Jakarta Tomcat. It is a fairly bare-bones application server. More sophisticated open source Internet commerce application servers can be purchased from dealers such as Red Hat.

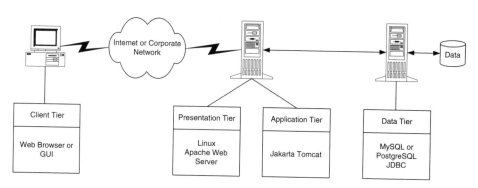

Figure 13–16 *An open source N-tier solution.*

In Figures 13–17 and 13–18 we show various combinations involving proprietary software. In Figure 13–17 we show a mixed IBM/Microsoft architecture. The operating system is Windows 2000 and the presentation server is IIS. The application server is IBM's WebSphere and the DBMS is IBM's DB2. The architecture illustrated in Figure 13–18 is an all Unix/Java proprietary architecture. The operating system is Solaris from Sun; the Web and application server are the Java-based BEA WebLogic product; the database is Oracle9*i*.

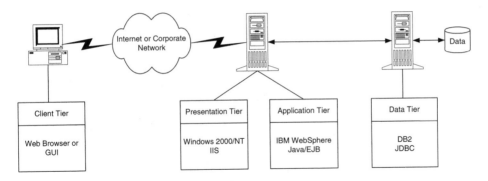

Figure 13–17 A "mixed" N-tier solution.

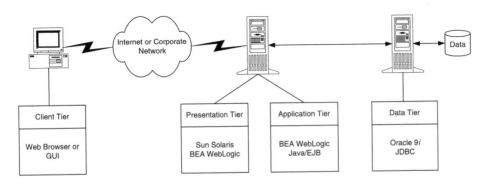

Figure 13–18 A second "mixed" N-tier solution.

SCALING AND WEB FARMS ....

The five nines (99.999), scaling, Web farms, clusters, 7/24/365, are terms constantly appearing in ads in the popular press such as *The Wall Street Journal* and *Business Week*. They are all related to the reliability of a Web site. Even if you are not part of the IT function, it is important to understand them and know if your Internet business applications can scale. There is a humorous IBM commercial where Bob, evidently a marketing executive, is confessing his ignorance of an important aspect of Internet business. He is saying, "We made this commercial—we were going to be rich—millions of hits to the Web site." But, unfortunately for Bob, "the site crashed, I forgot to warn the Web guys." What was the problem? The site did not scale.

Scalability is a measure of a Web site's ability to expand capacity in order to handle increased traffic without a significant reduction in performance. Closely related to scalability is *reliability*. Reliable means that the computer is up and running. When people talk about the five nines for a server they mean that the server is up 99.999 percent of the time. Thus, scaling relates to the performance of an application, and reliability relates to whether or not the application is up and running. In this section we focus on load balancing and Web farms—two techniques for building scalable, reliable Web sites.

If a Web site cannot handle either the current or anticipated load, there are two ways to increase capacity: either by scaling up or scaling out. These are also called, respectively, vertical and horizontal scaling. Vertical, or scaling up, means getting a bigger and faster computer. With vertical scaling you buy a true mainframe, a big machine with lots of memory and processors. There are two problems with this solution. First, it is a very expensive solution. Mainframes can run into the millions of dollars. More importantly, getting a big mainframe is like putting all of your eggs in one basket (or in computer lingo—a single point of failure). If the mainframe goes down, so does your site.

More common today is horizontal, or scaling out. Horizontal, or scaling out, refers to distributing the load on a Web site across many computers. Horizontal scaling may involve partitioning or service scaling that divides services up among different computers. For example, one server acts as a mail server, another as a Web server, and so on. Once the servers are partitioned based on tasks, *load balancing* is used to further partition requests (say, for a Web page) evenly across a cluster of servers (also called nodes) where any one of the servers is capable of handling the request. The servers in a cluster are often quite small (no larger than a pizza box) and mounted in a rack on top of each other. In the old days we had a large, climate controlled room with a single big mainframe. Now we have a large, climate controlled room with stacks of small computers. The advantage of a lot of small machines is that when one crashes it does not significantly affect the performance of the system. Also, it is possible to slowly scale the system up by adding as many machines as needed. This is much more cost effective than buying a huge mainframe.

Tech Talk

Cluster: A cluster is a set of independent servers that act as a single machine—they have a common network address and are capable of performing the same task (e.g., serving up a Web page).

Tech Talk

Web farm: A set of one or more server clusters.

We discuss three approaches to load balancing requests across a cluster of computers. The first is called round-robin DNS. We studied the domain name system in Chapter 4, "Internet and Web Technology." Recall that the DNS server takes a domain name such as ibm.com and "resolves" it into an IP address. A DNS server can be configured to associate a sequence of different IP addresses with the same domain name, and then rotate through the sequence when queried. For example, if there are three Web servers, each with a distinct IP address, the three IP addresses are entered into the DNS server and associated with the same domain name. The DNS server then rotates among the servers, assigning the addresses when requests for the domain name come in. Ideally, this gives each server one-third of the load.

There are two problems with round-robin DNS. First, frequently or recently used IP addresses are often cached with a local DNS server specific to a company or ISP. This means that the locally-cached IP address is used by the company or ISP rather than the IP address provided by the round-robin DNS server at the destination site. This defeats the purpose of the round-robin DNS server. An even bigger problem is that the DNS server cannot truly balance the load on the servers, because it is not monitoring their usage. In fact, a Web server may be down with the DNS server unaware of this fact.

A second, and better solution, for load balancing is to use a dedicated hardware device. This is illustrated in Figure 13–19. A load balancing switch such as the Cisco LocalDirector sits between the firewall and a Web cluster. The load balancing switch has an IP address and requests to the Web cluster are sent to this switch. This switch is a sophisticated hardware/software device that constantly "pings" all of the servers in the cluster to measure their usage. Then, when a request comes in, the switch allocates the request to a server using routing algorithms based upon server usage.

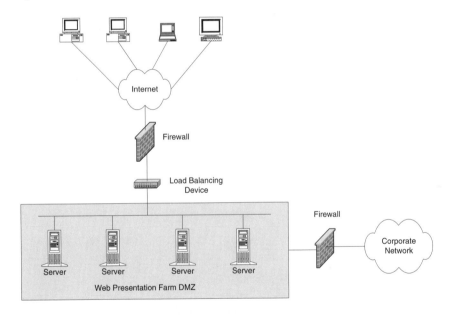

Figure 13–19 Hardware-based load balancing.

PCs/workstations are also used for load balancing. For example, IBM's Network Dispatcher software routes requests in a manner similar to the Cisco LocalDirector switch. One problem with this solution is that there is a single point of failure. If the load balancing switch or computer goes down, the cluster cannot be used. In many cases a redundant switch or computer is used to improve reliability. This investment in hardware is not cheap.

A third solution, which does not require any load balancing hardware in addition to the Web cluster, is Windows 2000 NLB (network load balancing). This is an operating system/software solution. This solution requires each server in the cluster to run Windows

2000 Advanced Server or Windows 2000 Datacenter. With this approach there is an IP address for the cluster, and each server in the cluster also has a unique IP address. When a request comes in to the cluster, *every server* in the cluster receives the request. (See Figure 13–20.) Then the NLB software uses an algorithm to determine which server will process the request. Generally, it is the server with the smallest current load. Contrast this with the hardware load-balancing approach in Figure 13–19. With NLB, requests are not routed to a specific server; rather, requests are discarded at the servers not selected for processing the request. This is very efficient because filtering requests is often faster than routing requests. A big plus of NLB is that there is no single point of failure. If a server goes down or is taken out of the cluster, requests are automatically directed to the other servers in the cluster. Furthermore, the load balancing is done within the cluster and additional load balancing hardware is not required.

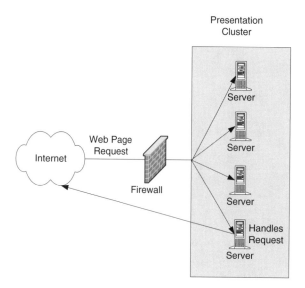

Figure 13–20 NLB: Network Load Balancing.

It is often desirable to put the application and database servers behind the corporate firewall for added protection. In Figure 13–21 we illustrate a second cluster of servers behind a second firewall. This is the application server cluster. These application servers perform the business logic function by running COM+ software components. Windows 2000 Advanced Server and Datacenter provide load balancing capabilities for the application servers. This is called CLB (component load balancing).

In Figure 13–21, the Web request that comes into the Web server cluster is processed by the second server in the cluster. Each of the Web servers in this cluster keeps a routing table. This routing table is constructed by polling all of the application servers every 200 milliseconds and ranking them by response time. The Web server then passes off the request for a business logic component to the component server that registered the shortest

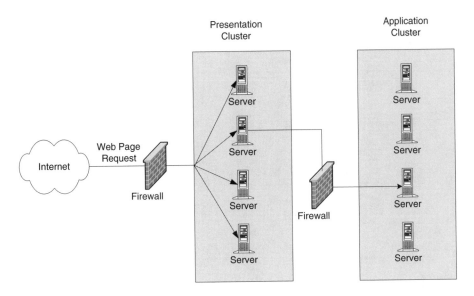

Figure 13–21 CLB: Component Load Balancing.

response time. In the Java world, the presentation and application servers may also be separate machines. For example, IBM's WebSphere has a component, Servlet Redirector, for forwarding Servlet and JSP requests to the application server.

Load balancing increases the reliability of a system because if one machine goes down the traffic is switched to another machine. Load balancing is good for allocating a substantial amount of TCP/IP traffic to different servers. However, some applications are not well suited to load balancing. An example is making queries to and updating a database. Performing this task across multiple machines makes locking and concurrency control difficult. A second example is a print server. If there were multiple machines acting as a print server for the same printer, then two print jobs could get scheduled simultaneously. The reliability of some server services is best handled using a *failover cluster*. A failover cluster is illustrated in Figure 13–22. This example is a two-node cluster. One machine is the primary database server and the other is the backup database server. They are using a shared data source and Fibre Channel technology. (See Figure 12–22 and the discussion of SAN technology in Chapter 12, "The Power of Databases.") If the primary server fails, then with failover technology in place, the applications running on the primary server are automatically migrated to the backup node and restarted. This architecture is also important when making upgrades. It allows upgrades to be made on the primary server with no downtime experienced.

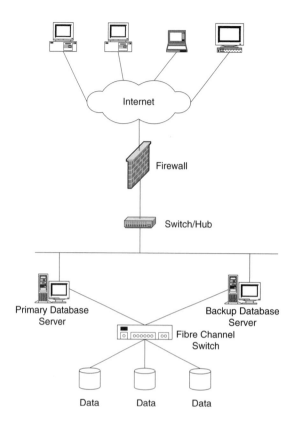

Figure 13–22 A two-node failover cluster.

FUTURE TRENDS AND IMPLICATIONS ....

As we mentioned in the chapter introduction, a very important trend is the growing dichotomy between Microsoft and the Java world. This is going to affect every company,
large and small, involved with Internet business. Witness the decision by Microsoft not to
include the Java virtual machine in its latest release of Internet Explorer and the Windows
XP operating system. Now that we have studied the various technologies that are available,
let's summarize the advantages and disadvantages of each approach.

Microsoft Strengths:

1. Most corporations use the Microsoft Windows operating system on their desktop
   machines. By using Microsoft technologies on the server side, a corporation is able
   to stay with one vendor and operating system. This is a big win in terms of IT
   support personnel.

2. Microsoft solutions are cheaper than many of the competing proprietary solutions. For example, SQL Server is a much cheaper database than either of its competitors, DB2 from IBM and Oracle9*i*. The Web server IIS is free and the ASP application server is also free.

3. The Microsoft technology is easy to implement. It is very easy to get applications up and running with ASP technology. With the newer ASP.NET you are executing compiled code and there is no longer the performance disadvantage associated with running interpreted code.

Microsoft Weaknesses:

1. You are committed to one platform. The Windows 2000 family is Intel chip-based. You cannot, for example, run any of the Windows servers on the Sun servers which use RISC chip technology.

2. Until recently, the most significant problems with Microsoft server software were that it did not scale and was not reliable enough for important applications. Early reviews of the Windows 2000 family indicate that reliability and scaling are no longer problems.

Java/Unix Strengths:

1. The big one—write once, run anywhere. With Java you are working with an open standard. You can run Java on any variation of Unix and also on the Windows platform.

2. The majority of the most reliable and scalable Internet business systems to date are Java based. Java application servers such as BEA Systems' WebLogic running on Sun servers have an outstanding reputation for reliability and scaling.

3. Java is a true object-oriented language and an excellent choice for rapid development. Many classes/objects have been written in Java and it is easy to build on the work of others.

Java/Unix Weaknesses:

1. A proprietary Java-based platform such as Sun hardware, an Oracle database, and BEA WebLogic application server is very expensive.

2. With a Java solution you will probably have to deal with at least two vendors, one for the server software and one for your operating system. If you choose to run Unix on your servers and Windows on your desktop machines, you must support two different operating systems.

The discussion above applies to server technologies. When developing client applications we recommend being agnostic—use JavaScript or Java Applets; avoid VBScript and ActiveX components.

We conclude the chapter with one of the hottest topics in Internet business—Web services. A lot is being written about Web services in the popular press. What are they? First, we provide some motivation. The Web browser is a great device—easy to use and ubiquitous. However, it has a very limiting user interface. If you use a browser, the user interface must be rendered in HTML or downloaded as a Java Applet. A browser was designed for document presentation rather than the user interface for applications. One nice thing about desktop applications is that they have a dedicated user interface for the task at hand. For example, when you work with Microsoft Word the user interface allows you to see the document as it will actually appear when printed. Why not combine the best of both worlds and allow desktop applications to interact directly with the Internet?

Another problem with the browser is that it is designed so that humans can interact with programs running on a server. However, in many cases there is need for a program, with no human interaction, to use the Internet to access another program offering a "service." For example, organizations like Visa and MasterCard might wish to provide a Web service for credit card verification that would be used by shopping cart software components. It has even been suggested that one day your refrigerator will use a Web service to order milk when it detects you are running low. Ideally, we would like to use the power of the Internet to allow one application to talk to (i.e., use) another application. Loosely speaking, a Web service is an application available to another application over the Internet.

More precisely, a Web service is a software component accessible to client programs using HTTP and XML. If two pieces of software are to communicate with each other two things are necessary. First, there must be a protocol for exchanging or transferring information. Second, there must be a precise format for the information that is transferred between client and server. If this communication takes place over the Internet, the logical choice for the transfer protocol is HTTP and the logical choice for formatting the information is XML. In order for a client to use a Web service component it is necessary for the client to know the API for the Web service; in other words, it is necessary for the client to know the methods provided by the component and the parameters that the methods require. The description of the Web service API is in XML format.

This very brief introduction to Web services leads naturally into the next chapter on Internet business software, in which we discuss middleware and business-to-business integration. Web services and Internet technologies are becoming key business-to-business integration technologies.

14 Enterprise Application Software

In this chapter ...

THE IMPORTANCE OF APPLICATION SOFTWARE

Most people associate Internet business with Internet commerce—the selling and purchasing of goods through Web sites. But some of the most compelling advances in Internet business have taken place on the back end of business, linking the internal processes of a company and helping them work more efficiently. Many of these advances, like ERP (enterprise resource planning), which links a company's internal processes like accounting, finance, and human resources, and SCM (supply chain management), which links a company with its suppliers, distributors, and customers, began as non-Internet solutions in the early 1990s. But the integration of the Internet in the late 1990s turned these solutions into powerful competitive weapons. Through the Internet, relevant data like customer orders or sales could be input immediately into the system and be instantly available to all users. These solutions were expensive and required the commitment of top management and intensive retraining of employees, but when they worked, the financial rewards to the bottom line were significant.

We begin our discussion of enterprise application software with the section, "From MRP to ERP." ERP is one of the most important pieces of enterprise application software. We trace ERP from its roots as software for material requirements planning (MRP) to its present form as software tightly integrated with the Web. In the Internet business age firms must operate efficiently in order to compete effectively. A crucial aspect of this is an efficient supply chain which is discussed in the section, "Supply Chain Management." A third important piece of enterprise application software is discussed in the section, "Customer Relationship Management."

It is unlikely that any company will use one piece of software to meet all of its corporate computing needs. Even if a company were to try, it is unlikely that all of its business partners would use compatible software. In the real world, companies need to link systems from different vendors with their older legacy systems and with the systems of their trading partners. How is this done? Through middleware. In the section, "Middleware," we discuss software for integrating applications within a company and between companies. The Internet is having a big impact on middleware. In the section, "New Age Middleware: Web Services," we talk about middleware based on HTTP and XML standards. As usual, we conclude the chapter with a section on "Future Trends and Implications."

FROM MRP TO ERP . . . .

In the mid-to-late 1990s, companies were up against a formidable challenge. The problem of Y2K loomed large, and the introduction of the Internet to business put added pressure on CEOs and CIOs to shore up their computer systems and automate business processes. The problem was compounded because many firms had outdated and disparate legacy systems. These legacy systems served each department separately, did not communicate with each other, and were burdened with outmoded hardware and methods of data gathering. This situation led many companies to turn to ERP (enterprise resource planning) systems to overhaul their computer systems and integrate business processes into one seamless whole.

ERP systems, which can command anywhere from tens of thousands to hundreds of millions of dollars, were seen as the panacea for many firms looking for a way to surge ahead of competitors who also faced the same challenges. Rather than face Y2K and the advent of Internet commerce in a piecemeal fashion, some companies opted for a major overhaul through ERP. With ERP, a company no longer had to enter data about an order multiple times as it passed through customer service, production, inventory, invoicing, accounts receivable, and shipping. It was Y2K compliant; data only had to be entered once, sales could close more quickly, products could ship more quickly, payments could be received more quickly, and all the business processes would be much more efficient, saving time and money.

. . . .

MRP

ERP has it roots in a production scheduling technique called MRP (material requirements planning) developed in the 1960s by Joseph Orlicky. MRP is used to calculate a production schedule for manufactured items that have many parts, like an automobile. The three major components to an MRP system follow.

1. Bill of material construction. The bill of material is a listing of the components in each assembly and sub-assembly of a product. For example, if the end product is a six-cylinder Honda Accord, then a sub-assembly of the car is the engine, a sub-assembly of the engine is the pistons, etc.

2. Bill of material explosion and netting of requirements. Explosion refers to the process of taking the demand for the end product and converting it into demand for each item in the bill of material. For example, each unit of demand for the car translates into one unit of demand for the car engine, which translates into six units of demand for pistons, etc.

3. Time phasing and lot sizing. Once the net requirements are known for each item in the bill of material, the lead time for producing each item is used to calculate a demand schedule. Next, a lot sizing algorithm is applied to calculate production lot sizes based on cost considerations.

MRP eventually evolved into MRP II, which added a capacity planning module to MRP. Then MRP II evolved into BRP (business requirements planning), which is designed to include other functions of the firm such as finance and marketing into the production planning process. Finally, BRP evolved into ERP, which resulted in production planning being only one aspect of the ERP system. ERP is truly MRP on steroids.

ERP systems have the capability to automate the following business functions:

- Database management
- Data warehousing

- Payroll management
- Self-service human resources
- Time management
- General ledger
- Mobile financials
- Accounts payable
- Accounts receivable
- Asset management
- Property management
- Self-service financials
- Process manufacturing
- Project billing
- Project costing
- Project resource management
- Budget planning
- Materials management
- Forecasting
- Distribution
- Transportation
- Procurement
- Business portals
- Sales management
- Warehouse management

It is easy to see how an ERP overhaul can be a breathtakingly complex and expensive endeavor. Not only must the necessary hardware and software be purchased, auxiliary expenses for installation and training must also be covered. In many cases, ERP projects have gone over budget with hidden costs for training, integration and testing, data conversion and analysis, consulting, staffing, retaining trained implementation teams, waiting for the return on investment, and post-installation havoc rearing their ugly heads months, if not years, after the initial installation. In one Meta Group study of total cost of ownership (TCO) of ERP, 63 small, medium, and large companies were surveyed. It was found that the average TCO was $15 million, with TCO ranging from $400,000 to $300 million. The study also arrived at a figure for the average cost per user: a heart-stopping $53,320 [93]. In the face of high costs and extended implementation times, the stories of failed ERP projects are legion. In Chapter 3, "Software Is Everywhere," we mentioned the downfall of the pharmaceutical company FoxMeyer after it installed ERP software from SAP. In addition, an ERP implementation at Whirlpool fouled up the shipping system and left appliances on loading docks for a full eight weeks. Hershey Foods experienced difficulty meeting its production schedule for Halloween after an ERP implementation. Similarly, Volkswagen implemented an ERP system that caused delays in parts shipment and buildup of costly inventory. In a Meta Group study of net present value (NPV) of ERP projects, 60 percent of respondents reported negative returns on their investments [84]. A Deloitte Consulting survey of 64 Fortune 500 companies found that one in four admitted they suffered a drop in performance when their ERP systems went live [93]. Boston Consulting Group interviewed more than 100 executives who directed ERP projects from 1996 to 1999 and found that only one in three thought the experience was positive; one in ten actually fired their ERP vendors mid-project. One former SAP executive, who resigned in 1998 because he was tired of being chewed out at client meetings, admitted, "Of the hundreds of millions clients spent on SAP installations, in a lot of cases there was little or no value being derived by clients [111]."

Yet SAP boasts that more than 22,000 enterprises worldwide have successful ERP implementations and are enjoying returns on investment up to 89 percent or more. In SAP's words, "For SAP customers, the move from many separate, disjointed systems to one central software system that integrates many parts of a company results in streamlined efficiency and huge cost savings. In addition, enormous business benefits derive from achieving standard business processes within and outside an enterprise [111]." Despite the stories of failure and the tumbling stock prices of some of the leading ERP vendors like SAP, PeopleSoft, and Baan, many companies young and old, like Indian Motorcycle Company and grocer A&P, are investing millions to overhaul their IT systems with an emphasis on ERP. What separates the success stories from the failures? Are there steps that can be taken to ensure a successful implementation?

The first thing a company must consider is whether ERP makes sense for its business processes. An ERP implementation begins with an assumption about the way business processes work in a company. It then takes the necessary steps to make those processes more efficient. If your current business practices fit well with those assumptions, your chances for success are increased. If your practices differ greatly from the assumed model, it will be like trying to fit a square peg into a round hole and implementation will be difficult. Your company of course has the option of changing its processes to fit the model, but retraining employees can be an enormous undertaking, especially if they are reluctant. Thus, a primary consideration should be fit, rather than price, for the wrong fit can lead to escalating hidden costs.

As is the case with any other large-scale software implementation, it is necessary to perform the due diligence task before the contract is signed. The system should be flexible enough to scale with your company, serving all employees and customers as your business grows. It should be user-friendly to minimize training. Customization should be kept to a minimum to avoid implementation and maintenance problems. Talk to other companies who have implemented ERP systems, both successful and not, to determine the responsiveness of an ERP vendor. Does it have a 24/7 customer and tech support service? How long does it take to respond to calls for help or information? How often are upgrades necessary? Finally, determine the TCO to the best estimate possible, taking into consideration the hidden costs mentioned above.

While ERP focuses on a company's internal processes, the proliferation of Internet commerce with its emphasis on the customer has prompted some companies to integrate the internal with the external. Combining Internet commerce with ERP has been a subject of intense focus by some of the leading ERP vendors. Companies are scrambling to link their front end processes with their back end in one seamless application, much in the way that ERP meshed all internal processes. Thus, the problem of integrating offline legacy ERP systems with newer online systems for Internet commerce has loomed large. Many CIOs find that Internet commerce data are not easily analyzed in its legacy ERP systems, and ERP data cannot be pushed through to its Internet commerce system.

Some companies have chosen to integrate the systems in-house. David Ramsey, CIO of PSS World Medical Inc. (PSSI), a distributor of medical products to physicians, needed to link the company's Internet commerce applications to its ERP system (J.D. Edwards's OneWorld B73.3) and make that system available to the sales force. The main problem was incompatible data formats. PSSI hired two independent J.D. Edwards consultants and formed a team that would build middleware (more on middleware in an upcoming section) between the two systems. Because the two systems were not directly linked, maintenance could be performed on the ERP system without shutting down Internet commerce activities [130].

Others have looked to their ERP vendors to implement new Internet commerce systems that would integrate well with their ERP systems. A successful integration story comes from Specialized Bicycle Co. in Morgan Hill, CA. In 1995, Specialized turned to Oracle for an ERP system that would upgrade its manufacturing and financial processes. In 2000 it was using Oracle 10.7 and planned to upgrade to Oracle11i. When Specialized was being threatened by competitors with Internet commerce systems in place, it decided to fight back with its own. It decided to implement Oracle's iStore, which not only provided a Web storefront, but could facilitate the flow of information into its legacy 10.7 system. Specialized CIO Ron Pollard engaged an implementation partner, FutureNext, based in McLean, VA, to help with the iStore implementation, which was completed in 40 days. Now inventory information is fed to iStore, and customers can check their orders online [130].

There are a number of ERP vendors making the transition to offer integrated Internet commerce applications. SAP has developed mySAP.com for its Internet strategy. Oracle has gone beyond pure database solutions to enter the wider software solutions business. Oracle, as we have seen, has taken steps to integrate Internet commerce solutions with its standard back end software. PeopleSoft eStore manages B2B and B2C sales and self-service and can be integrated with backend business processes to provide a multichannel sales and customer self-service solution. Dutch company Baan's iBaan OpenWorld integrates disparate applications into an environment for Internet business and customer fulfillment. These companies and others are leading the way for total ERP integration, including Internet business.

. . . .

LEADING ERP AND INTERNET INTEGRATORS

- **SAP**, arguably the leading ERP vendor, boasts successful implementations in the tens of thousands. It has introduced mySAP.com to integrate ERP systems with Internet commerce.

- **Oracle** has transformed its pure database business to enter the wider software business, including ERP. It can integrate front end Internet commerce applications with back end ERP.

- **PeopleSoft** offers eStore to combine B2B and B2C Internet commerce with back end business processes. It is a multichannel sales and customer self-service solution and can help you manage your customer relationships, manage supply to meet demand, and generate additional revenue.

- **Baan's** iBaan gives users and companies their own 'business portal' that gives multiple applications, data sources, the Internet, intranets and extranets—the entire value chain—in one single view. It offers one source for multiple users.

SUPPLY CHAIN MANAGEMENT . . . .

If ERP was about integrating all the business processes internal to a company, supply chain management (SCM) is about integrating all processes external to the company and linking them to internal processes. It is about linking the company to its suppliers, distributors, manufacturers, and customers to create one seamless process that helps to cut costs and increase revenues. This is done by holding far less inventory, receiving payments more quickly from customers, and drastically cutting the time it takes to process an order.

The principles of SCM are based on the inventory management concept of "just-in-time" initiated by the Japanese, particularly in automobile manufacturing, in the 1980s. The idea was that parts would be ordered and delivered and a final product manufactured in response to demand so that inventory levels would be kept to a minimum. Previously, manufacturing held that demand would be forecast based on previous sales, products manufactured based on these forecasts, and the finished item would be "pushed" through the system to sell the quantities produced. Parts for the finished product would also be ordered far in advance because little coordination took place between the manufacturing and ordering processes.

With just-in-time, the manufacturing process began with customer demand. In response to demand, manufacturers would order parts from suppliers, assemble them, and ship them off to meet demand. Thereby, a product would be "pulled" through the system, beginning with the customer's order. This cut inventory costs not only of the final product waiting to be sold, but also of parts. Of course, this required a much closer relationship between the manufacturer and suppliers, as suppliers would have to be immediately responsive to the manufacturer's orders. This type of relationship had been nurtured for decades in Japan, whereas the concept was relatively new in the United States and elsewhere.

Two decades later, SCM takes just-in-time to a new level. The Internet has connected manufacturers, suppliers, distributors, and customers in ways that never before seemed possible. With SCM, everyone in the supply chain can have access to customer demand information almost instantaneously (in "real time" some would say) and act accordingly. This does not only work for manufacturers. Retailers, too, can use SCM to help reduce inventory levels and be more responsive to their customers. Point-of-purchase information at the cash registers can be automatically entered into the SCM system and alert suppliers to merchandise levels (also part of the SCM system) to step up their production process to manufacture their products and supply them to the retailer. In this way, everyone in the supply chain can react immediately and efficiently to demand.

SCM systems can include the following modules:

- Strategic planning

- Demand management

- Supply management

- Fulfillment planning

- Fulfillment execution

- Fulfillment monitoring and control

- Profit optimization

- Pricing optimization

- Revenue optimization

- Supplier relationship management

- Product life cycle management

- Knowledge management

- Performance measurement

- Logistics

- Procurement

- Inventory planning

- Order promising

- Production planning

The general SCM model clearly requires very close relationships among suppliers, manufacturers, and distributors. In the Internet business environment, all in the supply chain must agree on and adopt computing standards. The manufacturer must convince its suppliers to change their ways of doing business, in many cases at the supplier's expense, in order to accommodate SCM. Many times this is accomplished by promising the suppliers more business if they adopt the SCM system. Orders previously issued via fax and telephone are automatically transmitted via the Internet, which reduces the time and staff necessary to keep the supply chain moving. Paper reports and invoices, communicated via fax or the postal service, are no longer required. Data, instead, are instantaneously updated.

Of course, like other large-scale, enterprise-wide software implementations, SCM is difficult to achieve. It is costly, necessitates retraining many employees and weaning them off the telephone and fax, and may require a complete reorientation of the way a company operates. It faces many of the same problems we discussed earlier with ERP—it requires the commitment of all top management, and employees may resist the implementation. But with SCM, the problems are compounded because not only employees must be sold on the idea, but also those external to the company like suppliers, distributors, and customers. It requires not only cooperation among external partners, but good communication and trust. Instead of simply trying to extract the best deal from an external partner, all involved will have to share data and work together to benefit all parties.

STRAIGHTENING THE BULLWHIP EFFECT OF SCM

Adding to the difficulty of achieving a successful SCM system is the "bullwhip effect," which increasingly distorts the projections of end demand as the projections travel up the supply chain. Demand projections for an SCM system are often made for a fixed period of time, say, a week or a month, which are inaccurate estimates in and of themselves. The problem is magnified further up the supply chain, because with every step in the chain, suppliers are planning to accommodate the projection and have some extra safety stock on hand. By the time the projection reaches the end supplier, projections are so distorted they cause excessive inventory and labor requirements. Internet-based SCM solutions, whereby suppliers in the chain can access actual demand data immediately, are helping to straighten the bullwhip effect.

Despite the challenges inherent in an SCM implementation, many companies have installed SCM successfully and many more have SCM in their future plans. Sanjiv Sidhu, founder of i2 Technologies, one of the leading SCM suppliers, claims that i2's 1,000 or so customers will realize a $75 billion payback by 2005. AMR Research predicts that the SCM market will total $7.8 billion in 2001, an increase of 45 percent over the previous year [120]. Cisco Systems, the San Jose, CA-based networking equipment maker, has implemented one of the best known Internet-based supply chains. Over 90 percent of its orders come through the Internet and fewer than 50 percent are touched by the hands of a Cisco employee. A customer order triggers orders to Cisco's suppliers, distributors, and contract manufacturers for parts and subassemblies. Assemblers create the finished product, apply a bar code, match it to the customer's order, ensure that specifications are met, and ship the product to the customer. Cisco outsources as much manufacturing as possible so it can concentrate on core activities: engineering and marketing. Cisco reports that administrative overhead has been reduced from $100 per order to $5 or $6. As a result, AMR Research reports that in 1999 Cisco brought in $713,000 per employee, whereas the average for the Fortune 500 was $192,000 [92].

MAJOR SUPPLY CHAIN MANAGEMENT SOFTWARE SUPPLIERS

- **i2 Technologies** was founded on making manufacturing planning more efficient and valuable. It claims that its solution suite is the only end-to-end solution that integrates forecasting, planning, and execution capabilities with complete supply-chain-wide visibility.

- **Manugistics** has more than 20 years experience in supply chain management, from computer time-share to the first commercial supply chain applications to the transition to client/server to the emergence of Internet business. It claims to have pioneered the technology that supports intelligent supply chain decisions.

- **SAP** starts with B2B private exchanges and continues with integration of SAP and non-SAP solutions which might help solve your ERP and SCM integration problems. SAP's solutions cover supply chain networking, planning, coordination, and execution. You can also integrate mySAP customer relationship management (CRM is discussed in the next section) with its SCM system.

- **PeopleSoft** SCM solutions help with high value-adding activities like collaborative product management with suppliers and customers. These solutions include efficiencies in manufacturing, sales and logistics, supply chain planning, supplier relationship management, and Internet procurement.

The synergies between an SCM and an ERP system can be great if managed well. In most cases, a company will have an ERP system in place and will want to add an SCM implementation. Some companies, like SAP and PeopleSoft, provide both systems, so if you went with one of these for your ERP system, integration will be easier. If you didn't, you will probably have to have customized software so that data can be easily exchanged between the two systems. This problem will be eased if your ERP system was based on XML standards, which is rapidly becoming universal. There are many challenges to implementing SCM, but if done successfully the rewards are great. Peter Nygard, founder of Nygard International, a Toronto-based women's clothing manufacturer, estimates that profits have been boosted by $10 million annually thanks to SCM. Says Nygard, "We can gather information and make decisions based on what is actually selling, with a snap of a finger, as opposed to philosophizing and assuming [120]."

CUSTOMER RELATIONSHIP MANAGEMENT.......

Many have complained about the level of customer service on the Internet. According to a Gartner Group survey of online customer service, 73 percent of respondents rated it "fair," and not one rated it "good" or "excellent [109]." Contrary to what some might believe, Internet retailing is not a vending machine. It's not as though a customer clicks on some buttons, fills in payment information, and the goods show up at the doorstep, much as a can of soda rolls out of the mouth of a vending machine after you deposit some coins and press a tab. In many cases, there's a lot of service involved between the customer's visit and the satisfied customer, whether visible or not. In a brick and mortar store, the service can be provided by knowledgeable and responsive salespeople who answer your every question and guide you step-by-step through your purchase. On the Internet, what can be done?

One solution is CRM. CRM stands for customer relationship management, which helps companies serve their customers better (and become more profitable) by developing stronger relationships with them. The business mantra of the early 21st century has focused on the customer. While customers have of course always been important to a company, Internet use in business has brought customer service to a new level. The ability to track a customer's movements, receive customer feedback instantaneously, and analyze reams of customer-related data have heightened expectations of the level of customer service provided. In short, data make the difference.

Data make a difference because companies now have unprecedented insight into customers' desires and behaviors and can tap into that insight to cross-sell and foster customer loyalty. Not only can past purchases be documented, even window shopping and purchase considerations without a sale can be recorded, which does not yet occur in brick and mortar stores. But CRM is about much more than mere software that gathers and analyzes data. CRM is a strategy, a combination of technology and human resources that can enhance everything from sales and marketing to transactions and fulfillment. Implementing CRM may require that a company completely rethink its goals and objectives. How many minutes on average will it allow a customer to wait when he calls a call center or emails an inquiry? What kinds of data does it want to collect on customers? How does it want to use those data? Answering all of these questions can bear on the entire culture of a company.

A CRM strategy first requires an analysis of all functions of a company. It is necessary to analyze the way it views and works with not just its customers, but with its employees and partners. A company must consider all the ways it communicates with customers, and determine to what degree it wants to be customer-focused. Then, it should implement CRM in stages, perhaps beginning with a call center, expanding toward email correspondence with customers, eventually directing the entire company's processes toward servicing the customer. All data gathered from these efforts must be integrated to come up with a clear, total picture of the customer and to arrive at the appropriate responses.

CRM systems can include the following modules:

- Web storefronts
- Order management
- Customer self-service
- Field service
- Sales force automation
- Marketing automation
- Partner relationship management
- Pricing
- Auctions
- Mobile sales
- Business analytics
- Help desk
- Call center
- Customer portal

Clearly, any CRM implementation requires the support of top-level management. The company must be completely aligned toward the customer in order to be most effective at CRM. Businesses everywhere are realizing that they can no longer get away with mediocre customer service or with trying to sift through disparate kinds of customer data. Forging an integrated whole to go beyond the expected levels of service is what many companies are aspiring to do. One way in which a company is implementing CRM is Chase Manhattan's mining of data for demographic and psychographic profiles of customers to see not only what products and services to pitch to certain customers, but what level of service to provide. If you're an up-and-coming attorney at a leading law firm in New York and a customer at Chase, you may receive better rates on investments and promotions than someone who doesn't hold as much promise of becoming a millionaire as you. Chase has implemented CRM to analyze data from its tellers, ATM machines, Web site, and telephone service representatives to determine whose calls go to the head of the line and get white-glove service. Chase claims that implementing CRM strategies such as these has led to a 4 percent increase in the retention of high-net-worth customers from January to June of 2000 [138].

Some companies have even gone as far as to appoint a "customer czar" or CCO, chief customer officer. The Meta Group has projected that by 2003, 25 percent of all Global 2000 businesses will have a customer czar. The Gartner Group has predicted that by 2003, 15 percent of all U.S. companies will have a CCO or equivalent. Cisco Systems was one of the first to appoint such a position. Since 1991, Douglas Allred, Senior Vice President of Customer Advocacy, has overseen Cisco's customer service, product design, and IT groups, all in the name of customer service. Yet, most large corporations have yet to initiate a comparable position. Much as the chief knowledge officers and chief quality officers of decades past have gone by the wayside, so might a CCO be a temporary position. Allred cannot overstate the importance of creating such a position: "If your customer satisfaction is decreasing, you're in a death spiral," he said. "Customer satisfaction equals customer loyalty. If you really understand that notion, you will systematize your organization around continually increasing that metric [160]."

LEADING CRM VENDORS

- **Siebel Systems** claims that its customers generated increased revenues using its software and reported a 21 percent increase in customer satisfaction levels. It scored the highest in a Gartner Group rating of top CRM applications for large companies [128].

- **PeopleSoft** claims that its PeopleSoft 8 is the first CRM solution to provide immediate, seamless integration among customer, financial, supply chain, and employee management systems. Because the application is built on a pure Internet architecture, all the user company needs is a Web browser.

- **E.piphany** claims that its E.5 system is the only Web-based, intelligent CRM solution that coordinates and unifies in real time all inbound and outbound interactions with B2C and B2B customers. It provides a single view of the customer and integrates data across all customer interactions.

- **J.D. Edwards's** "collaborative commerce CRM" is a B2B solution that optimizes planning, marketing, sales, fulfillment, delivery, and service. The company offers sales force and marketing automation, partner relationship management, and storefronts as parts of its CRM arsenal.

As you might imagine, a full CRM implementation can be very expensive. A Data Warehousing Institute survey of more than 1,600 business and IT professionals found that $500,000 was roughly the median CRM project budget. Thus, while about half of CRM budgets fell under the half-million dollar mark, the survey also found that a few respondents had CRM project budgets of over $10 million [37]. Sometimes companies roll out expensive CRM projects only to find that the employees refuse to use them. According to a CRM consultant, one telecommunications company equipped more than 1,000 sales representatives with a CRM application to the tune of $10,000 per user. One year later, fewer than 100 were using the system [128].

Reasons for failure of CRM implementations range from poor communications to lack of management support, to opposition by customers concerned about "big brother" looking over them. It is essential to garner the support of all those connected to the CRM strategy before implementing it. This may be the hardest task of any CRM implementation. One of the myths about CRM is that it is all about technology. True, it does require a fair amount of software and hardware to implement, but the key to a successful implementation is the people behind it. As Ned Liddell, Monster.com's Vice President for Business Applications Development, put it, "CRM is not for the weak spirited. It requires a lot of management and money [128]."

MIDDLEWARE...................................

This chapter is about enterprise software. We have focused on several broad categories such as ERP, SCM, and CRM. In this era of computing, software applications do not operate in a vacuum. Consider the following examples.

- In recent years, numerous retailers with telephone-ordering-based catalog businesses have included a Web ordering component. How is the Web system integrated with the telephone order entry system? When the online order gets entered and completed, how is this information communicated to the customer?

- A company has a legacy payroll system based on the COBOL programming language. How can it integrate this legacy system with a new ERP system?

- A company needs to integrate its SCM system with the ERP system of a supplier so that orders are automatically sent to the supplier when inventory levels hit their reorder points.

- Airline and car rental reservations are complementary and logically bundled together. In early 2000, Southwest Airlines approached Dollar Rent-a-Car about the possibility of integrating their two reservations systems [115]. This presented a problem because Southwest's technology was based on Sun Solaris Unix and Dollar Rent-a-Car technology was Windows based.

These are four simple examples of companies needing to integrate different software applications in a distributed environment. This is done using *middleware*. We define middleware as software used to integrate two or more software applications running over a network. Or, put another way, middleware is the nonnetworking software that allows distributed applications to communicate with each other. The first two examples illustrate EAI or enterprise application integration, which is the integration of firm-wide business process and IT systems. The second two examples illustrate B2Bi or business-to-business integration. As the name implies, B2Bi is about integrating applications between two or more distinct companies. In this section we concentrate on technologies that have traditionally been used for EAI. In the next section we concentrate on modern, Web-based technologies, which are appropriate for either EAI or B2Bi.

There are several ways to think about how to integrate two different software applications. Consider Figure 14–1. In this figure, there are two applications and each application consists of presentation, business logic, and data. Often, the most straightforward approach

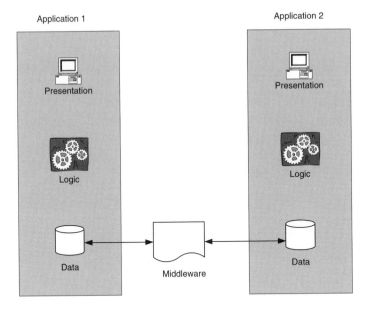

Application 1   Application 2

Presentation   Presentation

Logic   Logic

Data   Middleware   Data

Figure 14–1 Data-based integration.

in integrating two applications is through middleware that converts data files from Application 1 into the data format used by Application 2 and vice versa. For example, assume Application 1 records dates using the two digit format $mm/dd/yy$ (recall all of the time and money spent on the Y2K problem) and Application 2 formats dates using four digits for the year. An example of middleware is a program that reads the data file with the two digit dates and converts it to a file with the four digit format.

Unfortunately, there are several reasons why it may not be practical to work at the data level of different applications, i.e., access the data directly. First, data are often stored in a proprietary binary format. If the data format used by an application is proprietary, it is necessary to reverse-engineer the process used to store the data if you want to access the data directly. Even if the data format used by an application is not proprietary, the data format often changes when the application is upgraded. This would require rewriting the middleware to use the new format. Instead, most vendors provide an API (application program interface) so the application's data files can be accessed. The purpose of of the middleware is to implement the API to get the data. Second, in the case of B2Bi, it is unlikely that one company will allow another to have direct access to its corporate database. For example, a vendor's shopping cart software needs to verify a credit card number. Clearly, the bank will not give the vendor full access to its database. Rather, the bank provides an API through which the query can be made. This is illustrated in Figure 14–2 where middleware is gluing together the business logic of each of the different software applications. We discuss several broad categories of middleware.

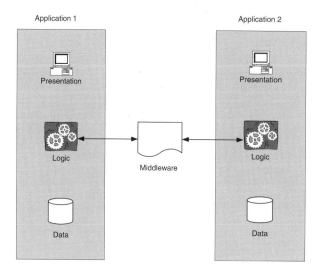

Figure 14–2 Logic-based integration.

Enterprise application software typically comes with an API, which we discussed in Chapter 13, "Internet Business Architecture." This interface is a set of methods that can be called by middleware over a network. Recall from our discussion in Chapter 3, that a method is a procedure (or function) that takes data and operates on it. Methods perform the work needed to get things done. For example, the method

```
GetSkuNum(''15467'');
```

might return the string:

```
<sku>
    <skunum>
        15467
    </skunum>
    <price>
        $57.63
    </price>
    <supplier>
        Acme Auto
    </supplier>
</sku>
```

A programmer writes middleware in a language such as C++ or Java. The middleware makes calls to the application through the API and gets the required data. These calls are named remote procedure calls (RPC). They are remote because one program is calling another over a network.

Tech Talk

IDL: interface definition language. An IDL is used to describe the API of a component. The IDL gets compiled into client and server stubs that are linked into the client and server programs. These stubs convert parameters of the methods into a string of bits that are sent over the network.

Over time, and with the continuing emphasis on object-oriented programming, RPCs have been replaced with distributed components. We discussed distributed components in the previous chapter. A good example of middleware component technology is Microsoft's ADO middleware. Using ADO, a programmer can write middleware that uses ADO objects such as a *record set*. A record set is a set of records in a database that satisfy a set of criteria specified in a SQL command. We also talked about application servers in the previous chapter. An application server is also a good example of middleware software. The application server is a container for a set of components. This can get complicated because in many cases we have middleware talking to middleware. For example, if we use active server pages to get data out of a SQL database, we have the ASP middleware communicating with the ADO middleware communicating with the OLE DB middleware that communicates with SQL server.

. . . .

CICS: The Mother Of Application Servers

CICS (customer information control system): Software developed by IBM back in the days of the mainframe. It is perhaps the most widely used transaction processing monitor of all times. It was the forerunner of modern application servers. Recall from Chapter 12, "The Power of Databases," that a transaction is a set of tasks treated as a single unit of work performed by a DBMS. Either the entire set of tasks is executed (a commit) or none is (a rollback). CICS is a layer of middleware software with an easy-to-use API for executing transactions against a DBMS.

At the present time there are three major distributed component technologies or standards used to build middleware. They are CORBA, COM+/DCOM, and Java RMI. CORBA stands for common object request broker architecture. It is a standard for component to component communication set forth by the Object Management Group and is not a software product. CORBA allows for a component written in one programming language (e.g., C++) to use methods of a component written in another programming language (e.g., Java). The IDL is compiled into files that get linked and compiled into the client and server components. Recall from Chapter 13 that COM+ is the Microsoft technology for distributed components. DCOM is distributed COM, or as Microsoft says, COM on a wire. Finally, Java RMI is Java remote methods invocation. It is the Java technology for allowing a component to call another component's methods over a network. Unlike CORBA, with Java RMI both components must be written in Java.

The middleware component technology we have discussed has two features. It is application-to-application communication and it is synchronous. Application 1 makes a call to Application 2 and waits for a response. However, there is another type of middleware called MOM (message-oriented middleware) that is application-to-queue communication and is asynchronous. (See Figure 14–3.) MOM software is to application software what email is to people. As long as the email message conforms to certain standards, it does not matter what email program the individuals use in sending/reading the email. The same is true for MOM. By communicating with a queue rather than directly to another application, applications can communicate with each other even if there is a network or server failure. Prominent MOM software includes IBM's MQSeries, Microsoft's MSMQ, and TIBCO's Rendezvous. Part of the J2EE standard includes JMS (Java messaging service), which is a Java API for connecting Java programs to message-based middleware such as MQSeries. We give an illustration of messaging middleware when we discuss BizTalk in the next section.

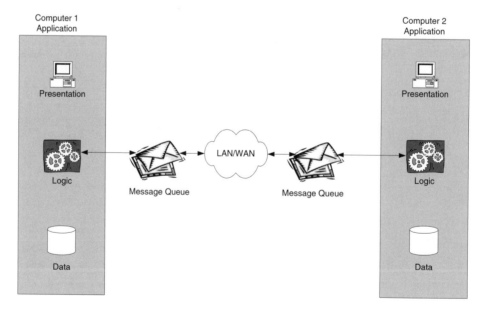

Figure 14–3 Message-oriented middleware.

NEW AGE MIDDLEWARE: WEB SERVICES........

Middleware is about distributed components. A Web service is a software component available over the Internet. More precisely, a Web service is a software component accessible to client programs using HTTP and XML. If two pieces of software are to communicate with each other two things are necessary. First, there must be a protocol for exchanging or transferring information. Second, a precise format for the information that is transferred between client and server is necessary. If this communication takes place over the Internet the logical choice for the transfer protocol is HTTP and the logical choice for formatting the information is XML. In order for a client to use a Web service component it is necessary for the component to expose its interface to the client; in other words, expose the methods provided by the component and expose the parameters that the methods require. The description of the interface is in XML format.

There are three key ingredients of Web services. They are 1) protocol, 2) description, and 3) discovery. We cover each of these in turn.

The key Web service *protocol* is SOAP (simple object access protocol). SOAP is yet another middleware standard. It is an alternative to CORBA and COM+/DCOM. SOAP is a completely open standard and is not owned by any company. It is based on the HTTP and XML protocols. Refer back to Chapter 4, "Internet and Web Technology," where we discussed the HTTP protocol. The HTTP request message from client to server contains 1) a request line, 2) header information, and 3) a body. We illustrate a SOAP request in the Technical Appendix.

Basically, a Web service takes Internet technology and removes the constraint that the client software must be a Web browser. An important feature of Web service technology is that it uses the HTTP protocol. Thus, if the client software is based on Web service technology it is necessary to open network connections on only the port (number 80) used by HTTP. This allows network administrators to cut off the other ports and improve security of the network.

Description is the second ingredient of Web services. Web services are distributed component software. Company A will use Company B's Web service. This means that Company B must clearly describe and publish the interface of its Web service. A Web service is described using WSDL (Web service definition language). In order to use a Web service, the client software must know how to use the Web service interface. The client must know what methods are available and what parameters are passed back and forth. The WSDL is the IDL for Web services. The WSDL is, not surprisingly, in XML format. Among other things, the WSDL contains an XML schema that lists all of the methods, their parameters, the server name, location of the Web service, etc.

Finally, the third ingredient of Web services is *discovery*. How do we know what Web services are available? We need a yellow pages or Yahoo! for Web services. One initiative is UDDI (Universal Description Discovery and Integration). The UDDI initiative is the result of an industry consortium, uddi.org, for developing a registry of Web services. This organization includes many of the key heavyweights such as Ariba, IBM, Microsoft, and Sun. Both IBM and Microsoft have a searchable registry database. One can search by various categories such as business name, service type, or D-U-N-S reference number.

It looks like a promising future for Web services. Major players such as Hewlett-Packard with its Netaction software suite, IBM with its Web Services Toolkit, Microsoft with its Microsoft .NET, and Sun with its ONE (Open Net Environment) are all emphasizing development tools for Web services.

SOAP is a standard for sending XML data using HTTP. Now what if two companies wish to exchange purchase orders and invoices using SOAP? Clearly, the SOAP message must contain (in XML format) information on the intended destination, the sender of the message, what the message is about, a receipt mechanism to acknowledge delivery of the message, an identifier for the package, a timestamp, expiration date, etc. In short, in order to facilitate B2Bi we need another standard to use with SOAP. This standard is *BizTalk Framework 2.0*. Unlike SOAP and XML, BizTalk Framework 2.0 is not a W3C standard. It is a standard being floated by vendors such as IBM, IONA, and Microsoft. A SOAP envelope document has two parts, a header and a body. The BizTalk Framework 2.0 consists of a set of BizTalk XML tags that go into the header of a SOAP envelope. These tags provide information on the intended destination, what the message is about, the sender of the message, a receipt mechanism to acknowledge delivery of the message, an identifier for the package, a timestamp, expiration date, etc.

. . . .

biztalk.org

BizTalk Framework 2.0 is a set of rules for tags in a SOAP header. BizTalk Server is a Microsoft product for EAI and B2Bi. A third member of the BizTalk family is `biztalk.org`. Both BizTalk Framework and BizTalk Server are designed to facilitate the exchange of XML-based information between trading partners. The object of `biztalk.org` is to serve as a schema repository.

The idea is for companies within an industry, e.g., chemical or financial, to form a coalition and agree on XML schemas. For example, in the financial industry we might have an XML schema representing an option on a stock. The schemas are published at the `biztalk.org` Web site. Companies that wish to exchange XML information can then download the schemas and use the schemas to format the XML data contained in the body of a SOAP envelope. To use an analogy, `biztalk.org` is to XML schemas what `uddi.org` is to Web services.

Not to be confused with the BizTalk 2.0 Framework is Microsoft's BizTalk Server. This product is designed to facilitate the exchange of interfirm and intrafirm information. For example, a company might have a piece of component software that writes purchase order information to a file. One can configure BizTalk Server to poll a folder for the presence of an XML file with purchase order information. When BizTalk Server reads the file it could call a distributed component to apply business logic to the data in the file. An example of the business logic is to query a database and find the least expensive supplier for the product. Then BizTalk Server could send a purchase order to the supplier using any number of protocols such as HTTP, FTP, SMTP (email), or MSMQ. BizTalk Server could then process the return invoice from the supplier. BizTalk Server is designed to use XML with SOAP/BizTalk Framework envelopes. However, BizTalk Server is very flexible and can work with plain text files or EDI.

Marks & Spencer is a very large retailing conglomerate in the United Kingdom. Its database center is based on the IBM CICS and MQSeries technologies. Marks & Spencer has numerous suppliers with widely varying computing platforms. It has integrated point of sale data at all of the retail outlets with its corporate databases and applications using BizTalk Server. The point of sale transactions are aggregated and sent to corporate headquarters as XML messages using MSMQ. There, the XML messages are processed and examined by BizTalk servers that route them to the appropriate applications.

FUTURE TRENDS AND IMPLICATIONS............

We have discussed CRM—customer relationship management. This is essentially Internet commerce (B2C) software. There is now a trend to extend this idea into the Internet business (B2B) world. Partner relationship management (PRM) is analogous to CRM but designed to improve relationships with business partners. Many CRM and ERP software companies are getting into this area, and there are companies whose central focus is PRM. For example, Siebel has a PRM product called eChannel. This software allows for the development of a Web portal for partners. One feature of this portal is a set of tools for partners of a vendor to service end customers on behalf of the vendor. Partners can even route service requests on behalf of the customers to the portal to be handled by the vendor.

Other companies have similar products. At one point, Maytag had decided to sell directly to customers using a B2C Web portal. This quite naturally led to considerable resistance from Maytag's reseller partners. Because of this resistance, Maytag reversed course and used PRM software from Comergent to establish a portal that encouraged end users to buy from Maytag resellers. When an end customer selects a model, he is given a list of reseller sites from which to select. The Comergent product allows Maytag to integrate its site with those of its resellers and offer information about service agreements, disposal policies, etc. (See Fraone [52].)

One problem with enterprise software is the integration of different systems. If you are starting from scratch, you could implement ERP, SCM, and CRM systems from a single vendor such as PeopleSoft or SAP to ease the problem. However, if you have a legacy system, like ERP, it may not integrate well with the SCM or CRM system you wish to purchase. We discussed earlier in this chapter how some companies handled this problem. Another trend is to seek out an ASP (application service provider) aggregator like Jamcracker, which we mentioned in Chapter 7, "Getting Your Business Online." An ASP aggregator provides a variety of software through the Internet and ideally writes the code to integrate different applications so that the end user is able to share data among them. If aggregators deliver what they promise, this should allow for greater flexibility in selecting different systems. Of course, with an aggregator you are restricted to its software offerings. Most companies, however, seem to be going the one-vendor route or are writing their own middleware. The trend toward ASPs has yet to take off as some predicted.

We have already discussed how Microsoft is attempting to extend its monopoly in the desktop market to the back end. In particular, it is competing in the server (presentation, application, and database) and middleware markets. More and more firms are going to have to choose between the Microsoft world and the Java/Unix world. We summarize the various technologies available in Table 14–1.

Table 14–1 Microsoft versus Java/Unix

Software	Microsoft	Java/Unix
Operating System	Windows 2000 Family	Unix/Linux
Languages	C#, C++, VB	Java
Runtime	CLR	Java Runtime Engine
Component Specification	COM+, DCOM	J2EE, CORBA, RMI
Component Software	DLL, ASP	JavaBeans, Servlets
DBMS	SQL Server	Oracle, DB2
Web Server	IIS	Apache, iPlanet
Application Server	ASP, BizTalk, Commerce Server	WebLogic, WebSphere
Dynamic HTML	VBScript, ActiveX	JavaScript, Java Applets
Database Connectivity	ADO, OLE DB	JDBC
Message Queues	MSMQ	MQSeries, JMS

Part 5

Appendix: Additional Help

In this last part of the book, we help you pursue Internet business technology in greater depth. In the Technical Appendix we cover more in-depth information on representing numbers in digital form, IP addressing, object-oriented programming, XML, JavaScript, Active Server Pages, Web services, and middleware technologies. In Suggested Reading we provide a brief annotated bibliography on a wide variety of Internet business-related books, chapter by chapter. In the Glossary we include definitions of key terms used in the book. This glossary is provided for your ease of reading and reference.

A   Technical Appendix

In this appendix ...

STORING FLOATING POINT NUMBERS · · · · · · · · · · ·

If you'll recall from high school math and chemistry, in scientific notation in base 10 (the number system we humans use, which probably originates from the fact that we have 10 fingers to count on), the number $-.8125$ is represented as -8.125×10^{-1} and the numbers -8.125 (the mantissa) and -1 (the exponent) are stored.

However, because of the binary nature of computing (using 0s and 1s), base 2, not base 10, is used on the computer. This requires a more complex formula that may tax your memory of exponents and the base 2 number system. If you don't completely understand the rest of the section, it's okay. We just want you to appreciate how all numbers can be expressed as 0s and 1s.

In computers, the noninteger numbers are stored as the product $s * M * B^{(e-E)}$. In this expression s is the *sign bit* (0 for a positive number or 1 for a negative number), M is called the *mantissa*, B is called the *radix*, and $e - E$ is the *exponent*. In the exponent term, E is a fixed integer called the *bias*. Generally, $B = 2$, although on the IBM 360/370 the $B = 16$. In a typical 32-bit word used to represent a number, the sign bit is a single bit, the exponent e is stored as an eight-bit positive integer, the mantissa is 23 bits, and E is equal to 127. Since e is a positive integer, the exponent $e - E$ can be positive, negative, or zero.

As with the mantissa in scientific notation, the bit pattern in the mantissa for the binary system must be "normalized." Consider the analogy with base 10. The number $-.8125$ could be represented as -8.125×10^{-1}, or as $-.8125 \times 10^{0}$, or as $-.08125 \times 10^{1}$. The possibilities are endless. In base 10, with scientific notation, we normalize by having one nonzero digit to the left of the decimal point, e.g., -8.125×10^{-1}. Normalization is also necessary in binary. In the binary case, 1 is the only nonzero digit. Thus, if we used scientific notation in base 2, the digit to the left of the decimal point is always 1 for any nonzero number. Since it is always 1, there is no need to store it. It is called a phantom bit.

Consider the following 32-bit representation of $-.8125$:

$$1 \ 01111110 \ 10100000000000000000000$$

In this example, the first bit, the sign bit, is $s = 1$ (so it is a negative number), the second set of 8 bits is the base 2 representation of the number $e = 126$, and the mantissa, represented by the last 23 bits is 1.101 (recall the phantom leftmost bit $= 1$) where $B = 2$ and $E = 127$, so $s * M * B^{(e-E)}$ is

$$-1 * 1.101 * 2^{126-127} = -1 * 1.625 * 2^{-1} = -.8125.$$

where $M = 1.101$ is the base 2 representation of 1.625.

THE IP ADDRESSING SYSTEM · · · · · · · · · · · · · · · · · · ·

Whenever you use the Internet, you are making use of TCP/IP and packet switching. In order to use TCP/IP software for packet switching, each computer needs a unique IP address so that each packet has a forwarding address and a return address. An example IP address is `128.135.130.201`. All IP addresses have this format: four three-digit numbers separated by three periods. This is called *dotted-octet* notation. Each number (octet) is between 0 and 255 because one byte of memory (eight bits) is used to store each of the four parts of the IP number. Recall from our discussion of the binary number system in Chapter 2, "What Do I Need to Know about Hardware," that eight bits can store $2^8 = 256$ values, so if we store unsigned integers, one byte can store any integer from 0 to 255. In the IP addressing system, the IP address is divided into two parts: a network address and a host address on the network. Specifically, the IP address has the form

```
network:host
```

in the hierarchy of parts. For example, in the IP address 128.135.130.201, the network address is 128.135. This is the address that all computers in the University of Chicago network share. The host IP address may be further subdivided into a subnetwork and machine number. For example, in the host number 130.201, the 130 denotes a particular local area network (Stuart Hall) and 201 is the machine number in that local area network.

IP addresses are divided into three main classes: A, B, and C. The class determines which set of bits is used for the network number, and which set of bits is used for the host number. This, in turn, determines how many host computers there can be on a network. This is illustrated in Table A–1:

Table A–1 Field Allocation in an IP Address

Address Class	Network Address	Host Address
A	octet1	octet2.octet3.octet4
B	octet1.octet2	octet3.octet4
C	octet1.octet2.octet3	octet4

For example, in the IP address 128.135.130.201, the number 128.135 is the network address so this is a class B address. The number of networks and hosts with each type of address is summarized in Table A–2. The higher the class, the more computers you can have on a network. Unfortunately, the higher the class, the scarcer the network number. For example, there are a maximum of 128 networks with a class A address. They are obviously only for the largest firms. Most medium to large companies have a set of class B network addresses. A small company requires only a class C address. A firm obtains these IP addresses from an Internet service provider (ISP). The Internet service provider receives the authority to resell IP addresses from ICANN (Internet Corporation for Assigned Numbers and Names).

With the incredible growth of the Internet, IP addresses are becoming scarce. A new addressing scheme, IPv6, based on 64-bit numbers instead of 32-bit numbers is being developed. In many organizations the problem of a lack of IP addresses is remedied by assigning IP numbers in a dynamic fashion; that is, a computer is not given a permanent IP address. Rather, when the computer boots up on a network, it is assigned a number from a pool of numbers. This reduces the number of addresses needed at any one time.

Table A–2 IP Address Classes

Address Class	Leading Bits	Bits in Prefix (Network)	Max Number of Networks	Prefix Range of Values	Bits in Suffix	Max Hosts per Network
A	0	7	128	0–127	24	16777216
B	10	14	16384	128–191	16	65536
C	110	21	2097152	192–223	8	256

Separate networks are connected by routers. IP addresses are used by routers to forward packets. These routers use routing tables to see where a packet should be sent. The routing table may be static or dynamic. As the name implies, a static routing table will always route packets with the same destination the same way. With dynamic routing, the router will alter the routing table as conditions (such as congestion) of the network change.

OBJECT-ORIENTED PROGRAMMING ....

In this section, we provide more detail on the example of object-oriented programming from Chapter 3, "Software Is Everywhere." Recall the concept of a class. A class is an abstraction of an object. It contains methods and data. Below is the Java source code for the class Account in the example.

```
class Account{
   double new_balance, old_balance, int_rate, tax, tax_rate;
   void calcbal()
   {
      new_balance = old_balance*Math.exp(int_rate);
   }
   void calctax()
   {
      tax = tax_rate*(new_balance - old_balance);
   }
}
```

The class Account has two methods and five data members. The first method, calcbal(), takes the data members old_balance and int_rate and applies the continuous compounding formula to them using the Java built-in function Math.exp(). This results in a new data member, new_balance. The second method, calctax(), takes the data members old_balance, new_balance, and tax_rate and calculates the tax owed. No objects have been created yet. The following source code creates an object dcrockett:

```
class  InterestExample
{
   public static void main(String[] args)
   {
```

```
// Create dcrockett object
Account dcrockett = new Account();
dcrockett.old_balance = 1000.0;
dcrockett.int_rate = 0.09;
dcrockett.tax_rate = .31;
// calculate the new balance
dcrockett.calcbal( );
System.out.println("Crocketts balance="+dcrockett.new_balance);
// calculate the taxes
dcrockett.calctax();
System.out.println("Crocketts tax="+dcrockett.tax);
```

An instance of the object dcrockett in the class Account is created by the line

```
Account dcrockett = new Account();
```

In the lines following Account dcrockett = new Account(), note the use of the "dot" notation. For example,

$$dcrockett.tax\_rate = .31$$

sets the data member tax_rate in the class Account equal to .31 for the object dcrockett. The line dcrockett.calcbal() calls the calcbal() method in the class Account and calculates the new balance based on the specific data member values for object dcrockett.

Now let's try to understand inheritance and polymorphism. The method calcbal() calculates the new balance based on the continuous compounding formula. Let's create a new class that uses periodic compounding. The source code for the new class AccountPeriodic follows.

```
class AccountPeriodic extends Account
{
   int num_periods = 12;
   void calcbal()
   {
   new_balance = old_balance*Math.pow(1.0 +
   int_rate/num_periods,num_periods);
   }
}
```

The line of code that defines the new class is

```
class AccountPeriodic extends Account
```

The keyword extends is crucial. It says that the new class AccountPeriodic inherits the methods and data members from the class Account. This means, for example, that we can use the method calctax() in our new class and do not have to rewrite any code. This is called inheritance. However, we want to calculate the new balance differently, so notice how the formula for `calcbal()` in the class `AccountPeriodic` overrides the method `calcbal()` in the class `Account`. Now let's create an object in each class. This is done in the following source code:

```
class  InterestExample
{
    public static void main(String[] args)
    {
        //Create dcrockett object
        Account dcrockett = new Account();
        dcrockett.old_balance = 1000.0;
        dcrockett.int_rate = 0.09;
        dcrockett.tax_rate = .31;
        // calculate the new balance
        dcrockett.calcbal( );
        System.out.println("Crocketts balance="+dcrockett.new_balance);
        // calculate the taxes
        dcrockett.calctax();
        System.out.println("Crocketts tax="+dcrockett.tax);
        //
        //Create wtravis object
        AccountPeriodic wtravis = new AccountPeriodic();
        wtravis.old_balance = 1500.0;
        wtravis.int_rate = 0.08;
        wtravis.tax_rate = .39;
        wtravis.calcbal();
        System.out.println("Travis balance="+wtravis.new_balance);
        wtravis.calctax();
        System.out.println("Travis tax="+wtravis.tax);
    }
}
```

Notice that `wtravis` is an object in the class `AccountPeriodic`. Two key lines of code to focus on are

> `dcrockett.calcbal()` and `wtravis.calcbal()`.

How does the Java code know which `calcbal()` method to invoke? A feature of object-oriented programming called polymorphism ensures that the correct method is invoked. Since `wtravis` is an object in the class `AccountPeriodic`, Java knows to call the correct method associated with this class. Pretty neat!

MORE ON XML ....

In this section, we expand on the example illustrated in Figure 5–9 in Chapter 5, "Languages of the Internet," and explain how XSLT works. Following is the example XML file, `doowop.xml`, that we would like translated into HTML so the information can be displayed as a table on a Web page:

```
<?xml version="1.0"?>
<?xml:stylesheet type = "text/xsl" href = "doowop.xsl"?>
<CATALOG xmlns ="x-schema:doowop.xdr" genre="Doo Wop">
  <RECORD>
    <TITLE>In The Still of the Night</TITLE>
    <GROUP>The Five Satins</GROUP>
    <YEAR>1956</YEAR>
    <PRICE>15.00</PRICE>
  </RECORD>
  <RECORD>
    <TITLE>The Duke of Earl</TITLE>
    <GROUP>Gene Chandler</GROUP>
    <YEAR>1962</YEAR>
    <PRICE>5.50</PRICE>
  </RECORD>
  <RECORD>
    <TITLE>Angel Baby</TITLE>
    <GROUP>Rosie and the Originals</GROUP>
    <YEAR>1961</YEAR>
    <PRICE>25.00</PRICE>
  </RECORD>
  <RECORD>
    <TITLE>One Summer Night</TITLE>
    <GROUP>The Danleers</GROUP>
    <YEAR>1958</YEAR>
    <PRICE>7.50</PRICE>
  </RECORD>
  <RECORD>
    <TITLE>The Closer You Are</TITLE>
    <GROUP>Earl Lewis and the Channels</GROUP>
    <YEAR>1957</YEAR>
    <PRICE>17.00</PRICE>
  </RECORD>
  <RECORD>
    <TITLE>Over the Mountain, Cross the Sea</TITLE>
    <GROUP>Johnnie and Joe</GROUP>
    <YEAR>1957</YEAR>
    <PRICE>11.00</PRICE>
  </RECORD>
  <RECORD>
    <TITLE>Can I Come Over Tonight</TITLE>
    <GROUP>The Velours</GROUP>
    <YEAR>1956</YEAR>
    <PRICE>9.50</PRICE>
  </RECORD>
</CATALOG>
```

Following is the file `doowop.xsl` that translates the XML file `doowop.xml` into HTML so it can be displayed in a browser.

```
<?xml version="1.0"?>
<xsl:stylesheet  xmlns:xsl="http://www.w3.org/TR/WD-xsl">
<xsl:template match="/">
<html>
<head>
<link rel="stylesheet" type="text/css" href="doowop.css" />
</head>
<body>
<h1>The <xsl:value-of select="CATALOG/@genre" /> Catalog</h1>
<table border="2">
<tr>
<td><b>Title</b></td><td><b>Group</b></td>
<td><b>Year</b></td><td><b>Price</b></td></tr>
<xsl:for-each select="CATALOG/RECORD">
<tr>
<td><xsl:value-of select="TITLE"/></td>
<td><xsl:value-of select="GROUP"/></td>
<td><xsl:value-of select="YEAR"/></td>
<td><xsl:value-of select="PRICE"/></td>
</tr>
</xsl:for-each>
</table>
</body>
</html>
</xsl:template>
</xsl:stylesheet>
```

The resulting Web page display of the HTML that is generated from the XML code in `doowop.xml` using the XSLT code above is in Figure A–1.

There are several key aspects to the transformation. First, we have added the line

```
<?xml:stylesheet type = "text/xsl" href = "doowop.xsl"?>
```

to the original XML file, `doowop.xml`. This is the line that instructs the browser to use the file `doowop.xsl` to transform the XML. Next, notice the title The Doo Wop Catalog in Figure A–1. This was generated from the line

```
<h1>The <xsl:value-of select="CATALOG/@genre" /> Catalog</h1>
```

in the file `doowop.xsl`. The XSLT command `value-of select` reads the `genre` attribute value for the `CATALOG` element in file `doowop.xml` and puts it in the heading. This way we can use the XML file for different forms of music, e.g., jazz and classical, and generate the appropriate heading without editing any HTML.

How does the table in Figure A–1 with the record data get generated? The XSLT command `<xsl:for-each select="CATALOG/RECORD">` instructs the browser to loop over all of the `RECORD` elements in `doowop.xml`. Then the commands

Figure A–1 The XML file displayed in Internet Explorer using XSLT.

```
<td><xsl:value-of select="TITLE"/></td>
<td><xsl:value-of select="GROUP"/></td>
<td><xsl:value-of select="YEAR"/></td>
<td><xsl:value-of select="PRICE"/></td>
```

select the appropriate element value from doowop.xml and load it into the table. We have been able to separate the data from the formatting!

Next, we illustrate the use of schemas. Following is a schema for the example file doowop.xml. This is an example of an XML-DR (XML-data reduced) schema, which is supported by Microsoft. Note that this file is an XML file. The schema names every element and defines the type of data (dt) it is. For example, note that the element YEAR is defined as an integer and the element PRICE is defined as a floating point number. There is also XML Schema that the W3C has recently approved as a W3C Recommendation. Microsoft is also going to support the W3C XML Schema.

```
<?xml version="1.0"?>
<Schema name="CATALOG"
xmlns="urn:schemas-microsoft-com:xml-data"
xmlns:dt="urn:schemas-microsoft-com:datatypes">
<ElementType name="YEAR" content="textOnly" model="closed"
dt:type="int">
</ElementType>
<ElementType name="TITLE" content="textOnly" model="closed">
</ElementType>
```

```
<ElementType name="RECORD" content="eltOnly" model="closed">
<element type="TITLE" maxOccurs="*" minOccurs="0"/>
<element type="GROUP" maxOccurs="*" minOccurs="0"/>
<element type="YEAR" maxOccurs="*" minOccurs="0"/>
<element type="PRICE" maxOccurs="*" minOccurs="0"/>
</ElementType>
<ElementType name="PRICE" content="textOnly" model="closed"
dt:type="float">
</ElementType>
<ElementType name="GROUP" content="textOnly" model="closed">
</ElementType>
<ElementType name="CATALOG" content="eltOnly" model="closed">
<AttributeType name="genre">
</AttributeType>
<attribute type="genre"/>
<element type="RECORD" maxOccurs="*" minOccurs="0"/>
</ElementType>
</Schema>
```

JAVASCRIPT AND CLIENT PROGRAMMING ....

In this section, we give a very simple illustration of what can be accomplished through the use of scripts. In this example, we show how to put values dynamically into a table on a Web page. Consider the following segment of HTML. The document object model for this HTML is illustrated in Figure A–2. Note the tree-like structure. For example, the `table` object is a child of the `body` object. This document object model consists of the elements and element attributes that make up the Web page. The elements are accessed through JavaScript.

```
<body  onload = "getdata()"  >
<p id="par1"> Please fill in the table below: </p>
<table    id="table1"  onclick="changeColor()">
    <tr>
        <th id="col1">Age</th>
        <th id="col2">Social Security Number </th>
    </tr>
    <tr>
        <td id="txtage"> </td>
        <td id="txtssn"> </td>
    </tr>
</table>
<p id="par2"> Click anywhere on the table to
change color and center the table.</p>
</body>
```

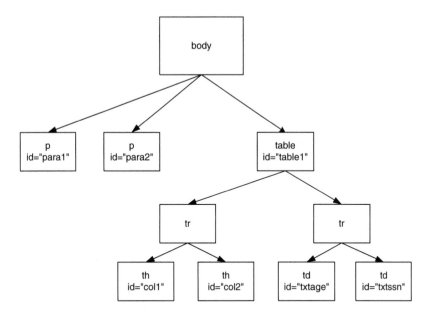

Figure A–2 Object diagram of HTML.

The following script is a simple illustration of how JavaScript may be used.

```
01 <script type = "text/javascript">
02     function getdata()
03     {
04        table1.border="7";
05        var age = prompt("What is your age", "");
06        txtage.innerText = age;
07        var ssn = prompt("What is your Social Security Number","");
08        txtssn.innerText = ssn;
09     }
10 </script>
```

Note from the document object model in Figure A–2 that the id for the first column in the first row is txtage and the id for the second column in the first row is txtssn. The script in lines 05 and 07 asks the user for an age and social security number, respectively. The user response is then put into the table using lines 06 and 08.

JavaScript also makes use of *events*. Events might be loading a Web page, clicking a mouse, moving a mouse over a link, etc. Each of these events can trigger the execution of JavaScript. For example, the HTML line <body onload = "getdata()"> "triggers" the getdata() function in line 02 of the JavaScript. The getdata() function creates pop-up windows that ask the user for an age and a social security number. This function is defined in lines 02 through 09.

The HTML line `<table id="table1" onclick="changeColor()">` triggers the `changeColor()` function in JavaScript, which changes the color of the table when the user clicks the mouse anywhere on the table object. The `changeColor()` function is in the following script.

```
<script type = "text/javascript">
function changeColor()
{
    table1.bgColor="red";
    table1.align="center";
}
</script>
```

ACTIVE SERVER PAGE TECHNOLOGIES ....

In this section, we illustrate the ASP.NET (active server page) technology that is part of the new Microsoft .NET initiative. Searching a database using a Web form is a common and important Web-based task. Consider the following HTML document, `contacts.aspx`, which displays the form that enables a user to search a database.

```
<%@ Page Src="contacts.aspx.vb" Inherits="Contacts"%>
<!DOCTYPE HTML PUBLIC "-//W3C//DTD HTML 4.0 Transitional//EN">
<html>
<head>
<title>
Contact List
</title>
</head>
<body>
<form id="Form1" method="post" runat="server">
    My E-Mail List
<p>
    <asp:TextBox id="TextBox1" runat="server">
    </asp:TextBox> Input Person's Last Name
</p>
<br/>
<p>
    <asp:Button id="Button1"  runat="server" Text="Submit">
    </asp:Button>
</p>
<br/>
<p>
    <asp:DataGrid id="DataGrid1" runat="server" >
    <HeaderStyle Font-Size="Medium" Font-Bold="True"
     HorizontalAlign="Center"></HeaderStyle>
```

```
        </asp:DataGrid>
</p>
</form>
</body>
</html>
```

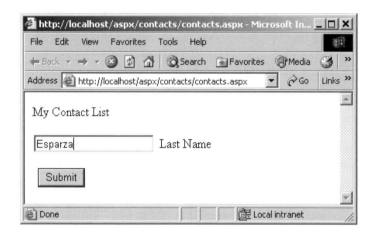

Figure A–3 Active server page to search database.

The display of this HTML appears in Figure A–3. This example illustrates an important feature of ASP.NET—the separation of HTML (formatting) from code that executes the database search. The first line of the HTML file, `contacts.aspx`, contains the name of the source code file `contacts.aspx.vb`. Following is this source code file. It is a Visual Basic (vb) program that implements the logic for the database search.

```
Private Sub Button1_Click(ByVal sender As System.Object, _
ByVal e As System.EventArgs) Handles Button1.Click
    Dim kConnection As SqlConnection
    Dim kCommand As SqlCommand
    Dim kSQL As String
    kConnection = New SqlConnection("Server = _
    gsbkxm;uid=sa;pwd=*******;Database=contacts")
    kSQL = "Select FirstName,LastName,eMail From Contacts _
    Where LastName = '" & TextBox1.Text & "'"
    kCommand = New SqlCommand(kSQL, kConnection)
    kConnection.Open()
    DataGrid1.DataSource = kCommand.ExecuteReader()
    DataGrid1.DataBind()
    kConnection.Close()
End Sub
```

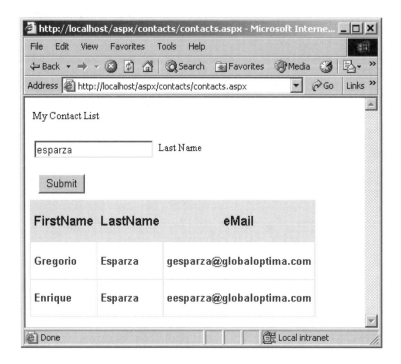

Figure A–4 Response to Search on `esparza`

This code is executed when the user clicks on the submit button of the form in Figure A–3. Using this code, a connection is established with the server `gsbkxm`, which has a SQL Server database called `contacts`. A search of the database is triggered, which looks for entries in `LastName` in the `contacts` database that match the text entered by the user in the TextBox of the form in Figure A–3.

The result of the search appears in Figure A–4. Two records were found with the `LastName` of `esparza`. The results of the search are generated using the `DataGrid` object of the Visual Basic file above. The `DataGrid` object is an ASP.NET reusable object for displaying the records that result from a database search. The necessary formatting information for the `DataGrid` object appears between the `<asp>` tags in the HTML document `contacts.aspx`.

JSP (Java server page) and Java Servlet technology for adding features to Web pages is very similar to ASP technology, and can accomplish the same task. For example, it is possible to have a Web page similar to the one illustrated in Figure A–3 where clicking on the submit button triggers a JavaBean application to search a database and return the records matching the LastName of `esparza`.

WEB SERVICE EXAMPLE ....

In this example, we illustrate in detail a mortgage calculation using a Web service. The Web service responds with the required monthly payments on a mortgage when a user enters the amount borrowed, the length of the mortgage (in years), and the interest rate. The client software communicates with the Web service by making an HTTP POST request. The HTTP POST request comprises a header and a body. The necessary data for making the request (the amount borrowed, the length of the mortgage, and the interest rate) are encapsulated as part of an XML file in the body of the HTTP POST request. The header of the HTTP POST request is:

```
POST /asmx/mortgage.asmx HTTP/1.1
Host: gsbkxm
Content-Type: text/xml; charset=utf-8
Content-Length: nnnn
SOAPAction: "http://gsbkxm/MonthlyPayment"
```

The header information contains the name of the server, gsbkxm, the directory, and name of the Web service, /asmx/mortgage.asmx, and the SOAPAction, which is the method named MonthlyPayment. Thus, the Web server running on the machine gsbkxm knows to pass off the HTTP POST request to the mortgage.asmx Web service. The source code for the Web service mortgage.asmx follows. This source code is in C# and makes the mortgage calculation.

```
using System;
using System.Web;
using System.Web.Services;
[WebService(Namespace="http://gsbkxm/")]
public class Mortgage : System.Web.Services.WebService
{
    [WebMethod]
    public double MonthlyPayment(double years, double intrate,
                                 double amount)
    {
        double payment;
        double periods ;
        periods = 12.0;
        intrate = intrate/periods;
        years = years*periods;
        payment = (amount*intrate)/(1.0 -
        System.Math.Pow(1.0 + intrate, -years));
        return payment;
    }
}
```

In order to calculate the monthly mortgage, it is necessary to know the interest rate (intrate), the length of the mortgage in years (years), and the amount borrowed (amount). These data are sent to the Web service in a SOAP envelope. The SOAP envelope is in the body of the HTTP POST request. The envelope is an XML file containing all of the necessary information to run the Web service.

The following illustrates the SOAP envelope in the body of the HTTP POST request. If, for example, the interest rate is .0725 for a 30-year mortgage and $50,000 is borrowed, the body of the HTTP POST request contains a SOAP envelope with these data:

```
<?xml version="1.0" encoding="utf-8"?>
<soap:Envelope
xmlns:xsi="http://www.w3.org/2001/XMLSchema-instance"
xmlns:xsd="http://www.w3.org/2001/XMLSchema"
xmlns:soap="http://schemas.xmlsoap.org/soap/envelope/">
  <soap:Body>
    <MonthlyPayment xmlns="http://gsbkxm/">
      <years>30</years>
      <intrate>0.0725</intrate>
      <amount>50000</amount>
    </MonthlyPayment>
  </soap:Body>
</soap:Envelope>
```

This mortgage calculation could also very easily be accomplished using a Web form. But the Web service is more general—any client software can use this mortgage Web service. The only requirement is that the client send a SOAP message in the format illustrated above. The GUI for such a client is illustrated in Figure A–5.

Figure A–5 Client software display of mortgage calculation form before HTTP POST request.

When the Submit button is clicked, the HTTP header and SOAP envelope are sent over the Web to the server machine gsbkxm. Following is the code executed by the event of clicking the Submit button in Figure A–5. (Note: The code intrate =

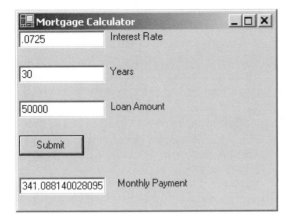

Figure A–6 Client software display of mortgage calculation form after HTTP POST request.

CDbl(TextBox1.Text) in line 08 takes the text entered into the first text box and converts it to a double precision number; similarly for years and amount in lines 09 and 10, repectively.)

```
01 Private Sub Button1_Click(ByVal sender As System.Object, _
02    ByVal e As System.EventArgs) Handles Button1.Click
03    Dim mortgage As New gsbkxm.Mortgage()
04    Dim years As Double
05    Dim intrate As Double
06    Dim amount As Double
07    Dim payment As Double
08    intrate = CDbl(TextBox1.Text)
09    years = CDbl(TextBox2.Text)
10    amount = CDbl(TextBox3.Text)
11    payment = mortgage.MonthlyPayment(years, intrate, amount)
12    Label3.Text = CDbl(payment)
13 End Sub
```

The Web service mortgage, running on a server, takes the years, intrate, and amount data and calculates the monthly payment. It then returns the following XML file to the client with the payment value. The client software reads this XML file and displays the result as shown in Figure A–6.

```
<?xml version="1.0" encoding="utf-8" ?>
<double xmlns="http://gsbkxm">
    341.08814002809504
</double>
```

BIZTALK AND MIDDLEWARE ....

In this section, we motivate the power of BizTalk Server and messaging middleware through a simple example. Assume that Company B is a supplier for Company A. In this example we illustrate how Company A sends a requisition to Company B. (This example is based on the Northwind tutorial file that is part of BizTalk Server.) The first step of the process is for Company A to create a requisition file containing the necessary information in XML format. The second step is to place the .xml requisition file into the folder c:\xmlpoll on a Company A computer running BizTalk Server. BizTalk Server can be configured to poll the directory c:\xmlpoll for the presence of files with an .xml extension. In Figure A–7 we show the display for configuring BizTalk to poll the directory c:\xmlpoll.

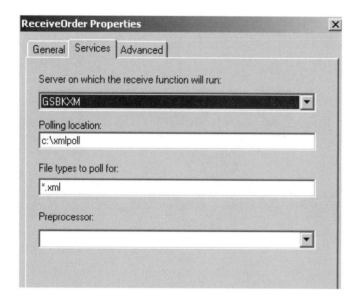

Figure A–7 Location for Biztalk polling.

When BizTalk Server detects a new requisition file in the c:\xmlpoll folder, it packages it into a SOAP envelope, creates a message queueing object, and sends it to a Company B server. In Figure A–8 we show the message queue on the Company B server. On the left of the screen, note the name of the queue companya_po located right above the highlighted "Queue messages." On the right of the screen is the actual purchase order labeled PO >From Company A.

Once the purchase order arrives at the Company B server, software on the server reads the message queue and gets the purchase order. The following is a very simple piece of code for doing this:

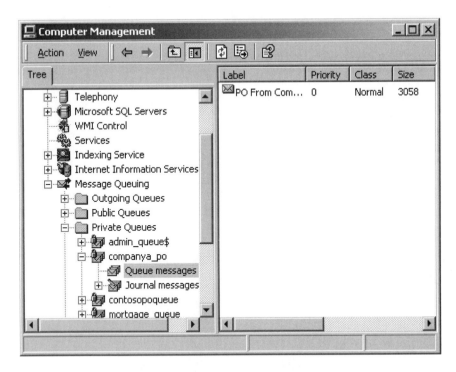

Figure A–8 Message queue on supplier (company B) computer.

```
private void button1_Click(object sender, System.EventArgs e)
{
  string sMsgBody = "";
  string path = "gsbkxm\\PRIVATE$\\companya_po";
  System.Messaging.ActiveXMessageFormatter bFormat = new
  System.Messaging.ActiveXMessageFormatter();
  MessageQueue q = new MessageQueue(path);
  System.Messaging.Message Msg = q.Peek(new TimeSpan(0,0,0,10));
  sMsgBody = bFormat.Read(Msg).ToString();
  label1.Text = sMsgBody;
}
```

In this code, the software opens the message queue companya_po and reads the purchase order. The purchase order in XML gets put into the variable sMsgBody as a string of characters. The character string is parsed, separating it into tags and data. The data are examined in detail, which allows Company B to take action on the purchase order. If Company B also had BizTalk Server, it could process the message queue automatically and send an invoice back to the message queue on the server for Company A.

B Suggested Reading

This book has a large bibliography. In this appendix we list some selected readings for each chapter that expand on material in the book.

Of general interest

- Readers with an historical bent will enjoy *Silicon Boys* [88] by David Kaplan. It is an engaging history of the great technology companies in Silicon Valley.

- *Dealers of Lightning* [75] by Michael Hiltzik is a thorough history of the major breakthroughs at Xerox PARC. From the GUI to Ethernet, this is where it was discovered.

- Robert Cringely provides both an entertaining and informative history of modern personal computing in *Accidental Empires: How the Boys of Silicon Valley Make Their Millions, Battle Foreign Competition, and Still Can't Get a Date* [33].

- In *The Road Ahead* [53], Bill Gates writes about what he was thinking as he led Microsoft to its role as the superpower in software. An excellent read.

- *Nudist on the Late Shift* [20] by Po Bronson is a humorous slice of life in Silicon Valley.

Chapter 2: What Do I Need to Know about Hardware?

- For a very broad coverage of hardware and computing in general, we recommend *The Essential Guide to Computing* [169] by Garrison Walters.

- For more detail on hardware issues, see *How Computers Work* [174] by Ron White.

- For even more detail on hardware, see *The Winn L. Rosch Hardware Bible* [140] by Winn Rosch.

- A history of computers from UNIVAC in 1945 through the desktop/workstation is thoroughly provided in *A History of Modern Computing* [26] by Paul Ceruzzi.

Chapter 3: Software Is Everywhere

- *Microsoft Secrets* by Michael Cusumano [34] is an excellent work about the software industry in general, and Microsoft in particular.

- Cusumano's more recent book, *Competing on Internet Time* with D.B. Yoffie [35], provides a good blow by blow account of what was happening inside Netscape as it was battling Microsoft.

- For readers interested in the software management/development process, there is the all-time classic *The Mythical Man-Month* [21] by F.P. Brooks Jr., the project manager for the IBM System/360 and OS/360. From this book we get Brooks's Law: "Adding manpower to a late software project makes it later."

- In *Decline & Fall of the American Programmer* [184], Ed Yourdon writes about the trend to move U.S. software development outside the United States and what is necessary for American software factories to remain world-class.

- Yourdon's follow up book, *Death March* [185], is also a very valuable resource for anyone involved with software development projects.

- For another peek inside the world's largest software house, Microsoft, we recommend *Show-Stopper* [186] by Pascal Zachary, which describes the race to create the Windows NT operating system.

- For even more practical advice about managing software projects, see *Dynamics of Software Development,* by Jim McCarthy, former director of the Microsoft Visual C++ Program Management Team.

- For a look into the open source movement and the development of the Linux operating system see *Rebel Code: The Inside Story of Linux and the Open Source Revolution* by Glyn Moody.

Chapter 4: Internet and Web Technology

- For a captivating history of the development of ARPANET and the Internet, see *Where Wizards Stay Up Late* [66] by Katie Hafner and Matthew Lyon.

- For a perspective of the Web by the man who invented it, see *Weaving the Web* [12] by Tim Berners-Lee.

- The Paul Andrews book, *How the Web Was Won* [5], is about how Microsoft became aware of the importance of the Internet.

- *Breaking Windows: How Bill Gates Fumbled the Future of Microsoft* [8] by David Bank details the struggle within Microsoft over the role of Windows versus the open standards of the Internet.

Chapter 5: Languages of the Internet

- There are numerous books on HTML. A good starter book is *The Web Wizards's Guide to HTML* [101] by Wendy Lehnert.

- A more complicated book with material on XML, XHTML, and writing scripts is *Internet & World Wide Web: How to Program* [38] by H.M. Deitel, P.J. Deitel, and T.R. Nieto.

- For readers interested in using XML within the new Microsoft .NET environment we recommend *XML for ASP.NET Developers* by Dan Wahlin.

Chapter 6: Web Site Design and Content

- For advice on Web design from the usability guru himself, see *Designing Web Usability: The Practice of Simplicity* by Jakob Nielsen [123].

Chapter 7: Getting Your Business Online

- The reader wanting more technical detail about telecommunications should consult *The Essential Guide to Telecommunications* [39] by Annabel Dodd.

- For everything you wanted to know, but were afraid to ask, there is the monumental *Encyclopedia of Networking & Telecommunications* [148] by Tom Sheldon.

Chapter 8: Rethinking Internet Business Models

- A good book on Internet strategy is *Information Rules: A Strategic Guide to the Network Economy* by C. Shapiro and H.R. Varian [147].

- To learn how to make the most of virtual communities, see *Net Gain: Expanding Markets Through Virtual Communities* by J.Hagel III and A.G. Armstrong [67].

- For more Internet strategy, see E.I. Schwartz's *Webonomics: Nine Essential Principles for Growing Your Business on the World Wide Web* [142].

- For still more Internet strategy, see *Opening Digital Markets: Battle Plans and Business Strategies for Internet Commerce* by W. Mougayar [118].

- Yet another Internet strategy book is *Unleashing the Killer App: Digital Strategies for Market Dominance* by L. Downes and C. Mui [40].

Chapter 9: Security and Internet Business

- The classic book in the area of ciphers and code breaking is the monumental tome *The Code Breakers* [87], by David Kahn.

- For a book with a good description of the modern public and private key systems, see *The Code Book* [150] by Simon Singh.

- For a book with an historical bent, we recommend *Crypto* [103] by Steven Levy. This book is a look into the delightful cast of characters such as Whitfield Diffie, Martin Hellman, Jim Bidzos, Phil Zimmermann, the RSA team, and James Ellis, all of whom brought secure encryption to the general public.

Chapter 10: Internet Business Transactions

- For more detailed information on Internet payment systems, see *Electronic Commerce* by Pete Loshin, John Vacca, and Paul Murphy [108].

Chapter 11: Marketing on the Internet

- For a lively, engaging read on permission marketing, see Seth Godin's *Permission Marketing* [58].

- For more on viral marketing, see Godin's *Unleashing the Ideavirus* [59].

- For an excellent textbook on Internet marketing, see Ward Hanson's *Principles of Internet Marketing* [73].

Chapter 12: The Power of Databases

- A standard classic textbook on databases is *An Introduction to Database Systems: Volume I* [36] by C.J. Date.

- A recent book on data warehousing with an emphasis on Internet business is *e-Data: Turning Data into Information with Data Warehousing* by Jill Dyché [41].

- For more on data mining, see *Data Mining Your Website* [113] by Jesus Mena.

Chapter 13: Internet Business Architecture

- Readers interested in the Java approach to application servers should consult *Java Server Pages* [129] by Larne Pekowsky.

- Readers interested in Microsoft back end architectures should consult *Professional Windows DNA* [16] by Christopher Blexrud et. al.

- We recommend *Deploying and Managing Microsoft .NET Web Farms* [17] by Barry Bloom for readers interested in the nitty gritty details of Web farms.

Chapter 14: Enterprise Application Software

- Readers interested in more detail on software integration within the enterprise should consult *Enterprise Application Integration* by D.S. Linthicum [105].

- For material on software integration between companies, see *B2B Application Integration: e-Business-Enable Your Enterprise* [106], also by Linthicum.

- A good book on middleware and integration architectures is *IT Architectures and Middleware* [19] by Chris Britton.

Web Sources:

- To look up the definitions of computer- and Internet-related terminology, see www.techweb.com and www.whatis.com.

- For breaking technology news and information on products, see www.cnet.com and www.zdnet.com.

- For general interest articles on technology- and Internet-based business, turn to www.business2.com (*Business 2.0*), www.fastcompany.com (*Fast Company*), and www.cio.com (*CIO Magazine*).

- The following popular press sites have special sections on technology:

  - www.nytimes.com (*The New York Times*)

- www.wsj.com (*The Wall Street Journal*); (requires subscription)
- www.businessweek.com (*Business Week*); (requires subscription for some access)

- For more information by the authors on topics related to this book, go to www.globaloptima.com. If you have comments or questions about this book, please write to the authors at InternetBusiness@globaloptima.com.

C Glossary

3PL (third-party logistics provider) A company that provides transportation and other logistical support for order fulfillment

4GL (fourth generation language) A nonprocedural programming language; nonprocedural programming language commands state what is to be accomplished, not how to accomplish it; SQL is a good example

ACL (access control list) A list used to filter packets on a network; packets with addresses that do not have permission based on the list are not allowed in or out of the network

ADO (ActiveX data object) A Microsoft API used for accessing databases

advertising model An Internet business model that offers content (e.g., news, stories, data) free on a Web site but charges for advertising

AES (advanced encryption standard) An encryption standard recently adopted by the U.S. government that is based on a very secure single key encryption algorithm

algorithm A precise, step-by-step, numerical procedure for solving a problem

affinity portal An Internet portal built for a group that shares a common interest, such as a labor union or college alumni association

ALU (arithmetic logic unit) The part of the microprocessor that controls mathematical operations

API (application program interface) A specification for a program that describes how other programs or an operating system should communicate with it

Applet A Java program that requires a Web browser in order to run

application Software designed to perform a task; examples include desktop applications such as word processing and spreadsheets, and enterprise applications such as ERP and SCM

application server Software designed to extend the functionality of a Web server; e.g., run components written in Java, VBScript, C++; also a "container" for business logic components; also called an app server

ARPA (Advanced Research Projects Agency) A federal agency founded in 1958 that created the network ARPANET, which was to become the Internet

ASCII (American Standard Code for Information Interchange) The standard code for representing text in digital form as 0s and 1s; is universal and virtually any piece of software capable of creating documents can read an ASCII file; files containing ASCII data are often called text files; contrasts with unicode

ASP (application service provider) A company that provides software as a service over the Internet

ASP aggregator A company that provides a variety of software as a service over the Internet and ideally writes code to integrate the different software systems so they can communicate with each other

ASP (active server page) A Microsoft technology for adding code such as VBScript to Web pages (the code is processed and run on a Web server); designated by an .asp extension

assembly language A second generation programming language that uses codes (called op codes or operand codes) instead of 0s and 1s to communicate with computers

authenticator A means of computer security that is an alternative to passwords; sometimes uses something the user possesses, like a card, and something the user knows, like a PIN (personal identification number)

B2B (business-to-business) Refers to transactions (usually commercial) on the Internet between two companies

B2C (business-to-consumer) Refers to transactions (usually commercial) on the Internet between a company and a person

bandwidth Transmission capacity of an electronic line like dial-up service, DSL, or cable; usually expressed in bits per second

big impression A banner ad on a Web site that is business-card sized and set off to the upper-right-hand corner of a page

binary file A file that uses all eight bits of a byte; contrasts with simple ASCII text files which use only seven bits of a byte

biometrics A form of computer security that uses body prints, such as a retinal scan or fingerprints, instead of a password to authenticate a person

bit The smallest unit of information on a computer; represented by "0" if an electrical is not flowing through a transistor, or "1" if it is

bit depth The number of bits a pixel uses to store color; true color requires 24 bits; a set of pixels is used to store a picture in bitmap graphics

bitmap graphic A means of storing graphics using pixels, which are cells of a grid on a computer screen that together form a picture; also called raster graphic; contrasts with vector graphic

BizTalk A standard set of tags for exchanging information in SOAP envelope headers for Web services; the BizTalk Framework 2.0 consists of a set of BizTalk XML tags that go into the header of a SOAP envelope; these tags provide information on the intended destination, the sender of the message, what the message is about, a receipt mechanism to acknowledge delivery of the message, an identifier for the package, a timestamp, expiration date, etc.

blinding factor A mathematical algorithm used in digital currency so that the sender of the currency remains anonymous

BLOB (binary large object) A field in a database that may include text, images, audio, and video; many modern DBMSs allow BLOB fields

boot What a computer does when it is turned on and the operating system is loaded into main memory

bot A program used by a search engine to read Web pages and create new entries for its index by following links in the hypertext; also called a crawler or spider

brick and mortar company A traditional company with physical buildings and stores; contrasts with a dot-com which is a pure Internet company that exists only on the Web

bricks and clicks An Internet business model that combines online and offline commerce; also called click and mortar

bulky box A banner ad on a Web site that is large and square and set in the middle of a page amidst text

byte A standard unit of measure on a computer; a byte is eight bits

bytecode A Java compiler compiles source code into bytecode; is independent of the operating system and is distributed to users with different operating systems; runs on operating system-dependent virtual machines

cache Computer memory capable of high speed transfer; used to temporarily store instructions and data in order to speed up instruction execution and data retrieval

CD-ROM (compact disk-read only memory) A type of secondary storage used to hold text, graphics, and sound; holds approximately 650MB

certificate authority An organization trusted to sign public keys; VeriSign is a well-known certificate authority

chip A very thin silicon wafer containing millions of transistors; functions as a CPU in a computer or can be specially designed to run any number of smart devices such as calculators, PDAs, and smart cards; also called integrated circuit or microprocessor

cipher An algorithm used to encode plaintext into ciphertext; two of the most common ciphers are substitution and transposition

ciphertext Text encrypted for security purposes that is generated by applying a cipher to the plaintext

circuit switching Establishing a connection between two points for the duration of a message exchange using a specific path; the technology behind POTS

CISC (complex instruction set computer) A chip design for desktop computers that reduces the number of times an instruction must be fetched from RAM, but requires more complex instructions; as access times to RAM decreased, chip design led to RISC which fetches instructions more often but uses more simplified instructions

class A term used in object-oriented programming that refers to an abstraction of a real world object and describes the essence of the object; e.g., think of a pattern for a suit cut for a particular individual as a class; contrasts with object

click and mortar An Internet business model that combines online and offline commerce; also called bricks and clicks

client/server computing A kind of computing whereby a client computer uses a server computer for either data or computing; see weak or thin client and strong or fat client; also called distributed computing

CLR (common language runtime) Software that manages the execution of the code compiled by Microsoft's .NET languages, VB.NET, C#, JScript.NET, and managed C++

cluster A group of computers linked together in a high-speed network acting as a single computer

colocation A service that provides climate control, backup, and upkeep for a company's hardware that is not located on the company premises

command line interface A type of interface for an operating system that relies on commands that the user must type in to use the operating system; contrasts with GUI

COM+ (component object model) The Microsoft technology that provides the necessary "plumbing" so that software components can talk to each other

compiler An application that runs on a programmer's computer that takes the instructions in the source code written by the programmer and converts them into a set of machine language instructions that the computer can read; creates a stand-alone application that the end user can purchase and use on a computer; contrasts with interpreter

component An application that interfaces with another application through an API

content model An Internet business model that charges Web site users for content (news, stories, stock quotes, etc.)

cookie A text file stored on the client machine that is designed to uniquely identify a visitor to a Web site in order to deliver customized information; a creation of Netscape

cooperative multitasking The ability of an operating system to appear as though it were performing multiple processes at the same time by dividing the time of the CPU into thin slices whereby the *process* that is executing controls when it can be interrupted; contrasts with preemptive multitasking

CORBA (common object request broker architecture) An API standard for component-to-component communication set forth by the Object Management Group; CORBA allows for a component written in one programming language (e.g., C++) to use methods of a component written in another programming language (e.g., Java)

CPU (central processing unit) The "brain" of the computer that comprises the control unit and ALU (arithmetic logic unit) and does the "computing"; also called micro-processor

crawler A program used by a search engine to read Web pages and create new entries for its index by following links in the hypertext; also called a bot or spider

CRM (customer relationship management) A software-based system that helps companies serve customers better (and ideally become more profitable) by developing stronger relationships with them

cryptography The study of encryption and decryption

CSS (cascading style sheet) A means of separating the formatting from the content of a Web page; with a CSS, formatting commands for tables, headings, paragraphs, etc., are stored in a separate file; multiple Web pages can refer to the same CSS, which gives a consistent look and feel to the Web site

data cube A presentation of data in a data warehouse that makes the data much more accessible

data mart A data warehouse that is subject-specific and normally used by a single department or group of users within a company

data mining Finding patterns in data that can be used as information, particularly customer information for marketing

data warehouse A repository of historical, multidimensional, aggregated data

DBMS (database management system) A suite of software tools for creating, updating, querying, and backing up corporate databases

denial of service attack A malicious act in which the perpetrator floods a server with requests for authentication using false return addresses that the server cannot find; the server gets "hung" waiting for responses from the false addresses

DHTML (dynamic hypertext markup language) Refers to the combination of HTML, style sheets, scripts, and Java Applets used to create dynamic Web pages; there is no DHTML standard supported by the W3C

digital Refers to data, whether text, a movie, a song on a compact disc, or a graphic, that have been translated into 0s and 1s (representing electrical charges in a transistor) so they can be stored and transmitted by a computer

digital certificate Used in computer security to prove that you are who you say you are; usually the owner's public key digitally signed by a certificate authority; also a "seal of approval" used in online credit card transactions to authenticate a merchant or a customer that is digitally signed by a trusted third party such as a bank or certificate authority

digital coin A bank-signed serial number sent to a merchant to authenticate and validate digital currency used by a customer

digital currency The online equivalent of cash whereby purchases can be made easily and anonymously with no possibility of being traced

digital signature A method used to guarantee that a file (or email) has not been tampered with and that it was sent by owner of the private key used to sign the file (or email)

distributed computing A kind of computing whereby a client computer uses a server computer for either data or computing; see weak or thin client and strong or fat client; also called client/server computing

DMZ (DeMilitarized Zone) A network in a company where the publicly available servers reside; is protected by a firewall and therefore more secure than an unprotected network, but not as secure as the internal corporate network where important data are kept (the internal network is protected from the DMZ by an additional firewall)

DNS (domain name system) The system used on the Internet to resolve domain names (e.g., gsbkip.uchicago.edu) into IP addresses (e.g., 128.135.130.201)

DTD (document type definition) A file used to validate XML files by ensuring that the elements and attributes in the XML file are consistent with those defined in the DTD

domain name A name used by organizations or individuals to uniquely identify themselves on the Internet; the domain name is resolved by the DNS into an IP address

DRAM (dynamic random access memory) A type of memory in a computer that needs a fresh electronic charge every few milliseconds; not as fast or expensive as SRAM; when people refer to the amount of RAM on a computer (e.g., 128 MB), they are usually referring to DRAM

drill down Get a more detailed view of data by clicking on various dimensions in a data cube

drop shipper A company that fulfills orders for another by shipping goods produced by the former and sold by the latter directly to the customer

EAI (enterprise application integration) The integration of firm-wide business process and IT systems; the integration process is usually based on middleware

ECML (electronic commerce modeling language) A standard for electronic wallets developed in 1999 by industry heavyweights such as American Express, Compaq, IBM, MasterCard, Microsoft, etc.; was never widely adopted

EDI (electronic data interchange) A forerunner of online data exchange that was developed to exchange purchase orders and invoices between companies electronically rather than on paper

EJB (Enterprise JavaBean) An API specification from Sun Microsystems for Java-based application server components

electronic wallet An online device that holds a user's ID, means to pay, and billing and shipping addresses; can be used for quick data entry when filling out a form to make an online purchase

e-logistics An industry that provides third-party fulfillment, transportation, and other logistical support using the Internet

enterprise portal A portal designed specifically for a company's employees that offers human resources documents, calendars of events, conference room reservation forms, databases, sales force tools, newsletters, etc.

ERP (enterprise resource planning) A software-based system that links together all of a company's internal processes such as order taking, fulfillment, financial management, and human resources; began as MRP and has been extended to include Internet commerce

ethernet A LAN technology that retransmits packets of data after they "collide" when being sent to and from different computers in a network

extranet A private network connecting a company with customers or business partners; often based upon TCP/IP

fat client A paradigm of client/server computing whereby the client is responsible for most of the computing and data storage; the client is a reasonably powerful desktop PC, or perhaps even a workstation; also called a strong client; contrasts with weak or thin client

Fibre Channel A technology for connecting servers with data storage devices; designed for very fast data transfer, up to 4 Gbps

firewall Hardware and software used to secure a network against attack; three main technologies are packet filtering, proxy servers, and stateful filtering

flash memory Nonvolatile memory found in newer computers that can be updated quickly because it is erased and rewritten in units of memory called blocks; faster than older ROM which is erased and rewritten at the byte level

freeware Software that is free (no charge) but copyrighted so there may be restrictions on its redistribution and use; contrasts with free software

free software This concept originates with Richard Stallman who founded the Free Software Movement in 1984; in this context, free does not mean zero price; the word free means that the owner of free software is free to use the software, copy it, modify it, and distribute it; also called open source software

FTP (file transfer protocol) A protocol for exchanging files over the Internet that is often used to download software; nonanonymous FTP requires an account name and password to access files on a server while anonymous FTP does not

fulfillment The process of filling a customer's order that has come to include not only on-time delivery of the correct order, but also email notification to a customer that an order has been received and shipped, as well as a mechanism by which the package can be tracked

gateway page An HTML page designed expressly to secure a high ranking for a Web site on search engines

Gb (gigabit) 2^{30} or 1,073,741,824 bits

Gbps (gigabits per second) 2^{30} or 1,073,741,824 bits per second; used to measure bandwidth

GB (gigabyte) 2^{30} or 1,073,741,824 bytes; most high-end PCs now come with at least 10 gigabytes of memory on the hard drive

GIF (graphics interchange format) A common bitmap graphic file format on the Web that handles only 8-bit color; slowly being replaced by PNG; developed by the W3C

GNU (GNU's not Unix) The GNU project is an effort to write a free, portable, Unix-like operating system; Linux is a Unix kernel that uses GNU software

GPL (general public license) A license often used to distribute open source software such as Linux; the GPL is designed to ensure that software obtained under the GPL is redistributed without adding any restrictions on its use

GUI (graphical user interface) An interface for an operating system that allows a user to click on images and graphical icons with a mouse to get things done; originally developed at Xerox PARC but commercially introduced in the Macintosh in 1984; contrasts with command line interface

hash function A one-way (cannot reverse to get original message) function that takes a variable length input message and distills it into a fixed length message digest; there is an extremely low probability that two distinct inputs will produce the same digest; used to verify that a message has not been tampered with

HTML (hypertext markup language) A language that tells the browser how to display text and graphics on a Web page

HTTP (hypertext transfer protocol) A high-level protocol used to exchange information between a browser and a server; uses TCP/IP to locate and make a connection between the browser and the server

HTTP server A server that serves up Web pages to a browser; also called a Web server

hypertext Allows a person to read or explore a Web document in a nonlinear fashion; hypertext contains "links" to other text; by following the links, the reader is not constrained to follow any particular order

ICANN (Internet Corporation for Assigned Names and Numbers) An organization established by the United States Commerce Department for the purpose of making the Internet run smoothly; this organization has responsibility for allocating and managing IP addresses and domain names

IDL (interface definition language) Used to describe the API of a component; the IDL gets compiled into client and server stubs that convert method parameters into a string of bits sent over a network

interface The part of the operating system that allows a user to interact with the computer; also called user interface or shell

Internet2 A joint government, university, and industry project to create an Internet that will exchange multimedia data at high speed (the first Internet was designed to exchange text)

interpreter An application that translates the "English-like" instructions of the source code into machine language the computer can understand by executing the source code directly, line by line; contrasts with compiler

intranet An organization's intranet is a network available only to members of that organization; often based upon TCP/IP

IP address A 32-bit (4 byte) number assigned to a computer so a packet of data can be sent to and from the computer using the Internet protocol; each byte is expressed as a three-digit decimal number; e.g., 128.135.130.201

ISO (independent sales organization) A company that provides merchant accounts and credit card services, usually at higher rates than banks because they bear a higher level of risk

ISP (Internet service provider) A company that provides an Internet connection for a user (company or individual)

J2EE A suite of Java API specifications from Sun Microsystems for Servlets, server pages, Enterprise JavaBeans, database connectivity, etc.

Java An object-oriented programming language developed by Sun Microsystems; a very popular language for B2B applications; used to write Java Applets, which add functionality to a Web page; Java source code compiles into bytecode rather than a platform-dependent machine language

JavaBean A Java class that has been compiled into an independent component that can be called from within a JavaServer page; used to add functionality to an application server

Jaz drive A type of secondary storage for a computer from Iomega that can hold 1-2 GB

JDBC (Java database connectivity) A component API that allows Java programs to make SQL queries to databases such as Oracle and DB2

JPEG (joint photographic experts group) A bitmap graphics file format on the Web; uses a compression scheme for photographic images

JRE (Java runtime environment) Consists of a Java virtual machine and important Java classes and libraries that, when installed, allows users to run Java applications on their computers

JSP (Java server page) A technology for adding functionality to a Web page that uses HTML, Java code, and tags that reference JavaBean components; the page is compiled into a Java Servlet that is run by an application server

Kb (kilobit) 2^{10} or 1,024 bits

Kbps (kilobits per second) 2^{10} or 1,024 bits per second; used to measure bandwidth

KB (kilobyte) 2^{10} or 1,024 bytes; used to measure a computer's memory

killer app A term for any hot, revolutionary computer application tool in great demand; short for killer application

kernel The part of the operating system that controls how the computer works; responsible for file management, memory management, peripheral control, process management and scheduling, and network communication control; contrasts with shell

L1 cache A kind of memory located on the microprocessor that acts as a temporary staging area where data and instructions are held before being used by the control unit and the ALU in the CPU; more expensive than RAM

L2 cache A kind of memory located between the microprocessor and RAM; more expensive than RAM

LAN (local area network) A communications network consisting of cables, computers, and network devices confined to a very small geographic region such as a single building or floor of a building

last mile Refers to the Internet connection between the ISP and the user

legacy application An application written for and running on an older (usually mainframe) computer that must be integrated with or replaced by a newer application

LMDS (local multipoint distribution system) A wireless last-mile technology that broadcasts in the part of the spectrum centered at 28GHz; the bandwidth is in the OC-1 to OC-12 range; a line-of-sight technology with a range of two to four miles

load balancing Distributing requests (say, for a Web page) evenly across a cluster of servers (also called nodes) where any one of the servers is capable of handling the request

lossless compression A form of data compression for faster transmission of audio, video, and some imaging whereby no data are lost; contrasts with lossy compression

lossy compression A form of data compression for faster transmission of audio, video, and some imaging whereby some data are lost; contrasts with lossless compression

machine language The first generation of programming languages, the syntax of which consists of strings of 0s and 1s conforming to the circuitry of the computer

macro A sequence of commands, menu selections, and keystrokes that are stored and can be assigned a name or key combination

main memory A group of RAM chips in a computer where program execution and data processing take place; also called memory

mainframe Today the term refers to a large computer or computer system; in the late 1940s and into the 1950s a single mainframe filled an entire room and relied on vacuum tubes for computing power; the term is being replaced by enterprise server or supercomputer

MAP (merchant account provider) A company that provides the accounts for merchants into which revenues from credit card sales are deposited by the cardholder's bank

markup language A language that uses a set of commands to describe how text should be displayed, or to give meaning to the text; examples are HTML and XML; contrasts with WYSIWYG (what you see is what you get)

Mb (megabit) 2^{20} or 1,048,576 bits

Mbps (megabits per second) 2^{20} or 1,048,576 bits per second; a unit used to measure bandwidth

MB (megabyte) 2^{20} or 1,048,576 bytes; used to measure a computer's memory

m-computing (mobile computing) Computing using handheld wireless devices; usually provides Internet access

memory A group of RAM chips in a computer where program execution and data processing take place; also called main memory

memory bus The part of the computer that connects the CPU and main memory through which instructions and data come in and go out of the CPU; also called system bus

message digest A compact, fixed-length (usually 128-bit or 160-bit) "fingerprint" of a long, variable-length plaintext created by applying a hash function to the plaintext; if the original plaintext is tampered with, applying the same hash function to the tampered plaintext will produce a different message digest from applying the hash function to the original plaintext; used to verify that a message has not been tampered with

meta language A language used to define other languages; XML is an example because it defines XHTML

method A function or procedure that operates on data; for example, a method might be used to price a call option; in object-oriented programming, classes are made up of methods and data

microcommerce A segment of Internet commerce whereby the price of each transaction ranges from one cent to roughly $10; usually aggregates transactions so that the user is billed for a single monthly amount

micropayment A payment in microcommerce in the range of one cent to roughly $10; many are usually aggregated so that a monthly statement is presented to the user

microprocessor The primary logic device in a modern PC; a CPU on a single silicon chip

middleware Software that allows one application to communicate with another over a network

MMDS (multichannel multipoint distribution service) A wireless last-mile technology that broadcasts in the 2.2 to 2.4 GHz spectrum; the bandwidth ranges from 128 Kbps to 3 Mbps and has a reach of up to 30 miles

MOM (message-oriented middleware) Middleware that is application-to-queue communication and asynchronous; MOM software is to application software what email is to people

Moore's Law An empirical observation of Gordon Moore of Intel that the computing power of a new chip doubles every 18 months

MP3 (MPEG-1 audio layer-3) One of the best-known compression schemes for reducing sound files to a fraction of their original size; well-known because of the battle fought between Napster—a Web site from which music could be downloaded free as MP3 files and shared among users—and major recording studios over copyright infringement

MQSeries IBM's message-oriented middleware product

MRP (material requirements planning) A production scheduling technique developed in the 1960s that is used to calculate a production schedule for manufactured items that have many parts, like an automobile

MSIL (Microsoft intermediate language) The Microsoft .NET languages (VB.NET, C#, JScript.NET, and managed C++) are compiled into MSIL; much like Java bytecode in that the MSIL is platform independent; it is the job of the CLR to execute this code on the appropriate platform

MSMQ (Microsoft message queue) A Microsoft message-oriented middleware product

MSP (managed service provider) A company that provides hardware and networking as well as maintenance of the hardware and network as a service to other companies; in many instances, a company will use an MSP to host its Web site

MSP (merchant service provider) A general term that covers MAPs and ISOs; will usually offer more than merchant accounts

multiprocessing The ability of a single operating system to manage multiple processes simultaneously without sharing time slices from a single CPU; requires two or more CPUs so that each CPU can be completely devoted to performing a single process

multitasking The ability of an operating system to appear as though it were performing multiple processes at the same time, but in reality divide the time of the CPU into small time slices, each devoted to a different process, in rapid succession so as to give the appearance of multiple processes occurring simultaneously

multithreading The ability of an operating system to work on multiple subprocesses within a single process seemingly simultaneously

multiuser The ability of an operating system to support multiple users "concurrently," which means that each user is allocated very small time slices alternately by the CPU so that from the users' standpoints they appear to be accessing the operating system simultaneously

namespace Used to qualify tags in XML documents in order to prevent confusion when XML documents are exchanged

NAP (network access point) A switching point in a large city where the very high bandwidth network backbones of major telecommunications companies meet

NAS (network attached storage) A storage device typically attached directly to an ethernet LAN and assigned an IP address; the NAS device may be a server appliance that performs duties in addition to storage, or it could be a dedicated storage device

NAT (network address translation) Software used by proxy servers and routers to replace the IP address in a packet with the IP address of the proxy server or router and forward the packet

NC (network computer) A very weak client computer interacting with a server over the Internet that some predicted would replace desktop computing (the PC)

newsgroup An asynchronous way of exchanging information among multiple users over the Internet; usually formed around a topic of interest, from archery to zen

Nielsen approach A means to track visitors to a Web site from the client side that requires installing software on client machines to see where users are going when they surf the Internet

nonlinearity A quality of the Web that there is no straight-line path from beginning to end when surfing the Web as there is with viewing a television program or listening to a song on the radio

nonprocedural language Nonprocedural programming language commands state what is to be accomplished, not how to accomplish it; SQL is a good example

nonvolatile memory Memory in a computer that keeps its content even if the power to the computer is turned off; examples are ROM and flash

object A term used in object-oriented programming that refers to an instance of a specific class; e.g., if the class is a call option, an object in this class might be a call option for Procter & Gamble expiring in December 2002

Object Management Group The not-for-profit consortium that produces and maintains computer industry specifications; manages the CORBA standard

object-oriented programming Refers to a programming language that allows reusable software modules called objects that can be easily modified or extended for use in different applications; examples include Java, C++, and C#

OC (Optical Carrier) A term used to refer to different bandwidths; ranges from OC-1 (51.85 Mpbs) to OC-192 (9.952 Gbps), typically for fiber optic cable

OLAP (online analytical processing) A type of data processing for *analytical* purposes that is used on multidimensional, aggregated data, usually a data warehouse; contrasts with OLTP

OLE DB (object linking embedding database) A software component that provides an API or interface for communicating with a data source; there are OLE DB data providers for SQL Server, Oracle, and Access

OLTP (online transaction processing) A type of data processing for *operational* purposes; requires up-to-the moment records that are found in a highly normalized, relational database; contrasts with OLAP

one-to-one marketing Personalized marketing to a single customer rather than marketing to the masses or to a target audience; more easily realized using the Internet

open source software Software, for which the source code is available to copy and/or modify and redistribute; also called free software

operating system Software that controls how the computer works (the kernel) and how the user interacts with the computer (the shell)

opt in To give permission on a Web site to receive information (usually product) from the Web site or to have one's personal information distributed to other companies

opt out To decline on a Web site to receive information (usually product) from the Web site or to have one's personal information distributed to other companies

P2P (peer-to-peer) Refers to transactions (usually file sharing or payments) on the Internet between two persons

P3P (privacy preferences project) An attempt by the W3C to establish an industry standard for Web users to gain more control over how a Web site uses information about them

packet Messages and files sent over the Internet are broken into packets and then reassembled in the correct sequence when they reach their destination

packet filter A type of firewall that uses a static ACL to limit inbound or outbound packets of a network based either on their IP address or port; contrasts with stateful filtering, which dynamically builds a table that determines which packets are let in and out

packet switching A means of sending data over the Internet by "breaking" the data into packets that are numbered, addressed, and forwarded so that they can be sent separately and reassembled at the destination in the correct sequence

parser Used to read an XML file and construct an appropriate tree structure; if there is a mistake in the XML syntax, the parser will give an error message

passphrase A long password, usually consisting of several words strung together

P-card (procurement card) A credit card for a company used for purchases

PDA (personal digital assistant) A wireless handheld device that functions as a computer and is used in m-computing

permission marketing Marketing to a customer who gives permission to a company to send product information and advertisements

pervasive computing Ubiquitous computing that allows one to download or upload information of every kind in everyday life using "smart" devices networked to provide a single continual seamless computing experience

pipelining A means to speed up a computer by having one part of a chip fetching instructions, another part decoding instructions, and another part executing instructions, all at the same time

pixel A cell of a grid that is turned on or off in bitmap graphics; each pixel stores data on color or black-and-white, and a grid of pixels creates a graphic representation of a picture; the continuous lines and shapes of the picture are approximated using a finite number of pixels but the pixels are close enough together so that the eye is "tricked" into seeing a continuous line or shape

PKI (public key infrastructure) Consists of a server, where public keys are stored, and a key management system; key management includes issuing keys, a key certification system, and revoking keys

plaintext The original message between a sender and a receiver that is encrypted (then called ciphertext) for security purposes before being sent

POP (point of presence) The location of a presence of an ISP; in making a last-mile connection a company must connect from its LAN to the ISP's POP

pop-under window A window (usually an advertisement) that is created when a user logs on to a Web site; opens up "underneath" the main browser window and remains on the screen even after the user shuts the browser down

pop-up window A window (usually an advertisement) that pops up on the screen as a user is browsing a Web site

port A line into and out of a computer or a network device that receives and transmits data

portal A single "gateway" site that offers a search engine, email, chat rooms, real time news and stock updates, weather, virtual malls, and personalization; an Internet business model that makes money from advertising on the portal

POTS (plain old telephone service) Standard telephone service used in a dial-up connection for the Internet

power user A user who requires a very high-end desktop PC

preemptive multitasking The ability of an operating system to appear as though it were performing multiple processes at the same time by dividing the time of the CPU into thin slices whereby the *operating system* controls when a process is interrupted in order to run another process; contrasts with cooperative multitasking

private key A recipient of an encrypted message (ciphertext) uses his private key to decrypt the message that was encrypted by the sender using the recipient's public key (the recipient's public key is often published on a server); a private key is often based on the prime number factorization of a very large integer; a private key is also used to digitally sign documents; a private key must be kept secret by its owner

PRM (partner relationship management) A software-based system designed to improve relationships with business partners; analogous to CRM; many CRM and ERP software companies are getting into this area, and there are companies whose central focus is PRM

procedural language A high-level, third generation programming language that uses instructions to precisely spell out, step-by-step, exactly what operations the CPU is to perform

process A set of resources that is created by an operating system and used to manage a program when it executes

programming language A type of application software used to write instructions to a computer for performing a task

protocol A set of rules for exchanging messages over a network so that computers on the network can communicate with each other

proxy server A type of firewall used to protect computers behind a firewall from an intruder by replacing their IP addresses with the IP address of the proxy server; may also be used to cache frequently viewed Web pages

public domain software Software that is free and carries neither copyright nor restrictions on redistribution

public key A sender of a message uses the recipient's public key (often published on a server) to encrypt the original plaintext message; the recipient uses his private key to decrypt the encrypted message (called ciphertext); a public key is often based on a very large integer; a public key is also used to verify a digital signature

RAID (redundant array of independent disks) A hard drive that appears as one drive, but data are written across two or more drives; the data are divided among the multiple drives using a process called stripping

RAM (random access memory) A group of memory chips in a computer that serves as the main memory; this is where the data and instructions for an executing program are stored; also called DRAM

raster graphic A means of storing and displaying graphics using pixels; also called bitmap graphic

RDRAM (Rambus dynamic random access memory) A kind of RAM Intel developed for the Pentium 4, which Intel claims has greater performance than SDRAM

real time A term used to describe an immediate response, usually by a computer or system; communication or transaction processing without delay

RISC (reduced instruction set computer) A chip design for desktop computers that makes more frequent fetches for instructions in RAM but uses more simplified instructions; was developed as RAM access times decreased; contrasts with CISC

RMI (remote method invocation) The Java technology for allowing a component to call another component's methods over a network; unlike CORBA, with Java RMI both components must be written in Java

ROM (read only memory) Nonvolatile memory that permanently stores instructions and data even without power; holds a piece of the operating system that allows the computer to boot

root server A server that serves up IP addresses for top-level domains; there are multiple copies of root servers throughout the world to make this process more efficient

router A network device used to route or forward packets between LANs and WANs

RSA algorithm A mathematical algorithm that serves as the basis for one of the most widely-used public key cryptosystems in Internet security; named after its inventors from MIT: Ron Rivest, Adi Shamir, and Leonard Adleman

SAN (storage area network) A storage system that is a separate subnetwork attached to a data center using a high-speed transport technology called Fibre Channel

Say's Law A law in economics that states supply creates its own demand; e.g., as computers have become more powerful and available, they have created tremendous demand for their use

scalability A measure of a Web site's ability to expand capacity in order to handle increased traffic without a significant reduction in performance

scale To size up to meet a growing company's needs; often refers to hardware and software needs

schema A file written in XML used to validate XML files by ensuring that the tags in the XML file are consistent with those defined in the schema file; an alternative to DTD

SCM (supply chain management) Software designed to link a company with its suppliers, distributors, manufacturers, and customers with the objective of cutting costs and increasing revenues

screening router A router that uses an ACL to filter packets in and out of ports on a network for security purposes

scripting language A programming language written for interpreters; usually less complicated than a full-blown programming language designed for generating compiled applications; examples include VBScript and JavaScript, which are used to add functionality to a Web page

SDRAM (synchronized dynamic random access memory) Very fast DRAM synchronized with the clock of the CPU

secondary storage The hard drive and removable external storage for a computer such as diskettes, Jaz drives, Zip drives, and tapes

server log file A text file kept by a Web server for visitor tracking purposes; a W3C standard format for Web server log files includes the time, client IP address, the method, the URL, and the result of the request

Servlet A program written in Java designed to extend the functionality of a Web server; runs as part of a Java application server

SET (secure electronic transaction) A form of security for online credit card transactions that is designed to authenticate both the merchant and the customer through signed digital certificates issued by a trusted third party such as a bank or certificate authority

set-top box A cable television device that sits on top of a television and gives the user access to the Internet

shareware Copyrighted software that is distributed on a "try-before-you-buy" basis; often the downloaded software can be used for free until an expiration date; sometimes there is no trial period and users are on their honor to purchase the software if they decide to keep it

shell The part of the operating system that enables the user to interact with the computer; also called interface or user interface; contrasts with kernel

SIMD (single-instruction, multiple-data) An important technique for making microprocessors faster that executes the same arithmetic operation (e.g., add or multiply) on multiple data streams simultaneously; examples of SIMD microprocessors include the Intel MMX and the Pentium III

skyscraper A tall, skinny, vertical banner ad usually found on the right-hand side of a Web page

smart card A card (usually plastic) with an embedded chip that has many uses, ranging from identification for security measures to a tool for commerce (if the chip holds data on the monetary value available to the holder of the card); examples include phone cards and gift cards

sniffer program A tool in networking that records and analyzes packets on a LAN; also one of the most common technical means to steal a password, whereby a computer is infected with a virus or worm (the sniffer program) that captures keystrokes; the program covertly records a password typed out on the keyboard and sends the password back to the perpetrator

SOAP (simple object access protocol) A Web service protocol that is an open middleware standard; distributed applications communicate with each other using HTTP and SOAP envelopes consisting of data in XML format

source code Source code is the set of "English-like" instructions that tell the computer exactly what to do; the source code is usually compiled into executable programs

spam Email advertising that is sent without the recipient's permission; usually unwanted and proliferates because sending email is inexpensive compared to other forms of advertising

spider A program used by a search engine to read Web pages and create new entries for its index by following links in the hypertext; also called bot or crawler

spoofing A kind of security breach whereby the perpetrator gains access to a system by sending packets with the IP addresses of trusted machines; hackers routinely break into systems to steal confidential information and sometimes blackmail the owner of the information

SQL (structured query language) A standard data manipulation and query language that all of the major database systems use

SRAM (static random access memory) Memory that holds its content as long as power is being fed to the computer; more expensive and faster than DRAM and does not require fresh electronic charges every few milliseconds

SSL (secure socket layer) A form of security for online credit card transactions; designed to encrypt and decrypt HTTP data between the merchant and the customer

SSP (storage service provider) A company that provides storage hardware either on-site or off-site, and provides maintenance and monitoring

stateful filtering Dynamic filtering of packets being transmitted in and out of a network; dynamically builds a state table that determines which packets are let in and out; contrasts with packet filtering, which uses a static ACL to filter packets

stored program The concept pioneered by the mathematical genius John von Neumann that a computer works by executing a set of instructions on data, and that both the instructions and the data are stored in main memory

strong client A paradigm of client/server computing whereby the client is responsible for most of the computing and data storage; the client is a reasonably powerful desktop PC, or perhaps even a workstation; also called a fat client

subprocess A sequence of instructions to execute within a process, e.g., printing and editing "simultaneously" in a word processor creates two subprocesses; multiple subprocesses for the same process share memory space and system resources; also called a thread

subscription model An Internet business model that sells content (e.g., news, stories, data) on a Web site to users on a subscription basis

supercomputer The fastest and most powerful computer money can buy, often well over a million dollars; can rapidly perform an extremely large number of numerical calculations; used for weather simulation models, atomic research, gene research, and the solution of very complex systems of equations in business applications (e.g., financial modeling)

superscalar Refers to a microprocessor with multiple pipelines

system bus The part of the computer that connects the CPU and main memory, through which instructions and data come in and go out of the CPU; also called memory bus

tag The element of HTML that instructs the browser how to display information

TCO (total cost of ownership) The total cost of owning computers, which includes updating and maintaining software, establishing help desks, and training users for new upgrades, which may dwarf the cost of just the hardware and software

TCP/IP (transmission control protocol/Internet protocol) The standard protocol used for the Internet; the network protocol invented by Vint Cerf and Bob Kahn

Telnet An Internet protocol that enables communication between a thin client and a Telnet server; the computing is done on the server while the client sees a command line interface; widely used, especially in Unix environments

text file A file containing ASCII data; uses only seven out of eight bits of a byte to represent the 128 ASCII characters; contrasts with a binary file, which uses eight bits

thin client A paradigm of client/server computing whereby the server has all of the data, and all of the applications execute on the server; the user of the client terminal sees a "desktop" display just like on a regular PC, but the software is actually running on the server and sending a graphical image to the client terminal; the client's only task is to display sets of colored pixels; also called a weak client; contrasts with strong or fat client

thread A sequence of instructions to execute within a process, e.g., printing and editing "simultaneously" in a word processor creates two threads; multiple threads for the same process share memory space and system resources; also called a subprocess

token A small hardware device embedded in a card or key fob that authenticates a user of a system and allows access

top-level domain The three-letter suffix at the end of a URL; e.g., `.com`, `.edu`, `.net`

transaction A set of SQL statements treated as a single operation for a DBMS; e.g., withdrawing money from a bond fund and investing it in a stock fund online, both treated as a single transaction

transistor In a computer a transistor opens or closes a circuit that determines whether 0 or 1 is stored; the computer registers "0" if an electrical charge is not flowing through a transistor and "1" if it is

true color A way to display color on a computer screen that uses three bytes for each pixel: one for red, one for green, and one for blue (any color on the spectrum detectable by the human eye can be represented by a mixture of these three colors)

UDDI (Universal Description, Discovery and Integration) An initiative to create a registry for Web services by an industry consortium, uddi.org, that includes many of the key heavyweights such as Ariba, IBM, Microsoft, and Sun

unicode A coding scheme for representing text that uses 16 bits, rather than 7 bits, to represent a character; allows for representation of over 65,000 characters; contrasts with ASCII

Unix The most popular operating system for servers; because Unix was developed as a nonproprietary system and freely given away, there are many variants of Unix; considered to be the most reliable operating system

URI (uniform resource indicator) A string of characters used to identify a resource; a URL is an example; another example is the string of characters in the root element of an XML file to qualify the name tags

URL (uniform resource locator) The "address" of an Internet resource; must follow a very specific syntax; there are three parts to a URL: the Internet protocol used (e.g., HTTP, FTP, or Telnet), the address or name of the server, and the location and name of the file on the server

user interface The part of the operating system that enables the user to interact with the computer; also called interface or shell

vector graphic A means for storing and displaying graphic objects by describing the object in terms of circles, rectangles, lines, and other geometric shapes; two advantages of the vector scheme over the bitmap scheme are that it is easy to scale and size shapes, and graphics stored as vectors require much less memory than bitmap graphics; the disadvantage is that it cannot store photographic images easily

viral marketing A type of marketing that uses customers to spread the word about a product; word-of-mouth amplified by use of email among customers

virtual machine Interprets and runs Java bytecode on a user's operating system; operating system-dependent; any user with a browser has the virtual machine appropriate for the computer

VLIW (very long instruction word) A means to improve the speed of a microprocessor by fetching and decoding long words—e.g., a 64-bit word that is composed of two 32-bit instructions—and processing these instructions in parallel; an extension of SIMD

volatile memory Memory in a computer that holds its content as long as power is being fed to the computer; examples are DRAM and SRAM

vortal A portal designed to meet the disparate needs of a specific industry; contains industry news, the latest technologies, newsgroups, a means of buying and selling industry-related products, etc.; examples include Plasticsnet.com and Ventro.com

VPN (virtual private network) A private network that uses the public Internet; to ensure privacy, it makes use of encryption and authentication; offers a company the ubiquity of the Internet but added security

W3C (World Wide Web Consortium) An organization for promoting Web protocols and standards; it oversees XML, HTML, XSL, SOAP, and XHTML specifications

WAN (wide area network) LANs connected together over a larger geographical region, perhaps the world

weak client A paradigm of client/server computing whereby the server has all of the data and all of the applications execute on the server; the user of the client terminal sees a "desktop" display just like on a regular PC, but the software is actually running on the server and sending a graphical image to the client terminal; the client's only task is to display sets of colored pixels; also called a thin client; contrasts with strong or fat client

Web farm A set of one or more server clusters

Web server A server that serves up Web pages to a browser; also called an HTTP server

Web service A software component accessible to client programs, or other components, using HTTP and XML

well formed Refers to an XML document that satisfies the requirements of basic XML syntax

WSDL (Web Service Description Language) Description (using XML) of how a Web service is used; this document "exposes" the Web service API; it is an IDL for SOAP components

WYSIWYG (what you see is what you get) A type of application, usually a word processor, whereby what is displayed on the screen is an accurate representation of what gets printed; an example is Microsoft Word

XHTML (extensible hypertext markup language) The next generation of HTML written in XML that combines the markup and formatting ability of HTML with the rigor of XML; used to segue from HTML to XML

XML/EDI (extensible markup language/electronic data interchange) A hybrid system that allows traditional EDI documents to be converted to XML-based dialects which allows the features of XML to be incorporated into legacy EDI systems; some EDI vendors include XML translation capabilities as part of their systems

XML (extensible markup language) A markup language that is rapidly becoming the universal language of business; gives meaning to data by the creation of tags; is object-oriented and can be used with scripting languages; with XML a Web developer can easily separate the data from the formatting and content of a Web page

XML Schema An XML schema that is a recommendation from the W3C

XSL (extensible stylesheet language) There are three components to XSL: the first component is XSLT, the second component is the XPath language used for accessing parts of the XML document, the third component is an XML formatting vocabulary

XSLT (extensible stylesheet language transformation) A language used to transform XML documents into HTML

Zip drive A type of secondary storage for a computer from Iomega; a 3.5-inch removable disk that can hold 100–250 MB

Bibliography

[1] Bruce Abbott. Software failure can lead to financial catastrophe, September 29, 2000. `www.idg.net/english/crd_software_259925.html`.

[2] Elinor Abreu. Center of attention, December 13, 1999. `www.thestandard.com/article/0,1902,8048,00.html`.

[3] Airwise.com, May 6, 1999. `news.airwise.com/stories/99/05/925996895.html`.

[4] Jason Aloia. Desperately seeking webheads, August 2000. `www.ecompany.com/articles/mag/print/0,1643,6839,00.html`.

[5] P. Andrews. *How the Web Was Won*. Broadway Books, New York, NY, 1999.

[6] Julia Angwin. Orbiscom tackles concerns about e-commerce security, January 18, 2001. `interactive.wsj.com/archive/`.

[7] Associated Press. MIT course materials free over Web, April 4, 2001. `www.nytimes.com/aponline/national/AP-MIT-Web.html`.

[8] D. Bank. *Breaking Windows: How Bill Gates Fumbled the Future of Microsoft*. The Free Press, New York, NY, 2001.

[9] Paul Baron. On distributed communications: Introduction to distributed communications network, August 1964. `www.rand.org/publications/RM/RM3420/`.

[10] Randy Barrett. E-tailers caught in card squeeze, April 10, 2000. `www.zdnet.com/filters/printerfriendly/0,6061,2524002-35,00.html`.

[11] S. Berinato. "7 reasons the PC is here to stay". *CIO Magazine*, June 1, 2001.

[12] Tim Berners-Lee. *Weaving the Web: The Original Design and Ultimate Destiny of the World Wide Web*. Harper Business, New York, NY, 2000.

[13] M.W. Berry and M. Browne. *Understanding Search Engines: Mathematical Modeling and Text Retrieval*. SIAM, Philadelphia, PA, 1999.

[14] Christina Binkley. Checked out, May 21, 2001. `interactive.wsj.com/archive/retrieve.cgi?id=SB989952732632012944.djm`.

[15] Kathi Black. The new magic number: $1,000,000,000, January 29, 2001. `www.thestandard.com/article/display/0,1151,21723,00.html`.

[16] C. Blexrud, M. Bortniker, J. Crossland, D. Esposito, J. Hales, W. Hankison, V. Honnaya, T. Huckaby, S. Khristich, E. Lee, R. Lhotka, B. Loesgen, S. Mohr, S. Robinson, A. Rofail, B. Sherrelll, S. Short, and D. Wahlin. *Professional Windows DNA*. WROX Press Ltd., Birmingham, UK, 2000.

[17] B. Bloom. *Deploying and Managing Microsoft .NET Web Farms*. SAMS, Indianapolis, IN, 2001.

[18] Lisa Bowman. Hotmail spam filters block outgoing e-mail, January 18, 2001. `news.cnet.com/news/0-1005-202-4523924-0.html`.

[19] C. Britton. *IT Architectures and Middleware*. Addison-Wesley, Boston, MA, 2001.

[20] Po Bronson. *The Nudist on the Late Shift*. Random House, New York, NY, 1999.

[21] F.P. Brooks, Jr. *The Mythical Man-Month: Essays on Software Engineering*. Addison-Wesley, Reading, MA, 1982.

[22] Beth Snyder Bulik and Jennifer Gilbert. Digital marketing hits the mainstream, March 20, 2001. `www.business2.com/content/magazine/marketing/2001/03/12/27669`.

[23] William M. Bulkeley. Software uses patterns made on keyboard, mouse to target ads to individual users. *The Wall Street Journal*, May 25, 2001.

[24] J.D. Camm, T.E. Chorman, F.A. Dill, J.R. Evans, D.J. Sweeney, and G.W. Wegryn. Blending OR/MS, judgment, and GIS: Restructuring P&G's supply chain. *Interfaces*, 27:128–142, 1997.

[25] Laura Carr. 100 numbers you need to know, November 13, 2000. `www.thestandard.com/article/display/0,1151,20128,00.html`.

[26] P.E. Ceruzzi. *A History of Modern Computing*. MIT Press, Cambridge, MA, 2000.

[27] James Christie. E-logistics delivers, July 18, 2000. `www.redherring.com/index.asp?layout=story_generic&doc_id=RH1550010555`.

[28] Thomas Claburn. The banner ad is dead. (ok, not really.), February 12, 2001. `www.zdnet.com/filters/printerfriendly/0,6061,2677309-103,00.html`.

[29] Don Clark. Start-up will sell Web addresses to bypass Internet bureaucracy. *The Wall Street Journal*, March 5, 2001.

[30] E. Codd. A relational model for large shared data banks. *Communications of the ACM*, 13:377–387, 1970.

[31] Computerweekly.com. Hershey SAP roll-out leads to losses of $60.4m. *computer-weekly.com*, November 11, 1999.

[32] Edward Cone. Kicking asp, December 2000. `www.wired.com/wired/archive/8.12/jamcracker_pr.html`.

[33] R.X. Cringely. *Accidental Empires: How the Boys of Silicon Valley Make Their Millions, Battle Foreign Competition, and Still Can't Get a Date*. Harper Business, New York, NY, 1996.

[34] M.A. Cusumano and R. W. Selby. *Microsoft Secrets*. Free Press, New York, NY, 1995.

[35] M.A. Cusumano and D.B. Yoffie. *Competing on Internet Time*. Free Press, New York, NY, 1998.

[36] C.J. Date. *An Introduction to Database Systems: Volume I*. Addison-Wesley, Reading, MA, 1990.

[37] Stewart Deck. What is CRM?, May 1, 2001. `www.cio.com/research/crm/edit/crmabc.html`.

[38] H.M. Deitel, P.J. Deitel, and T.R. Nieto. *Internet & World Wide Web: How to Program*. Prentice Hall, Upper Saddle River, NJ, 2002.

[39] Annabel Z. Dodd. *The Essential Guide to Telecommunications*. Prentice-Hall PTR, Upper Saddle River, NJ, 1999.

[40] L. Downes and C. Mui. *Unleashing the Killer App: Digital Strategies for Market Dominance*. Harvard Business School Press, Boston, MA, 1998.

[41] J. Dyché. *e-Data: Turning Data into Information with Data Warehousing*. Addison-Wesley, Boston, MA, 2000.

[42] Stefani Eads. How to get Web sites shop-shape, November 22, 1999. `www.businessweek.com/bwdaily/dnflash/nov1999/nf91122d.htm`.

[43] William Echikson. The fashion cycle hits high gear, September 18, 2000. `www.businessweek.com:/2000/00_38/b3699071.htm?scriptFramed`.

[44] eCompany Staff. What works, August 2000. `www.ecompanynow.com/articles/mag/print/0,1643,6864,00.html`.

[45] Renee Ferguson. Alternative online payments here to stay, December 8, 2000. `www.zdnet.com/zdnn/`.

[46] Carol Ferrar. Two more e-tailors pull online operations offline, June 15, 2001. Gartner Group Report FT-13-9172.

[47] Adam Feuerstein. Changing face of online retail, July 18, 2000. `www.upside.com`.

[48] Emily Fitzloff. Email marketing at a price, January 26, 2001. `www.business2.com/content/channels/marketing/2001/01/26/25307`.

[49] Emily Fitzloff. Web ads reach all-time high, January 23, 2001. `www.business2.com/content/channels/marketing/2001/01/23/25098`.

[50] Vincent Flanders and Michael Willis. *Web Pages That Suck: Learn Good Design by Looking at Bad Design*. Sybex, Alameda, CA, 1998.

[51] Brand Fortner. *The Data Handbook: A Guide to Understanding the Organization and Visualization of Data*. Springer-Verlag Telos, Santa Clara, CA, 1995.

[52] Gina Fraone. Keeping partners together, April 9, 2001. `techupdate.zdnet.com/techupdate/stories/main/0,14179,2704180,00.html`.

[53] Bill Gates. *The Road Ahead*. Penguin Books, New York, NY, 1996.

[54] Jennifer Gilbert. Cheap tricks, February 6, 2001. `www.business2.com/content/magazine/marketing/2001/01/29/25384`.

[55] Jennifer Gilbert. When brands get burned, January 23, 2001. `www.business2.com/content/channels/marketing/2001/01/15/24638`.

[56] Kim Girard. The battle over renting software, February 1, 2000. `news.cnet.com/news/0-1008-200-1538592.html?tag=st.ne.1002`.

[57] A. Glossbrenner and E. Glossbrenner. *Search Engines for the World Wide Web*. Peachpit Press, Berkeley, CA, 1999.

[58] Seth Godin. *Permission Marketing*. Simon & Schuster, New York, NY, 1999.

[59] Seth Godin. *Unleashing the Ideavirus*. Do You Zoom, Dobbs Ferry, NY, 2000.

[60] Lauren Goldstein. Build your e-business, December 1999. `www.business2.com/articles/mag/print/0,1643,6132,FF.html`.

[61] Jeffrey Graham. Five challenges of interactive marketing, April 3, 2001. `www.business2.com/content/channels/marketing/2001/04/03/29452`.

[62] Matthew P. Graven. Leave me alone. *PC Magazine*, January 16, 2001, 151–159.

[63] Jay Greene. Microsoft's big bet. *Business Week*, pages 152–163, 2000.

[64] Dan Greening. Data mining on the Web. *Web Techniques*, pages 41–46, January 1, 2000.

[65] Neil Gross, Marcia Stepanek, Otis Port, and John Carey. Glitches cost billions of dollars and jeopardize human lives. How can we kill the bugs? *Business Week*, December 6, 1999.

[66] K. Hafner and M. Lyon. *Where Wizards Stay Up Late: The Origins of the Internet*. Touchstone, New York, NY, 1996.

[67] J. Hagel III and A. G. Armstrong. *Net Gain: Expanding Markets Through Virtual Communities*. Harvard Business School Press, Boston, MA, 1997.

[68] David P. Hamilton. Faulty software disables modems on Hewlett-Packard and Gateway laptops. *Wall Street Journal*, February 22, 2001.

[69] Michael Hammer and James Champy. *Reengineering the Corporation: A Business Manifesto*. Harper, New York, NY, 1994.

[70] Saul Hansell. A front-row seat as Amazon gets serious, May 20, 2001. `www.nytimes.com`.

[71] Saul Hansell. Now that we're still here, where do we go? 7 answers, February 28, 2001. `nytimes.com/2001/02/28/technology/28HANS.html`.

[72] Evan Hansen. Microsoft's stake in the AOL-Amazon deal, July 25, 2001. `news.cnet.com/news/0-1005-200-6671199.html?tag=tp_pr`.

[73] Ward Hanson. *Principles of Internet Marketing*. South-Western College Press, Cincinnati, OH, 2000.

[74] Matt Hicks. When ASPs go sour. *eWeek*, April 29, 2001.

[75] M. Hiltzik. *Dealers of Lightning: Xerox Parc and the Dawn of the Computer Age*. HarperCollins, New York, NY, 1999.

[76] Robert Hof. Commentary: Desperately seeking search technology, September 24, 2001. `businessweek.com`.

[77] Hoovers.com. Hoover's company capsule for eBay inc., June 7, 2001. `cobrands.hoovers.com`.

[78] G.V. Hulme. Virus costs estimated at $10.7 billion, September 6, 2001. `www.informationweek.com/story/IWK20010906S0003`.

[79] Ibm.com. `www.ibm.com/press/prnews.nsf/crawler/255CA70D126DD45085256840005A554F`.

[80] Idc.com. Computer operating environments coevolve, August 8, 2000. `www.idc.com/itforecaster/itf20000808.stm`.

[81] Intel.com. `www.intel.com/intel/museum/25anniv/hof/tspecs.htm`.

[82] Bob Ivins and Tim Reed. Opinion: Comparing systems to server logs, January 18, 1999. `www.adage.com/interactive/articles/19990118/article3.html`.

[83] Greg Jaffe and Gary McWilliams. EDS wins huge, five-year contract to develop network for the Navy, Marines. *The Wall Street Journal*, October 9, 2000.

[84] Bill Jeffery and Jim Morrison. ERP, one letter at a time, September 1, 2000. `www.cio.com/archive/090100_ea_content.html`.

[85] Del Jones. Y2K's cost a bargain at $100B, November 18, 1999. `www.usatoday.com/life/cyber/tech/ctg686.htm`.

[86] Paul Judge. How I saved $100 million on the Web, February 2001. `www.fastcompany.com/online/43/ideazone.html`.

[87] D. Kahn. *The Codebreakers: The Story of Secret Writing*. Scribner, New York, NY, 1996.

[88] David A. Kaplan. *The Silicon Boys and Their Valley of Dreams*. William Morrow & Company, New York, NY, 1999.

[89] Faith Keenan. Giants can be nimble, 2000. `www.businessweek.com/2000/00_38/b3699121htm?scriptFramed`.

[90] Faith Keenan. Is your data safe from disaster?, September 24, 2001. `businessweek.com`.

[91] Gregg Keizer. Cnet reviews 5 online payment services, June 26, 2001. `www.cnet.com/software/0-5421322-8-6335860-1.htm.?tag=1d`.

[92] Christopher Koch. The big payoff, October 1, 2000. `www.cio.com/archive/100100_payoff_content.html`.

[93] Christopher Koch, Derek Slater, and E. Baatz. The ABCs of ERP, December 22, 1999. `www.cio.com/research/erp/edit/122299_erp.html`.

[94] R. Konrad. Data mining: Digging user info for gold, February 8, 2001. `www.zdnet.com/zdnn/stories/news/0,4586,2683567,00.html`.

[95] Susan Kuchinskas. The end of marketing, November 14, 2000. `www.business2.com/content/channels/marketing/2001/01/15/24638`.

[96] Susan Kuchinskas. More for less, September 12, 2000. `www.business2.com/content/magazine/indepth/2000/08/22/16720`.

[97] Susan Kuchinskas. One-to-(n)one?, September 12, 2000. `www.business2.com/content/magazine/indepth/2000/08/22/19107`.

[98] David Lake. Quick and easy, February 26, 2001. `www.thestandard.com/article/display/0,1151,22342,00.html`.

[99] Stacy Lawrence. Forget Christmas: E-commerce takes Q1, April 28, 2000. `www.thestandard.com/article/0,1902,14602,00.html`.

[100] Jennifer Lee. eBay University: Part school and part tent meeting, June 14, 2001. `www.nytimes.com/2001/06/14/technology/14ebay.html`.

[101] W. Lehnert. *The Web Wizard's Guide to HTML*. Pearson Education, Inc., Upper Saddle River, NJ, 2002.

[102] Eric J. Lerner. Can anything stop the transistor? *The Industrial Physicist*, June 2000, pgs. 18–21.

[103] Steven Levy. *Crypto*. Viking Penguin, New York, NY, 2001.

[104] Martin Lindstrom. E-tail-retail battle: And the winner is. . ., October 19, 2000. `www.clickz.com/article/cz/2636.html`.

[105] D.S. Linthicum. *Enterprise Application Integration*. Addison-Wesley, Boston, MA, 2000.

[106] D.S. Linthicum. *B2B Application Integration: e-Business-Enable Your Enterprise*. Addison-Wesley, Boston, MA, 2001.

[107] Laura Lorek. Russian Mafia threat, July 16, 2001. `www.zdnet.com`.

[108] Pete Loshin, John Vacca, and Paul Murphy. *Electronic Commerce*. Charles River Media, Hingham, MA, 2001.

[109] Nora Macaluso. Study: E-tailors flunk customer service test, August 9, 2000. `www.ecommercetimes.com/perl/printer/3982`.

[110] Dylan McClain. Job forecast: Internet's still hot, January 30, 2001. `www.nytimes.com/library/financial/01working-mccl.html`.

[111] Josh McHugh. Binge and purge, June 2000. `www.business2.com/articles/mag/print/0,1643,6580,00.html`.

[112] Joseph McKendrick. Priceline.com: An inside look at the reverse auction master, January 1, 2000. `www.ecomworld.com/global/includes/content/print.cfm?contented=51`.

[113] J. Mena. *Data Mining Your Website*. Digital Press, Boston, MA, 1999.

[114] Cade Metz. Usability. *PC Magazine*, March 6, 2001.

[115] Microsoft.com. Rental car company creates elegant link to airline system using Microsoft, April 13, 2001. `www.microsoft.com/BUSINESS/casestudies/b2c/dollarrentacar.asp`.

[116] Microsoft.com. SPAR Handles AG transforming vast amounts of raw data into valuable business intelligence, May 23, 2001. `www.microsoft.com/servers/evaluation/casestudies/spar.asp`.

[117] Cynthia Morgan. ASPs speak the corporate language, October 25, 1999. www.computerworld.com/cwi/Printer_Friendly_V.../0,1212, NAV47_STO37371-,%00.htm.

[118] W. Mougayar. *Opening Digital Markets: Battle Plans and Business Strategies for Internet Commerce*. McGraw-Hill, New York, NY, 1998.

[119] Ian Mount. This way to oblivion, April 2001. www.ecompany.com/articles/mag/print/0.1643,9583,00.html.

[120] Ian Mount and Brian Caulfield. The missing link: What you need to know about supply-chain technology, May 2001. www.business2.com/articles/mag/print/0,1643,11253,00.html.

[121] Eric Nee. How to tell your ASP from your elbow, May 2000. www.ecompany.com/articles/mag/print/0,1643,6621,00.html.

[122] Netcraft.com. www.netcraft.com/survey/.

[123] Jakob Nielsen. *Designing Web Usability: The Practice of Simplicity*. New Riders, Indianapolis, IN, 2000.

[124] Stefanie Olsen. 'Spam King' leads new trend in annoying promotions, February 5, 2001. news.cnet.com/news/0-1005-201-4687442-0.html?tag=btmprm.

[125] Stephanie Overby. Survivor III, May 1, 2001. www2.cio.com/archive/050101/survivor_content.html.

[126] William J. Pardi. *XML in Action*. Microsoft Press, New York, NY, 1997.

[127] Andy Patrizio. XML passes from development to implementation, March 26, 2001. www.informationweek.com.

[128] Susannah Patton. The truth about CRM, May 1, 2001. www2.cio.com/archive/050101/truth_content.html.

[129] L. Pekowsky. *Java Server Pages*. Addison-Wesley, Reading, MA, 2000.

[130] Lee Pender. The missing link, June 15, 2000. www2.cio.com/archive/061500_link_content.html.

[131] Don Peppers and Martha Rogers. *The One to One Future*. Doubleday, New York, NY, 1993.

[132] Don Peppers and Martha Rogers. The physical-virtual future, April 28, 2000. www.intelligententerprise.com/000428/feat1.shtml.

[133] Don Peppers and Martha Rogers. The 'store' is everywhere, February 6, 2001. www.business2.com/content/channels/marketing/2001/01/29/25298.

[134] Stacy Perman. E-tailing survival guide: OK, forget the whole damn thing, December 2000. `www.ecompany.com/articles/mag/print/0,1640,8786/8938,00.html`.

[135] Carol Pickering and Kim Girard. A confederacy of consultants, August 8, 2000. `www.business2.com/magazine/2000/08/17945.htm`.

[136] Andrew Pollack. For coders, a code of conduct, May 3, 1999. `www.nytimes.com/library/tech/99/05/biztech/articles/03code.html`.

[137] Poor Richard's. `topfloor.com/pr/freeinfo/shop.htm`.

[138] Michelle Rafter. Know thy customer, November 6, 2000. `www.thestandard.com/article/0,1902,19689,00.html`.

[139] Aaron Ricadela. Microsoft claims Win2000 reduces TCO. *Information Week*, February 14, 2000.

[140] W. L. Rosch. *Hardware Bible*. Que, Indianapolis, IN, 1999.

[141] Cheryl Rosen. Visa unveils smart card, July 31, 2001. `www.informationweek.com/story/IWK20010731S0016`.

[142] E. I. Schwartz. *Webonomics: Nine Essential Principles for Growing Your Business on the World Wide Web*. Broadway Books, New York, NY, 1997.

[143] Scia.org. Welcome to the SCIA Internet ad. `www.scia.org/aboutSCIA/InternetAd.htm`.

[144] Dianne See. Building community on the Web, September 28, 1998. `www.thestandard.com/article/0,1902,1793,00.html`.

[145] Michael Selz. Insight enterprises finds success mixing Internet, human advice, April 3, 2001. `interactive.wsj.com/archive`.

[146] Stephen Shankland. IBM exceeds expectations with supercomputer. *CNET News.com*, June 28, 2000.

[147] C. Shapiro and H.R. Varian. *Information Rules: A Strategic Guide to the Network Economy*. Harvard Business School Press, Boston, MA, 1999.

[148] T. Sheldon. *Encyclopedia of Networking & Telecommunications*. Osborne/McGraw-Hill, New York, NY, 2001.

[149] David Shook. Comparing the big three of clicks-and-bricks, October 5, 2000. `www.businessweek.com`.

[150] S. Singh. *The Code Book*. Anchor Books, New York, NY, 1999.

[151] John G. Spooner. IBM taking Moore's Law by the horns. *ZDNN*, August 11, 2000.

[152] Jim Sterne. Making metrics count, April 3, 2001. `www.business2.com/content/channels/marketing/2001/3/26/28396`.

[153] Anne Stuart. Clicks & bricks, March 15, 2000. `www2.cio.com/archive/031500_click_content.html`.

[154] Sun.com. `www.sun.com/products/staroffice/vision.html`.

[155] Don Tapscott, David Ticoll, and Alex Lowy. Internet nirvana, December 2000. `www.ecompany.com/articles/mag/print/0,1643,8850,FF.html`.

[156] Bob Tedeschi. A fresh spin on 'affinity portals' to the Internet, April 17, 2000. `www.nytimes.com/library/tech/00/04/cyber/commerce/17commerce.html`.

[157] Bob Tedeschi. Why purchasing agents turned out to be hard to herd, February 28, 2001. `nytimes.com/2001/02/28/technology/28TEDE.html`.

[158] Owen Thomas. Yahoo delivers bad news, March 7, 2001. `www.ecompany.com/articles/web/print/0,1650,9699,00.html`.

[159] Dylan Tweney. The defogger: Whip, beat, and stomp your data into submission, May 2001. `www.ecompanynow.com/articles/mag/print/0,1643,11256,00.html`.

[160] Steve Ulfelder. Do you really need a customer czar?, May 2001. `www.darwinmag.com/read/0501012/czar_content.html`.

[161] J. D. Ullman. *Principles of Database and Knowledge–Base Systems: Volume I.* Computer Science Press, Rockville, MD, 1988.

[162] Paco Underhill. *Why We Buy: The Science of Shopping.* Simon & Schuster, New York, NY, 1999.

[163] Nick Usborne. The death of permission, February 20, 2001. `www.business2.com/content/channels/marketing/2001/02/12/26190`.

[164] Kate VanScoy. New money models, July 17, 2000. `www.zdnet.com/pccomp`.

[165] JP Vellotti. Outsourced software, March 19, 2001. `www.zdnet.com/products/stories/reviews/0,4161,2692076,00.html`.

[166] Ken Vollmer. Don't believe the hype: EDI and XML are just perfect together, January 15, 2001. `www.internetweek.com/columns01/beat011501.htm`.

[167] Ken Vollmer. The Internet will determine the future of EDI, July 20, 2001. `www.internetweek.com/columns01/beat072001.htm`.

[168] Constantine von Hoffman. Stand (pick) and deliver, April 15, 2000. `www2.cio.com/archive/041500_stand_content.html`.

[169] E.G. Walters. *The Essential Guide to Computing.* Prentice-Hall PTR, Upper Saddle River, NJ, 1997.

[170] Charles Waltner. B-to-b e-payment offers benefit to marketplaces, November 13, 2000. www.informationweek.com.

[171] Bernhard Warner and Miguel Helft. Portals start to feel the heat, May 1, 2000. www.thestandard.com/article/0,1902,14412,00.html.

[172] Thomas Weber. New Web search tools offer useful shortcuts, nice twists, October 1, 2001. interactive.wsj.com/archive/retrieve.cgi?id=SB1001883437365887000.djm.

[173] Kimberly Weisul. Web software failure rates as high as 30 percent, September 17, 1998. www.zdnet.com/intweek/daily/980917c.html.

[174] R. White. *How Computers Work, Millennium Edition.* Que, Indianapolis, IN, 1999.

[175] M. Wilson. *The Difference Between God and Larry Ellison: Inside Oracle Corporation.* William Morrow, New York, NY, 1997.

[176] Wired News. SAP sued for firm's collapse. *Wired News*, August 27, 1998.

[177] Roberta Witty and William Malik. Security TCO model helps with more than cost savings, June 12, 2001. Gartner Group Report FT-13-9070.

[178] Troy Wolverton. Glut of goods lowers some eBay prices, June 7, 2001. news.cnet.com/news/0-1007-202-6216964.html.

[179] World Bank Group, 2000. devdata.worldbank.org/external/dgprofile.asp?RMDK=0&SMDK=1&W=0.

[180] XML/EDI Group. XML/EDI: the e-business framework, July 31, 2001. www.xmledi-group.org/xmledigroup/executive.htm.

[181] Rutrell Yasin. Banks add digital ids, July 5, 2001. www.internetweek.com/story/INW20010705S0002.

[182] Rutrell Yasin. E-payment deja vu, July 20, 2001. www.internetweek.com/newslead01/lead072001.htm.

[183] Eric Young. B-to-B's broken models, November 6, 2000. www.thestandard.com/article/0,1902,19693,00.html.

[184] Ed Yourdon. *The Decline & Fall of the American Programmer.* PTR Prentice Hall, Englewood Cliffs, NJ, 1993.

[185] Ed Yourdon. *Death March: The Complete Software Developer's Guide to Surviving "Mission Impossible" Tasks.* Prentice Hall PTR, Upper Saddle River, NJ, 1997.

[186] G.P. Zachary. *Show-Stopper! The Breakneck Race to Create Windows NT and the Next Generation at Microsoft.* The Free Press, New York, NY, 1994.

Index